slight H2O damage

6⁵⁰

ALSO BY ALBERT ROSENFELD

Prolongevity

The Second Genesis: The Coming Control of Life

The Quintessence of Irving Langmuir
(Reissued as Men of Physics: Irving Langmuir)

Responsible Parenthood (with Gilbert W. Kliman)

Mind and Supermind (Ed.)

Science, Invention & Social Change (Ed.)

PROLONGEVITY II

Prolongevity II

An Updated Report on the Scientific Prospects for Adding Good Years to Life

ALBERT ROSENFELD

ALFRED A. KNOPF   NEW YORK   1985

THIS IS A BORZOI BOOK
PUBLISHED BY ALFRED A. KNOPF, INC.

Library of Congress Cataloging in Publication Data

Rosenfeld, Albert.   Prolongevity II.

Includes index.
1. Longevity.   2. Rejuvenation.   3. Aging.
I. Title.   II. Title: Prolongevity 2.   III. Title:
Prolongevity two.
QP85.R653   1985   612'.68   84–48662
ISBN 0–394–534755–1

Prolongevity published October 6, 1976.
Updated, expanded and revised edition, *Prolongevity II*,
published June 24, 1985.

Manufactured in the United States of America

FIRST EDITION

For my wife,
Lillian,
after thirty-six years.

Looking forward
to the next thirty-six.

CONTENTS

INTRODUCTION
AND ACKNOWLEDGMENTS

GERONTOLOGY, the scientific study of the aging process, is one of the most important frontier areas in current biomedical research. As a science journalist, I had been following its erratic progress with great fascination for a number of years when, in 1975, the time seemed to me ripe for a popular synthesis. The result, a year later, was *Prolongevity*. The intent was not to describe in exhaustive detail an entire science, but, rather, to explore the most recent developments, experiments, and theories that might serve as combined reportage, interpretation, and responsible speculation. I tried to keep the reportage as clear and accurate as possible, and to separate it from what was purely interpretative and speculative. To take on such a task, especially in an area where there was little consensus among the credentialed experts, required a certain presumptuousness; but without a willingness to presume, very little scientific information would ever be conveyed to the public. I did a great deal of homework over a long period of time and sought advice and instruction from many of the leading investigators in gerontology and related areas of biology. They often disagreed with one another, as was apparent in the course of my research, but the response to the book was nevertheless gratifying. The scientific community was for the most part laudatory, despite some of the book's relatively surprising statements. In fact, a few of the scientists I spoke to in the course of this revision were kind enough to say that they regarded *Prolongevity* as "still the classic" in its field.

I have continued to stay in touch with aging research in the years since then, writing, lecturing, consulting, serving (often as the only nonscientist) on scientific advisory committees. Yet, it was only when I was well into the research for this updated edition that I realized how substantial a revision would be required—so much so, as it turned out, that the publisher has decided to call the new version *Prolongevity II*.

It is not that striking breakthroughs have been made in the intervening years. It is rather that new knowledge has continued to accrue, and the result has been a trend toward consensus and convergence (nothing yet like unanimity, of course) among gerontologists. The credibility gap has also narrowed; more people are beginning to understand and to believe that something can be done about the aging process, that we are not as a species forever doomed to undergo the ravages of senescence. This realization is partly the cause and partly the result of a number of new books with titles like *Life Extension*, *The Life Extension Revolution*, and *Maximum Life Span*, and the appearance of new organizations devoted to aging research such as the American Longevity Association (ALA), the American Foundation for Aging Research (AFAR), and the Fund for Integrative Biomedical Research (FIBER), not to mention the work and support of the still-fledgling (ten years old) National Institute on Aging (NIA) itself.

In *Prolongevity* I felt I had to devote a fair amount of space to justifying my conviction that the science of genetic engineering would one day progress to the point where genes could be modified, transferred, or deleted so that a genetic "clock of aging," if it could be identified, might thus be adjusted in any way we chose to define as beneficial. Genetic engineering has moved ahead with such incredible speed over these few years that the first halting experiments I was at such pains to describe are now ancient history. In fact, what genetic engineering can do has now been so well demonstrated and accepted that not much space needs to be spent justifying its capabilities. This is one area not only where much speculation has become fact, but also where fact has surpassed speculation. So the progress of science has just as often led me to delete material from, as to add material to, this new edition.

Nevertheless, *Prolongevity II* does contain an entirely new major section. Whereas the earlier version was divided into two main parts, called "Can We Do It?" and "Should We Do It?," circumstances now require an additional part (the new Part Two) called "Entering the Age of Prolongevity." For one thing, there has been a shift of research emphasis, especially on the part of the NIA, from a preoccupation with the pathology of old age to a new focus on healthy old age. This change in perspective has brought—or, rather, revealed—good news, relatively unappreciated as yet, to the effect that with a bit of luck we may already have the means to live out long lives and yet escape both physical and mental decrepitude. Moreover, just enough new research and testing have been done to warrant a cautious foray into mapping out a personal prolongevity program—something I was unwilling to do the first time around. The regimen I have sketched out for myself is relaxed enough to allow someone who possesses less than an iron will to follow it with reasonable consistency.

To make room for some of the new material, I had to trim some other areas that, though interesting, were not really central to the book's major themes. One example is the cryonics movement, whose members advocate the freezing of people after death in the hope that future biomedical science will be able to bring them back to life. The cryonics movement is still covered, as a fascinating phenomenon, in chapter 20, "The Immortalists," though treated in much less detail than before. The book is, after all, about prolongevity, not immortality.

Something needs to be said about that word—"prolongevity." I would have said more about it in the original edition had I known it was going to serve as the book's final title: when I didn't like the editors' favorite title and they didn't like mine, we compromised. The word is of course an elided combination of "prolong" and "longevity." Because it has come to be associated with my book and hence viewed as *my* word, I feel obliged to point out that the word existed before I wrote about the subject. It was coined by Gerald J. Gruman for his Harvard doctoral thesis, "A History of Ideas About the Prolongation of Life: The Evolution of Prolongevity Hypotheses to 1800," published in the December 1966 issue of *Transactions of the American Philosophical Society*. Gruman defined prolongevity as "the significant extension of the length of life by human action." (In papers leading up to his thesis, he had variously defined prolongevity as "the belief that it is possible to lengthen significantly the span of life," and "the hope that science may be able to extend greatly, perhaps indefinitely, the length of life." All the definitions are related, of course; and I guess I like the first one best—the one he finally settled on himself.) To designate an individual who believes "that prolongevity is both possible and desirable," Gruman suggested the term "prolongevitist," which, despite its unwieldiness, has actually been used by a few writers. I doubt that it will catch on. I have tried shortening it by a syllable to "prolongevist," but it doesn't help much. Until a more felicitous term is invented, some phrase like "advocate of prolongevity" will have to do.

I remain aware, now as before, of how much has been omitted. But the book does not, and never did, attempt to encompass all of gerontology; it has, rather, dwelt selectively on those themes in aging research that offer the hope, even the probability, that the goal of prolongevity can be realized, at least partially, and in the not impossibly far-off future.

One thing that became abundantly clear to me in the wake of the first book's publication—especially during my numerous appearances on radio and TV programs around the country, the kind that feature live audiences and call-in questioners—was that not everyone is ecstatic over the prospect of prolongevity. There is distinct and understandable concern about the consequences—and that is what Part Three of this book is all about.

I am of course deeply indebted to all those whose writings I have studied, but I want to extend my particular thanks to the people who have generously and cheerfully granted personal interviews; allowed me to visit their offices, homes, and laboratories; answered my phone calls and letters; and referred me to other valuable sources of information. In some cases the communication may have amounted to no more than a single conversation or an exchange of letters; in others, it entailed hours or even days at a time of intensive talk and shared speculation, as well as subsequent communications and revisits in order to clarify points of confusion or to give one investigator the opportunity to respond to a challenge raised by another.

I shall not attempt to list my numerous benefactors—though most of them will appear somewhere in the pages of the book, or at least in a bibliographical mention. For one thing, it is difficult to express degrees of gratitude where this is not really measurable; for another, I would not want anyone to be blamed for the views expressed here—unless a given view can be clearly attributed to a specified individual. None of my sources or mentors was given the opportunity to read the book in its entirety before publication. The responsibility for any errors of fact or interpretation—always a risk in a work of this scope—must be borne by the author alone.

A note on style: An editorial decision was made to drop the designation "Dr." throughout the book, mainly because just about everyone mentioned is a doctor of one kind or another. As a rule, in the main text of the book, the investigator's full name and affiliation are given the first time she or he is mentioned, but usually not thereafter. Similarly, the full names of institutions are often abbreviated on repetition; thus, for example, the Gerontological Research Center in Baltimore becomes GRC/Baltimore, the State University of New York at Buffalo becomes SUNY/Buffalo, and the University of Texas Medical Branch at Galveston becomes UTMB/Galveston.

My research required the use of a number of different libraries. My special thanks, however, are due the March of Dimes Birth Defects Foundation for providing easy access to indispensable journals and books, particularly in the area of genetics. I am deeply grateful, too, to Emil Frey, director of the Moody Medical Library at UTMB/Galveston for permission to use the superb facilities of one of the nation's very finest medical-school libraries.

Virtually every writer owes much to a good editor. In my case, that debt is to Charles Elliott of Knopf, a long-time friend as well as a sharp-eyed editor who not only blue-penciled my prose with sure expertise and sensitivity but also probed for inconsistencies of fact and the validity of sources.

Finally, for rendering the details of the task much easier than would otherwise have been the case, my heartfelt appreciation to Dina Gutierrez for her typing and secretarial services, and her unerring eye for the author's typos.

And, of course, to Lillian, for putting up with it all for so long.

—A.R.
New Rochelle, N.Y.

FOREWORD

"Every day you get older—that's a law."
—Butch Cassidy to the Sundance Kid

BUILT INTO the beginning of life is the end of it.

Every individual who is born into the world inevitably follows a predictable course, unless his life is cut short by accident or disease. He develops to maturity, remains at a productive plateau for a given number of years, then gradually declines, ages, dies.

I say "inevitably" because this is what has always happened to every human being who has lived on earth. A conspicuous minority remain vigorous longer than others, some notable random examples from recent history being Bertrand Russell, George Bernard Shaw, Margaret Sanger, Winston Churchill, Albert Schweitzer, Leopold Stokowski, Marianne Moore, Pablo Picasso, Grandma Moses, Arturo Toscanini, Konrad Adenauer, Wanda Landowska, Georgia O'Keeffe, Pablo Casals—men and women who remained creative and productive into their eighties and nineties. Others seem not only to remain vigorous in their later years, but actually to live out a longer lifetime. Pockets of impressive longevity have been reported in the Soviet Republic of Georgia, in the Himalayan heights of Hunza in Kashmir, and among the Andean Indians of the Vilcabamba Valley in Ecuador. In all these places, quantities of hardy individuals claim to have survived well past the century mark—some into the 120s, 130s, 140s, and even beyond, but these more extreme claims have been convincingly disproved. Nevertheless, in these populations, unusual numbers of women and men do seem to live at least through their eighties and nineties, and in unusual good health by our standards.

Even in the United States, where more than 10 percent of the population is now over sixty-five, an estimated twenty-five thousand to thirty-two thousand* men and women are a hundred years old or older—and, in this group, the women outnumber the men by better than two to one. Of those Americans over sixty-five, 86 percent are afflicted with one or more of the chronic degenerative diseases. But few observers emphasize the reverse side of these statistics: 14 percent do *not* have such diseases. Though all old people eventually fall prey to deteriorative changes, many seem to escape the major ravages of aging until they are very old indeed. Why is it that one man is bald and toothless twenty years sooner than his next-door neighbor? Is his neighbor just lucky, or is long life somehow written into his genes?

Some animals are unusually long-lived. The Galápagos tortoise, for instance, can go on for well over 150 years, and may live into the beginning of a third century. Some trees of the arid American West are believed to have endured for hundreds, even thousands, of years. In the mid-1950s, Edmund Schulman of the University of Arizona's pioneering Laboratory of Tree Ring Research began finding bristlecone pines in California that were nearly a thousand years older than the oldest known sequoias—until then rated the most ancient living things on earth. In 1957, Schulman—only a year before his own death at the age of forty-nine—discovered a bristlecone pine nearly five thousand years old, with its tree-ring data going back to the time of Nineveh and Babylon. In the "childhood" of those trees, the Pyramids were just being built. Since then, desert creosote bushes have been found that, experts calculate, are *twice* as old as Schulman's bristlecone!

It is possible that someone may yet turn up a living organism that predates even these Methuselahs of the plant world, perhaps some bacterium that has remained frozen under the polar icecap. Although we know of no organism that has lived forever—no person, no animal, no plant—there exists in every living organism an essential component that does appear to "live forever." It is DNA, deoxyribonucleic acid, which maintains headquarters in the nucleus of each living cell. With its celebrated "double-helix" architecture,

---

* As estimated by the United States Census Bureau after the 1980 census.

DNA is the master molecule of heredity—in fact, of all life. It is what the chromosomes and their constituent genes are made of. DNA is the molecule from which all life on earth seems to have sprung, from its dawn in prehistory through all the millennia of evolution, from protozoa to dinosaurs to people, all of whose "genetic codes" have been surprisingly alike.

DNA is millions and millions of years old—yet shows no signs of old age. As far as we know, DNA is the only organic substance in the universe that possesses the information to ensure its own virtual immortality. DNA has the unique ability to duplicate itself, again and again, almost without limit—as long as there are materials available from which it can manufacture new copies of itself. Following the genetic manual of instructions that is encoded biochemically into its molecular structure, it knows how to take what it needs from the environment and put it together as more DNA—and also the other things it needs, such as proteins, to keep alive the body it inhabits.

In the normal pattern of our lives, we mature, marry, have children, grow old, and die. The DNA in our cells may grow old along with us (at least, we believe it does), but it maintains its immortality—though occasionally changing some of its characteristics—by renewing itself in the mother's egg and the father's sperm. These combine to create a new individual who will carry on, unbroken, the chain of human life.

It is as if DNA *used* us to keep *itself* going. It discards individuals as blithely as a snake sheds its successive skins after they have outlived their usefulness, and simply continues its own life in the next generation. We like to think that *we* use DNA, that it is our way—or nature's, or God's—of perpetuating the human race. One might just as readily speculate that the purpose of human life is to perpetuate DNA!

We do take it as natural law that the outcome of every lived-out life must be aging and degeneration as precursors of death. But scientists have demonstrated in the past that even natural laws are subject to human amendment, once we learn how they work. Now that we have begun to fathom DNA's game, perhaps we can learn, by manipulating the genetic information, to use our new knowledge to gain some measure of immortality for ourselves—to use DNA rather than permit ourselves, passively resigned to our "fate," to continue to be used by it.

Every species of multicellular organism seems to have a fixed life span—but "fixed" under usual circumstances does not necessarily mean immutable under all circumstances. In fact, a number of experiments in recent years have suggested convincingly that there is nothing absolute about life's preordained endpoint in time. And this conviction has come about through experiments using relatively crude techniques that are a long way from the sophisticated control implied in schemes for manipulating the DNA.

If you restrict the diet of rats during early development, for example, to what would normally be deemed a semistarvation level (though still containing adequate nutrition), you extend their life spans. If you hook an old rat up to a younger one by a surgical procedure called "parabiosis," so that the two share a common blood circulation as Siamese twins do, the older rat lives considerably longer than his un-hooked-up littermates. An old cockroach, similarly linked to a young roach by parabiosis, will regain its youthful capacity to regenerate severed limbs. If you feed antioxidant compounds to mice or suppress the activity of their immune systems in certain circumstances, you retard the rate of aging. If you lower the temperature of certain cold-blooded creatures by a few degrees, they live longer. A combination of cooling and diet restriction at different periods of its development will triple the life span of the rotifer (a microscopic water-dwelling organism).

If you transplant skin cells from an aging animal to a younger one of the same species, then, as that one ages, retransplant the skin to another young one, and so on in serial fashion, the transplanted cells will outlive their original donor by a wide margin. If you add certain ingredients to the culture medium of human cells in tissue culture, the cells will live longer than they normally would— "normally" in this instance referring to the usual artificial conditions of life in laboratory tissue cultures.

There is a rare childhood disease called "progeria" in which the victim shows many signs of premature senescence in early childhood and dies of apparent old age in his early teens. If the aging process can thus be speeded up by accident, can it perhaps be slowed down by design?

All very fascinating, true enough.

But rats, roaches, and rotifers aren't people.

And isolated cells in tissue culture are not the same as whole living organisms.

And the course of a rare disease is not necessarily related in any way to what happens in the normal aging process.

And there is no unanimity among the experts as to what causes aging and what, if anything, might be done about it. In fact, the standard cliché used to be that there seem to be as many theories about aging as there are gerontologists.

Nevertheless, there has been some noticeable convergence among theorists, and growing agreement on the kinds of research that might test the validity of their hypotheses within reasonable periods of time, at reasonable expense. Moreover, the gerontologists themselves—those scientists who specialize in the study of the aging process—show every sign of mounting optimism and excitement as they pursue their far-flung investigations.

This book, as it surveys current gerontological research and theory, will explore the obvious question about the prospects of slowing down or even abolishing old age, and of significantly extending the vigorous years of our lives. The central question, of course, is whether or not we can really hope to do it. If that answer is affirmative, we will then have to examine the ethical question implied by the new biological possibilities—whether we *should* proceed to do it, just because we can. And we will want to make some guesses as to when we might expect the advances to occur, as well as what the consequences might be—personal, national, global—when the new knowledge begins to be acquired and applied.

Any consideration of consequences must of course be classified as sheer academic speculation unless the plausibility of success can first be reasonably documented. Hence the largest portion of the book will be addressed to that first crucial question: whether or not we can feasibly hope to succeed.

The subject of gerontology is vast and complex, and in such constant flux that it cannot be studied like a fly in amber, all details known and visible, but must be caught, as it were, in flight. Moreover, there is still much disagreement among students of the new knowledge, who often challenge one another's facts and observations, as well as the interpretation of those facts and observations. Nevertheless, they do so with an air of good cheer, confident that the situation is only temporary. Gerontologists of all schools can see ahead to a time when the kind of facts they can all agree upon will be in hand. Whichever theories of aging turn out to be correct, all researchers hold out high hopes that the answer will suggest ways to intervene.

The first advances will probably be limited in their application, but each significant advance should accelerate the acquisition of further knowledge and understanding. Eventually we will harness DNA and its genetic code to our own ends. When we have begun to do that, it is likely—for reasons shortly to be spelled out—that we will be well on our way to the final conquest of old age. There could, as we shall see, be a hormonal regulator of aging that might be discovered and manipulated without disturbing the DNA at all—at least, not directly. Long before we arrive at these stages of know-how, however, even relatively modest initial successes could be significant in terms of good years added to each individual's life.

P A R T   O N E

CAN WE DO IT?

"But the lengthening of the thread of life itself, and the post-ponement for a time of that death which gradually steals on by natural dissolution and the decay of age, is a subject which no physician has handled in proportion to its dignity."

—Francis Bacon,
The Advancement of Learning

"What happens to young flesh to make it old? I pinched the skin on the back of my hand, and it stayed up like a ridge of putty, only slowly flattening out. Loss of elastin. But what's elastin? Why do we lose it? What chemical breakdown or slowdown occurs, what little manufacturing plant fails or goes on strike?"

—Wallace Stegner,
The Spectator Bird

"It should be the function of medicine to have people die young as late as possible."

—Ernst Wynder, Epidemiologist,
President of the American Health Foundation

1

THE GERONTOLOGIST AS CAPTAIN AHAB

"LIVING things," according to the distinguished British zoologist J. Z. Young of the University of London, "act as they do because they are so organized as to take actions that prevent their dissolution into the surroundings." This is especially true of those highly developed living things called people, who, moved by psychology as well as biology, are equipped not only to observe but also to worry about the early signs of their dissolution into the surroundings. So moved and so equipped, they put forth great efforts—and encourage the medical profession to do the same in their behalf—to remain intact and keep their surroundings out where they belong.

Most of us, I think, believe intuitively that nature is on our side in these efforts: if only we would behave in accordance with nature's designs, assuming we knew what they were, then all would surely go well with us. Indeed, many sages, ancient and modern alike, have equated good health with "living in harmony with nature," an outlook they have prescribed as guide and governor of our everyday lives. In this implied scheme of things, a benevolent nature designs the human organism to go on as long as possible—perhaps forever; but the wear and tear of our days and years, exacerbated by our own follies, gradually slows us down and eventually does us in.

Is this an accurate portrayal of nature's game? Or has nature, rather, served its own purposes by *programming* us to run down and die by means of a preset "clock of aging"? It begins to look as if, in the matter of individual longevity, nature may not be on our side after all. At least, more and more gerontologists are coming around to the view that we are programmed to die, that the end of life really *is* built, genetically, in to its beginning. But this realization, if it is true, doesn't lead them to despair. On the contrary, it provides grounds for hope.

"Aging and death do seem to be what nature has planned for us," says Bernard L. Strehler, of the University of Southern California. "But what if we have other plans?" Strehler makes it plain that *he*, for one, has other plans. He characterizes death as a kind of Moby Dick, a tough, remorseless leviathan—never before conquered, to be sure, but still conquerable—and himself as one of the numerous Captain Ahabs out to get the great white whale. "And sooner or later," he vows, "we *are* going to get him!" He sounds both convinced and convincing as he plants his feet firmly on deck (he is actually standing, as he speaks, on the decklike wooden porch of his home in Agoura, California), looking every centimeter the tall, ruddy shipmaster, his eyes fixed on a far horizon. (In this case, the actual horizon—Malibu Lake's—is close at hand; and the ruddiness of Strehler's countenance is due more to a slight though chronic elevation in blood pressure than to the weathering effects of sun and wind.)

"I really hate death," he says, as we move back into the house. It is a straight-faced remark. He speaks with no trace of irony or resignation but, rather, in the testy, indignant tone one might use to complain about, say, air pollution, or graft at City Hall. "Death may be in accord with nature's plan so far. But there is no absolute principle in nature," he declares flatly, "which dictates that individual living things cannot live for indefinitely long periods of time in optimum health.

"I first became aware of death, with some sense of how unfair and how irrevocable it is, when the minister of our church died," he recalls. "I was not quite five years old when that happened." Young Bernie had already gone to bed when he heard his parents crying in the living room. He went halfway down the stairs, sat for a moment in puzzlement, then asked, "Why are you crying?"

"Reverend Tiersch has died," his mother told him.

Bernie was not sure what that meant, but he started crying, too. His parents hastened to assure him there was no need to be sad, really, that Reverend Tiersch was a good man and had certainly now gone to heaven to join Jesus. We all die sooner or later, they told him, and the upright minister now had a much better life to look forward to than was available on earth. Bernie, still sniffling, went back to bed thinking: If death is such a great thing for the minister, why are they still crying?

When Bernie was about seven, he and his brother had barely had time to grow attached to a mongrel named Skippy when the dog got distemper, started having convulsions, and finally had to be shot by a policeman in the family's back yard. That evening, Bernie's brother, who had been told that Skippy had gone to heaven, prayed that he, too, could die, so he could join his pet. "I found this innocent prayer most disquieting," says Strehler, "because my brother had, in fact, nearly died not long before that in a whooping-cough epidemic." A few years later the Strehler boys—and Bernie in particular—formed a much closer and longer-lasting attachment to their new dog, a fox terrier named Duke. When Duke died (of peritonitis, the aftermath of wounds suffered in a battle with a much larger dog), Bernie was desolate. And angry, too. "I remember thinking: Is this really necessary? Can't something be done about it?"

At this point in the story, Strehler pauses to hand me a few Xeroxed pages out of a book published in 1943. They contain an essay called "Immortality," written by himself at the age of seventeen, when, as a student at Central High School in Johnstown, Pennsylvania, he was awarded a Westinghouse Science Scholarship. "Immortality—that magic word is, I believe, the key to the direction which will be taken in the next great step forward in science," the essay begins. "From time immemorial man has sought, without avail, a way to eliminate or reverse the effects of time on the human body. . . ."

It goes on to speak of a "protoplasmic desire for unending existence." Art and religion, literature, music, and philosophy "are all, whether so intended or not, the mediums by which we propagate our personalities and ourselves," resulting in a kind of "thought immortality." But this kind of vicarious immortality, lived through the awareness of posterity, "is not enough for man, for the innate property of protoplasm, self preservation, must be satisfied. Man will never be contented until he conquers death." After a quick survey of some of the relatively sparse gerontological data that existed in the early 1940s, the final paragraph reads: "From this and other data I have come to the conclusion that senility and death are as a race, and that through scientific research we shall eventually be able to remove the sorrows of death from the human mind." not the inevitable ends of human existence, either as individuals or

A remarkable essay for a seventeen-year-old.* And here is Strehler, nearly forty years later, still talking in the same manner. There have been a few doubts along the way, but by and large he has held on to his dream. Some critics might regard Strehler's loyalty to his teen-age vision as merely a failure to outgrow his adolescence. Is he prey to simple illusions, like Ponce de León hunting for the Fountain of Youth or some alchemist seeking to brew an "elixir of life"? Thomas R. Cole of the Institute for the Medical Humanities at UTMB/Galveston reminds us that this country, during the years from 1890 to 1920, saw a flowering of enthusiastic support for prolongevity based on claims that were soon disproved. Are the grounds for Strehler's optimism any more substantial? He has every reason to believe so, outlandish as his declarations may sound.

His confidence is based on the new tools of biology, and on the rapidly proliferating knowledge of the basic processes of life, including human life. Strehler has done pathbreaking work of his own in gerontology, some of which will be described presently; he has written a seminal book on the subject, *Time, Cells and Aging*; and had President Richard Nixon not vetoed the bill that would have established a National Institute on Aging in 1972, Strehler would certainly have been a candidate for its directorship. The research he has carried out, along with the mass of new information provided by numerous other investigators in the intervening years (which he keeps track of partly by editing the journal *Mechanisms in Ageing and Development*), has only served to confirm and strengthen Strehler's early optimism.

Moreover, he is far from alone in his views. A growing number of his colleagues—many of whom have expressed themselves on the subject independently of Strehler, and perhaps even prior to him— are now willing to countenance the belief that to grow old physiologically, merely because the calendar has marked the passage of

---

* In *Maximum Life Span*, published in 1982, gerontologist Roy L. Walford of UCLA reports that he wrote a similar article, also at the age of seventeen, for his high-school magazine, in which he said: "Elders have received positively no gain from science concerning expectant life span . . . [but] death is not a necessary adjunct of living matter."

sixty, eighty, or even a hundred years, may not, after all, be an inevitable consequence of human life. Many believe, further, that we contain within ourselves a mechanism, an elusive clock of aging, whose working secrets are no longer necessarily beyond our understanding or our tampering.

Dylan Thomas advised his father: "Do not go gentle into that good night / Rage, rage against the dying of the light." To which the writer Alan Harrington, in *The Immortalist*, responds: " 'Do not go gentle into that good night' does not apply here. Rather aim not to go at all; mobilize the scientists, spend the money, and hunt death down like an outlaw."

This exhortation fairly describes what Strehler's aims have been: to mobilize the scientists, spend the money, and hunt death down like an outlaw. He has been reinforced in his determination by further events in his personal life, not least of which was the death of a small daughter by drowning.

Having long since recruited himself for the effort, Strehler has spent a lot of time and energy propagandizing, particularly among fellow scientists. Other gerontologists, many of whom we will meet in due course, have been similarly evangelistic. The job has not been easy. "Gerontology," as Strehler has lamented, "used to be too frequently associated in people's minds with quacks and dubious rejuvenators. It was considered a not-quite-respectable branch of biology to choose as a career." (As he said that, I remembered a British geneticist telling me that gerontologists were, by and large, "a ragbag lot.") But investigators with unassailable credentials have continued to move into the field. And now that the United States finally has an official National Institute on Aging, established in 1974 as part of the National Institutes of Health, new people continue to be lured to where the money is.

"Who has not felt a nostalgic or desperate longing to see the 'I' perpetuated in some form," Strehler has written, in *Perspectives in Biology and Medicine*, "to live beyond the pale of what we know as real?" Later in the same series of sketches, Strehler— who yearns for prolongevity in the same shameless, articulate manner as ever did the late Miguel de Unamuno—bursts into poetry:

> *Do men truly, truly go to dust and speak no more*
> *When breathing stops?*

And again:

> *Time (Oh, Time) I curse your ugly hours*
> *And would wring a respite*
> *From your bloodless pursing lips!*

Bernie Strehler—a good and gentle man, despite his size and booming voice to match—does have to keep a watchful eye on his blood pressure. And he smokes too much. When his friends chide him for not taking better care of himself (he knows he should) and working too hard (he knows he does), he smiles and—ever mindful of himself as Ahab, and death as the great white whale—replies, "Maybe I'll get him before he gets me."

Few gerontologists—even among the avant-garde, which Strehler represents—would predict the outright abolition of death. But many would certainly go along with the more modest forecast that old age, with all its attendant aches and ills, may well be abolished, and the life span extended, perhaps for a substantial number of years.

2

SENESCENCE AS A CURABLE DISEASE

GERONTOLOGISTS take pains to emphasize that they are not practitioners of the medical specialty of "geriatrics," which concerns itself primarily with the study and treatment of old people's diseases. Gerontology (*geron* is Greek for "old man") seeks, rather, to prevent people from getting old at all. It studies the aging process itself, and in *all* species.

The two areas do overlap, of course, especially since an increasing number of gerontologists are finding it useful to take a somewhat geriatric view of the matter—that old age itself is just another disease. It is a disease everyone gets, to be sure, and the individual who survives all the other diseases invariably succumbs to this one. But just because a disease is universal and has always been fatal does not—in this revised reasoning—make it inevitably so. Merely to think about aging as a degenerative ailment, rather than as man's eternal and preordained fate, is to put it in the category of a medical problem—something your doctor may some day hope to do something about.*

---

* As historians Gruman and Cole point out, prolongevity advocates have often in the past thought of aging as a disease to be treated, perhaps abolished. "Most persons in our society," writes philosopher Arthur L. Caplan of the Hastings Center, "would be loath to see aging classified and treated as a disease. Much of the resistance to such a classification derives from the view that aging is a natural process and that, like other natural processes, it ought not, in itself, be the subject of medical intervention and therapeutic control." Caplan argues that aging is no more natural or inevitably untreatable than any other human disease. Emerson considered old age "the only disease," the one into which "all others run."

Another way of expressing one of gerontology's unabashed aims, then, is this: to cure or prevent the disease we now call old age, or senescence. Its other major aim—to extend the human life span—is puzzling to many people who, aware that we already do live a lot longer than we used to, ask: Hasn't the human life span already been extended? The answer is that it has not. What has been extended is the *average life expectancy*. We do live much longer, on the average, because we have eliminated so many of the diseases and circumstances that used to kill us off prematurely in such large numbers. But the life *span*, the maximum longevity of the individual, has remained essentially unchanged.

In ancient Greece, for instance—let's say Athens in the age of Pericles—the average life expectancy was something like twenty-two years, but individuals did live to ripe old ages in those days, too. The number of the elders was small enough, however, to render them an elite in most ancient societies, where their seasoning was rare and their wisdom prized. They made up the powerful kosmoi of Crete, the ephors of Sparta, the archons of Athens. A Greek who reached the age of seventy in the fifth century B.C. had just as many years left to live—perhaps more, since he had to be tougher to have survived so long under such conditions—as does the seventy-year-old of today, who has merely reached his average life expectancy.

Sophocles wrote *Oedipus Rex* when he was seventy-five, and won the last of his many dramatic prizes at eighty-five, still going strong. And he needed no contemporary equivalent of Masters and Johnson to tell him that men of that age were still sexually effective. He not only kept his bed and bones warm with the famous hetaera Theoris (who was succeeded at an even later date by Archippe) but also became a father again. In fact, his legitimate son, Iophon, suspecting he might be disinherited in favor of Theoris or her child, tried to have his aging father declared incompetent. But Sophocles satisfied the court he was sound in mind by reading them a few choruses from the drama he was in the midst of composing—probably *Oedipus at Colonus*, which he finished at eighty-nine, a year before his death. Such vigorous longevity can be found today, but it is still rare. The maximum life span has *not* been extended. And our contemporaries who reach seventy, eighty, and ninety probably have just as many aches and failings as the ancients did, though there may be a few more medications available to ease their more troublesome symptoms.

The fact that so many of us *do* reach seventy and beyond (74.2 years was the official average life expectancy for the United States in 1981) is what makes us more aware than ever how universal are the ravages of the process of aging—ravages that made even Sophocles, for all his honors and amours, a thoroughgoing pessimist in his declining years.* We have plenty of opportunities to observe the inexorable nature of these aging changes, their variety, their sheer multiplicity, and their interlocking complexity. In the face of all this, most traditional gerontologists have maintained an unshakable conservatism, despite the boldness of their stated goals. The prevailing view, understandably, has been that, considering the multifaceted nature of the aging process, it would be foolish to count on any significant progress toward final answers until countless further generations of painstaking experimentation shall have passed.

Typical of this cautious outlook, even among scientists not reputed to be especially conservative, is the conclusion of a 1962 paper in *Proceedings of the Royal Society*. Its author, anatomist P. L. Krohn of England's University of Birmingham, after describing a brilliantly original series of experiments designed to study the effects of transplantation on aging tissue, finally notes: "Nothing has been said to imply that problems of old age are likely soon to be solved by this approach. The solution will probably come as slowly and insidiously as the ageing process itself."

But the spirited avant-garde that Strehler represents is strong in its conviction that significant progress can be made within our own lifetimes, within this century. How *much* progress? How significant? How soon? There is no way to forecast with precision. But the more confident gerontologists do not rule out the possibility of buying a little extra time for themselves personally while waiting for the larger

---

* Though long-lived, Sophocles was no advocate of prolongevity. He wrote in *Oedipus at Colonus*:

> *Who craves excess of days,*
> *Scorning the common span*
> *Of life, I judge that man*
> *A giddy wight who walks in folly's ways.*

advances to be accomplished—much as a leukemia victim might hope for the larger breakthroughs to occur while he is in remission.

Scientists who a few years earlier would have deplored such speculations as being in the realm of the quack and the con man are now distressed that the general public just won't give serious credence to the new possibilities. If people begin to believe in them, progress will certainly occur more rapidly. Alex Comfort is among those who have consistently argued not just that a project to slow down aging is feasible but that it could be carried out for relatively modest sums of money.

What worries some gerontologists more than public attitudes is the skepticism of some of their own biologist colleagues, who have regarded them somewhat pityingly, as if they were, like O'Neill's boozers in *The Iceman Cometh*, deluding themselves with wild pipe dreams. Listen, for example, to Lewis Thomas, president of the Memorial Sloan-Kettering Cancer Center and professor of pathology and medicine at the Cornell University College of Medicine, giving a major address before the American College of Surgeons in Houston on March 27, 1974 (italics mine): "If we are not struck down, prematurely, by one or another of today's diseases, we live a certain length of time and then we die, and I doubt that medicine will ever gain a capacity to do anything much to modify this. *I can see no reason for trying, and no hope of success anyway.* At a certain age, it is in our nature to wear out, to come unhinged and to die, and that is that." It is not that I would ever have singled out Lewis Thomas, of all people, as representing the old-fogey school of biology. Quite the opposite. He is one of the more liberal and forward-looking members of the biomedical community, a man of great vision and imagination, the author of such marvelously insightful books of biophilosophical essays as *The Lives of a Cell.**

There exists, in biomedical science (and practically everywhere else, too), a phenomenon I think of as The Josh Billings Syndrome. The name derives from Billings's celebrated observation: "The trouble with people is not that they don't know, but that they know so

---

* Since 1974, Lewis Thomas has considerably modified his views about gerontological prospects. In fact, he serves on the Scientific Advisory Committee of the Fund for Integrative Biomedical Research (FIBER), whose focus is the facilitation of research on aging; and gives talks and writes articles on aging with, it seems to me, something close to a prolongevity bias.

much that ain't so." The syndrome may be defined as the collection of tendencies that lead even the most authoritative experts (in fact, *especially* the most authoritative experts) to let what they think they know get in the way of what they might learn. If they know something ain't so, it ain't hardly worth looking at—right? They forget that what they know now ain't necessarily so forever. Thus they weigh future possibilities on the basis of present knowledge, techniques, and assumptions.

A biologist may know, for instance, how staggeringly difficult it is to carry out a certain biochemical operation to get a relatively simple piece of information. The prospect of acquiring information that is incredibly more complicated, even with the most sophisticated techniques at his command (techniques that, he tends to forget, may look very crude in the light of later discoveries), seems impossibly remote, and—as a leading expert in the field—he doesn't mind saying so.

Thus we debate matters such as genetic engineering, the notion that we may one day be able to manipulate our genetic material for our own purposes. This capacity could be vital to any total solution to the aging problem, as I will explain in later chapters. We had already taken our first halting laboratory steps toward genetic engineering when *Prolongevity* was first published, in 1976. Even so, the difficulties looked so intractable that Nobel-caliber minds and talents such as Jacques Monod in France and Sir Macfarlane Burnet in Australia—both of whom had made impressive and original contributions to our current understanding of biology—did not hesitate to predict that truly efficient genetic engineering would probably be forever beyond our grasp. Yet the astonishing and unforeseeable biotechnological breakthroughs of the past few years have actually put it within our grasp—or at least within our reach.

So experts such as Monod and Burnet and the legion of distinguished scientists of similar persuasion can be wrong and frequently are. Arthur C. Clarke was only half joking when he promulgated his "law" holding that whenever an expert insists that a problem is impossible to solve, he is certainly premature and almost certainly mistaken.

As Lewis Thomas has written, "The difficulties are more conspicuous when the problems are very hard and complicated and the facts not yet in. Solutions cannot be arrived at for problems of this sort until the science has been lifted through a preliminary, turbulent zone of outright astonishment. Therefore, what must be planned for, in the laboratories engaged in the work, is the totally unforeseeable. If it is centrally organized, the system must be designed primarily for the elicitation of disbelief and the celebration of surprise."

In any scientific endeavor, skepticism and caution constitute simple good sense. An eager young theorist, on fire with a Big Idea, may well be in danger of failing to consider the magnitude of the potential obstacles and, in his naïve enthusiasm, may rush ahead in the expectation that his experiments will carry him from Hello to Hallelujah in a straight line. But not many scientists, not even very young ones, sin in this manner. There is more danger that mature, experienced, eminent scientists—surer of what they know—will pronounce the goals of others to be impossible, or so remote as not to be worth the expenditure of immediate effort or attention.

It is hard to think of anything that exists in our civilized lives that would not once have been declared impossible. Look at the 350 passengers aboard a jumbo jet. See them lifted aloft and carried across the ocean in a few hours—carried in comfort, too, fed a sumptuous meal, shown a movie, given a choice of seven stereo listening channels. That implausible series of events does, as we know, happen routinely every day, many times a day, in many parts of the world. One would not have to go very far back in time to find the world's sanest, most knowing authorities, confronted with such a description, declaring that such a technological—and social—feat was among the more preposterous and unattainable fantasies they had ever heard.

Let's take another example, this time from the realm of pure theoretical physics: the case of the neutrino. In 1931, studying the disintegration phenomenon known as beta decay, Wolfgang Pauli could account for everything except a half-unit of "spin." This was intolerable, because it violated the law of the conservation of angular momentum and energy. So, as an admitted "accountant's trick" to make the atomic books balance, Pauli invented the neutrino (Fermi's name—"little neutral one"), a most curious subatomic "particle." Since all it possessed was that half-unit of spin, it had no rest mass, no electrical charge, no magnetic moment, no way of interacting with any other particle except by the most improbable chance.

How improbable? Physicists calculated that an average neutrino would pass through *fifty light-years of solid lead* before the chance interaction took place. Imagine the thick lead shielding around a nuclear reactor. Imagine it extending—the lead shield thickening, in a solid, unbroken mass—out beyond the sun, out beyond Alpha Centauri, out as far as light could travel nonstop through the galaxy in fifty years—and to the neutrino, all that might as well be empty space! Trillions upon trillions of neutrinos might pass through the earth in a split second, and no particle on earth would be the wiser for it.

Obviously, the neutrino would always remain a purely theoretical particle, since no one could even imagine the means by which it might ever be detected. But then some new and unforeseen things came into being: (1) nuclear reactors, which, if neutrinos existed, should be emitting enormous quantities of them, sufficient quantities to increase the chance of an occasional interaction; (2) liquid scintillating compounds, full of protons packed at unprecedented densities, thus further increasing the chance of interactions; (3) photomultiplier tubes, which amplify detection capabilities several millionfold.

Now, neither nuclear reactors, scintillating compounds, nor photomultiplier tubes were devised with the neutrino in mind. But once they all existed, it occurred to two Los Alamos physicists, Frederick Reines and Clyde Cowan, that they might be put together for particular purposes. Reines and Cowan did so, in a brilliantly imaginative and painstaking series of experiments, and behold, they detected the neutrino. (They actually detected the *anti*neutrino first— but let's not complicate the story unnecessarily.) That happened in 1956, exactly twenty-five years after the invention of the particle that could never possibly be detected.

To have pronounced the neutrino forever undetectable was obviously (we now see) premature. Yet there were much better grounds for doing so than for making a similar mistake about the goals of gerontology, a field in which one does not have to count on future technological windfalls of similar magnitude to make the search feasible, in which one can already begin to envision the experimental programs that must be carried out to achieve the desired ends, and in which encouraging evidence has indeed been coming in at an accelerating rate.

It is not that gerontologists of the old school—and they still undoubtedly represent the majority view—are given to making fatuously negative statements about the possibilities of success; otherwise, they would probably look for a different line of work. They simply are skeptical that any clock-of-aging theory, any genetic program, can truly encompass all the bewildering occurrences that accompany human aging: the wrinkle and sag and flab, the stoop and shuffle, the dimming and dulling of eye and ear, while, out of sight, the lungs, heart, arteries, liver, kidneys, brain, and all other organs and systems function ever more slowly. Connective tissue gets tough and fibrous. The whole organism loses substance; it shrinks. It copes less ably with stress. It falls prey more easily to cancer, arthritis, cardiovascular disease, diabetes, autoimmune disorders, senile dementia, infection. This has always seemed to be the natural and inevitable outcome of life, and the more cautious gerontologists— though hoping for eventual success—doubt that we will be in a position to do much more about our mortal predicament for a very long time to come.

Among the many well-respected gerontologists who, as we shall see, have no need for a genetic clock of aging to explain senility and death is Robert R. Kohn of Case Western Reserve University in Cleveland, distinguished author of *Principles of Mammalian Aging.* As we sat chatting a few summers ago, in the front lobby of the Jackson Laboratory in Bar Harbor, Maine, where we were both attending a short course in genetics, Kohn expressed the belief that the wearing down and wearing out of the organism and its parts through mere exposure to the world over a long period of time may be sufficient, in itself, to account for all the phenomena of aging.

This view is simply (perhaps oversimply) illustrated by what Sir Peter Medawar—who, among his other numerous contributions to biology, was the first to link genetics and aging—has called the "broken test-tube" theory of aging. Suppose one were to study the life experiences of a large "population" of test tubes undergoing routine use in a laboratory. Though test tubes are inanimate objects possessing no organic aging mechanisms, some might crack or break easily through some inherent structural weaknesses (birth defects?). Others would periodically be damaged or broken through chance or accident. Some of these would still be used for varying periods of time despite cracking, chipping, or corrosion. Others would be discarded and have to be replaced. Some could better withstand the strains—or would, by chance, undergo fewer strains—than others, and thus would last much longer. But eventually the entire original population of test tubes will have "died," and one could then plot a "survival curve" of aging and death. Does this not bear a strong resemblance to what happens to human populations? Logical enough, admittedly. And also consistent with observations, up to a point. But far from sufficient to explain all that happens either in the laboratory or in real-life circumstances.

Because the older explanations leave so much still unexplained, interest in the avant-garde view has been growing in research laboratories all over the world. This view is easy to summarize. Though even avant-garde gerontologists differ in the details of their schemes and their persuasions, they are clearly coming together in the common convictions (1) that there does exist within us an identifiable "clock of aging," a genetically determined program dictating that we will age and die, and the rate at which this will occur; (2) that we have an excellent chance of discovering the location (there may be more than one) of the clock of aging, as well as the nature of its operating mechanisms—and how to interfere with them to our own advantage; (3) that, moreover, all this can begin to happen, not centuries from now, but *now*, if only the research can be carried out; and (4) that senescence may thus be started on its way to obsolescence.

3

THE GENETICS OF LIFE—
AND MAYBE DEATH

NATURE does, of course, program us to survive, but only up to a point. That point is the production of offspring and the rearing of those progeny to the realization of their own procreative capacities. It would appear that nature has an unflattering lack of concern for our preservation as individuals, except as instruments to ensure the perpetuation of the species. Even that may be surmising too much. So many species have come and gone in the earth's lifetime that we are well advised not to regard the human race as possessing a guaranteed future.

What nature does seem to do, however—once a species has gone to all the evolutionary trouble of coming into being—is to give that species a fighting chance, if only through sheer extravagant multiplication. Many of the lower orders are notorious for the thousands upon thousands of eggs they produce in order that a few may survive. In fact, it is clear that only a few are *meant* to survive.

Nature is nothing if not redundant. A queen termite may, during her long reign, produce as many as 500 million eggs. Edwin Way Teale has calculated that if all the eggs generated by a single aphid in a single year were to develop into full-grown individual aphids (which are not very large creatures) and laid end to end, they would stretch for trillions of miles out into the galaxy. In our own case, nature demonstrates its prodigality by supplying the female ovary with many more thousands of oöcytes than can ever ripen into eggs, while a single ejaculation of semen may release somewhere between

100 million and a quarter of a billion spermatazoa, in the hope that one may survive the journey's hazards and attain its goal. We also get plenty of chances to try again, and again—a privilege not afforded the male praying mantis, for instance, whose mate bites off his head while the very act is in progress. There are many more human conceptions than there are births; we can only estimate the quantities of spontaneous abortions that occur unbeknownst to the potential parents. And of course many more babies are born than survive to the age of procreation, though our continuing intervention has now radically altered the statistics.

Nature's wildly improbable experiments with species do seem to be more random than directed, though we are far from having enough data to arrive at such a teleological conclusion. In any case, no matter how unwieldy, inefficient, or cruel the experiment may seem in human terms, if a given design works in terms of simple propagation, the resulting creature tends to survive. There is a certain species of silkworm, for example, that takes many months of development to reach the spinning stage. Once it does, it eats not, neither does it sleep; all its genes are turned on to doing nothing but spinning silk for its protective cocoon. Eventually out squeezes a moth, unfolding into a creature truly beautiful to behold—who, if a mate happens along in time, copulates once, lives for a few days, and dies. All that buildup for a flickering propagative opportunity.

The Pacific salmon is a powerful orange-red fish equipped to muscle its way like a decathlon champion through all obstacles. A veritable antigravity machine, it swims upstream against the rapids, jumps up and over waterfalls as it moves with undistractable compulsion to its spawning grounds. Once spawning has taken place, this magnificent embodiment of piscine strength, health, and beauty—having discharged its procreative obligations—grows old with obscene suddenness. Senility sets in virtually overnight, and within two weeks the great gold fish is dead.

The fate of the Pacific salmon is an extreme example of nature's loss of interest in the individual once reproduction is assured. We human individuals require more time, since our task entails more than just seeing that a mess of eggs are safely deposited and fertilized. Human children come, as a rule, one at a time. And each must be carried for many long months inside its mother, and nurtured for many long years by its parents. This program offers the less prolific human propagators a fair chance at success with far fewer offspring.

The individual human life may be likened to one of NASA's planetary "fly-bys"—a comparison that has grown popular in gerontological circles. NASA has launched many space vehicles designed to fly by Venus, Mercury, Mars, or Jupiter. The craft's mission, in each case, is to fly past the planet and, as it does so, with its sophisticated array of instruments, monitors, and cameras, to pick up and send back all possible information about the target planet's composition, density, terrain, atmosphere, temperature gradients, seismic activity, gravitational and magnetic fields, and whatever else the scientists are able to investigate. The space engineers design the vehicle and all its instruments with great care and precision. If everything does not survive the long and dangerous trip in good enough condition to function properly when it arrives, then the whole effort has been wasted. So all systems are meticulously monitored all the way to the planet; the data that are sent back constitute a treasury of new knowledge; the scientists and engineers are elated. But when the fly-by's task is done, the designers lose all further interest in the vehicle. They have their "baby." The vehicle may travel out into space for a long time; its instruments may even continue to function for a while, but nobody cares. In some fly-bys, a self-destruct mechanism may be installed to ensure that the vehicle's life comes to an explosive end at a predestined moment.

It is a reasonable analogy. Unlike the planetary fly-by, however, we are sentient vehicles, and *we* care about our individual fates, even if the designer no longer does. Moreover, we are intelligent, and have been accumulating sufficient knowledge about our own workings to give us hope that we can now begin to do something to modify what was formerly beyond human intervention.

We have had some limited success, as already noted. In ancient Greece, the average life expectancy of twenty-two was enough to guarantee the continuation of the species. But we have gone on, over recent centuries, to raise this expectancy beyond the scriptural three score and ten. Now we know we can do even better, extending not just expectancy, but the actual life span. We can discover what keeps this fly-by from functioning after its official mission is complete (by DNA's standards?); and we can perhaps restore those functions, or prevent their running down. If there is a self-destruct mechanism aboard—as many believe—we can find it, and abort or dismantle it.

To understand how it is that we age and die, we must first understand how it is that we live at all, how it is that—going against the entropic trend, defying the Second Law of Thermodynamics, which governs the nonbiological universe, blithely increasing the complexity of its organization instead of petering out into an amorphous chaos—a single-celled organism, the original fertilized egg, guided by a compact set of genetic instructions in its nucleus, can develop into a thinking, feeling creature made up of some sixty trillion or more variegated and marvelously orchestrated living cells. The living cell, and the genetic information concentrated in its nucleus, will play a critical role in our exploration of the aging process.

But before we talk of the cell—or of the body as a population of cells—it is worth a little time and attention to dispel a widespread mistaken impression: that the body is made *entirely* of cells, and of nothing but cells. In fact, much of the body is composed of material not contained in cells. "If it became possible to remove miraculously all cells from the body, as well as all free fluids," writes Macfarlane Burnet in *Genes, Dreams and Realities*, "one would have something that was still the shape of a man and probably still as difficult to disintegrate." The noncellular portions of the body are composed of crystalline minerals (bones and teeth) and fibrous proteins such as collagen and elastin, which constitute a large part of the body's connective tissue and help hold the bones together. All these are made up of protein molecules and, though not cellular themselves, were originally produced by cells and are repaired by cells—until the cells can no longer repair them. So it is still the genetic information in the cells on which the welfare and very existence of these noncellular materials depend. These fibers, these protein molecules, are all products of the same set of genetic instructions contained in the original egg.

The reason I place such emphasis on this last point is the claim occasionally raised in objection to any cellular theories of aging: if this material is not cellular, and it does age, then how can the "clock of aging" be within the cell? The answer is that if the instructions for building and repairing these extracellular materials can be within the cell, so can the program for their aging. The contractor who built the building can also tear it down.

The cells that make up the human body are so diverse in their sizes, shapes, functions, and what would appear to be their basic natures that an innocent observer, examining them under the microscope, might well take them to be entirely different and unrelated species of one-celled organisms. Yet they all contain the same package of genetic information, which dictates what they do, when and how they do it, and perhaps when and how they *stop* doing it.

The fertilized human egg, the initial and initiating cell, contains in its compact nucleus forty-six chromosomes. These make up a fantastically miniaturized data bank, the entire manual of genetic instructions by means of which—assuming proper food and fuel, and the absence of disastrous accidents—the single cell that is the fertilized egg will convert itself into a multitrillion-celled adult human being. (Whether the resulting individual is to become a woman or a man is also already decided, depending on whether or not the fertilizing sperm has brought a male-producing Y chromosome to the union.) The chromosomes are composed of DNA molecules, whose spiral lattices are chemically coded with the individual's entire hereditary future in detail,* as well as the specific information each cell needs to carry out its day-to-day activities. It has been estimated that this information, translated into English print, would fill a couple of dozen sets of the *Encyclopaedia Britannica*.

And, mind you, *all* this information, every detail of it, is supposed to be copied *exactly*, each time the cell divides. The presumption is that, if the individual has grown to normal maturity, every cell in his body does in fact contain the entire genetic manual—though any particular cell uses only part of it.

After the first few cell divisions of embryonic life, new cells already begin to "differentiate"; that is, they become a bit more specialized. Indeed, if they all used all the genetic information, an aimless, amorphous growth would result, rather than a patterned development, and the embryo would be spontaneously aborted. Very early in embryonic life, certain genes (a gene is the information contained on a particular segment of the DNA molecule) begin to be "switched off," inactivated chemically—perhaps covered up

---

* The individual's actual future cannot be predicted from the genetic information alone, because the detailed outcome is contingent on the interaction of the genes with their environment at every step along the developmental pathway. The genes, then, represent what the individual *may* become.

physically—by certain proteins made especially for the purpose. (These "repressors" act as if they were removed at appropriate times by "derepressors," which thus turn the gene on again.) During embryonic and fetal development, genes are being constantly switched on and off, so that cells "know" when to divide and when to stop dividing.* (Later in life, when cells lose this genetic control, they may proliferate blindly and become cancerous.)

Though the chromosomes are made of DNA, a series of proteins dwells intimately in the nucleus alongside the DNA. The structure and function of some of these proteins are still largely unknown. Together the DNA-protein complexes are part of the "chromatin." Intensive investigations around the world have suggested that these nuclear proteins are what turn the genes on and off, perhaps by causing the DNA to uncoil or unfold at critical times to make genes physically accessible. Some genes, it is believed, may turn on only once in the cell's lifetime, providing the blueprint needed for one specific chemical product, then turn off again forever. The exact "start" and "stop" signals for some genes are beginning to be known—knowledge whose importance can hardly be exaggerated.

Cells are constantly dying and being replaced during the entire prenatal period. In fact, more cells die before birth than die at death! Joan M. Whitten of Northwestern University, writing in *Science*, emphasizes the importance of cell death to the proper formation of arms, legs, fingers, and toes—or, for that matter, the limbs and digits of any vertebrate species. When, at a critical point in digit formation, a chemical interfering with cell death is injected into an experimental animal embryo, the digits, intended to be formed with spaces between them, grow together in webbed fashion instead. Whitten had saved the lives of the cells that were programmed to die, but, in so doing, she had crippled the animal! Such "life-saving" mistakes occur during human embryonic development and result in birth defects.

Whitten carried out experiments of her own with insects, in which embryonic cell death was believed to be much less frequent and important. But she found a "dramatic" incidence of cell death, "wholly unexpected for the insect," and concluded that "death clocks

---

* Barbara Migeon of Johns Hopkins reported in 1984 that in women one of the X chromosomes is inactivated in the egg cells as in all other cells—but in the egg cells only, the other X is later reactivated (derepressed).

and their genetic programming seem to function in establishing shape in the insect as they do in vertebrate morphogenesis."

She then notes two contrasting types of programmed cell death. "In the vertebrate limb the death clocks function on time even when the tissue is transferred to a host of different age," which she takes as strong proof that "the timing of the vertebrate death clock is independent of external factors." When insects metamorphose from one stage to another, however, cell death is triggered from the outside—by hormones; in this case the cells are already differentiated, but have built-in receptors programmed to initiate cell death on hormonal signal.

Whitten's conclusions were supported by pathologist J. N. Webb of the Edinburgh Northern Hospital Group in Scotland in experiments aimed at discovering the mechanisms by which cell death occurs in embryonic muscle cells. Such cell death, writes Webb in *Nature*, "takes place in a highly predictable manner and all the evidence points to it being genetically controlled." Webb believes that the programmed death of these cells "must . . . serve a function which is probably crucial to the subsequent healthy development and growth of that tissue." The failure of the death switches to operate on schedule may result in their switching on at a later time of life. This anachronistic turn of events could cause a disease such as muscular dystrophy. In that case, Webb believes, the disease could be looked upon "as a normal process, but one occurring at the wrong time in the individual's life span—or else one which has not been repressed."

The course of embryonic development demands that cells of all types keep dying while new ones are created to shape the growing organism. In biology, growth is not the mere accretion of cells but, rather, the transformation, through time, of the developing being from one stage to the next to the next. If cells can be killed off in such wholesale quantities by a genetic program at the beginning of life, there is no reason this cannot continue to take place at a decelerated rate throughout life—with perhaps another spurt of acceleration toward the end of it. When the silkworm turns into a moth, enormous quantities of cells must die and new ones be created to bring about the birth of a being that bears no resemblance to the one from which it emerged.

Holger P. von Hahn of the Institute of Experimental Gerontology in Basel, Switzerland, has proposed the existence of genes that specifically regulate aging.* And it is not surprising that genetic on/off switching devices figure importantly in some theories of aging, including Strehler's. In the embryo and fetus, the switches are important not just for cell division and its cessation, but also so that each cell will know how to carry out its specific program as a skin cell, a muscle cell, or whatever specialized role is ordained for it.

In the adult organism, some cells go on dividing, and thus replacing themselves, throughout life. These are called "mitotic" cells (from "mitosis"—division—from the Greek word *mitos* [thread]; as the cell divides, its nucleus appears to split up into small threads). Others never divide again once the organism is full-grown. These are called "postmitotic" or "resting" cells. In between are other cells that do not ordinarily divide, but can begin doing so again when circumstances demand it. Liver cells serve as a good example of this in-between category. They appear to be postmitotic, but if a piece of the liver is cut away or damaged, the division switches are somehow turned on again in response to the challenge, and they spring into action until the missing piece is regenerated, at which point they turn off again. (A salamander can regenerate a lopped-off limb in this fashion. Some biologists believe it will one day be possible for human amputees to do likewise, once we know enough about on/off switching.)

Among the mitotic cells that divide throughout life are the outside or surface cells, such as skin cells and the epithelial cells that line the gastrointestinal tract. It may seem strange to hear the gut and stomach—which we usually think of as our innermost innards—referred to as being "outside." Yet, in a sense, they really are. The entire tract that has to do with eating, digesting, and eliminating runs all the way from the mouth to the anus in a single, unbroken space. It is a tube that, though it changes shape as it goes, is still a definable and visible structure, a continuous tunnel that opens to the outside world at both ends. Food gets into the body's *real* innards only by seeping through the tunnel's permeable walls. So the lining

* George M. Martin of the University of Washington School of Medicine in Seattle has estimated—based on a study of all the known genetic disorders—that as many as seventy genes may be involved in aging. But, as we shall see, a number of investigators—among them USC's Bernard Strehler, NIA's Richard G. Cutler, UCLA's Roy Walford, and Florida's Leonard Hayflick—believe that the "clock of aging" could be contained in a very few regulatory genes, or even a clustered "supergene."

of this tract *is* like an outside surface, and its cells are in many ways similar to skin cells. At any rate, all these surface cells keep dying off and replacing themselves through continuing cell division. So do the blood cells—red as well as white—including the lymphocytes, the cells of the body's immune system.

Among the postmitotic cells—those that never do divide again—are those of the muscles and nervous system. After a myocardial infarction (a heart attack), part of the heart muscle may be irreparably damaged—irreparably because these cells, unlike liver cells, are *not* switched on to regenerate themselves. A few researchers have been trying to "teach" heart cells how to regenerate in tissue culture; if they succeed, the hope is that heart cells in the living body can be taught to do the same. After a stroke, when brain cells are denied oxygen and therefore die, or when parts of the brain are damaged by any other means, this same incapacity to regenerate renders the damage permanent. In fact, under perfectly normal circumstances of aging, it was once estimated that as many as 100,000 brain cells a day die off after the age of thirty-five—hardly a negligible loss, even though the brain cells initially number in the billions. The subject of brain-cell death, however, especially regarding the daily numbers involved, is a matter of some controversy; it has been seriously challenged by Alex Comfort, among many others. But the major fact about postmitotic cells is that, once they die, they are dead and gone forever.

Any theory of cellular aging must encompass both mitotic and postmitotic cells, as well as those in-between categories, in all their astonishing diversity of types. Many decry the idea that there could be a single genetic clock of aging located in the nucleus of each cell, which is one of the popular theories: if such a clock existed, they argue, how could it account for the different ways in which these cells age and die? This raises no theoretical difficulty, for me. If the same packet of DNA can program the cells to develop so differently, and to live such different existences, it can surely program them to age and die differently as well. It is, in fact, exactly what one would expect.

4

THE PROTEIN ASSEMBLY LINES

BECAUSE cells are programmed so differently, often in response to specific triggering by hormones, one wonders that they have any activities in common at all. But they do, of course. And one activity they share universally is the making of proteins. In fact, it can be said that when a typical cell (mature, though still young and healthy) is functioning according to program, its principal business is the manufacture of proteins (usually referred to in scientific papers as "protein synthesis"). Each cell makes many different kinds of protein—out of amino acids, which are broken down from the proteins we eat—and it makes them, by and large, for two purposes: to rebuild its own substance, and to export them for the needs of other cells. Endocrine cells, for example, make hormones—which are also proteins—for export to other cells. There are body cells, of course, that do not engage in the export trade. *All* cells, however, whether they continue to divide throughout life or whether they have stopped dividing for life, must keep on manufacturing protein to replace their own structural material in the constant breakdown and buildup we call metabolism. Food serves us here both as construction materials and as fuel to run the cell's internal-combustion engine. Like a car's engine, however, the cell's engine also requires oxygen, which is delivered regularly by the red blood cells.

We have already noted that every cell, with the specialized exception of the red blood cell, has a nucleus, which serves as headquarters for the DNA. DNA has long been a household monogram, and I have been using the term freely since the book's introduction.

Nevertheless, I'll remind you once more that DNA is deoxyribonucleic acid, the master molecule of heredity, uniquely capable of replicating, of making exact copies of itself. It is what the chromosomes and genes are made of.

The other important nucleic acid is RNA, ribonucleic acid, quite similar to DNA in structure and coding. But whereas DNA is a double-stranded helix, RNA is single-stranded and cannot make copies of itself. RNA—which comes in at least three or four varieties, as well as varieties within varieties (there are some sixty types of "transfer RNA" alone)—cannot make a useful move without explicit instructions from DNA.*

RNA operates both within the nucleus and outside it—in the "cytoplasm," which is the main body of the cell. Out in the cytoplasm are a number of different kinds of "organelles"—the generic name for cell parts that are neither in the nucleus nor part of the "cell membrane." The nucleus and each organelle are surrounded by protective membranes of their own. The cell's membrane is its wall, though in mammals this is not a solid wall, as it is in most plants. It used to be thought of simply as the containing envelope that kept the cell's cytoplasm from spilling out into the general environs. But the membrane is now seen to be a very dynamic "wall" indeed, full of entrances and exits, mazes and secret passageways, guard towers, sentry boxes, and sets of signals and passwords by which strangers are admitted or kept out—all in all a highly complex and functional part of the cell. The specific nature of the membrane needn't concern us for the moment, nor need the cytoplasm, except as the site of protein manufacture.

A cell, remember, is essentially a protein factory. All proteins are made of the same twenty-or-so amino acids broken down from food, though not all proteins contain all the amino acids. Among

---

* An exception had to be made to this rule with the startling discovery of the enzyme known as "reverse transcriptase," for which Howard Temin of Wisconsin and David Baltimore of MIT shared the 1975 Nobel Prize. This enzyme does what its name implies: it reverses the usual process, enabling the message of RNA to be transcribed into the form of DNA. Thus "retroviruses," the improbable microorganisms that harbor this enzyme, can infect animal and human cells, and, by utilizing the genetic material of the host organism, cause DNA (which the viruses themselves do not possess) to be made from the viral RNA. After many years of study, retroviruses have only lately begun to be suspected of causing—or at least contributing to the causation of—cancer and other human diseases.

the more important kinds of proteins are "enzymes," which come in thousands of varieties and serve as catalysts for the step-by-step chemical reactions of every cell in every living organism. There is a different enzyme for each little step. This is what keeps our metabolic engine going at a slow-burning rate. Without enzymes we would heat up and go critical, like a nuclear reactor with the cadmium safety rods pulled out. If a vital enzyme is missing or inoperative—through some molecular error or genetic defect—an entire cellular chain reaction may come to a halt, or never begin.

The basic process of protein manufacture, oversimplified, is this: DNA orders and uses RNA to make proteins out of amino acids, with the help of enzymes. That's the essential story. The genetic instructions are carried from the nucleus and executed in the cytoplasm, where the amino acids (very small molecules) are put together (on organelles called "ribosomes," which serve as assembly workbenches) into the much larger protein molecules. DNA, RNA, and proteins (including enzymes) are all large molecules, with complicated three-dimensional configurations. When the assembly line is functioning efficiently, the cell is healthy; and there is no theoretical reason why, with luck, it could not go on functioning this way in perpetuity.

These large molecules are not only the intelligent supervisors but also the workers with the know-how to keep the protein assembly lines moving. If the director of the plant, DNA, never leaves its headquarters, it must transmit instructions accurately. It can only do so through chemical coding, permitting its executive director, RNA, to copy the master code from its (DNA's) own content, and entrusting it to deliver the instructions intact. DNA's orders are spelled out in a simple four-letter code—though the combinations are complex. The same is true of RNA, except that one of its code letters is substituted, thus making five code letters in all—three of them common to both DNA and RNA, one unique to each.

It takes only three letters to designate a given amino acid. The order of the letters is all-important, just as it is in any language. If we take the English letters *o, d,* and *g,* and place them in that order, *odg,* the result is meaningless. We get a nonfunctional nonword. Rearrange the letters, however, into *dog,* and they suddenly take on meaning, evoking the image of a familiar, tail-wagging animal. Rearrange the letters yet again, and we come up with *god,* a radically different order of meaning. Using the same three letters, we have gone from no meaning at all to an animal to a deity. Some combinations (z, l, m) are meaningless no matter how you arrange them, while others (a, r, t) tend to form meanings without much trouble. In biology, as in all science, the quantity of information—which includes its arrangement—dictates the quality of the result. Arrangement, or errors in arrangement, of the genetic letters in a cell can make the same drastic difference as errors in English spelling. One misplaced genetic letter on the RNA chain can mean an error in one amino acid, therefore an error in the finished product. That product could be an enzyme, which, if it failed to do its catalytic job at a critical step, might bring to a halt a whole sequence of activities. The further activities that depended on the completion of *that* sequence of activities could thus not begin to take place. The cascading effect could result in an "error catastrophe"—which is one of the major theories of aging, put forth by Leslie E. Orgel of the Salk Institute. If the smooth functioning of the protein assembly line constitutes life, then interference with that functioning is what defines aging—the running out of life.

The important point to make here is not so much that an explicit genetic code exists, but that we are learning to "read and write" in it. We know that things do go wrong with the cell's protein factories. We are now maneuvering ourselves into a position where we can not only detect *when* something has gone wrong, but perhaps can pinpoint specifically *what* has gone wrong and begin to do something about it.

That is what molecular genetics is all about. It represents our major long-range hope for the cure and prevention of a variety of ailments, all the way from birth defects to cancer and the cardiovascular diseases. In fact, many of these late-in-life ailments, including cancer, heart disease, stroke, arthritis, diabetes, senile dementia, autoimmune disease, and a host of other degenerative diseases, are increasingly seen to have genetic components (though they are not simple, single-gene defects such as cystic fibrosis or sickle-cell anemia) and therefore might all be characterized, in a sense, as being birth defects. Aging research encompasses the whole spectrum of molecular-genetic research. The power to understand and manipulate the genetic information, a power growing by the day, will produce many ancillary payoffs, some now unforeseeable, before the aging process itself is finally elucidated.

Many current theories of aging are directly related to what can go wrong, and where, in the process of protein making. Some major theories focus on the genes, on the DNA: The original genetic instructions could be faulty. Or other genes may fail to function—such as those charged with repairing accidental breaks in the protein-making genes, or those responsible for switching the protein-making genes on or off at the appropriate times. Errors could occur in copying the genetic information from DNA to RNA, or in transmitting the information—which of course means literally transporting it—out into the cytoplasm. Or at any step along the devious way to the assembly line, or at any point on that complex and precision-demanding assembly line itself.

Where—and when—the trouble occurs represents only one aspect of the problem. Trouble could occur, as time goes on, at any point in the process. The other aspect is why it occurs. Running contrapuntally through all theories of aging are a pair of controversial themes, either of which is in harmony with most of the observed facts. One holds that damage to the genetic machinery or errors in the protein-making process are the result of accident and incident, of wear and tear. The competing view, as we know, holds that most of the damage and errors expressed in the aging cell are dictated by the genes themselves; the on/off switches shut down certain genes and thus the critical activities they control*—or they bring *new* genes into play that start dismantling or disrupting the protein assembly lines so that the organism runs down by explicit program. In the latter case—with life and its demise all part of a single genetic package—if we could control the DNA, *all* the DNA, then we should be able to keep those assembly lines moving. Maybe not forever, but for an impressively long time.

---

* The role that proteins themselves may play in this on/off switching process will be discussed in chapter 13.

5

THE CELL AS A MACHINE THAT WEARS OUT

AMONG those who believe that gerontology has resolved many of its contradictions and now is ready to move decisively ahead has been D. F. Chebotarev of the Soviet Union's Institute of Gerontology in Kiev. In fact, on the occasion of the Ninth International Congress of Gerontology, held in Kiev in 1972, Chebotarev expressed his firm conviction that gerontology "has now reached its concluding stage of accumulating practical material to be used for inferring profound theoretical generalizations."

We are, however, just at the beginning of this "concluding stage," and all the requisite "practical material" is not likely to be accumulated for some time to come. Hence the theoretical generalizations being propounded are seldom in agreement with one another. But no wonder. The visible signs of physiological aging, as well as the easily measurable running down of internal functions, are so many, and so varied—in fact, as another Soviet gerontologist, A. V. Nagorny, pointed out, each kind of tissue seems to have its own peculiar "handwriting of aging"—that a multiplicity of theories is to be expected. Nathan Shock, dean of American gerontologists and long-time director of NIH's Gerontological Research Center (GRC) in Baltimore—now the research arm of the National Institute on Aging—who was also a prominent figure at the Kiev conference, believes that aging must be looked upon "as a complex phenomenon which may require different explanatory principles for different aspects of the process."

When one begins to look at aging theories, one must turn to the work of Alex Comfort, who, in addition to being one of the world's leading gerontologists, has been in the business of collecting, analyzing, and expounding theories of aging longer than almost anyone around. Comfort has gained most of his more recent fame—and fortune, too—as an amateur sexologist, through his authorship of the best-selling *The Joy of Sex* and *More Joy of Sex*. Several years ago, just about the time *Prolongevity* was being completed, Comfort transplanted himself from his native England to California. Now, as *Prolongevity II* is being completed, he is preparing to go back to London. It was not a case of "rejection phenomenon" or "graft-versus-host" disease; in fact, his time in the United States, which included the writing of his sex books, was busy and productive. Those who know of Comfort only in his sexological incarnation may have been puzzled by previous mentions of him in a book on aging research. But all of his professional credentials are in gerontology, and they were earned over most of the years of his life to date through his labors at the University of London. In the States, he has continued to teach—for instance, in the gerontology program at UCLA—and to edit the journal *Experimental Gerontology*. He has always been a prolific writer, too, including novels, essays, and poetry. But his largest body of work has been on the subject of aging. His technical output has been prodigious, and he has written numerous reviews and surveys of the field, culminating in his highly regarded book *The Biology of Senescence*.

The summer before he moved to California, I had lunch with Alex Comfort at his favorite Indian restaurant, near the University of London. Though he had no pet theory of his own, Comfort seemed at the time to be leaning, with Strehler and the others, toward the idea of genetically programmed aging. As we discussed one aging theory after another, he kept returning to a point that both amused and frustrated him: many theorists, even those who do not believe in a genetic program, tend to select a single aspect of aging out of the diversity of possibilities as *the* primary cause of aging. "What is so frustrating," said Comfort, "is that you can seize upon almost any given feature of aging and invent a theory based on it. From one single aspect, it seems that you can usually derive most of the others!"

The other side of this, of course (as already suggested), is the argument that *no* theory of aging is necessary, inasmuch as senescence can easily be accounted for on the basis of accumulated accidents, errors, and wear and tear over time. The cell, after all, is a machine, so why should it not simply wear out, just as an automobile does? The whole body, for that matter, is a machine—though not a simple nuts-and-bolts kind of machine—and the same argument would be applicable for the same reasons.

But the way even a nonbiological machine wears out is not so simple as it might appear. Another British investigator and theorist, John Maynard Smith of the University of Sussex, in considering single-cause versus multiple-cause theories of aging, uses the automobile analogy to clarify some of the major problems: "As a car grows older," he writes in *Proceedings of the Royal Society*, "the cylinders, the gearbox, the body work, the electrical wiring, all deteriorate. But the deterioration of each of these 'organs' is to a large extent independent of the others, as is shown by the fact that a gearbox from an old car, if put into a young one, would not be rejuvenated, and a gearbox from a young car put into an old one would not deteriorate any more rapidly. Thus ageing in motor cars is multiple in nature."

However, there is a large "but": "We can imagine circumstances," he goes on, "in which a single theory would be appropriate. Suppose that a new car was fed with petrol, oil, grease and water, but that the battery was never charged. It would soon show a number of symptoms of senescence, in the starter motor, the ignition, the lights, the traffic indicators. Yet these would all be symptoms of a single ageing process, and could all be cured by a single measure—changing the battery."

Later in the same discussion, Maynard Smith returns to the motor-car analogy: "It may be true that different 'organs' age as a consequence of the same physical processes, even though ageing is 'multiple.' . . . In fact, only two, perhaps three, physical processes (abrasion, corrosion, and metal fatigue) are likely to be involved. Although the engine and gearbox age independently, both do so primarily because of mechanical wear, and the life of both might be extended by a single treatment—for example, an improved lubricant. Similarly, even if it proves that in animals different organs age independently, they may do so as a consequence of similar changes at a cellular level."

What kind of changes?

Alex Comfort, who is personally more attracted to the genetic-clock idea because the *rate* of aging in organisms of the same species is so stable, has nevertheless speculated that aging in cells might be due to a kind of blurring of the genetic information over long periods of time. He has likened this process to what happens with repeated photocopying, where successive copies made from copies that are made from yet other copies will be of lower and lower quality. If a similar blurring or dimming effect occurred in cell division, then "the new cells produced by an old man would in some way be less viable than the new cells produced by him when he was a child." This effect, however, would only explain what happens in cells that continued to divide after maturity; and, as another gerontologist once put it, "No one ever dies of dead skin." Comfort's Xerox analogy would thus not apply—and it is clear from his own later papers that he agrees—to the senescence of the critical postmitotic cells, which are not required to undergo the hazards of continuing replication throughout life. Since copies need never be made again once these cells mature, the "blurring" phenomenon would certainly have to be ruled out as a principal aging mechanism in creatures whose bodies are made entirely of nondividing cells. Maynard Smith offers the fruit fly as an example: "Since there is no cell division in adult *Drosophila*, mutations due to miscopying cannot occur."

Errors can and do occur, however, which have nothing to do with the DNA's making copies of itself. Damage can be *inflicted* on DNA—or, for that matter, on any of the cell's large molecules—in many ways by sources outside the cell, or as a by-product of the cell's own activities. Some of the damage is reparable, some not.

Our quick survey of the DNA-RNA-protein chain, sketchy as it was, makes it obvious that DNA damage would be a likely candidate for a theory of aging. DNA is the storehouse of genetic knowledge as well as the director of its applied uses. Moreover, a number of experiments over the years have suggested that the progressive breakdown of genetic material with aging is not just a theory. As one example, Tracy M. Sonneborn and his associates at Indiana University, studying the reproductive capacities of paramecia during the 1950s, found that the older the parents, the smaller was the percentage of vigorous offspring they could produce. Any injury to the DNA molecule, especially to those segments of it that dictate protein synthesis, could have serious consequences for the welfare of the cell—unless, of course, the cell was finished forever with that particular piece of information. An instance cited by the late Howard J. Curtis of the Brookhaven National Laboratory: "If the gene for eye color is mutated in a liver cell, nothing of consequence will result."

We know that changes—mutations—do occur in DNA. They may be caused by many factors not in the original genetic program: viruses, potent chemicals, extreme heat, radiation (cosmic or manmade). Mutations can be good or bad—"good" or "bad" being variously defined under varying circumstances—and the outcome of evolution for a given species may depend on how the good and bad balance out. To influence evolution, mutations must occur in the germ cells—sperm or egg—in which case they are "genetic" mutations, capable of being passed on to ensuing generations. A mutation in other body cells is called a "somatic" mutation, which affects only that one, already existing person; this is the type believed to be implicated in individual human aging.

Anyone may, in the course of his lifetime, accumulate mutations in cells anywhere in his body. The late Leo Szilard, when he turned his ingenious mathematical-physicist's mind to biology in 1959, theorized that chance mutations in the genetic material, perhaps caused by the random impact of cosmic rays tearing through the cells' nuclei over a lifetime, could gradually damage—or even kill outright—one cell after another until the organism began to run down and finally not enough viable cells were left to sustain it. Szilard's theory applied specifically to nondividing cells. Inasmuch as Szilard's calculations would have resulted in a roughly identical life span for most people, he further theorized that variations in life span occurred largely because people started out in life with differing quantities of already inherited DNA faults. "However," argued biochemist M. S. Kanungo, of India's Banaras Hindu University, "this theory does not explain why identical twins do not die within a year [of each other]." Other criticism has since pretty well invalidated Szilard's theory, but it served as a valuable stimulus for aging theory at the time.

Soviet gerontologists have also intensively investigated what happens to DNA with age. In summarizing these results in 1972, Kharkov University's V. N. Nikitin concluded that, "using the present methods of extracting and analysing native DNA samples, no unambiguous and clear answer has been received to the question of the age dependence of DNA molecules and the 'residual proteins' associated with them."

Nevertheless, a damaged, blurred, misshapen, or somehow weakened DNA molecule—or many of them, in cases of gross chromosomal damage—is central to the somatic-mutation theory of aging, which was most carefully worked out by Howard Curtis, who was a close observer of chromosomal damage caused by radiation. With its DNA unable to convey accurate instructions, the cell's protein factory might muddle through, erratically turning out products of uncertain quality, or it might just shut down. "Indeed," Curtis felt, in 1966, "from what we now know, it appears that the only way in which a permanent change, short of death, can be effected in the cell is by a change in the DNA or chromosome structure. All other damage can be repaired."

But it turns out that all other damage *cannot* necessarily be repaired, and that there are other ways, short of mutation and death, by which the cell can be permanently changed. Most gerontologists today feel that the somatic-mutation theory does not really stand up to close critical scrutiny. One argument is that, given that most of the genetic material in mature cells is switched off anyway—since the cell never needs the information again (as in Curtis's own example of the liver cell and eye color)—random damage to most of the DNA would have no effect on protein manufacturing, and thus none on the aging process, either. Strehler, basing his critique on work done by A. G. Sacher at Oak Ridge as well as in his own laboratory, is among those who have discarded the somatic-mutation theory. And Maynard Smith, using mathematical reasoning—which gave the theory its original power—has pretty well demolished it, in Comfort's view.

Moreover, a number of recent experiments and calculations have convinced many that mutations occur much less frequently than was formerly assumed. And of the mutations that do occur, most are probably not permanent; we have known, at least since 1960, thanks to Ruth Hill's work at Columbia University, that DNA creates its own self-repair enzymes. These enzymes would be manufactured, like any other protein on the assembly line, on instruction from the "repair genes." They probably correct most mutational damage before the faulty information can be transmitted. It is true that the cell's repair capacity can be virtually knocked out by a single massive dose of radiation. Yet it is not significantly diminished if the same quantity of radiation is administered in small doses over a period of time. Normal wear and tear would be most unlikely, at any point in life, to include a traumatic event of such severity and suddenness as to inactivate all the repair genes at once.

Paradoxically, this very repair capacity is what makes investigators such as Boston University's F. Marott Sinex reluctant to give up the somatic-mutation theory altogether. He is intrigued by the as yet inconclusive evidence suggesting that only a relatively few genes—perhaps four in all—seem to control the entire mechanism of DNA repair. In that case it would not require a large number of unlucky "hits" (as Szilard called them) to impair the function of these crucial genes. Thus information loss in aging would be due not so much to the extent of DNA damage as to its loss of ability to repair the damage.

It makes good evolutionary sense, of course, to suspect that all cells are not equal in their self-repair capabilities. Cells of the skin, gut, and bone marrow—which keep replacing themselves by division—would seldom last long enough to undergo the kind of steady wear and tear that results in dangerous accumulations of damage. Hence they would have little need to require an always-at-the-ready fix-and-patch team. The highly specialized cells, however, which are assigned many important duties and must, because they no longer reproduce, try to last as long as the organism does, are in quite a different situation. Their long-term repair needs are great, and it stands to reason that evolutionary experience would have taken due note of this.

Zhores A. Medvedev, the brilliant and courageous Soviet gerontologist who has been working in England for the past several years, considers DNA damage from another standpoint. At any given time, most of the DNA in the cell's nucleus is unused. Much of it is in fact redundant—never used at all, at least not in protein manufacture. Samuel Boyer III of Johns Hopkins University believes that this "junk DNA," as it has been called, may represent the critical evolutionary information that dictates whether the creature possessing it will turn out to be a mouse, a monkey, or a man. In any case, there also seem to be redundant, reiterative DNA sequences for the protein-making genes, so that one could take over if another were damaged, though not all genes are repeated with the same frequency, and some may not be repeated at all.

It would be as if, in a football game, some players had many substitutes on the bench, while others had few or none. A team that had only one expert punter and place kicker, if he suffered injury, would simply have to do its best without the services of a kicker. If, as the game went on, other players were injured—and their substitutes as well—the team would play under increasing handicaps, until finally, perhaps without a center or a quarterback, they would lose the game by default. Medvedev has suggested that genes without substitute sequences would be the most vulnerable. If such a gene were damaged, and if the information thus irretrievably lost contained an indispensable piece of the protein recipe (to switch metaphors), then the protein factory would, to that extent, be handicapped.

Bernie Strehler also believes that the repetitive sequences of DNA may be important in aging. He had set out in 1972, with one of his students, Roger Johnson, to disprove the somatic-mutation theory. But he "did not rule out another possible type of damage, the gradual loss of copies of certain genes that exist by the hundreds, side by side in each cell's DNA. Although the idea seemed improbable to us," he recalls, in the 1973 *Science Yearbook*, "we set out to test it by comparing the number of copies of one such gene in brain cells from young and old beagles. The repetitive gene that we chose produces a major constituent of ribosomes, ribosomal RNA (rRNA)." Strehler and Johnson found that

> the brain cells of old dogs contained about 30 percent fewer copies of the gene than did those of the young dogs. We also measured the number of copies of the gene in other tissues of these animals, and found that all of those tissues whose cells had stopped reproducing (brain, heart, skeletal muscle) showed similar decreases. However, none of the tissues whose cells were still reproducing (liver, kidney) showed a decrease.
>
> In other words, the protein-making machinery of heart cells, brain cells, muscle cells, hormone-producing cells, sex cells, cells that produce antibodies, and all other nonreproducing cells may stop working effectively for the same reason—too few ribosomes. [Ribosomes, remember, are the cytoplasm's assembly-line workbenches.] If further studies should establish this as a universal accompaniment of aging in higher animals, extending the healthy life span might be achieved by increasing the number of ribosomes available in the cells of critical tissues.

Following these experiments, Strehler and others in the late 1970s and early 1980s studied the postmortem tissues of human heart and brain, and were able to demonstrate fairly convincingly that this

loss of ribosomal RNA in postmitotic cells was as true for humans as for dogs. Prior to this work, Strehler had believed that the DNA molecules—which originally dictate the manufacture of RNAs as well as proteins, including the materials that make up the ribosomes—are not really damaged or destroyed, but merely switched off by inhibiting substances so that the information needed to make the RNAs and the proteins is no longer available. But the newer studies showed that the ribosomal *DNA* was also being lost—or permanently inactivated through some such process as cross-linkage—so that the resulting deficits might well be irreversible.*
Moreover, the losses, on the average, would add up to something like half the ribosomal genes by the age of 100. But with so many extra copies of the gene, does the loss matter? Apparently so. Strehler points out that even if we possess, say, 300 copies of a ribosomal gene in a given cell, and 150 are lost by the age of 100, that would only be an average figure. Some cells may have lost close to 100 percent of their copies of the gene, perhaps well before the age of 100. So real functional deficits might occur, especially in the aging individual under great stress. Interesting to note, Susumo Ohno of the City of Hope, in Duarte, California, has put forth a theory suggesting that *only* those genes with multiple copies are responsible for aging because, when there is only a single copy of the gene, he believes, it is replaced as soon as it is knocked out!

Thus Strehler feels that the ribosomal story may be a special case of gene wipeout rather than turnoff. He believes that the ribosomal genes could, in fact, be among the central keys to the decline of postmitotic cells because, as he wrote in 1982 (the italics are his), these genes *"are required in order for ANY protein synthesis to occur."* (The ribosomes, remember, are the workbenches where all of the cell's proteins are assembled.) If Strehler's hunch about the special nature of these genes is borne out, then that still leaves viable his original notion that many of the deficits of aging are the result of turned-off genes and hence reversible. Holger von Hahn's findings in Switzerland, and his interpretation of them, seem to bear out Strehler's thesis. Von Hahn found that the DNA double helix is much more stable—that is, harder to break apart—in aging cells,

---

* They would not be irreversible, that is, by merely turning the genes back on, though they could still be reversible by, say, breaking the cross-linked bonds, or by replacing the lost or inactivated DNA via genetic engineering.

and he decided that this stability was "dependent on the presence and the binding of certain proteins. It appears that in old nucleo-protein a particular protein fraction is bound to DNA in such a way as to increase the energy required for the separation of the two strands in the helix. Since strand separation is a necessary step in the mechanism of transcription, blocking this process necessarily blocks transcription, and thus leads to a loss of genetic information for the cell." (This phenomenon could also, of course, turn out to be the result of, say, cross-linkage.)

Strehler hypothesizes that the cell is programmed to start man-ufacturing, at a certain point in life, the very substances that then proceed to switch off the critical genes. The "damage" is thus not random or accidental but, rather, the purposeful carrying out of the genetic program. Some plants and insects are definitely known to possess "mutator" genes which are programmed to produce mu-tations in their own DNA, but such genes have so far not been found in human chromosomes. Strehler's view, if correct, is a much more hopeful one, since the genes are still present and intact, though covered up, rather than being changed irreversibly. It is, then, only necessary to *un*cover them and thus switch the genes on again to make them function as efficiently as in their "youth."

Even if all the DNA in the cell were to remain perfectly intact throughout life, however, information loss could still occur else-where—and the results would be the same as if the DNA itself were deficient. There are, as we have already seen, other molecules that DNA relies on to carry the protein-making instructions out into the assembly lines. These are the several varieties of RNA, and certain enzymes—especially those required to make more RNA, or to help RNA make more proteins (including more enzymes). These mol-ecules are charged with transcribing and translating the genetic in-structions. As long as they remain in efficient working order, they can readily repair damage to *other* molecules. But damage to one of these key molecules would be irreparable. It would be like knock-ing out someone on the assembly line—or en route to it—who was the only one who knew how to do some particular job. If he were crippled, or absent, components would come off the line improperly assembled, or production might come to a confused halt as every-thing jammed at a given point.

You may already have recognized this as another way of describ-ing what was earlier referred to as the "error-catastrophe theory" of the Salk Institute's Leslie Orgel. Orgel—like Comfort, an Englishman transplanted to California—has also made major contributions to theories about the origins of life on earth. Though Orgel now believes there may be mechanisms at work that could prevent error catastrophes from occurring—and is the first to say that the newest experimental evidence is inconclusive and often confusing—his hypothesis, even more than Szilard's, has served a powerful enzymatic function of its own in aging theory. For a while, hardly a review article on aging research in any technical journal failed to take Orgel's theory into serious account—a statement that cannot be made for many aging theories. Moreover, it stimulated an enormous quantity of fruitful research. At the National Institute of Medical Research at Mill Hill, London (where Medvedev also works), Robin Holliday, in collaboration with C. M. Lewis and G. M. Tarrant, carried out a series of experiments with cells in culture. Their results seemed to corroborate Orgel's error theory, as did similar studies carried out by B. I. Goldstein in the Soviet Union.

Nevertheless, as Orgel later pointed out, "It may not be possible to separate the contributions to cellular ageing caused by errors of protein synthesis from those due to the accumulation of somatic mutations. Errors of protein synthesis must occasionally lead to the formation of 'mutator' DNA polymerase molecules which replicate DNA inaccurately. Conversely, some mutations . . . must reduce the fidelity of protein synthesis. Thus inaccurate protein synthesis and inaccurate DNA synthesis are coupled phenomena."

The same dual interpretation can be applied to many other experiments—for example, the findings of Harriet and David Gershon at the Technion-Israel Institute of Technology in Haifa. The Gershons' studies of mice and nematodes showed a consistent "accumulation with age of altered, partially active, or catalytically inactive enzyme molecules"—results that would fit either the error theory or the mutation theory. There were some suggestions, at the end of 1969, that many proteins might be one-shot creations, that is, made to last for the lifetime of the cell. This was based on some fascinating experiments at Sussex by Maynard Smith and his associates A. N. Bozcuk and Susan Tebbutt, which showed that, in the fruit fly *Drosophila*, just as there were cells that never divided again, so there were large quantities of protein (the structural protein of the thoracic flight muscles, for instance) that did *not* turn over—i.e., were not broken down and resynthesized. In that case, error catastrophes occurring in, say, RNA would not cause aging; nor would mutations in the DNA. Only damage to—or the ultimate wearing out of—the irreplaceable protein itself would be critical.

But *Drosophila* is different from vertebrates in many respects— one, already mentioned, being that the body of the adult is made entirely of nondividing cells. Maynard Smith still believes that the one-time-only protein deterioration "provides a sufficient cause of aging in *Drosophila*," but adds: "Unfortunately the wearing out of non-replaced protein structures is unlikely to be the major cause of aging in vertebrates."

The one universal element in all observations and theories about aging is that something goes wrong, somewhere along the line, with components of the DNA-RNA-enzyme-protein assembly line. Attempts to replace damaged or error-ridden cellular components, whether in the nucleus or elsewhere, have provided the basis for a number of controversial rejuvenation therapies. The celebrated Swiss "cell therapist" Paul Niehans, for example, injected fresh sheep-embryo cells into his aging patients—many of them rich and famous. The late Benjamin Frank, a New York physician, claimed success with diets that provided everything that failing cells might need— nucleic acids, enzymes, and proteins—packaged into a single meal. Critics objected that, inasmuch as food is all broken down in the liver anyway and reaches the cell as raw materials, efficient cell machinery is still required to put it all together again.

Here again, Strehler's outlook may be the most hopeful. If his surmise is correct, it may well be possible to "awaken the sleeping genes" so that they would be as good as new, capable of correcting any kind of errors, wherever they might occur, however catastrophic they might be adjudged in today's cellular circumstances. In this context, it is worth describing briefly an earlier experiment of Strehler's, this time with his student Michael Bick (who has since moved on, first to Harvard, then to the Roche Institute of Molecular Biology). They worked with the cotyledons (first leaves) of the soybean plant, a convenient experimental tool because the cotyledon has a life span of just three weeks, from the day the seed sprouts to the day of the leaf's withering and death (falling off the plant). Strehler and Bick found that transfer RNA (tRNA) molecules had no trouble binding with the amino acids leucine and tyrosine at the age of seven days. But by the age of twenty-one days, they had a great deal of trouble doing so. Even more interesting, the older cotyledons contained *new* substances not present in the younger ones—substances that *inhibited and inactivated the enzymes* that normally attach the amino acids to the tRNA molecules! Strehler took this as clear evidence of a specific genetic aging program: genes had been turned on to create the enzyme-inactivating substances at the right time (or perhaps the wrong time, from the leaf's viewpoint). Strehler's answer, again: control of the on/off switching mechanisms.

Kanungo and his colleagues in India have put forth a similar theory, featuring genetic on/off switching as both a probable cause and a possible cure for aging. Orgel, too, gives cautious support to the genetic-clock theory, but warns, in *Nature*, that "it seems unwise, in the absence of experimental evidence, to take for granted the idea of 'programmed obsolescence' in man and other mammals."

Just as Orgel sees the interrelationship of DNA errors and protein-making errors, and the feedback between them, so does he emphasize the mutual impact of these errors with other kinds of damage in the cell's cytoplasm and membrane—and, for that matter, with the aging of the body's noncellular material. An increasing number of gerontologists are in agreement. Virtually every aspect of aging seems to exaggerate and acccelerate the other aspects. Hence Comfort's complaint that you can use almost any facet of aging to explain all the others.

As a case in point, on the same day I had read a paper of Comfort's in which he reiterated the wry comment I heard from him in London, I picked up a copy of *Science* in which William Bondareff and Robert Narotzky of the Northwestern University Medical School in Chicago report some careful experiments with rat brain cells. They were, in this instance, concentrating on measuring the *spaces* between cells. It turns out that the space between senescent brain cells is, on the average, only half that between the cells of younger adults. Starting with this information alone, I tried playing Comfort's game: what functions do these spaces serve? Because the brain contains essentially no connective tissue, the spaces are probably critical in the transport of all sorts of chemicals as well as in all-important communications among the neurons. (This chemical transport *is* known to be reduced with age.) With shrinking space between the cells, they obviously cannot function as well—and the resulting increase in pressure and density must also change the cell's physical configuration and produce adverse effects in its molecular activities, including protein manufacture. We know that the welfare of all the body's cells and tissues is dependent upon the control functions of the brain. If those decline, then all physiological functions begin to deteriorate. Ergo, the cause of aging is the shrinkage of spaces between brain cells.

Bondareff and Narotzky did not offer this as a theory of aging—but see how easily they might have!

6

GARBAGE GLUT, FREE-RADICAL RAPE, AND THE SELF-TURNED-ENEMY

THE living human cell is a highly organized community of molecular citizens. As in most living communities, garbage disposal is an important function. But as the organism—the larger community that both governs and is dependent upon its citizenry—ages, the individual cell has an ever-harder time getting rid of its wastes in a routine and efficient manner. In many cells, especially those that no longer divide (nerve cells and heart-muscle cells are two examples), there is a steady buildup of cellular garbage, in particular a pigmented fatty substance called lipofuscin, discovered independently in a number of laboratories, including Bernard Strehler's, around 1958. Some investigators have attached great significance to the presence of lipofuscin in aging cells, but whether or not it is a true indicator of aging, or even perhaps a primary causal factor in the aging process itself, remains controversial.

At the annual meeting of the American Aging Association (called AGE for short) in 1983, Kalidas Nandy of the Veterans Administration Hospital in Bedford, Massachusetts, stated that lipofuscin was undoubtedly an indicator—indeed, a reliable "marker"—for aging, and that to acquire the ability to lower the lipofuscin content of cells could provide us with a powerful life-prolonging technique; Nandy has already done some preliminary experiments along these lines. At the same meeting, Michael Katz of the National Eye Institute went a step further, holding that lipofuscin accumulation is a *primary* factor in aging.

Most gerontologists, however, feel that lipofuscin is a result rather

than a cause of aging and that its deleterious effects are more theoretical than proved. In many cells lipofuscin does accumulate to a
point where it occupies 10, 20, or even 30 percent of the space, and
one can see how the cell might virtually choke on its own pollutants.
The working molecules would hardly have room to squeeze through,
and their performance would have to suffer. Nevertheless, a few
scientists—Dutch gerontologist C. F. Hollander for one—have cast
doubt on the role of lipofuscin as a specific cause of aging by pointing
to the fact that its granules sometimes show up even in the cells of
newborn infants. Here again, though lipofuscin is generally regarded
as a wear-and-tear product, Strehler puts much of the blame for its
buildup on the cell's genetic program. He cites the child victims of
Batten's disease—a genetic disorder—who store up vast quantities
of lipofuscin in their brain cells, are blind by the age of five,
and undergo steady mental deterioration until their premature
deaths.

Lipofuscin formation and accumulation are attributed by some
to the effects of "cross-linkage." In fact, one of the most durable
single-cause theories of aging is the cross-linkage theory, originally
proposed by Johan Bjorksten, director of the Bjorksten Research
Foundation in Madison, Wisconsin. Cross-linkage is the inadvertent
coupling of any two large molecules, inside or outside the cell. When
a pair of adjacent molecules are cross-linked at some point, the
cell's enzymes can often break them apart again. But irreversible
cross-linkage occurs more frequently with age, the repair enzymes
apparently diminishing either in quantity or in function. Cross-links
occur in proteins, enzymes, RNA, even in DNA, so they could be
the cause of both the somatic mutations and the error catastrophes
described earlier.

If someone were to throw a lasso over two adjacent workers on
an assembly line, and if they couldn't get the lasso off, they might
not be totally immobilized, but they certainly could not be expected
to do their separate assigned jobs. And they would, as more and
more of them "dropped out," clutter up more and more of the
available working space, making it ever more difficult for others
trying to carry out their normal tasks. In the cell, then, lots of cross-
linkages mean lots of work stoppages—and, finally, no work at all.
A few gerontologists—Robert Kohn is one—believe that the cross-
linking of molecules outside the cell (that is, in the spaces between
cells) and the consequent stiffening of connective tissue alone could

account for many of the functional losses of old age. A. A. Bogo-
molets, one of the founders of Soviet gerontology, attached similar
importance to the aging of connective tissue.

At least two other scientists independently suggested the cross-
linkage theory of aging: Frederic Verzar, a Hungarian who did most
of his work in Switzerland (some of it with von Hahn); and Major
Donald G. Carpenter of the United States Air Force Academy in
Colorado Springs. But Bjorksten—who first got the idea when,
as a young chemist for Ditto, Inc., he noticed a strange similarity between the "aging" of hectograph duplication film and
the aging of human tissue—has clear priority. For nearly forty
years now, Bjorksten has done painstaking research and continued
to elaborate his theory with great force, conviction, and documen-
tation.

In *Extended Youth*, an excellent book published in 1968, Robert
W. Prehoda introduced his chapter on cross-linkage with a glowing
tribute to Bjorksten. After comparing Bjorksten's theory to Einstein's in importance, he goes on to predict that "future history
books will describe the years of debate, slow acceptance, and the
dramatic breakthrough that was the beginning of a true understanding of the aging process." But one can't remind oneself too often
of Comfort's warning about the ease of parlaying a set of observations into a comprehensive theory of aging. In the few years since
Prehoda's book, the cross-linkage theory has lost much ground—
which is not to say that it couldn't regain it in such a mercurial field
of endeavor. Today it is possible to read major surveys of gerontological research and theory that contain no mention of Bjorksten
at all—a premature dismissal, surely. No one denies that cross-
linkage occurs or that it increases with age, but most gerontologists
now seem to agree with the judgment of Charles G. Kemendy of
the Bristol Laboratories in Syracuse, New York, that cross-linkage,
like lipofuscin accumulation, "is not a cause but simply a result of
aging."

Nevertheless, Bjorksten stands staunchly by the confident statement he made in a summarizing article published in 1971: "The
crosslinkage theory stands unique among the primary theories of
aging. It stands simply and without strained assumptions." It is, he
still insists, compatible with all other theories of aging. He an-
nounced at the time that no more work would be done to validate
a theory already substantially proved, and that henceforth he would

devote his efforts to finding and testing anti–cross-linking substances.

Bjorksten decided very early, however, that looking for cross-link inhibitors was the most difficult, if not an altogether fruitless, route to pursue. There was such a multitude of substances that could cause cross-linkage that it would be hard even to imagine what might serve as a universal inhibitor. One would have to try a forbiddingly large number and variety of possible inhibitors. The more sensible strategy, he decided, was simply to let the cross-links form, "then to dissolve all aggregates present, both normal and abnormal, by nonselective means . . . and administer this so slowly that the organism can replace what is normal, while the abnormal cross-linkages are not so restored." One possible approach would be to use enzymes small enough to penetrate the dense cross-link jungle and at the same time not so specific that they would act on only a narrow range of cross-linked aggregates. Bjorksten's recent research has confirmed that enzymes fulfilling these criteria do in fact exist, if one can discover how to employ them. Another plan is to use "chelation" techniques—that is, to use certain compounds that have a special affinity for a given metal and can thus latch on to that metal. Chelation would work only if a metal was responsible for the cross-linkage, but this is often the case.* For instance, Bjorksten believes—as others are also beginning to—that Alzheimer's disease, one of the most prevalent forms of senile dementia (though hardly anyone had heard of it at the time *Prolongevity* was published), is largely caused by cross-linkages, and that many of these cross-links are brought about by aluminum absorbed by the body and reaching the brain cells via diverse pathways. Thus an aluminum chelator might break up some of the cross-links responsible for Alzheimer's (assuming that theory is correct).

Yet a third scenario composed by Bjorksten as a possible means for attacking cross-links entails breaking them up through the artful use of free radicals (about which more in a moment). This approach would be the riskiest of the three, because free-radical damage is generally conceded to be one of the major causes of cross-linkage.

In fact, there has developed a well-worked-out free-radical theory of aging, a theory that looks better with each passing year. Its principal originator and proponent has been Denham Harman of

* For a note on "chelation therapy," see page 208.

the University of Nebraska School of Medicine in Omaha. Harman—like Strehler and Comfort a dedicated investigator as well as an evangelist for gerontology—was the founding father of AGE and still remains the center of organizing energy for the group. He should have felt pleased indeed to hear paper after paper at AGE's 1983 meeting vindicating the work he had pioneered back when many scientists were skeptical that free radicals even existed in living systems. While the cross-linkage theory has declined in influence, the free-radical theory has picked up an increasing number of advocates, including Aloys L. Tappel of the University of California at Davis, Lester Packer of the University of California at Berkeley, Paul Gordon (formerly of Northwestern), Harry Demopoulos of New York University, William A. Pryor of Louisiana State University, Richard G. Cutler of NIA, Jaime Miquel of the NASA Ames Research Center, and Richard A. Passwater, an independent investigator in Silver Spring, Maryland.

"Free radicals" are highly unstable atoms, broken-off pieces of molecules, or molecules with an electron stripped away. Because a free electron can hardly stand being unattached, free radicals tend to race frantically around the nearby cellular environs until they find other molecules they can attach themselves to. "A free radical," Alex Comfort once said, "has been likened to a convention delegate away from his wife: it's a highly reactive chemical agent that will combine with anything that's around." In some cases a free radical might more accurately be likened to a rapist. Its union with another molecule—ready or not (some molecules are more vulnerable than others, often depending on their momentary state of activity)—frequently amounts to outright attack. Though the lifetime of free radicals is usually measured in thousandths of a second, that is plenty of time for them to do considerable damage. To make matters worse, a free radical's assault on its victim is, more likely than not, so violent that it creates other free radicals, thus setting off a small chain reaction of devastation in the neighborhood. Pryor, for instance, has shown how easily a single free radical—formed by, say, a toxin—can generate up to a hundred molecules of hydroperoxide, all of them capable of producing damaging reactions.

Free radicals can split molecules in half, knock pieces out of them, contribute substantially to the buildup of lipofuscin, and garble the cellular information in a number of ways—only one of which is cross-linkage. Especially susceptible are the delicate cell-surface membranes, as well as the less extensive membranes that embrace the organelles within the cell's cytoplasm—particularly those organelles called "mitochondria," which serve as the cell's all-important energy machines. This peculiar vulnerability to free-radical damage is in part what led Harman to postulate that the mitochondria are the pacemakers of the aging process. "One quality that characterizes free radical action," Paul Gordon notes, "is that . . . free radicals do not appear to contain or reflect any useful biological information. Their action on membranes, therefore, represents the replacement of genetically determined order by randomness."

In the course of studying radiation damage in the 1950s, Denham Harman noticed that (1) radiation not only causes symptoms that look like mature aging in animals, but actually seems to shorten the life span; and (2) radiation creates an excess quantity of free radicals in cells. He wondered if the free radicals could be causing the aging effects. All cells produce small quantities of free radicals—small quantities, at least, compared with the consequences of radiation bombardment—*in the normal course of their everyday oxidation reactions*. If vast swarms of free radicals created in a single split-instant can significantly speed up the aging process, could relatively small quantities, spread over a long period of time, be responsible for normal aging?

Harman knew that, in various industrial processes, antioxidant substances were used to combat free-radical damage—to prevent the deterioration of leather, rubber, and synthetics, for instance, and to keep butter from turning rancid (T. L. Dormandy of London's Whittington Hospital has referred to free-radical cell damage as "biological rancidification"). At the beginning of his investigation, Harman was mainly concerned with reducing or treating radiation damage—which he was able to do by administering antioxidants such as 2-MEA (2-mercaptoethylamine), BHT (butylated hydroxytoluene), vitamin E, and a quinoline derivative called Santoquin; all are compounds that hold down oxidation reactions and mop up free radicals. When he became interested in the aging problem, Harman set up experiments with normal, unirradiated mice, and found that by mixing antioxidants into their food, he was able to keep them alive significantly longer than mice who did not get antioxidants. For a while he thought he had succeeded in extending the life spans of these mice, but as he studied the natural longevity of this strain with greater care, he finally concluded that he had merely stretched out their life *expectancy*, enabling them to come much closer to the end of their potential maximum life spans—still a notable accomplishment. (A Soviet researcher, N. N. Emanual of the University of Moscow, is the only scientist who still claims to have increased the *life span* of mice—by 25 percent with antioxidants.)

There may be high irony in one aspect of free-radical research: it turns out that polyunsaturated fats increase the cell's oxidation reactions, thus creating more free radicals and thus, presumably, more of all types of aging damage. The irony lies in the fact that, because of the implication of cholesterol in atherosclerosis and heart disease, millions of Americans—and now millions in other nations as well—have switched from saturated fats to polyunsaturated fats, in the interests of increasing our life expectancy by avoiding premature heart attacks. In doing so we may have contributed instead to the premature aging of all our cells. A number of scientists now hold this view. Demopoulos, for example, says, "If forced to choose between the two, I'll take cholesterol as the lesser hazard."

The study of free radicals in aging has revealed their potential importance in other medical areas as well. The evidence grows ever more convincing, says Pryor, that free-radical damage contributes to an increased risk of acquiring ailments as diverse as emphysema, cataracts, senile dementia, cardiovascular disease, and cancer. The case for a link between free radicals and cancer seems to have been bolstered by recent epidemiological studies suggesting that foods containing the antioxidant beta-carotene offer anticancer protection. Inasmuch as free radicals inflict damage to the molecular genetic apparatus—the disruption of which can mark the beginning of a cell's transformation to an abnormal state—it makes sense that the individual whose cells undergo this kind of damage runs a higher risk of developing a runaway malignant growth. In a cover article featured in *Science* in the fall of 1983, Bruce N. Ames of the University of California at Berkeley, one of the world's leading authorities on toxicology, reported that the everyday human diet contains a great variety of natural carcinogens—and that the damage they cause is mostly due to free radicals. Fortunately, many foods also contain antioxidant substances (though not enough to counter all the damage); moreover, the body possesses its own protective antioxidant enzyme systems—among them catalase, glutathione per-oxidase, and superoxide dismutase. In fact, as Cutler has empha-sized, not even the lowliest single-celled oxygen-dependent orga-nism could have survived without evolving some kind of internal antioxidant protection. Cutler, in an extensive study of a large di-versity of species, has concluded that life span itself is essentially proportional to the amount of antioxidant insurance a given species has accrued. A number of scientists have begun to experiment (a few, such as Demopoulos, quite vigorously) with antioxidant dietary supplements like vitamins B, C, and E, beta-carotene, glutathione, and selenium in an attempt to bolster the body's defenses against free-radical damage. These developments will be discussed at greater length in chapter 18.

Among the critical body systems that can undergo injury via the free-radical route is the immune system. Its lymphocytes are exposed to the same hazards as are the rest of the body's cells. This consid-eration leads us to yet another well-thought-out, highly developed theory of aging—the autoimmune hypothesis. Among its supporters and originators are Sir Macfarlane Burnet, and Takashi Makinodan of the Veterans Administration Hospital in Wadsworth, California. But its principal theorist, investigator, and elucidator has been Roy L. Walford of UCLA. With his shaven head, sweeping mustachios, and often gaudy (and always informal) outfits, Walford cuts a col-orful figure. Yet his personality is eminently nonflamboyant. He is a gentle, soft-spoken man, and as serious and hard-working a sci-entist as anyone in gerontological research, respected by those in the mainstream and in the avant-garde alike. Walford has occa-sionally undertaken expeditions to far places to gather exotic ex-perimental animals (such as the tropical fish *Cynolebias*); and he has used these travels as material for fiction, which a few editors have liked and even bought. The immune theory has been spelled out most convincingly by Walford in his book *The Immunological Theory of Aging*, published in 1969, updated and considerably mod-ified in his more recent publications, including his 1983 book, *Max-imum Life Span*.

We know that as we age our immunological defenses diminish and the incidence of autoimmune disease rises. This could mean: (1) that the immune cells themselves change through damage, error, or information loss of one kind or another in such a way that their powers of recognition fail them, and they can no longer distinguish between friend and foe—i.e., between the "self" and the "not-self"; or (2) that other cells of the body change, for the same reasons, to such an extent that they begin to "look foreign" to the immune cells and are thus attacked; or (3) both. The immunological theory will be discussed in another context in chapter 9, as will Walford's recent hunch that the genetic clock of aging, if there is one, may be located in the "supergene" that seems also to be the control center for certain vital immune functions.

The theories of aging are far from exhausted by this catalogue. A number remain undescribed, and a few unmentioned. But there is no need to be all-inclusive. The point is already sufficiently made that many viable theories of aging have now been worked out to a degree where they can be tested and either proved or disproved. Comfort has said that the free-radical theory, for one, can be disposed of one way or the other by a sizable short-term effort. That done, we could either drop it as a primary cause of aging (though it might still be a contributory cause) or else concentrate on it with fresh vigor.

It is clear, too, that these theories spell out many possible causes of aging that do not require a genetically programmed clock of aging. All these taken together—free radicals, cross-linkages, somatic mutations, error catastrophes, lipofuscin accumulation, autoimmune reactions, the stiffening of connective tissue, all the varieties of simple wear and tear—seem more than enough to account for the process of aging. In point of fact, any single one of these "causes," even if none of the others existed, could all by itself eventually result in the death of the organism.

Eventually, yes. But on schedule? If any one of these factors, or all of them taken together, told the whole aging story, wouldn't we expect to see much greater variations in the life span of a given species? Why doesn't a shrew, just an occasional shrew, live to be 150 or 200 years old, like the Galápagos tortoise? And why shouldn't a Galápagos tortoise, every now and then, wear out at the age of one and a half, as the shrew does?

And why, asks W. Donner Denckla, whose work we shall soon come to, should some classes of animals die sooner than others that have a higher metabolic rate, perhaps the surest measure of wear and tear?

And why, asks Leonard Hayflick, another key figure, are cancer cells immortal in tissue culture and normal cells not, though both are subjected to exactly the same conditions of wear and tear? Hayflick's own experiments with aging cells in culture have led him to the belief that "the fundamental events which orchestrate age-related changes are likely to be found in the genetic machinery." We now arrive at these experiments of Hayflick's. They are among the most fascinating, and the most controversial, in all of recent gerontology.

7

HAYFLICK AND THE CELLULAR AGING CLOCK

WHAT IS especially striking about Leonard Hayflick's work is that he was able to make his contribution to gerontology without ever doing an experiment on either human or animal subjects (which is precisely what some of his critics object to). To appreciate what he did and how he did it requires some understanding of how isolated cells in laboratory tissue cultures came to be scientifically acceptable as substitutes for whole organisms in certain types of research.

When Ross Harrison of Johns Hopkins first hit upon the idea, back in 1907, of trying to keep alive a fragment of frog nerve tissue by immersing it in the frog's own juices, he did not have in mind starting a biological revolution. He merely wanted to find out whether or not nerve fibers grew from single cells, a question that was in dispute. Harrison's experiment succeeded, and he did demonstrate that nerve fibers grew from single cells. As an incidental by-product of the experiment, he also proved—and herein lies the revolution—that tissue could be kept alive outside the body of the host organism. In this situation, the cells take their nourishment from the surrounding medium—whether it is natural (supplied by the body fluids of the host) or artifically concocted (nearly always the case in current experimentation)—and continue to proliferate in the best of health. If they are *not* in the best of health, speaking strictly from the donor's point of view (e.g., cancer cells), they proliferate even more readily.

This past quarter of a century has been an extraordinarily creative period in biology, and tissue culture, once its uses were understood, has been one of the most powerful tools for the acquisition of knowledge about living cells in an enormous variety of species. Human cells have of course been of special interest to medically oriented researchers.

The longest continuously maintained human cell strain in biology is the HeLa strain, begun by George O. Gey—also of Johns Hopkins—in 1951, and still thriving in laboratories all over the world. Gey took the first samples from a patient who had cancer of the cervix. ("He" and "La" were the first two letters of her first and last names—Henrietta Lacks, frequently misreported as Helen Lane.) Because the HeLa strain has proved to be unusually stable and extremely valuable for many specialized studies, the cancer cells of Henrietta Lacks are still undergoing nonstop multiplication thirty-three years after her death. They have undoubtedly divided and redivided to create many times the sixty trillion or so cells that originally made up her entire adult body.* Cancer cells cannot possess this kind of virtual immortality as inhabitants of a living body. Their uncontrolled growth, in fact, constitutes an act of suicide, since it kills the organism on which they depend for their life-support systems—much as the human species seems intent on doing with the planet earth. In tissue culture, the cancer cells, released from their bodily boundaries and supplied with an abundance of all their growth needs, can go indefinitely. Perpetuating oneself via the cultivation of one's cancer cells would not be anyone's choice of a way to achieve longevity. But in the case of Henrietta Lacks, could she have known, she might have been comforted by the fact that the entire human species has been the beneficiary of these studies.

Only mitotic cells, those that continue to divide in the living body, will continue to divide in culture as well. Postmitotic cells, such as mature brain and heart cells, do not begin dividing again on being transferred to culture; they remain in their "resting" state. Some attempts are being made, as already noted, to impart to them this capacity—to teach them to start dividing again, perhaps by reactivating turned-off genetic switches. This is, after all, what cancer

---

* In fact, HeLa cells have multiplied in many places they weren't wanted; even a few HeLa cells, when they contaminate another culture, will quickly take it over and spoil those cultures for further experimentation. Many investigators, unaware of this propensity of HeLa's, did their research on HeLa cells when they thought they were working with something else. This caused the retraction of much published data, especially after Walter Nelson-Rees of Berkeley revealed how dismayingly widespread HeLa contamination had become.

cells are good at doing, though in transferring their own proliferative capacities to neighboring cells, they render their neighbors abnormal as well.

Scientists have long suspected that the neoplastic (cancerous) transformation is brought about by altering the genetic on/off switches of the afflicted cell; the "stop dividing" signal, which was supposed to be posted forever, somehow gets taken down (derepressed). This suspicion has lately been magnified by the discovery that a number of enzymes and hormones that are normally present only in the fetus reappear again in adults who have cancer. In fact, these fetal chemicals have emerged as possible "markers" for the early diagnosis of certain types of cancer. O. W. Jones and his colleagues at the University of California at San Diego, for instance, discovered that a certain form of the enzyme thymidine kinase (TK), which otherwise appears only in prenatal life, also shows up in adult cancer tissue. Carcinoembryonic antigen (CEA) reappears apparently only in the victims of cancer of the gastrointestinal tract. Alpha-fetoprotein (AFP) is most likely to be found in liver-cancer patients, though AFP in the blood of an expectant mother may indicate a heightened risk that her offspring will be afflicted with a "neural-tube" defect, such as a spina bifida. AFP also turns up consistently in the rare immunological birth defect known as ataxia telangiectasia, whose victims have a very high predisposition to cancer. In their case, it is as though nature had forgotten to switch off the gene for AFP at the scheduled time. "That 'forgetfulness,' " as Joe Mori of the March of Dimes observes, "may be part of the hereditary defect. Such 'recall' of embryonic traits may be a feature of other diseases of adults as well." In the cancer cases, it seems logical that the TK, CEA, and AFP found in adults are the results of genes that had been switched off at the appropriate time in fetal development, presumably forever, but had now been switched on again through some fault or accident in adult life—either "caused" by the gene-scrambling effects of the cancer process, or the scrambled gene itself acting as a contributory cause of the cell's neoplastic transformation.

Any number of genetic "markers" denoting cancer predispositions have turned up since the publication of *Prolongevity*, and the last few years in particular have witnessed a worldwide outbreak of interest in "oncogenes"—specific genes capable of initiating the cancer process—most of it so far representing research on animals rather than humans.

The more cheerful aspect of this bad news is that Strehler may well be on the right track in his aging theories. If "permanently" switched-off genes can be reactivated to our disadvantage by cancer mechanisms, then we can learn to derepress others to our advantage—the desirable genes that will keep our vital cellular protein factories going full-blast. So far, the researchers who have had some limited success in inducing postmitotic cells to divide again in tissue culture have not been able to do so without transforming them to an abnormal state. But this kind of effort is only in its infancy, and there is every reason to feel confident that we will acquire the sophistication to turn on the "start" switches again while leaving the cell otherwise intact—and also to activate the "stop" switches when we know (or the organism knows) it is time for cell division to come to a halt once more. Something like this happens in wound healing. Cells multiply to repair the injury, then stop multiplying when the job is done. Because the repair mechanism is imprecise, some scar tissue remains. It would obviously be desirable to bestow the gift of self-repair upon the living heart. (Whether it would be an equivalent blessing for the brain is less certain, as we shall presently see.) Again, since 1976, rapid progress in recombinant-DNA and other genetic-engineering techniques has taught us a great deal about genetic on/off switching. And it is not always necessary to manipulate the DNA itself. In 1983, a team of NIH investigators were able, by using the drug 5-azacytidine, to turn on a long-repressed gene governing the manufacture of hemoglobin and thus improve the lot of five patients with severe inherited anemias.

There is a heartening aspect to the fact that cells that no longer divide in the body will not divide in culture, either: it suggests that there must be some relationship between what happens in culture (*in vitro*) and what happens in the living organism (*in vivo*). In that event, studies in the one state, where cells are convenient and accessible, will tell us something about the other, which is not just more complex but often out of experimental reach. How close is the relationship? That is a matter of continuing debate. Cells could not, of course, be expected to undergo the same experience in such contrasting environments. Cells in culture are living outside their normal context. They get no feedback from the other cells and organs that would ordinarily surround them. They are out of touch with the body's hormonal and nervous systems. They are sustained on artificial nutrients. For these and other good reasons, it would be surprising if their behavior and development did not differ in many respects from what they would be in the cells' natural habitat. Nevertheless, as a means of observing the workings of living cells and manipulating them at the whim of the investigator, tissue culture is unbeatable. Besides, no bioethical questions arise when experimenting with cell clones. ("Cloning" is a term much used these days. A clone is any growth of cells, usually from a single starter cell, that has come about asexually.)

A test-tubeful of cultured cells is not only cheaper, easier to handle, and more accessible to observation than an animal subject would be; there are many experiments that simply could not be carried out in any other way. How else could we watch viruses infect cells, or observe how cells resist them and how they succumb, or discover how normal cells may be transformed into tumor cells? Much of our newest cancer knowledge derives directly from tissue-culture studies. One can also use culture to *grow* viruses—as was done in developing the polio vaccine.

The uses of tissue culture are limited only by the imagination of the investigator (and the size of his grant funds). Cells can be fused and hybridized to make man-mouse combinations, or almost any other combination desired. In this manner genetic material is transferred and translocated, hundreds of gene sites are pinpointed precisely in the geography of the chromosomes, new genetic traits are imparted, and a truly marvelous repertoire of "genetic surgery" can be performed.

In tissue culture, cells can be punished to the limit—scalded, frostbitten, poisoned, loaded with allergens—in order to study the precise mechanisms of injury, and to test possible therapies for reversing or alleviating the damage. In fact, cell cultures provide an ideal testing ground for drugs of any kind and have long been routinely used for this purpose. As one example: Allan L. Goldstein, of the George Washington University Medical Center in Washington, is codiscoverer of the hormone thymosin (so called because it is produced by the thymus), which we will hear more about later because it may turn out to be of some importance in aging. But its initial use has been in the treatment of inherited immune-deficiency diseases. When thymosin was deemed ready for clinical trials (Goldstein was then at the University of Texas Medical Branch—UTMB—in Galveston), there were two possible candidates for the first treatment. One was a boy in Houston who had then been living in a plastic bubble for more than two years to keep him germ-free.* The other was a girl in San Francisco who had been hospitalized many times with recurring infections.

Any untried drug may (1) fail to work in human patients, or (2) cause adverse side effects. In the case of thymosin, animal studies had suggested it was relatively free of major hazards. Just the same, Goldstein and his UTMB collaborators were reluctant to use it on these children without some evidence, beyond the theoretical, that thymosin had a good chance of boosting their deficient immune systems. So they worked out a method for testing thymosin first in tissue culture. The Houston boy's cells did not form the telltale "rosette" shapes that indicate the production of immune cells (lymphocytes). This meant his bone marrow was not capable of manufacturing the incipient "stem cells" (perhaps because those genetic switches were mistakenly turned off), without which even thymosin cannot help the patient. There was no point in exposing him to even a small additional risk. The cells of the San Francisco girl, however, responded with a strong display of rosettes, indicating that stem cells were present; her deficiency lay in an inability to convert them to mature lymphocytes. She was treated with thymosin and has continued to receive regular doses; as of 1984, her infections still seem to be well under control, as she goes about her close-to-normal life.

When the first anti-aging drugs are tested, they will almost surely be tried initially *in vitro* to see if they can reverse the signs of aging in cultured cells. But do cells truly age in culture? And, if so, is the process the same as *in vivo?* Does the study of cells in culture have anything at all to tell us about the physiological deterioration and death of human beings? Some think not. Among the more outspoken is Donner Denckla, formerly of the Roche Institute and Harvard, creator of the best-worked-out hormonal-clock theory of aging (the "clock" being located in the brain). Denckla, originally an endocrinologist and a relative newcomer to gerontology, says, "I don't care what happens to cells in tissue culture. What is important is *what people die of.*" His own theory, a brilliant and promising one based on experimental data as well as logic, will be dealt with at some length later in this book. Briefly, he believes that the release

* This is the boy who died in 1984, at the age of twelve, after an unsuccessful bone-marrow transplant.

of certain pro-aging hormones by the pituitary at scheduled times of life is what causes aging. Inasmuch as cells in tissue culture are beyond the reach of any hormonal influences (unless hormones are deliberately added to the culture), whatever "aging" seems to occur *in vitro* is an artifact, not related in any meaningful way to the real thing.

Leonard Hayflick of the University of Florida, on the other hand, has founded the whole new discipline of "cytogerontology" (cellular aging) and has written papers bearing such titles as "Aging Under Glass." He firmly believes that the clock of aging lies within the nucleus of the individual cell. (In either case, the program is still genetically dictated.) Taking a stance directly opposite to Denckla's,* Hayflick declares that "the primary causes of age changes can no longer be thought of as resulting from events occurring at the supracellular level, i.e., at cell hierarchies from the tissue level and greater. The cell is where the gerontological action lies. I believe therefore that purely descriptive studies done at the tissue, organ and whole animal level, as they pertain to the biology of aging, are less likely to yield important information on mechanism than studies done at the cell and molecular level."

Who is right? Is the clock of aging—if one exists—a single entity located in the brain, governing the aging and death of all cells? Or does each cell carry its own genetic clock? Which theory—if either— is compatible with what is observed both *in vitro* and *in vivo*? Are the two theories as incompatible with each other as they appear to be? Do they in any way encompass the ideas of other, competing aging theories?

When Hayflick first turned his attention to the life spans of cells *in vitro*, in the late 1950s and early 1960s, the prevailing belief was that cells in tissue culture could live on indefinitely. This belief, which ruled with the strength of dogma, had been mainly propagated by the experiments of the late Alexis Carrel of the Rockefeller Institute. Carrel, besides his many real achievements—one of which earned him a Nobel Prize—had long been credited with an erroneous one: the continuous maintenance, over a period of more than thirty-four years, of a culture of chick-heart fibroblasts (the embry-

---

* Though I oppose Hayflick to Denckla for dramatic emphasis, as of this writing the two have never been in any direct personal confrontation; in fact, I am not sure they have ever met.

onic cells that later give rise to connective tissue). Carrel put the first little sliver of embryonic heart in a flask in 1912. As the cells multiplied in their special medium in culture after culture, they were religiously tended over the remaining thirty-three years of Carrel's life, and then not permitted to die out for nearly another two years. The word "religiously" is used here only half metaphorically. The tending of the cells was very like a religious rite. In fact, everything that went on in Carrel's lab took on a ceremonial air as his celebrity grew. He even made his technicians carry out their solemn high duties in flowing black robes with hoods. Though his theatricality was looked upon with distaste by many of his peers, he was unquestionably a great scientist; his data, and his interpretations of the data, were accepted without serious challenge. "From such experiments," says Morgan Harris, in *Cell Culture and Somatic Variation*, "came the widely heralded view of Carrel['s] that tissue cells are potentially immortal, if maintained as continuously proliferating strains *in vitro*."

Hayflick, then working at the Wistar Institute in Philadelphia, where he did his trail-breaking experiments, did not set out to challenge Carrel at all. He and a colleague, Paul Moorhead, were trying to study the effects of cancer-causing viruses on normal cells in culture. "The single missing link in this research plan," he later recalled, on accepting the Robert W. Kleemeier Award of the Gerontological Society in 1973,

> was the establishment of normal human cell cultures—a feat that, surprisingly, had not been satisfactorily accomplished in 1959. Since human tissue that is most easily available comes from operating theaters and is presumably abnormal, we turned to human embryonic tissue, not only because it represented presumptive normal tissue but because we reasoned that the likelihood of encountering unwanted latent viruses might also be reduced. . . .
>
> Until that time no one had determined that normal cells could be cultured by invoking a wide variety of criteria including chromosome analysis. Prior to these studies normal human cells were only presumed to have been cultivated.

Why the long hiatus? Earlier, as Morgan Harris explains, "the methods at hand were too laborious for routine use, and the necessity for a complex, undefined medium prevented the application of analytical techniques. Owing to such limitations, cell culture had for many years relatively little general impact, and was regarded more as an art than as a basic research tool in biology and medicine." By the time Hayflick came on the scene, the potential research uses of tissue culture had become much more widely recognized. The major surprise that grew out of his initial studies with Moorhead was "the finding that the normal cell populations grew and divided perfectly for many months, then slowed down, stopped dividing, and ultimately died."

As Hayflick repeatedly emphasizes, he was not the first to learn that normal cells in culture—unlike cancerous strains—had a finite life span. Other researchers had made the same observation on numerous occasions, but nobody believed them. In fact, they often disbelieved their own results. Any contradiction of the Carrelian dogma was assumed to be due to the investigator's sloppiness: the cultures must have become contaminated. As we now know, it was Carrel's cultures that were contaminated. His technicians, as they kept adding fresh chick-embryo medium to maintain the cultures, did not realize that their "pure" medium also contained a few stray cells, which thus were being constantly, albeit inadvertently, added to the cultures. Once, at a meeting in Puerto Rico, Hayflick encountered one of Carrel's former technicians, who told him that she, for one, had been aware of what was happening but hadn't dared to say anything because so much was at stake! Hayflick was more persistent than his predecessors. For one thing, he was certain, by virtue of repeated testing—as they perhaps could not have been— that he was working with a pure, uncontaminated medium and with truly normal cells.

Hayflick's embryonic fibroblasts consistently underwent about fifty divisions (varying between forty and sixty "population doublings") before they reached what Hayflick calls "Phase III"—the point at which division ceases. Though this happens over a period of months *in vitro*, it could be an accelerated model of what requires all the years of a person's life *in vivo*. The figure of 50 ± 10 (50 plus-or-minus 10) doublings has become celebrated as "the Hayflick limit," and his favorite strain of fibroblasts, the WI-38 strain,* widely used by others, has gained almost the same kind of fame in gerontological circles as the HeLa strain in cancer research. Once he

---

* WI for Wistar Institute, where they originated.

had convinced himself that "the finite lifespan of cultured normal human and animal cells was a manifestation of biological aging at the cellular level," Hayflick decided to pursue cytogerontology as his central research interest. He has continued at Stanford and at Florida what he began at the Wistar Institute—where others, notably V. J. Cristofalo, have continued to do original work in the same field. Over the intervening years, Hayflick has performed many variations on his first experiments, and so have investigators in hundreds of laboratories around the world.

Before he ever submitted any of his data for publication, Hayflick wanted to reassure himself triply that his Phase III phenomenon did not come about because of some unsuspected fault in his culture medium—or through mere statistical wear and tear. It is easy, in cell clones, to distinguish male cells from female. Only female cells contain the so-called Barr bodies, which are clearly visible in the sex chromatin under a microscope. Hayflick grew out a pure male strain, let them divide until they had lived out most of their expected life spans, then added a pure young female strain to the culture. After the time when the male cells could be assumed to have arrived at Phase III, Hayflick carefully checked the culture and found that the viable cells were now 100 percent female, still dividing vigorously on schedule. That clinched it. If there had been a contaminant present, it would not have discriminated against the male cells only, leaving the female cells intact. It would have killed male and female alike, and the survivors, if any, should have included both sexes.

Hayflick submitted his carefully compiled report to *The Journal of Experimental Medicine*, which he considered to be "the Cadillac of medical journals" at the time. It was rejected and returned with what amounted to a kindly pat on the head. "The largest fact to have come out from [*sic*] tissue culture in the last fifty years," the editor wrote, "is that cells inherently capable of multiplying will do so indefinitely if supplied with the right milieu *in vitro*." Though Hayflick usually neglects to mention it when he tells the story, the editor who signed the letter, ironically, was Nobelist Peyton Rous— whose own early work with the Rous chicken-sarcoma virus had a similar hard time getting acceptance, because everybody knew that viruses could not possibly cause the cancer (another example of The Josh Billings Syndrome). Hayflick did finally get his report published in *Experimental Cell Research*.

As further evidence of a cellular aging program, Hayflick put cells in deep-frozen hibernation for long periods of time without affecting the Hayflick limit. In an ingenious series of experiments, a number of cultures were placed in storage at liquid-nitrogen temperatures at varying "ages" (i.e., after a measured number of divisions); then thawed, a few at a time, over a period of a dozen years. In each case, the cells "remembered" where their lives had been interrupted—say, at twenty divisions—and proceeded to double another thirty or so times before reaching Phase III.

Hayflick has also cited other evidence, based on work done in his own lab and in many others—especially by a diligent team of investigators headed by George M. Martin at the University of Washington School of Medicine in Seattle. In general, when cell samples were taken from adults of varying ages, the older they were the fewer times the cells divided before they attained Phase III. The cells of a twenty-year-old tended to have more "life" left in them, by this standard, than those of a fifty-year-old. Yet the cells of even very elderly individuals still had a few doublings left, and this—if the life of a cell *in vitro* up to Phase III can be considered a valid paradigm—suggests that people rarely live out their potential life spans.

In 1969, Samuel Goldstein of the McMaster University Medical Center in Hamilton, Ontario, cultured the cells of a child victim of progeria—the cruel disease that mimics speeded-up senescence—and found that they had only a few doublings left this side of Phase III, like the cells of a very old man or woman. Other scientists, including the Seattle group as well as Robin Holliday in London, did similar experiments with the cells of people afflicted with genetic diseases that shorten the life span—Werner's syndrome, for example—and found that the cells' *in vitro* span was likewise shortened.

Later Goldstein, who had done the work on the shortest-lived cells (progeria cells), carried out further experiments with cells that should be the longest-lived, those of the Galápagos tortoise. These were skin cells rather than embryonic cells, and the four strains Goldstein was able to use achieved from 72 to 144 doublings before Phase III—significantly more than the human limit. At other research centers, embryonic cells from chickens and mice were found to divide fewer times in culture than human cells do—but not as few as would be predicted from their proportional life spans. The data on the cells of other species are still too sparse to establish any definitive correlations.

What else?

A number of experiments have been done in the "serial transplantation" of normal cells and tissues. As an animal ages, the tissue in question is transplanted to a younger animal (of the same carefully bred species, of course, to minimize chances of graft rejection); as that animal approaches senescence, the tissue is again transplanted to another young one. This goes on until the transplanted cells are no longer viable. The best-known of these experiments was the series done by P. L. Krohn at England's University of Birmingham with the skin cells of mice. Since then a variety of other cells have been serially transplanted, ranging from mammary tissues to lymphocytes and marrow cells—such as the well-known series carried out by David Harrison at the Jackson Laboratory in Bar Harbor, Maine.* In all these cases the cells lived longer than they would have in their original donors (long since dead), sometimes by as much as two or three lifetimes. But they all eventually died.†

These serial-transplantation results have been pointed to by Hayflick's critics as evidence that he was wrong. Caleb Finch of the University of Southern California, citing Krohn's mouse-skin data, asked: If those cells had a built-in life span, why didn't they die on

* The fact that cell lines transplanted from old mice functioned well in young animals, while young marrow did not noticeably improve deficiencies in aged mice, convinced Harrison that the aging of these cells could not be intrinsically timed but was, rather, dependent on the environment provided by the new host.

† This is still in dispute. One long-term lymphoid cell line was kept going continuously in culture for more than a decade by Kurt Hirschhorn and his associates at the Mount Sinai Medical Center in New York. Critics of this kind of research insist that all such cell lines are contaminated by the Epstein-Barr virus and are therefore abnormal. Hirschhorn insists that, virus-contaminated or not, these cells are normal by standard criteria, since the virus did not transform them into cancer cells.

This kind of discrepancy, along with David Harrison's experiments as well as the reports of various immunologists that some lymphocyte (T-cell) lines seem to continue far beyond the Hayflick limit, have fascinated and puzzled Roy Walford and his UCLA colleague Rita B. Effros. In a survey of the situation published in 1984, they conclude: "It may be that criteria applied to growth of fibroblasts and other cell types simply can not be applied to lymphocytes. On the other hand, there are several suggestions in the reports on long-term T-cell cultures that the successfully growing clone is a rare event and may even constitute an abnormal cell type. Thus it seems crucial that immunologists, cell biologists, and gerontologists consider and address two basic questions: Do lymphocytes follow different growth patterns from other cell types, thereby overthrowing the Hayflick limit as a general biological phenomenon? Are cultures of lymphocytes possessing 'infinite' life span really normal?"

schedule? There must be some "youth factor," imparted to the cells by their new hosts, others reasoned, that extended their life spans. I was present at a meeting in Bar Harbor where David Harrison was speaking. At one point, Robert Kohn—who was in the audience—said flatly to Harrison: "Your experiments have very neatly refuted Hayflick," and no one rose to refute Kohn.

Yet, to Hayflick, these transplantation findings serve as further confirmation of his cytogerontological thesis. He never claimed that the Hayflick limit *in vitro* applied to cells under other conditions. Obviously, human cells go through their *in vivo* lives at a much slower rate than they do in culture. The fact that transplantation increases the *duration* of a cell's life—"the passage of metabolic time," as Hayflick calls it—is interpreted by him and others, based on further experiments, as a slowing down of doublings.* Even if it were conclusively proved otherwise, Hayflick would not consider this any kind of refutation. He does not hold that there is no way to increase the life span; he is, rather, motivated by high hope that such ways will be discovered. To him, the fact of central importance that work such as Krohn's and Harrison's has demonstrated is that normal cells that have been carefully kept track of, growing not in culture but in the sites they normally occupy in the living body, *also* have finite life spans. In fact, when A. R. Williamson and B. A. Askonas of London's National Institute for Medical Research carried out serial transfers of an antibody-forming spleen-cell clone in mice, they proved to their own satisfaction that they had created a model demonstrating the limited life span of dividing cells *in vivo*. All this, in Hayflick's opinion, "circumvents arguments levelled at similar data obtained from the 'artificial' conditions of in vitro cell culture."

Critics eager to refute Hayflick find support in yet another, and quite different, set of experiments, which all involve the apparent extension of the cell's life span *in vitro* through the addition of various substances to the culture medium. Modest extensions of cellular life span (up to eighteen doublings beyond control cultures) have been achieved, for example, with cortisone and hydrocortisone by both A. Macieira-Coelho in France and Cristofalo in Philadel-

---

* As Hayflick likes to point out, he has deep-frozen cells for more than a dozen years before thawing—thus fantastically "increasing their life spans," but *not* increasing the number of doublings.

phia. Why should this be so? It is known that the making of RNA as well as ribosomes (those protein-assembly workbenches again) declines as cells age. Macieira-Coelho and his colleague E. Loria have speculated that cortisone and hydrocortisone may increase life span by maintaining the manufacture of ribosomes—and therefore of ribosomal RNA*—for longer periods of time. "It is interesting, however," as they note in their *Nature* report, "that when hydrocortisone is withdrawn from cells which have grown beyond the lifespan of the controls, the cultures die within two passages."

More recently, and even more impressively, Berkeley's Lester Packer, in collaboration with James R. Smith of the Veterans Administration Hospital in Martinez, California, appears to have *doubled* cellular life spans by adding vitamin E to the cultures. And the cells were still dividing vigorously when the experiment was terminated! The trouble was that no one else could duplicate the results of Packer and Smith; and when, on further attempts, they couldn't repeat it either, they withdrew their paper, thus officially erasing the data.

As I mentioned in the last chapter, antioxidants such as vitamin E are believed to slow down oxidation reactions and combat free-radical damage. Though the Packer-Smith experiments didn't pan out, the other experiments that achieved less dramatic extensions of cellular life spans *in vitro* still seem to lend strong support to Harman's free-radical theory of aging. They also seem to add weight to the suspicion of Harman and others that the cell's mitochondria— the organelles that serve as energy machines to power the cell, and where most of the oxidation reactions therefore take place—are critical to the aging process. If, indeed, free-radical damage is the principal cause of cellular aging *in vitro*, as the theory's proponents believe it to be *in vivo*, and if, further, the end result of the accumulated damage is the gradual cessation of cell division, then these extensions of the lives of cells in culture could be considered a reasonable demonstration—not only of the theory's validity, but of the powerful anti-aging potential of antioxidant therapy.

But are such ideas consistent with observed events in tissue culture? Is there any evidence that free-radical damage occurs at all *in vitro?* The evidence is indirect. Certainly cells in culture do undergo a stage of fairly rapid deterioration before they die, just as cells *in*

---

* The ingredient that declined so drastically in Strehler's aging beagles.

vivo do, suggesting the handiwork of free radicals. Hayflick's Phase III is not a clear-cut cellular event, a sudden cessation of all doubling at a precisely pinpointable moment. Even after all cells have stopped dividing—clearly beyond Phase III—"the culture," says Hayflick, "may linger for several weeks or months during which time the cells continue to degenerate to the point where they are all ultimately dead." And before the cells stop dividing altogether, the *rate* of division slows down, while the cells show many signs of senescence and the loss of vital functions. Even before the onset of this obviously degenerative pattern, biochemical tests can detect signs of damage and deterioration. When such observations were first reported, they were taken as evidence that Orgel's error theory was correct. The work of Holliday and of Macieira-Coelho particularly seemed to lend such support. "An error catastrophe process of this sort," wrote Macfarlane Burnet in *The Lancet*, "is the most likely interpretation of the cell-culture phenomenon known as the Hayflick limit"—though Burnet expressed the belief that such errors came about through somatic mutations, under genetic control. The same results led others to the conclusion that the Hayflick limit was *not* built in to the cell's genetics at all but, rather, was a reflection of what statistics would lead one to expect when large numbers of cells, in artificial circumstances, were allowed to accumulate damage over long periods of time: gradual degeneration, the slowdown of division, the end of division, and eventual death. Denckla is among those who favor this interpretation; and Medvedev earlier predicted the likelihood of just such a statistical amassing of errors. Hayflick disagrees, of course—and feels that he convincingly refuted such charges in advance, before he ever published his first paper, with his careful studies in culturing male and female cell lines.

Nevertheless, further credence was lent to these interpretations by a series of experiments done at the State University of New York at Buffalo by a British-born team, James F. Danielli and Audrey Muggleton, using a relatively immortal species of amoeba.* The basic question in cellular aging is the same *in vitro* as *in vivo*: is it the nuclear DNA that dictates the running down of the cell's mul-

---

* A species of amoeba is said to be "immortal" only in the sense that cancer cells are immortal: they go on dividing indefinitely. The individual "parent" cells continue to survive only in their progeny. A "mortal" species would be more like WI-38 cells, which stop dividing after a while.

tifarious activities, or is it, rather, that the cytoplasmic material—
the protein-making machinery and the mitochondrial energy gen-
erators—finally, under the steady beatings that mere living entails,
loses the capacity to follow the genetic orders? The Danielli-
Muggleton results seemed to prove the latter. They transferred cytoplasmic material from a *mortal* species of amoeba to the cytoplasm
of the immortal species—and, by so doing, conferred upon the immortals the gifts of old age and death!

But was the same true of human cells? Hayflick was eager to
devise an experimental test that could provide an unequivocal answer. Working with his Stanford colleague Woodring E. Wright,
with help from David Prescott of the University of Colorado, he
devised an elaborate laboratory technique for enucleating cells en
masse. There is a substance, called cytochalasin B, extracted from
mold, which can cause occasional cells to extrude their nuclei. Hayflick found he could considerably facilitate this process by spinning
WI-38 cells in an ultracentrifuge until they were subjected to gravitational forces 25,000 times greater than the G force that keeps us
on an earth that is spinning along in space. In a cell at 25,000 Gs,
the nucleus migrates through the cytoplasm out to the membrane,
where the cytochalasin B then pulls it the rest of the way through.
Under these circumstances, some 99 percent of the cells are enucleated. The remaining 1 percent are rendered incapable of further
division by being treated with the antibiotic mitomycin-C.

In other cells, again through a complex process, most of the
enzymes in the cytoplasm could be inactivated by treatment with a
poisonous substance, iodoacetate, while the nucleus generally remained intact. Then any two cells could be fused, using inactivated
Sendai virus to bring about the fusion—a standard laboratory method.
Employing such tools and techniques, Hayflick and Wright were
able to join a young nucleus with an old cytoplasm, and vice versa,
in diverse combinations and conditions. As they carried through
numerous variations of these experiments, Hayflick and Wright found
that in every case the number of doublings was dictated by the
transplanted *nucleus*. If the nucleus of a cell that had already divided
thirty times was placed in a very young cell, the resultant hybrid
would divide only twenty or so times. On the other hand, if a fresh
young nucleus—from a cell that had doubled, say, no more than
ten times—was put into an enucleated cell almost ready for Phase
III, it would then go on to divide another forty or so times before

Phase III actually set in. Unlike that of the amoeba, then, the life span of the human cell does *not* seem to be affected by old cytoplasm. But the hybridizing experiments seem to demonstrate beyond a reasonable doubt in Hayflick's mind that the genetic aging program resides solely in the nuclear DNA; and in 1983, at his new research laboratory in Florida, he was starting a concerted program directed toward discovering precisely where in the DNA the clock of aging is located. Others, including Walford, believe that they, too, are zeroing in on where that clock may be.

8

DENCKLA: THE CLOCK IS IN THE BRAIN

EVEN IF Hayflick's interpretation—which I for one find most convincing—is accepted as correct, it resolves the debate only for those who believe that the clock of aging is located in the individual cell. It does not, of course, satisfy a critic like W. Donner Denckla, who discounts Hayflick's work because he feels it has not provided any insights into how whole organisms age—and is therefore simply not very useful. For Denckla, the clock of aging is hormonal in nature and resides in the brain.

The first time I talked with Denckla, he was in his lab at the Roche Institute in Nutley, New Jersey, wearing an open-collared sports shirt and slacks, a bespectacled, boyish-looking Harvard man, enthusiastic and brilliantly articulate. He exhorted, expounded, defended, refuted, getting up to pace and gesticulate, stopping now and then to poke irritably at a large, washtublike vat with a complexity of glass tubing. This was a gadget he had designed for extracting the pituitary product he calls DECO (for "decreasing oxygen consumption" hormone), which he has deliberately refrained from referring to as the "aging" or "death" hormone, though others have not hesitated to do so. The gadget was giving him some mechanical difficulties, and he was impatient with the resulting holdup. Over the years since then, as Denckla has moved from Roche to Harvard to the National Institute of Alcoholism and Alcohol Abuse (NIAAA), he has remained dissatisfied with the degree of purification he has been able to attain. In 1983, through an unfor-

tunate freak of budgetary circumstance, he suddenly found himself
without a lab to work in, though others were continuing the effort.

Denckla's belief in a brain-based hormonal clock of aging has
begun to be shared by a number of investigators, including NIAAA's
Richard Veech, William Regelson of the Medical College of Virginia
at Richmond, Richard Cutler of NIA's GRC/Baltimore, Robert
Bolla of the University of Missouri in St. Louis, several Soviet
scientists, and Australia's Arthur Everitt, who, along with Denckla,
has pioneered this research frontier. The brain-based aging-clock
idea is supported indirectly by the similar views of USC's Caleb
Finch, who is convinced that one or more hormones must play a
large part in aging, and that certain small areas of the primitive
brain must be an important part of the clockwork. Also sympathetic
to this outlook have been James Bonner, now retired from the
California Institute of Technology, and a few of his former graduate
students.

I was on hand in Bonner's lab one late afternoon when he was
preparing to leave for Pasadena, where the first meeting of a small,
newly formed aging-research group was to be held. He invited me
along. The group consisted mainly of graduate students from both
USC and Caltech, surrounding the two principal figures, Bonner
and Finch. Though Bonner was the senior man, he was more the
molecular biologist whose long-time interest in the mechanisms of
genetic on/off switching had brought him to gerontology; whereas
"Tuck" Finch considered himself—and still does, and is so recognized by his peers—to be a dedicated, full-time gerontologist. In
any case, Bonner voluntarily took a side seat, and it was the younger
Finch who presided, a tall, gangly, open-collared guru, prematurely
balding, heavily red-bearded, full of an incandescent intelligence,
guiding his disciples down the hormonal path. The picture of guru
and disciples I have just painted is, I admit, a bit exaggerated—
Finch is not dogmatic, and his followers are not slavish adherents
of any doctrine—but such was my own impression of that evening's
meeting. The group was, well, not exactly *anti*-Hayflick, but certainly non-Hayflick in its orientation. Nor could the members be
described as pro-Denckla, though at that point it seemed to me they
were insufficiently familiar with Denckla's more recent experiments
and conclusions to center on him as the symbol of their own inves-
tigative thrust. By now, there is little likelihood that Finch is not
aware of Denckla's work and theories, but he still remains guardedly

aloof from Denckla's view of things. Finch, in 1984, is doubtful that any single "clock" governs aging. He leans to the view that there are clusters of aging processes which interact throughout life—a view that also holds some appeal for Roy Walford.

Just the day before that Finch-Bonner meeting, a little farther down the California coast, I had discussed Denckla's ideas with Roger Guillemin (who has since become a Nobel laureate) at the Salk Institute in La Jolla. Guillemin seemed startled to hear that someone was already actively trying to isolate "death hormones." His own research group had been thinking along somewhat similar lines, and though they so far had had no opportunity to pursue the hunch, it all made excellent sense to him. Guillemin was convinced, however, that if death hormones are released by the pituitary, this release would be triggered by "releasing factors" in the hypothalamus, located just above the pituitary—a sequence that now appears to be true for *all* hormones secreted by the pituitary. (This is the area of research Guillemin has pioneered so fruitfully.) Denckla believes that Guillemin may well be right, but that still leaves his theory not just intact but actually more hopeful in the long run, since releasing factors are smaller, simpler, and therefore easier to synthesize than pituitary hormones. At a later meeting in Miami, Nathan Shock also cited data that suggested to him that aging "must be regarded as a breakdown of endocrine and neural control mechanisms." Looking at what he considered to be the limitations of cellular-aging theories such as Hayflick's, Shock urged that more attention be given to what happens to the total organism.

Similar views have been espoused quite vigorously for some time in the Soviet Union, especially by V. V. Frolkis, who works at Chebotarev's Institute of Gerontology in Kiev. "The aging of an organism," wrote Frolkis in *The Main Problems of Soviet Gerontology*, "is not a simple sum of aging of its individual cells. At each new level of biologic organization appear not only quantitative but also qualitative features of the aging process. That's why the analysis of the neuro-humoral regulation (brain, nerves, glands, hormones) adapting the activity of the cells to the needs of the whole organism, is of primary importance for the purpose of understanding the essence of aging of a whole organism."

If the endocrine system is so heavily involved, is there, then, a "master gland" for aging? Sir Macfarlane Burnet had nominated the thymus, which controls the immunological surveillance system;

and this view gained considerable support from the work of Allan Goldstein with the thymic hormones—though Bar Harbor's David Harrison, as noted earlier, has pointed to a number of key experiments that cast doubt on the thymus as an intrinsically timed aging mechanism in itself. For similar reasons and others of his own, Donner Denckla prefers to regard the thyroid as the critical gland in aging—apart from the pituitary itself, which governs all the other endocrine glands. This is a belief he has arrived at through logic as well as experiment. After much study of autopsy data and death records, Denckla finds that people—in fact, all mammals—die through the failure of one or the other of two major body systems: the cardiovascular or the immune system. (This assumes that cancer is essentially an immunological disorder—or at least the result of a disruption of the immune system—as more and more researchers deem it to be. If this assumption proves incorrect, cancer will have to be added as a third and separate major cause of death.)

Denckla points out that people do not really die of heart failure, or kidney failure, or liver malfunction, or stroke; these are merely the end results of the failure either of the immune cells to do their job or of the blood vessels to deliver oxygen and nutrients where they are needed. There is only one gland that has a profound effect on both systems—the thyroid. Finch, too, has suggested that "a key candidate for a central endocrine change of aging . . . is the thyroid, whose obligatory role in central, autonomic, and endocrine functions is well documented."

Approaching the problem from another vantage point, Denckla carefully studied data on many species of animals, and found a fairly consistent correlation among five biological time elements: the heart rate, the metabolic rate, the time of gestation (specially defined), the time up to puberty, and the time from puberty to death. In all these time events, Denckla believes, the thyroid gland is of central importance because its product, thyroxine, is the *master rate-controlling hormone for all cells and tissues*. It governs the basal metabolic rate, the speed at which cells burn their fuel and consume their oxygen.

Moreover, says Denckla, the disease that most closely mimics premature aging in adults is hypothyroidism—lower-than-normal thyroid levels. The disease can be fatal if untreated, and the victim is more susceptible to infection, which suggests a diminished immune capability. We almost never see advanced cases of hypothyroidism these days, because thyroxine is prescribed as soon as a deficiency is discovered. But in the 1890s, when thyroxine was first administered, the reversals were quite dramatic: wrinkles disappeared, graying hair turned black or brown or red or blond again, resistance to disease returned to normal levels. Encouraged by these spectacular results, doctors started using thyroxine to reverse the symptoms of aging in the really old. But the treatment quickly went out of style because (1) it didn't work, and (2) the high dosage killed some of the elderly patients. Denckla's work sheds light on the reasons for this outcome.

Though Denckla is an analytical theorist, he bases his theories on experiments with more than twenty-five hundred rats of varying ages, some normal, some without ovaries, some without pancreases, some without adrenals, and so on. He has measured the metabolic rates of anesthetized animals under the most rigorously controlled conditions, making carefully computed adjustments for body weight, fat content, and other circumstances. He was able to demonstrate to his satisfaction that only the pituitary or the thyroid makes a difference in the metabolic rate (the thyroid being controlled by the pituitary); that the pituitary slows down the metabolic rate with age, not by failing to stimulate the thyroid to make its hormones but, rather, by releasing a blocking hormone (DECO) that prevents the cells from properly using the thyroxine that still circulates freely in the animal's bloodstream.

Denckla has since ascertained that aging men and women—if they are normal, not hypothyroid—are not short of thyroxine. Plenty of it circulates through the blood vessels, but the cells somehow cannot take it up and use it. Denckla believes that in people, as in rats, the pituitary gland begins at puberty to release the first of a series of those death or aging hormones—Finch calls them antithyroid hormones—that act at the cell membrane to keep thyroxine out.

In late 1975, just as *Prolongevity* was being readied for the press, Denckla told me of new experimental results, now long since published but at that time just being prepared for publication—results that reinforced his convictions. They demonstrated in a fairly startling way that aging changes could be turned back and youthful functioning restored in certain aspects of three major systems in animals—the immune, the cardiovascular, and the genetic.

The immune system's phagocytic activity—the characteristic engulfment of foreign material—goes down by five- or sixfold with aging in rats. That part of the immune system called "T-dependent," made up of the white blood cells known as "T-lymphocytes," also undergoes a major decline with aging. These T-cells not only fight off invading micro-organisms but are also believed to attack cancer cells. Denckla and his colleagues were able to restore (at least in part, and in some cases up to 80 or 90 percent) in his older rats immune functions, ranging from antibody reactions to graft rejection, to levels that would have been expected only in much younger rats.

This "restoration of juvenile competence" was achieved, like the other apparent reversals of aging, by (1) removing the pituitary, the presumed source of DECO, and (2) administering thyroxine! Giving thyroxine to normal animals with intact pituitaries had no such rejuvenating effects.

One result of cardiovascular decline is that the body's blood vessels lose much of their ability to relax and dilate in response to certain substances. The aorta in the rat, for instance, is already considerably less able to relax by the age of three months, and by six months the capacity is just about gone. Denckla surgically removed the pituitary from a rat nine months old—three months after its aortal relaxation response should have been gone. The response was not only restored, but for more than a year after surgery, even when the rat reached the age of twenty-four months—equivalent to about seventy years in human age—its aorta still retained the relaxation capacity normal for a four-week-old rat.

A measurement generally considered to be an index of overall cardiovascular competence is "maximum aerobic capacity" of the lungs. This capacity keeps diminishing with age in both rat and human. Here again Denckla was able, via the same surgical and hormonal-replacement techniques, to impart to a twenty-four-month-old rat the aerobic capacity normal for a three-month-old. Thus he suspects that most cardiovascular functions could be brought back to levels normal for the same creatures at younger ages if no DECO were around to interfere with thyroid uptake.

Not long after these first cardiovascular and immune experiments, Denckla was also able to report that youthful levels of the enzyme RNA polymerase in the liver—an enzyme that declines by fourfold with age in the rat—had also been restored. This offered strong, suggestive evidence that thyroxine was operating at the level of the genes themselves.

Reviewing all this and some related work in a lengthy chapter in the 1983 book, *Intervention in the Aging Process* (which he co-edited), William Regelson said flatly: "To my knowledge, this is the only demonstration of a confirmed, broadly based physiologic rejuvenation currently accessible to further research, exploration and eventual clinical intervention." And, later in the same chapter: "Currently, we know of no other theory of mammalian aging with this degree of clinical implication for aging intervention that can be rapidly tested for experimental validation. Clinical intervention can follow once the isolation and characterization of DECO have been accomplished."

It is worth emphasizing that these rats without pituitaries are seriously handicapped animals; they are, after all, deprived of all the vital products normally supplied by fully functioning pituitaries. But surgical removal of the pituitary is the only way Denckla has so far found, in the absence of a chemical blocking agent, to keep DECO out of circulation. He brings the animal back to some semblance of normality by administering a few of the "good" hormones it needs (without being certain what, precisely, the correct dosages are for normal rats). He gives them thyroxine, for instance, and a couple of the adrenal steroids to help keep them alive and functioning.

In one fascinating experiment, Denckla was able to compare the life spans of these handicapped creatures with the life spans of normal rats. At a time when he was working with 95 rats without pituitaries, he also had on hand 125 intact rats exactly the same age that he was able to use as a control group. At 34 months of age (a human of equivalent age would be pushing 95, an age at which only about 1 percent of his contemporaries would still be around), only 2 out of the 125 intact rats were still alive, compared with 20 percent of those whose pituitaries had been removed; there was, in a word, a tenfold increase in the number of survivors. (Unfortunately, funds ran out on the project, and these survivors could not be kept alive long enough for Denckla to observe what their maximum life span would have been. He has since noted, however, that when these pituitaryless animals die, many of them seem to die very suddenly, almost without warning, and with hardly any signs of prior deterioration.)

If the ravages of aging can be reversed in older animals by blocking DECO, can excess DECO bring on premature aging in younger animals? Denckla has never yet had on hand a supply of pure DECO, which has been maddeningly difficult to isolate. (For one thing, it clings tenaciously to growth hormone—whose activity it also seems to inhibit in some circumstances.) There has been only the crude extract of DECO to work with, and it takes about a hundred minced-up cow pituitaries to get enough of this extract—still contaminated by other hormones—to test thirty rats. Even so, this crude substance has rapidly brought on the predicted signs of aging in very young rats. The aging signs that are caused by DECO and apparently reversed by its blockage include not only various biochemical and physiological measurements but even overall traits grossly observable by sight and touch, such as the smoothness and texture of the animal's coat. In recent years, David Harrison, who was previously quite skeptical of Denckla's work, has been able to duplicate some of the results in mice without pituitaries. He was eager to try some of Denckla's crude DECO extract just when Denckla ran out of it and lost access to his source of it. Denckla believes, however, that his results would not be too difficult to duplicate.

But Denckla himself will not be the one to do it—at least, not for the present. Convinced by earlier advice from within NIA that his research was too unpopular there to allow a realistic hope for any significant support from that agency, he never submitted a formal grant proposal. Early in 1984, he was making desultory efforts to raise venture capital to support him in his own aging-research enterprise. But he soon ceased making even those efforts, and when I pressed him he finally admitted that he had really put his search for DECO and its inhibitor on hold indefinitely—for moral reasons. The more he thought about the potential consequences of placing in the hands of the public the ability to achieve perhaps indefinite prolongevity, the more he decided that the public—based on his observations of how other major discoveries had been handled—was not yet mature enough to deal with it. He had simply made a personal moral decision not to proceed! This decision does not, of course, bind others who might be inclined to pursue the work.

In any case, it is DECO—the "aging" or "death" or antithyroid hormone or family of hormones presumed to be the regulator of the genetic clock of aging—that Denckla was trying so hard to isolate, purify, and synthesize over the years. It is interesting to note, in this context, that the Soviet Union's V. V. Frolkis has reported that, with advancing age, the blood does contain increasing concentrations of substances that inhibit the functioning of the pancreatic hormones, much as Denckla believes that DECO inhibits the functioning of thyroid hormone. Frolkis also, quite independently, notes the decline with age of the body's ability to bind thyroxine.

A diminished supply of thyroxine within the cell would cause a number of critical imbalances. These imbalances could bring on— or at least allow the onset of—the destructive changes we associate with the aging process. Oxidation may be speeded up, creating more free radicals, thus more cross-linkages, more somatic mutations, more error catastrophes. More toxins may be produced, leaving more cellular garbage (including lipofuscin) than the cell can dispose of. Immune cells, too, become less efficient, sometimes attacking other cells, creating autoimmune phenomena, and adding to the general disruption. DECO may act on the thymic cells to cut down production of thymosin and other thymic hormones (perhaps even causing the shrinkage of the thymus, which occurs in everyone at a relatively early age), further impairing immunologic function and increasing the risk of cancer and lethal infection. The aging or death hormones might even operate principally at the level of genetic on/off switching. As Finch has pointed out, "Hormones influence cellular activities at both the nuclear and cytoplasmic levels of control."

Medvedev once postulated a built-in genetic death mechanism, and Howard Curtis even hypothesized the existence of death hormones, but he took it no further than the raw suggestion. There is nothing inconsistent in the idea that death hormones, if they exist, could be responsible for the changes of aging in all the varieties of both dividing and nondividing cells. The DNA in the original fertilized egg does in fact program all the body's cells to perform their astonishing multiplicity of tasks. Thus groups of differently programmed cells, which have already lived out radically different lives, may also "know how" to die differently. In a well-trained army— with units of infantry, artillery, cavalry, tank corps, air support, all ready to go—the commanding general does not have to issue specific detailed instructions an hour before the battle. All he needs to do is give the prearranged signal, and the programmed units all speed to their diverse and unique tasks—though coordinated by the original master battle plan. A death or aging hormone could, in a similar manner, command legions of cells to perform separate actions. It would not have to *cause* the specific detailed changes; it would simply *trigger* the sequences of events already programmed in the given cell. "The high level of adaptation of the organism," as Frolkis reminds us, "has been reached in the process of evolution due to the *centralization of the processes of regulation*, the centralization which on the one hand made it possible to unite the activity of individual cells, organs and systems in achieving a common adaptive effect and on the other hand to ensure within certain limits a degree of autonomy of their metabolism and functions against the background of these centralized reactions [italics mine]."

In Denckla's tidy scheme, however, at least one important question remains unanswered: how to account for the running out of the genetic program in cells in Hayflick cultures, which are certainly beyond the reach of any brain-based hormonal clock of aging? If Hayflick is right, can Denckla be? The two views seem irreconcilable. That's why proponents of hormonal theories are so often affronted by Hayflick's findings and have felt it necessary to question his data or to minimize their meaning. So has Denckla.

But Denckla may have inadvertently supplied an answer of sorts. On many occasions I have questioned him in his lab at Roche, or while he paced before his blackboard at home in Tenafly—and later at his home in Washington, D.C., and aboard his sailboat at Woods Hole. During these conversations he has often returned to the matter of why, to him, it makes so much sense to assume an underlying genetic program (an assumption he shares with Hayflick and many others) that sets the limit to how long any individual of a given species can live.

In puzzling over the possible evolutionary reasons for the existence of a substance like DECO, he speculates on why it was necessary to evolve a blocking agent for a hormone so vitally important to so many of life's processes as thyroxine. His tentative solution lies in the necessity for an animal to maintain a constant body temperature throughout life. "Young animals," he says, "have a very small body mass. They dissipate heat very quickly. Keeping the temperature within the rough limits—from 96 to 105 degrees (as measured rectally)—depends on the rate at which oxygen is burned, a function under thyroid control." From birth to adulthood an animal will grow, he says, anywhere from one to three orders of magnitude. "When that happens, there is an incredible increase in body mass along with an enormous relative loss of ability to dissipate heat. So my hypothesis is that DECO was originally a hormone designed to turn the thermostat down, in order not to have to be burning at full bore, using up all this energy just to keep the body temperature up. DECO slows the thyroid down and allows all those extra calories to go into growth, while ensuring that the animal won't cook inside its own skin." According to his preliminary studies, he told me during an interview for *Omni*, "if you had the metabolic rate as a fully grown adult that you had when you were two or three years old, you would have a temperature of roughly 110 to 115 degrees, which means your brain would be cooked."

Denckla's further evolutionary reasoning—admittedly not altogether original to him (in an inchoate form, at least, it dates back as far as August Weismann in the late nineteenth century)—goes something like this: The environment keeps changing as time goes on (more for land mammals than for sea creatures). In order to adapt to these changes, the species must evolve in favorable ways through genetic mutations. But evolution is a slow process. As the environment changes, there must be a sufficiently rapid turnover of generations to allow those characteristics best fitted for the changed conditions to be incorporated into the gene pool. Whether the population consists of pinworms, pterodactyls, or people, species survival requires a large enough quantity of individuals in any given generation to ensure that a significant number of them will be the beneficiaries of chance mutations that can be passed along, and a short enough life span to permit the necessary turnover. As Jonas Salk puts it in *Survival of the Wisest*, "Even though Death eventually wins over Life as far as the individual is concerned, Life wins over Death in the perpetuation of the species."

Thus Denckla believes there must exist "an absolutely fail-safe killing mechanism without which the species would not survive." Now, a fail-safe system in rocketry or weaponry means redundancy—backup systems that will take over in case the primary system fails to function. So it may be with our program for aging and death. Suppose Denckla is right, and the release of specific death hormones is the primary self-destruct mechanism. The cellular aging program could be a backup system, designed to set a second limit, in case the death hormones somehow failed to be released, or to be effective. Finally, if all else fails, wear and tear alone would do the job.

As Hayflick has suggested, "Normal cells have a finite capacity for replication, and . . . this finite capacity is rarely if ever reached by cells *in vivo*, but when freed of *in vivo* constraints can be reached *in vitro*." Hayflick's suggestion appears to be borne out by the conclusions of the noted German pathologist Ludwig Aschoff, who wrote in 1938, after long observation and hundreds of autopsies (the following is quoted in a paper by Finch):

> It is my conviction that natural death in human beings never occurs, or only in rare instances. Autopsies which have been made on the very old always show a pathological cause. In life the severe disease changes of those advanced in years are usually not felt. When I visited a 97-year-old man two days before his death, he showed so little the symptoms of a serious illness that I was convinced on hearing of his demise that at last I had seen a case of natural death. I was very surprised when I found at the autopsy stipulated by the deceased, a severe lobar pneumonia of at least four to five days' duration and numerous metastases from a malignant tumor of the thyroid gland. The old man had diagnosed none of these disorders in himself, although he was well equipped by training to do so and had carefully observed himself.

Aschoff's comments recall Denckla's impatience with what happens to cells *in vitro*: "I care what people *die of*." And what they die of are the "*in vivo* constraints" to which Hayflick refers. One can imagine that if Denckla's research were ever to result in the successful removal of these *in vivo* constraints—perhaps by preventing the release of, or directly inhibiting the action of, DECO— we might then live long enough to be in deadly danger from the cessation of division in, say, our skin or gut cells, which, with our current life spans, has never been a problem. If we solved such problems, we would still have wear-and-tear damage to contend with—which seems a formidable undertaking, though it might be less so if we learn to keep the repair genes switched on so the cells can simply continue to maintain the integrity of their systems indefinitely.

The idea that the cellular aging program might be a redundant, fail-safe backup system for a hormonal aging program is further bolstered, in my own view, by still another set of Denckla's own experimental and theoretical considerations; and this is what I meant by suggesting that he may have inadvertently supplied us with the answer to the apparent irreconcilability of his view and Hayflick's.

In his experiments with those thousands of rats, it was important for Denckla to develop the most meticulous possible set of metabolic measurements he could devise. Instead of the usual basal metabolic rate (BMR)—also known as the "resting oxygen-consumption rate"— Denckla evolved a finer measure, which he called MOC for *minimum* oxygen-consumption rate. He was thus able to pin down the specific thyroid-influenced component that accounted for the steep drop in metabolic rate with aging. He was also able to discern, separately, a much lower, much steadier "athyroidal component" of the metabolic rate, which was not affected by the presence or absence of thyroid hormone. This was essentially the same rate as that measured in animal tissues *in vitro*. Denckla calls this component the GMR, the *genetic* metabolic rate. Unlike the MOC, which is controlled by the endocrine centers of the brain, the GMR is controlled by the individual cell's DNA.

Thus it would appear that the MOC is a reflection of the brain-based clock of aging at work, whereas the GMR could well be the medium through which Hayflick's cellular clock operates in those WI-38 cell cultures. In the one case, the cells in the brain responsible for hormonal release are turned *on* at the appropriate times; in the other case, the genetic information required to keep the cell machinery functioning is gradually turned *off*. In both cases, it looks as if we come back to the on/off switching mechanisms in the DNA of individual cells. If all this is so, then Denckla is right; but Hayflick is also right. And Strehler, too. And Harman, and Orgel, and Burnet, and Cutler, and Regelson, and Comfort, and practically everyone else. At least it would appear that their theories are not wrong— merely incomplete.

It pleased me to note that Roy Walford, in his 1983 book, *Maximum Life Span*, has also independently come around to viewing with favor a "two-clock" theory of programmed aging, one of the clocks being hormonal and brain-based, the other cellular and residing in the DNA—and he has his own convictions about where in the genes the DNA clock is probably located.

Yet another possibility is that the clock of aging in the brain and the clock of aging in the cell (if either or both exist) are not really separate programs at all but, rather, a single, delicately orchestrated program; and that, under the unnatural circumstances of tissue culture, that part of the program that resides in the DNA of the individual cells expresses itself in an undisciplined solo performance—

or perhaps a smaller group performance, much as, say, a violin section, isolated from both the main body of the orchestra and the conductor, could still play out its score, uninterrupted by any on/off signals from the baton, from beginning to end.

It is worth mentioning here that, after Denckla's departure from NIAAA, his colleague Richard Veech has continued to pursue the work, and seems to have tentatively concluded that growth hormone itself acts like DECO and perhaps *is* DECO. Robert Bolla of St. Louis, who has collaborated with Denckla and championed his work, thinks that Veech's idea may not be too farfetched. But he prefers to believe that it is only one portion of the growth hormone, perhaps operating alone, that performs the DECO function, and this may be why it has been so difficult to separate DECO from growth hormone! Regelson, too, is attracted to this idea. But Denckla finds much fault with the hypothesis, one among several reasons being that DECO inhibits growth-hormone activity in some circumstances, and a hormone would not be likely to act as its own inhibitor.

Whether Hayflick or Denckla turns out to be right, or whether neither of them does, one can still see the coming together of data and ideas in overarching concepts that incorporate diverse theories of aging: genetic switching, cross-linkage, free radicals, autoimmunity, somatic mutations, error catastrophes. V. V. Frolkis has pointed out dryly that "the number of hypotheses is generally inversely proportional to the clarity of the problem." Now, with hypotheses fast converging, the problem has taken an encouraging turn in the direction of clarity.

9

HEREDITY AND IMMUNITY

LIKE Denckla, Macfarlane Burnet believes that aging and death "are essential to the evolutionary process, and the age at which they happen must be related to the life style of the species concerned." Yet many gerontologists, even those who lean toward a genetic program (Strehler and Orgel, for example), have been reluctant to accept the idea that evolution has dictated the precise control of the aging process. What, they ask, is the evolutionary advantage of programming organisms to deteriorate and die at such relatively advanced ages?

Evolution, they agree, must indeed have programmed us (much as the space engineers program their planetary fly-bys) to survive in reasonable health and vigor until our job is done—that is, until we have sired, borne, and reared the next generation; otherwise we wouldn't be here to argue the matter. But positive programming for propagation is not the same as the building in of self-destruct mechanisms to guarantee aging and death at specified times. Perhaps it is, rather, a case of simply abandoning the machine and letting it run down (again, like the planetary fly-by). If the Pacific salmon's machine begins to run down days after spawning, so be it. If the human machine takes some years to run down, so be that also.

Back in 1941, the late J. B. S. Haldane argued—in *New Paths in Genetics*—that evolution would be unlikely to select either for or against mutations that occurred in individuals after their reproductive lives were over. Even so, Finch speculates that our aging patterns may still be there, tied into genes that were selected in the past for whatever advantages they may have bestowed earlier in life, in terms of reproduction and species survival. In this scheme, aging would still be accidental, but genetically programmed nevertheless.

Suppose an automotive engineer wanted to design a car that would get off to a very fast start; to give it the necessary horsepower, he might have to supply an engine that could achieve speeds up to 150 or 200 miles per hour. A naïve observer with no knowledge of or insight into the engineer's problems might well wonder why anyone would have designed and built a car capable of such speeds when its prospective driver had no intention of going more than sixty. The "programmed" velocity, of course, was irrelevant, since the engineer's aim was simply getting the car off to a fast start.

Thus evolutionary nature may not have intended that any living creatures survive much past their reproductive days. It could rely on mere exposure to environmental hazards and stresses, including predators, natural catastrophes, and infectious organisms, to end individuals' lives quickly once their primary mission, procreation, was accomplished. Human organisms, naturally, require many years of nurture by parents or guardians before they reach adulthood. This quality of "neoteny," of being born in a still-incomplete condition (unlike the newborn giraffe, which can instantly run beside its mother) and continuing to develop in the external womb of the family, is believed to have come to pass in a relatively brief time (in terms of evolutionary history). At an equally "explosive" rate, and over roughly the same time scale, the human brain underwent a spurt of growth. As Stephen Jay Gould pointed out in *Ontogeny and Phylogeny*, these two developments were not unrelated. The larger brain may have been a prerequisite for acquiring the essentially human trait of long-term nurturance.

It may be that this requirement for extended nurture on the part of parents—without which few if any of their human progeny would have survived—is analogous to the problem of the automotive engineer I was imagining a moment ago. Even though there was no need for the car to go more than sixty miles per hour in order to get it off to the desired start, he had to design it so its potential maximum speed exceeded 150: there was no way of getting one without the other. We know that in ancient times the average life expectancy was well under thirty years—long enough, obviously, to ensure the turnover of generations that Denckla's theory requires.

So, though a life span of thirty years would work, it may be that there was no way the evolutionary "engineer" could have designed an organism—including the enlarged brain—that would be *sure* of lasting long enough to do the rearing and nurturing job without giving that creature a much greater maximum life span than was strictly necessary—say, a hundred years or more. The enhanced longevity thus would not have been so much the product of evolutionary selection as of, in the words of Richard G. Cutler, "a lack of any evolutionary selective pressure to do anything about it." Though he concedes that "there probably are genes that are importantly involved in aging," he believes that "these processes or genes were not selected specifically for the purpose to cause aging."

In the wild it is hard to find living specimens of aging animals; nevertheless, their species thrive. Even farm animals, protected as they are from the major dangers of wear and tear as well as predation, are not protected from us, their protectors, and we usually butcher them before senescence gets a chance to set in. Yet, as all zookeepers know, wild animals do grow old in captivity. And farm animals show all the signs of senescence when they are permitted to live long enough—as Mike Tumbleson demonstrated on the pig farm he ran for a while at the University of Missouri. But only a gerontological farm could afford to permit its animals to grow old. It would make no economic sense for an ordinary farmer to keep feeding and housing animals for years and years after they had attained their peak of productivity and marketability. There are, of course, rare exceptions, such as the thoroughbred race horse who has won a sufficient number of purses to earn a few years of serene pasturing. And most of us have seen our pets age and die.

We accept that all organisms—whether we can find aged specimens or not—*do* age eventually; and that, barring accidents, they age at a rate that is roughly species-specific. This universal fact seems, after all, to throw the odds in the direction of Denckla's failsafe mechanism. If organisms were really on their own without such a specific aging mechanism, and if they were lucky enough to survive for indefinitely long times (as indeed the planetary fly-bys are likely to, out in the vacuum of space), the earth might soon run out of room for newcomers with fresh genetic combinations. One can readily see that such an eventuality could be antievolutionary in its effects.

Hayflick would probably agree that evolution has built in a genetic aging mechanism. Daniel Dykhuizen of the Australian National University in Canberra, goes along with Hayflick's concession that (in Dykhuizen's words) "cell senescence itself, rather than senescence of the organism, is the genetically controlled and programmed event selected by evolution" and that senescence at the level of the total organism is a reflection of what happens in myriads of that organism's individual cells. Dykhuizen has put forth (in *Nature*) a fascinating theory to explain how the cellular clock permits cells to proliferate when necessary, as in wound healing, yet turns off division at other times—for instance, to limit the growth of the damaging plaques that form on the walls of arteries. He challenges the idea that the random accumulation of errors in cells can alone account for senescence—again, on the same grounds as Hayflick: the failure of "transformed" (abnormal or malignant) cells to age and die under the same circumstances. As we saw in the last chapter, this exceptional behavior is as true *in vivo* as *in vitro*. When normal skin cells or lymphocytes are transplanted from one animal to another—even to a younger specimen of the same breed—they may live longer than otherwise but they do die out, whereas cancer cell lines go on and on.

Roy Walford believes we may have something very important to learn about aging from transformed cells. Such cells are usually thought of as being cancerous, or at least precancerous. Walford admits that they are surely abnormal and even that they have taken the first step in the direction of malignancy. But the fact that they have taken this first step (the transformation to a true cancerous state is now known to be at least a two-step process) does not imply that the next step is inevitable—most particularly if the mechanism of transformation is under our own control. Walford's daring proposal is that we deliberately seek a method for inducing cells to take this first step along the way to transformation—but stop the process right there.

Cells are already being transformed *in vitro*, usually by means of viruses or carcinogenic chemicals. But this is done mainly for the purpose of learning how to *prevent* transformation from occurring in the human body. Walford is suggesting that we make it come about by design, but refrain from applying the knowledge until we have also learned to forestall the cell's continuing stepwise transformation to a state of uncontrollable malignancy.

The idea of deliberately rendering healthy cells abnormal may seem more than a bit bizarre, but only until we consider that the goal of gerontology is exactly that: to free ourselves of the normality that is senescence. If we can in fact turn on those genes that the clock of aging has turned off—or keep specific aging genes from being turned on, if that is the way it works—and if we can do this without producing cancer as a result, we will perhaps have gone a long way toward thwarting the genetic fail-safe mechanism (not to mention solving the cancer problem), thus bestowing upon our own cells the relative immortality that only transformed cells now enjoy.

Even if we could do what Walford proposes, the solution would seem to apply only to dividing cells. What of those other cells—the all-important ones whose loss of function is, indeed, more likely to kill us—which have stopped dividing? The fact that mitotic and postmitotic cells are so basically different in this respect does not preclude a single aging mechanism for both. "There are two schools of thought in gerontological research," as Hayflick explains in *Medical World News*. "One says we age because our cells that divide have lost that ability, so there's a loss of numbers; the other says we age because the cells that don't divide, like neurones and muscle cells, lose their functional capacity over a long period. But that's a false distinction, because the division capacity of cells *is* a function. So it's the *decrement of function*, whether it be manifest as a loss of doubling, loss of making enzymes, of what have you, that may affect aging."

The genes that stop cell division, then, may be the same genes that trigger aging in nondividing cells as well. What makes Walford hopeful is that in that case the transformation might be achieved by tampering with no more than *a few genes on a single chromosome*. At least, that is the situation in mouse chromosomes, and Walford feels there is good reason for assuming the same is probably true in human cells. "In the sense of structural gene similarities and differences," he writes, "man and chimp are more alike than dog and fox. For this reason of near identity, and also because of the relatively short evolutionary time period during which hominid life span has doubled, the mutations responsible for the doubling could only have involved a few genes. Furthermore, we know the mutation rate for genes of ape and man, and during a 100,000-year period at most only half of 1 percent of the genes could have mutated. The genetic 'program' for aging must therefore be written in only a few genes or gene systems, rather than involving the whole enormous hodgepodge of hereditary material. This is encouraging. It narrows the search."

Walford has a strong ally here in Richard Cutler, who has done some of the most original and rigorously analytical work in this field. Cutler agrees—as does Oak Ridge's A. G. Sacher, for much the same reasons—that a very few genes may be involved in the aging process. But Cutler thinks these are likely to be regulatory genes— genes that are not merely "structural" (that is, simply the carriers of codes for making specific proteins) but that govern the activities of whole clusters of structural genes. Moreover, he feels that, without having to wait for the genetic answers to be resolved, we can hope to retard the aging process by doing something about the *products* of known genes; thus, "methods to extend longevity may not have to produce something better or longer lasting that is lacking in human biology, but simply to enhance to higher levels those gene products that are already there. This . . . places aging intervention into the realm of possibility for the first time."

Meanwhile, Walford—and Hayflick, too, and no doubt others— are trying to hunt down those aging genes. Inasmuch as Walford, like Burnet, is mainly associated with the immunological theory of aging, we might expect him to select the genes involved in immunological control as being in control of aging as well. Walford has never claimed that the immune theory, as originally proposed, was the total explanation for human aging. But he has long felt that immune function and dysfunction, taken together with the built-in genetic controls as an added theoretical ingredient, could account for enough of the phenomena observed in the laboratory to lead to the conclusion that immunology is the key system in aging. His attention has been particularly drawn to a cluster of genes (earlier referred to as a "supergene") known as the "major histocompatibility complex," or MHC, which are bunched together on a single chromosome. These genes, once they were discovered and elucidated (resulting in a 1980 Nobel Prize shared by three scientists), were of special interest to surgical-transplant teams, who knew that any graft or transplant of skin or any organ would have a much better chance of "taking" if the donor's cells were compatible with those of the recipient. The MHC provided a valuable new tool for testing potential donors for their cell (histo-) compatibility with the patient needing the transplant; hence the original name for the new gene complex.

Because graft rejection is a major immune function, Walford wondered whether other immune functions might also be regulated by the MHC. Experiments carried out with his UCLA colleague George Smith demonstrated that other facets of immunity were indeed under the control of the MHC. Moreover, the Walford and Smith work with mice carefully bred so that the only genetic differences between one group and another were in the MHC, showed convincingly that the MHC was involved in the aging process as well, since one group of these mice outlived the other by a significant margin. In collaboration with another UCLA colleague, Kathleen Hall, Walford showed that the MHC also had a critical influence on DNA repair—a capacity now generally conceded to be somehow related to aging, though the connection was by no means clear when Burnet first suggested it in 1973. The MHC has now also been shown to have an influence on the body's own antioxidant systems, in particular the free-radical scavenging enzymes such as superoxide dismutase and catalase. With all this accumulating evidence, Walford's tentative nomination for the aging supergene is the MHC—though he of course recognizes that other such genes and gene clusters may also be involved in aging. The important point is that they are probably few in number, and therefore put the genetic aging challenge within potentially manageable limits.*

The immune theory originally dealt principally with the phenomenon of *auto*immunity, the immune system's propensity for attacking the body's own tissues. But that was only the first clue. More came from a series of experiments carried out by Ian C. Roberts-Thomas and his associates at Australia's Walter and Eliza Hall Institute and Royal Melbourne Hospital; they showed that the protective immunological response was consistently lower in old people than in young adults—and that in groups of old people of similar ages but different immune responses, the highest mortality occurred in those

---

* The idea of two genetic aging clocks—one based in the brain and powered by the hormone DECO, the other in the individual cell nucleus—has been discussed in chapter 8. Suppose MHC represented the cell clock. There is no reason why it would have to operate wholly independently and separately, as implied earlier; one of the ways in which DECO could work is by influencing the MHC (and possibly other "clock" supergenes) in individual cells. And if there is a small handful of brain cells that give the command resulting in the pituitary's release of DECO, it could be that the releasing trigger is the MHC in those brain cells. In short, the clocks could interact. It would be surprising if they did not in some way.

with least immunity. Research the world over—in Walford's lab at UCLA, in Burnet's at Melbourne, in Takashi Makinodan's at NIH and later at the Veterans Administration's Wadsworth Hospital Center in Los Angeles, by E. J. Yunis and his associates at the University of Minnesota and at Harvard, and by Robert A. Good's team at the Memorial Sloan-Kettering Cancer Institute in New York, to name a few—has yielded similar results, which, oversimplified, can be expressed in two brief statements:

1. As the organism ages, the protective efficiency of the immune system goes *down*.

2. As the organism ages, autoimmune responses go *up*.

It is as if the armed forces of a constantly beleaguered community (which fairly describes the human body in the real world) were to grow increasingly careless about keeping out or hunting down dangerous invaders—who thus became free to destroy and despoil at will—and, at the same time, were to attack their own fellow citizens. In that event, the formerly secure population would suddenly find itself set upon simultaneously by both the cops and the robbers.

There could be no more literal self-destruct mechanism than programming the body's most efficient destroyer cells to attack the body's "civilian" cells. Autoimmune responses now seem to account for much more than those diseases formerly officially recognized as being of autoimmune origin. Studies carried out by two members of Roberts-Thomas's Australian team (Ian R. Mackay and Senga Whittingham), in collaboration with J. D. Matthews of Oxford's Radcliffe Infirmary, strongly suggested that autoimmune factors contribute significantly to the development of high blood pressure, atherosclerosis, and other degenerative diseases of aging. Walford was able to extend the life span of mice by administering high doses of immunosuppressive drugs that lowered immune responses effectively. Seymour Gelfand and J. Graham Smith, Jr., of the Medical College of Georgia at Augusta, in considering why cortisone and hydrocortisone had "released from aging" cells *in vitro*, suggested that the immunosuppressive capacity of these drugs had been responsible. The trick, of course, is to lower autoimmunity without at the same time impairing the aging animal's ability to resist infection.

Some success has been reported in this area, too. For instance, Makinodan challenged the immune system of young mice by exposing them to bacteria. He then injected their lymphocytes into old mice—who were, as a result, able to resist lethal doses of the same strain of bacteria for many months. He has suggested that the day might arrive when human beings could deposit goodly stores of lymphocytes in the deepfreeze while their immune system is young and they are at their productive peak, then draw upon these for support as needed in their later years. Such cells, in addition to being healthy and active, would presumably be free of autoimmune "memories" that the body's aging lymphocytes may have developed in the intervening years.

Further support for the immune theory of aging—especially that aspect of it that regards immune *deficiency* as being of critical importance—comes from the results of experiments done with a short-lived breed of dwarf mice that, as part of their genetic shortcomings, are handicapped by low levels of immunity. To raise their immune levels, N. Fabris of the EURATOM Unit at Italy's University of Pavia, working with W. Pierpaoli and E. Sorkin at the Albert Schweitzer Research Institute at Davos-Platz, Switzerland, gave the dwarf mice injections of lymph-node lymphocytes. As a result, they were able to double—in some cases almost triple—the life expectancies of their subjects. Fabris, Pierpaoli, and Sorkin believe that the lowered immunity, and therefore the shortened life span, of these mice is due to genetic *endocrine* deficiency. They argue persuasively that an intimate and necessary link exists between hormones and the proper activation and functioning of the immune system. It is in fact through immunological advances that we have perhaps become most aware of the role that hormones play in aging.

We have long been familiar with the phenomenon of immunity and have made practical use of its principles through a variety of medications and vaccines. Yet it is only in the past quarter of a century that we have come to any real understanding of what those principles are and how the immune system works. The last decade or so especially has produced an explosive acceleration in our acquisition of immunological knowledge. To appreciate how hormones and immunity are related, and what this relationship has to do with the aging process, requires at least a minimal grasp of immune mechanisms; this minimal understanding is all I shall attempt to convey.

The key to human immunity lies in the small white blood cell called the "lymphocyte." The normal adult human body contains something like a trillion lymphocytes, and about ten million of these are being replaced by new ones every minute of every day—at least until the early stages of aging. Lymphocytes appear to originate mainly in the bone marrow, as immature "stem cells."

Large quantities of these, perhaps as many as a third or more, mature directly into the bloodstream and are called "B-lymphocytes" or "B-cells."* The main task of B-cells is the manufacture of "antibodies"—proteins whose major function is to fight bacterial infections. The body's B-cells are flexibly encoded to recognize virtually an infinite variety of potential invading substances ("antigens" are the proteins on cell surfaces that antibodies attack)—including synthetics that do not normally occur in nature at all. Once a B-cell is challenged by a foreign antigen, it starts to make antibodies to combat that specific antigen. From then on, it keeps making only that antibody and no other, and its descendants inherit the capacity to make the same antibody and to recognize the same antigen. That is why immunological memory can last so long.

The rest of the lymphocytes pass through the thymus, and for that reason are called "T-lymphocytes" or "T-cells." The thymus, the pinkish-gray mass located just behind the breastbone and just below the neck, shrinks rapidly to insignificant size beginning with the onset of puberty. Its function had always been anybody's guess, and modern doctors tended to look upon it as another useless vestigial organ, like the appendix. In fact, there was an unfortunate period in this century when physicians, who had seen only adult thymuses, used radiation to shrink thymuses mistakenly thought to be enlarged. But all that was changed by the ingenious research of several investigators working independently of one another—notably Robert Good, then working at the University of Minnesota, and Jacques Miller, then at England's Chester Beatty Institute. Their experiments clearly established that the thymus was of some importance to the body's defense system. Moreover, it soon became evident that *all* lymphoid tissue (which is where the lymphocytes live when they are not circulating) plays a role in immunity—including the tonsils, the adenoids, and the appendix!

But the thymus turned out to be the "master gland of immunity,"

---

* The "B" in "B-cells" does not stand for either bacteria or blood, interpretations that have sometimes appeared in print. Because, in the chicken, these cells were first found to be located in the bursa, their human counterparts were named "bursa-equivalent," or "B" for short.

which is why Burnet, one of the fathers of the immunological theory of aging, proposed the thymus as the master gland of aging as well. In agreement with him, as a result of their dwarf-mice studies, were the Italian-Swiss team of Fabris, Pierpaoli, and Sorkin. "Because immunological function is fundamental for survival," they wrote in *Nature*, "if its function declines before other body functions, it would be a major determinant in the ageing process.

"We emphasize here the possible importance of the thymus as a biological clock and of hormones for the ageing process of the lymphoid system. We evaluate the capacity of lymphocytes, whose formation depends on hormones, to prevent early death and ageing processes." As we have seen, lymphocytes were able to postpone aging and death in the dwarf mice.

"The full development of the thymus and the thymus-dependent lymphoid cells which can be induced by hormonal treatment in the post-weaning period," they continued, "results in the prevention of early ageing and considerable prolongation of life. . . . Therefore we wish to propose with Burnet that the thymus might be considered an important organ for ageing control of body tissues. One could predict then that the longer the thymus functions at its optimal level either as a producer of humoral factors and/or lymphocytes, the longer will be the life-span."

The T-cell, then, merits our special attention. A lymphocyte that passes through the thymus to become a T-cell does not make antibodies at all. It becomes, instead, a hand-to-hand-combat specialist. Whereas B-cells use antibodies as their chemical weapons, T-cells act as assault troops. They attack, surround, destroy, ingest, or in one way or another inactivate the invaders. They can do this directly—or indirectly, by producing lymphokines (substances we shall return to in a moment) that attract the white cells called macrophages, which hurry to join the battle, chewing up any intruders they encounter. Because they can act in this direct manner, the T-cell function is called "cell-mediated immunity" (in contrast to the B-cell antibody "humoral immunity" system). This is the kind of immunity involved in rejecting transplanted tissue and in killing cancer cells.

Most immunologists now believe what Burnet's fertile intellect, again, first hypothesized: that one class of lymphocytes is constantly carrying out an "immunological surveillance" of all the body's cells. As soon as a cell becomes malignant or even shows signs of premalignant changes, the T-cell scavengers move in, before the defective cell can begin to multiply. (Such activity would raise a problem for Walford's scheme of deliberately transforming cells to the first step toward malignancy: how to keep them from being destroyed by the body's immune system? The same problem will in any case have to be resolved if we are to overcome the aging body's propensity to autoimmune behavior.) It makes sense, then, that as thymus function declines with age, immune function also declines—and the incidence of cancer goes up.

While this understanding was being worked out in many laboratories and in many theorizing minds around the world, a team of scientists at the National Cancer Institute conducted a critical experiment. Into a newborn mouse without a thymus they implanted thymic tissue. But they put the tissue into a container with holes too small for a lymphocyte (or anything else of cell size) to get out. In spite of this barrier, *something* got through those tiny holes to stimulate the spleen and lymph nodes into making their own lymphocytes. That something almost had to be a hormone; and if that is the case, then the thymus was proved to be an endocrine gland.

Before 1960 such a hormone had not even been suspected. Now it became apparent that if a hormone released by the thymus could induce stem cells to mature into lymphocytes, then going through the thymus itself was not absolutely essential after all. Thus, if a child was born without a thymus, or if a patient later had to lose his (the thymus is sometimes removed as a therapeutic measure in, for instance, myasthenia gravis), the hormone alone might serve as an adequate substitute. Inasmuch as all thymuses shrink with age, often to the point where they can be found only by an expert, thymic hormones—if they existed—could conceivably render a service to almost everyone.

This brings us to thymosin, a discovery already mentioned in passing, but perhaps representing a story worth telling in more detail for at least two good reasons: (1) thymosin—or, more appropriately, the thymosins, because thymosin has turned out to be a whole family of hormones—may be one of the first important anti-aging drugs to reach the marketplace; and (2) the story illustrates how research in an area not officially related to gerontology at the outset can nevertheless make a major contribution to it—in the same way that gerontological research will make major contributions to, say, cancer research, genetics, and immunology, contributions that could be of greater importance than work done specifically to further knowledge in those fields.

By 1966, Allan L. Goldstein, a young biochemist then working at the Albert Einstein Medical College in New York, and his colleague and mentor, Abraham White, had discovered and isolated the hormone they named "thymosin." After White and Goldstein both left New York, they continued to coordinate their efforts for many years— until White's death in 1980. White went to Palo Alto, where he divided his time between Syntex Research and Stanford University. Goldstein meanwhile became director of the biochemistry division at the University of Texas Medical Branch (UTMB) in Galveston, where he quickly recruited a superb and dedicated team of young, energetic investigators. With a high-priority effort financed in part by the government, in part by foundations, in part by private Texas contributors, and in part by Hoffmann-LaRoche, Goldstein was able to crash ahead with the development of thymosin. Members of the team worked out new immuno-assays and new ways of extracting and purifying the hormone, and they ascertained that thymosin does circulate in the human bloodstream and decreases with age; and, further, that bovine thymosin is sufficiently similar to human to act on human cells. It was able to turn immature human stem cells into mature human T-cells. Soon nearly a hundred other laboratories around the world were participating in thymosin research; today the substance has begun to be used on human patients.

Meanwhile, Goldstein moved on to become chairman of biochemistry at George Washington University, taking his core group along with him. They have continued to work full-speed-ahead on the thymosins, synthesizing some of the key molecules and carrying out some clinical trials. Goldstein recently helped found a new research and development company, Alpha-1 Biomedicals (alpha-1 is one of the first molecules to have been identified in the thymosin family), in order to exploit the practical possibilities of his discoveries.*

The first patients to benefit will probably be those with genetic immune deficiencies. A few of these victims—those born without the capacity to make stem cells at all—may turn out to be beyond the reach of thymosin. For these, as mentioned earlier,

* I recently accepted Allan Goldstein's invitation to serve as a member of the board of directors of Alpha-1.

bone-marrow transplants, always tricky and hazardous procedures, may be the only alternative for some time to come. But for the majority of immune-deficient patients, thymosin should be able to help—just as the lymphocyte injections were able to help the dwarf mice—and even to restore them to complete immunological normality. As noted in chapter 7, the very first patient on whom thymosin was tried, a five-year-old California girl whose inherited immune deficiencies would almost certainly have led to her death by infections long ago without it, is still living a virtually normal, active life (she is a cheerleader for her high-school team) after ten years of therapy.

This promise became especially important in the year 1983, when the disease called AIDS—for "acquired (as opposed to inherited) immune deficiency syndrome"—suddenly surfaced as a major national health problem.

The thymosins, with their presumed capacity to boost the faltering immune system, may have direct benefits in other areas as well. One is cancer. If Burnet's immunological-surveillance theory is correct, then one or more of the thymosins may be able to restore the body's cell-mediated ability to hold off malignancy—or, short of that, to help cancer patients fight infections when potent anticancer drugs and radiation knock out their immune capacity. Such lab experiments as well as human clinical trials are already in progress, and they show some promise.

In the same manner, thymosin may hold off the aging process itself. The body's immunity, as we have seen, does decrease with age; so do the quantities of thymosin circulating in the blood—and so does the capacity of the thymus to make new lymphocytes. New supplies of thymosin added to the circulation should increase resistance to all kinds of infection, to cancer, to other deteriorative changes, as well as to stress, thus enhancing good health and well-being over a much longer period of years. This hypothesis, too, is already being tested in a preliminary way with aging cells in tissue culture—by Goldstein, Walford, and Makinodan, among others.

In recent years, investigators have learned that there are several kinds of T-cells with specific functions, and that, though T-cells do not themselves make antibodies, certain types of specialized T-cells can influence and regulate the production of antibodies by B-cells; for example, "helper" cells can do exactly that—help increase faltering antibody production—while "suppressor" cells can keep down antibody overproduction. At the University of Vermont, William Ershler has demonstrated that thymosin can stimulate human lymphocytes to make antibodies on being challenged by pneumonia and tetanus; this suggests a way of making vaccines more effective for the elderly, whose own immune capacities may be in sharp decline. Ershler's work so far has been in cultured cells and in animals, but he expects to begin human clinical trials soon. At Rome's Atomic Energy Center, Gino Doria and his associates used thymosin to stimulate elements of the immune system, including antibody production, in aging mice.

The anti-aging capacities of the thymosins could in fact turn out to be greater than the effects of merely boosting immune capacity. A series of experiments—some done in Goldstein's lab—have shown that thymosin acts by stimulating the production of "lymphokines" (hardly heard of when *Prolongevity* was published), substances like T-cell growth factor (now known as Interleukin II), interferon (one now also needs to say "the interferons"; everything seems to come in families), and other substances produced by lymphocytes, substances that have begun to be thought of as the natural drugs of the immune system. Other research, especially collaborations between Goldstein's group and NIH teams, underscores the versatility of the thymosins by showing that they act directly on the brain. When monkeys are injected with thymosin, for instance, their hypothalami, pituitaries, and adrenal glands are stimulated to secrete ACTH; cortisol; the body's natural opiate, beta-endorphin; and the chemical factor that dictates the release of luteinizing hormone. All this suggests that thymosin could affect the aging brain, as well as functions elsewhere that the brain controls.

It is easy to see that thymosin would be a promising therapy for that aspect of immunity which has to do with lowered efficiency, hence less protection, as we age. But what of those instances where the immune system is functioning very actively but against our best interests, as in the case of transplant rejection or autoimmunity? When tissue is grafted onto or into our bodies, we would wish those cells to remain unmolested; after all, we have had them transplanted on purpose, to improve our chances of good health and survival itself. But those cells are inarguably foreign, and the immune system goes after them with lethal intent. Could thymosin help?

If thymosin boosts immune capacity, would it not serve merely to accelerate graft rejection and worsen autoimmune attacks? One thing one might hope for is the development of an *antithymosin serum.** Under present circumstances, transplant teams use a variety of immunosuppressive techniques, some of them fairly radical, to knock out the T-cell system (and usually the B-cell system as well, since means have not been available to suppress them selectively). Antithymosin might be a gentler way to disarm the system—and then only the T-cell system, leaving the B-cells free to continue making antibodies against the bacterial infections that have killed many a patient after an otherwise successful organ transplant. Moreover, once all the old lymphocytes were wiped out, thymosin could stimulate the production of new, mature lymphocytes from stem cells. Since these new lymphocytes would not have inherited any of the old memories, they might very well accept the formerly foreign graft tissue as legitimate if "naturalized" parts of the body; in that case, no rejection would occur.

Another way to achieve the same kind of selective knockout of only one segment of the immune system might be through the use of "monoclonal antibodies"—almost unlimited copies of single, specific antibodies directed against single, specific antigens on a given protein molecule or cell surface. (The scientists who developed monoclonal antibodies in England, Cesar Milstein and Georges Kohler, shared the 1984 Nobel Prize.) Our knowledge of these antibodies, which has exploded in the few years since *Prolongevity*'s publication, offers not only a marvelously potent research tool but also the means for new kinds of diagnosis and therapy. Monoclonal antibodies directed at a specific T-cell antigen might be able to knock out only those target cells while leaving all others unmolested.

A similar effect might be achieved in autoimmune diseases. In such a disease, usually (though not invariably) late in life, autoimmunity may come to pass, as already mentioned, either because aging changes in the attacked cells render them no longer recognizable as members of the family by our lymphocytes (Makinodan believes this is what happens about 90 percent of the time) or be-

---

* In 1984, Goldstein's group developed a rabbit antiserum, as well as specific antithymosin antibodies, and were able to halt production of one of the lymphokines (Interleukin II) in young mice. In old mice, thymosin itself *stimulated* production of the same substance to levels normal for a young mouse.

cause aging changes in the lymphocytes have blurred their "judgment." In either case, fresh, newly constituted lymphocytes might again accept these changed cells as being part of the self rather than enemies. In autoimmunity, incidentally, this blurred judgment can occur in either B-cells or T-cells—in either the humoral or the cell-mediated immune system. In humoral autoimmunity the B-cells produce copious quantities of "autoantibodies." Yet even in a case like that, thymosin could possibly restore to normal levels the declining population of "suppressor" T-cells, whose job it is to inhibit antibody overproduction, and thus keep the B-cell factories in balanced control. Where autoimmunity is cell-mediated, with T-cells attacking other body cells—including perhaps other T-cells—the hope would reside, as in transplant rejection, with the development of antithymosin or with the use of monoclonal antibodies.

If it turns out, as many now suspect, that rheumatoid arthritis, pernicious anemia, late-onset diabetes, Hashimoto's thyroiditis, systemic lupus erythematosis, and multiple sclerosis, among others, are in fact autoimmune diseases, then thymosin—if it can defeat or even significantly ameliorate autoimmunity—could have an even broader impact, not just in delaying senescence but in making the later years considerably more comfortable.

10

HORMONES
AND ENZYMES

THOUGH DECO (not yet securely in hand) and thymosin are the most striking examples, other hormones have long been known to be involved—by virtue of either their presence or their absence—in the aging process. The rejuvenating effects of certain sex hormones, for instance, administered as replacement therapy when the natural supply has run down, are widely recognized. A pioneering researcher in this area used to be William H. Masters (of Masters and Johnson), before he shifted his focus from the impersonal biology of sex to its more intimate physiological and psychosocial aspects. A presentation he gave at the annual meeting of the American Gynecological Society in 1957 ("Sex Steroid Influences on the Aging Process," later published in the *American Journal of Obstetrics and Gynecology*) was probably the best survey available at that time. (Masters was also interested in thyroid and adrenal hormones in relation to aging.) Naturally, much work has been done since 1957, and the best summarizer of that information—to which his own work has of course contributed—has been USC's Caleb Finch, who is firmly convinced that "the extent of changes in the endocrine system has direct bearing on all theories of aging, as well as on the treatment of diseases in older persons."

Almost every experiment probing for clues to the link between hormones and aging has pointed to centralized endocrine control in the brain—and specifically to the hypothalamus and pituitary, which serve not only as the master control sites of the entire autonomous (endocrine) nervous system, but apparently as the major channels of communication with the central nervous system as well.

Much research has been devoted to the reproductive hormones. What has reproduction to do with the latter part of life? Isn't it all over by then? Exactly. That's what makes it a natural area for study. The sexual and procreative functions, especially in females, tend to be cyclical, and the organism arrives at a point in life where such cycles come to an end. Moreover, these cyclical functions are known to be regulated by specific hormones. A likely question for any investigator is: when the ovarian and estrous cycles in aging females come to a halt, does this represent a failure of the reproductive tract itself, or of the central endocrine control systems of the brain?

Seeking a solution, Joseph Meites and his associates at Michigan State University were able repeatedly to reactivate ovulation in female rats by means of electrical brain stimulation and the injection of various drugs and hormones. These rats were well past the age when ovulation could reasonably be expected to occur naturally— which is about twelve months (on a human scale, this would be about thirty years). These results clearly pointed to the brain centers as the sites of hormonal "aging" rather than the old ovaries them- selves—which, when properly stimulated, were perfectly capable of producing eggs.

Pursuing their own studies at USC, Finch and his group discovered that, when the seemingly worn-out ovary of an elderly female mouse is transplanted into a young female, the organ resumes its ovulatory cycles, showing convincingly that the ovary was not used up after all, once it was placed in a more congenial environment. On the other hand, when the reverse operation is done, the implantation of a young ovary into an old mouse, that youthful organ acts as if it had lived out its life in its new host; it loses the capacity to cycle. But something interesting happens if you concoct a totally novel scenario. Remove the ovary from a very young female mouse, then permit that mouse to grow old. Now, into *this* mouse, which has never in its life experi- enced ovulation, implant a new, young ovary. The ovary begins to cycle as if it were in a young mouse! Finch's interpretation of these results is that the area around the hypothalamus responds to the fe- male hormone estradiol (produced by the ovary to induce ovulation), but that there is a limited number of ovulatory cycles it can go through during its lifetime; then that area turns off, either through some kind of advance programming, or because after a certain number of ovu- latory cycles it simply runs down.

When a team at the University of Milan—A. Pecile, E. Muller, and G. Falconi—removed the pituitary from a young adult female rat and replaced it with the pituitary of an old rat, the young ovaries and uterus atrophied prematurely. Following these leads, and arriving at similar results and conclusions, Ming-tsung Peng and Hwe-ho Huang of Taipei's National Taiwan University transplanted both ovaries and pituitaries in several variations on the same theme. To clinch the matter, G. B. Talbert and P. L. Krohn in England—transplanting ova rather than whole ovaries—found that in young females old eggs could produce the same quantity and quality of normal offspring as young eggs could; whereas in old females young eggs were seldom able to produce offspring at all. The only question that remained, in the words of Peng and Huang (reporting their research in *Fertility and Sterility*), was "which part of the hypothalamic-pituitary axis plays the primary role in reproductive dysfunction in old female rats."

The hypothalamic-pituitary axis is of course not the only brain site where hormones are active. An international conference of neuroendocrinologists held in 1974 at the University of North Carolina School of Medicine made it clear that hormones are both active and interactive in many areas of the brain—though the interactions are often poorly understood; but the control centers do seem to reside in that restricted region. Of some interest, incidentally, especially when one considers Denckla's theories, is a presentation given at that conference by Walter E. Stumpf of North Carolina. "Thyroid hormones—or metabolites of them—which are thought to exert relatively little effect on mature brain tissue in contrast to the developing brain," Stumpf (and Lester D. Grant) reported in *Science*, "appeared to be localized in nuclei and cytoplasm of neurons almost throughout the entire mature brain." If thyroid hormones or their products are essential for the function of mature brain cells—which would seem to be the case in the light of this finding—and are present in both the nucleus and the cytoplasm of each cell, it certainly makes sense that thyroid deprivation would have a series of deleterious effects on those cells, which could take the form of cross-linkages, error catastrophes, lipofuscin accumulations, and other "causes" of aging. But let us return to that idea in the next chapter.

The experiments we were discussing a moment ago dealt almost entirely with the hormones of sex and reproduction, and it could be argued that these are quite special and may not be typical of all hormones. But, then, no hormones are "typical." Hormone function of any variety is a complicated business. Some hormones seem to have only one function; others have several. Some seem to act alone; others require interaction with further hormones. Some need to be triggered by others and/or may need in turn to trigger yet others before their assigned task can be carried out. How hormones act and react depends a great deal on the environment (which they may help create) in and around the endocrine glands, in the bloodstream which transports them, and in and around the target cells—which possess "hormone receptor sites" that may or may not be receptive at a given moment or whose receptivity may go up or down (mostly down) with age.

One of the strangest hormones to be associated with aging—and that association is very recent—is dehydroepiandrosterone or DHEA. Though it is the most abundant steroid hormone circulating in our bloodstream (at a given moment, there might be a thousand times as many DHEA molecules as, say, the much better known male and female hormones), until recently endocrinologists were reluctant even to classify it as a hormone; there was no known function for it, and it simply didn't act the way hormones are supposed to. Yet as far back as the 1950s it was known that DHEA production reaches its peak at the age of about twenty-five and declines steadily thereafter, going down virtually in a straight line with age. No other steroid hormone behaves this way. Research by Claude Migeon at Johns Hopkins, by birth-control pioneer Gregory Pincus, and by a team in Japan demonstrated that as life draws to its close, DHEA levels have gone down to about 5 percent of what they were at age twenty-five.

DHEA has come into its own in the past few years, in large part through the efforts of biochemist Arthur G. Schwartz of Temple University's Fels Research Institute in Philadelphia. Following up the work of others, Schwartz has helped show that DHEA may be effective in preventing several forms of cancer, as well as autoimmune reactions, diabetes, and obesity—and though the evidence that it retards aging is still quite sketchy, the hormone's other favorable propensities would still make it a good anti-aging substance, since offering protection against these other forms of disease and deterioration would surely improve the quality of our later years. Assuming, of course, that it really works.

There are two factors that may hold up the application of DHEA. One is its nonpatentability: there is usually no rush to compete for a drug that, because it is a known, natural substance, can't be patented. This handicap could be overcome if DHEA really were to live up to even a good fraction of its promise. The other is the fear of undesirable side effects. Since DHEA is a precursor of the sex hormones, it is possible that its use could result in overproduction of these potent substances and thus an increased risk of damage to, or even cancer of, the reproductive organs. Another biochemist, Norman Applezweig, who runs his own consulting business, and who has followed DHEA research as closely as anyone, doubts that these side effects would really occur. Even so, he agrees with Schwartz and others that it will be substances with a molecular structure similar to but not exactly like that of DHEA that are likely to get to market, not DHEA itself. Such substances, now rendered different from the natural DHEA molecule, would be patentable and might be tailored to keep DHEA's beneficial effects while eliminating the unwanted and possibly hazardous side effects. At least two companies have been formed, as of this writing, to exploit such possibilities.

In order for any hormone—whether it be DECO or DHEA, thymosin or thyroxine—to function successfully in any cell, whether in the nucleus or in the cytoplasm, it must set off or "induce" the appropriate enzyme activity. Because enzymes are so specific in their own functions, the study of "enzyme induction" has been a handy way to measure hormonal action—and especially to see how this action is affected by the passage of time. Richard C. Adelman of the Temple University Medical School in Philadelphia, who has been the leading investigator in this area, prefers to call what he measures "enzyme adaptation." It is well known that all mortal organisms adapt with increasing difficulty to environmental stress as they age. In fact, they have trouble adapting to any environmental change, because with approaching senescence change itself constitutes stress. And since change never stops, stress is fairly constant, until eventually death brings an end to that individual life as a historical entity.

As one of myriad examples of stress adaptation, the late Samuel Rosen, the New York ear surgeon famous for inventing the "stapes mobilization" operation that cures one type of deafness, liked to cite the manner in which human organisms adapt to noise. Noise is a form of stress, and we react to it not only with our auditory organs but with our cardiovascular systems as well. Rosen made many measurements among the inhabitants of many cultures, and established this relationship beyond doubt. "Whenever we hear a loud noise," he said, "our blood vessels contract. If the noise is continuous, then our vessels keep reacting. A young person's cardiovascular system—and ears—recover much more quickly than those of an older person. If I were to spend three hours in a discotheque with my son, my body would take much longer than his to return to normal."

On a cellular and molecular level, our biochemical adaptations also seem to slow down. Over many years, more than a hundred enzymes were studied and more than a thousand papers published; yet, though some tantalizing hints were turned up, the massive body of data led to no very helpful conclusions. That was the situation when Adelman appeared on the scene. In the case of one enzyme after another, when challenged with a given hormone, Adelman's careful investigations revealed that in rats aged from two to twenty-four months the "time of reaction"—the time it took the specific cellular enzymes to respond to the hormone—went up in proportion to the animal's age. Even in cases where the given enzyme activity finally reached the same level in an old rat as in a young one, it took correspondingly longer to reach that level. In order to make the kind of meticulous studies necessary to pinpoint where in the complex chain of hormone action the slowdown occurred, Adelman established a large colony of a specially bred variety of male laboratory rats known as the Sprague-Dawley strain. The rats were allowed to age normally, under protected circumstances, chiefly so that their enzyme adaptation could be studied as they grew older. Environmental conditions were kept as constant as possible, even to the extent that, throughout their lifetimes, a pasteurized, sterilized diet was provided whose components were rigidly controlled, so that none of the biochemical measurements could be attributed either to microbial infections or to nutritional differences.

With this system, as free of booby traps as human ingenuity could make it, Adelman proceeded with his studies, using various hormones and measuring the adaptive capacity of many enzymes. His most intensive investigations, however, centered on two hormones—corticosterone and insulin—and two liver enzymes—glucokinase and tyrosine aminotransferase (TAT). Adelman made this choice because it was known that: (1) the adaptive capacity of both enzymes can deteriorate with age; and (2) only in the presence of the two hormones can the activity of these particular enzymes be stimulated. As an example: if you administer glucose, you get liver glucokinase activity—but only if insulin is present. Adelman found that with carefully controlled injections of insulin to rats of various ages, there was no loss of glucokinase adaptability with aging. Both in magnitude of activity and speed of response, the twenty-four-month-old rats did as well as the two-month-old rats! Moreover, Finch and others, duplicating the experiment, got similar results. Meanwhile, Adelman's colleagues and students ascertained, in other painstaking experiments, that the binding of insulin to its receptor molecules in old liver cells was just as efficient as in young liver cells. So the problems in adaptation with aging were not in the responses of the cells or in the receptor molecules. Eliminating one possibility after another, Adelman arrived at the conclusion that the slowing of enzyme adaptation with age was due to either the lesser availability, or the lessened effectiveness, of the hormone itself—probably as a result of a deficiency at the hypothalamic-pituitary level.

While these experiments were in progress, other rats were being studied for their TAT activity in response to the adrenal steroid hormone corticosterone. Under ordinary circumstances, the pituitary first releases the hormone ACTH, which triggers the adrenal glands to secrete corticosterone into the bloodstream. When his rats were injected with ACTH, Adelman found that the old rats had just as much corticosterone circulating in their bloodstreams—and were able to maintain it at the same levels—as the young rats did. So the aging problem wasn't there, either. And the liver-cell enzymes were just as responsive to the hormone as glucokinase had been to insulin. Again, cellular-molecular failure was ruled out, and again, the hypothalamic-pituitary axis was implicated, because it seemed only logical that the pituitary must be releasing a reduced supply of ACTH.

A further experiment made the argument even more convincing. As an adaptive mechanism in a stress situation—such as a short period of starvation—higher levels of corticosterone would appear in the bloodstream. Adelman subjected his rats to just such a short period of starvation and found that in two-month-old rats corticosterone levels went up severalfold; at twelve months, the levels went up only slightly; and at twenty-four months of age, there was no response at all. Adelman looked for alternate explanations of these results. Could it be that food was of less importance to older rats, and the short period of starvation simply not very stressful? Adelman was soon able to ascertain that this was not the case. Without trying to follow him through the entire chain of further experimentation and reasoning, let's proceed to his conclusion (in a 1974 lecture before the annual meeting of the American Association for the Advancement of Science): "We have been able to demonstrate for the first time that a neuroendocrinological lesion of aging, probably localized within or near the hypothalamus, is capable of altering the pattern of liver enzyme adaptation."

Adelman's results are extremely encouraging, for a variety of reasons. One is that if aging bodies have an unimpaired capacity to maintain normal levels of hormones in their bloodstreams, and if the cells have an unimpaired capacity to receive and use them, then the probability is higher that anti-aging hormones, when administered, will restore cellular functions—which are, after all, not gone but only waiting for the necessary stimulation. This does not, of course, mean that *all* cell functions can be restored by hormones, though such an idea is not preposterous. (We should exercise caution in extrapolating liver-cell activity to other cells. Liver cells, remember, retain more regenerative powers than other postmitotic cells— e.g., nerve and muscle cells—and it's likely that fewer of their genetic switches are turned off permanently. For instance, Dieter Platt and his associates at the University of Giessen School of Medicine in Germany have studied the varying responses, with age, of lysosomal enzymes [the lysosome is one of the organelles in the cytoplasm of all cells]. They found that the lysosomal enzymes of the liver were, in general, much more stable than those of the spleen or the brain.)

Another hope that Adelman's work offers is a means for measuring physiological senescence via the cells' enzyme-adaptive capacities. His insulin studies should give us some important insights into "maturity-onset" diabetes, and his general approach should offer some clues as to why certain liver tumors can be chemically produced in aging organisms, not to mention new tools for determining both the safety and the efficacy of a variety of drugs and hormones in elderly patients. Dieter Platt was able to demonstrate, for instance, that lysosomal enzyme activity is quite age-dependent in its response to phenobarbital. A number of other German investigators got similar results with other drugs. These studies are corroborated by a long series of rat experiments carried out with amphetamines, barbiturates, tranquilizers, anesthetics, and anticonvulsants by Ryuichi Kato and Akira Takanaka at Tokyo's National Institute of Hygienic Sciences.

Virtually all the data from hormone and enzyme studies—though there remain vast gaps in our knowledge—have led Caleb Finch to at least partial agreement with Denckla: that the aging clock is in the brain, that it is located in the hypothalamic-pituitary endocrine-control center, and that whatever is responsible for the aging changes that occur there, they in turn produce a "cascade effect" of changes throughout the organism. This view of Finch's nicely fits an overall theory of aging put forth more recently by Douglas E. Brash and Ronald W. Hart of Ohio State University, who—avoiding either a strict wear-and-tear thesis or a genetic-clock theory—took a "systems view" suggesting that the process of aging consisted simply of ever-increasing cascade effects. Their view encompasses three major principles. One of them is the "principle of operating ranges." Every organ or system has a limited range within which it will work properly. The human body's optimal operating ranges occur, as might be expected, in the teens and early twenties. As the body grows older, virtually every change represents deterioration. Even small changes result in deviations from the optimal range, but we tend not to notice the difference until the changes and deviations have accumulated to the point where our adaptive and repair systems can no longer accommodate them and we can no longer ignore them.

The second principle, the one that most closely resembles Finch's cascade effect, is the "principle of propagation," which holds that any change resulting from aging will spread itself out to other parts of the body along a "senescent pathway." Thus, even a small change at the molecular or cellular level, if it influences an organ or system to deviate from its optimal operating range, is likely to propagate its effects elsewhere. This is true of free-radical damage, of lipofuscin accumulation, of cross-linkage, of error catastrophes, of somatic mutations, and all the other aging events we have talked about. This principle of propagation along senescent pathways is really the same basic truth that elicited Alex Comfort's remark that almost anything could appear to be a cause of aging—and could thus be shaped into a new theory of aging.

Brash and Hart's third principle deals with "rate-determining steps." Clearly, not all senescent changes are of equal importance. What gerontologists look for are "control points"—sites, substances, or functions that determine the rates at which other parts of the system function. The immune system, as we recognized in the last chapter, would be one such control point. But there may be other central control points—systems that act as rate determiners for the immune system itself.

There is nothing in these views, or in Finch's, that contradicts Denckla's further contentions. DECO—his family of aging-and-death hormones—if they exist, would be capable of causing aging changes anywhere in the body, including the hypothalamic-pituitary control centers (which thus literally self-destruct). They could turn off the thymus and interfere in other ways with immune functions. V. V. Frolkis, another advocate of the brain-endocrine clock and himself a brilliant and original investigator, has also shown that the same set of mechanisms may well be in control of the cardiovascular system. The immune and cardiovascular, remember, are the two systems whose failure, according to Denckla, is what kills us all. DECO, principally by denying the cells their thyroid (and perhaps their thymic) hormones, could theoretically do the whole job, since, as explained in chapter 8, thyroid hormones are the rate-controlling factors in both systems.

Still another Soviet researcher, V. M. Dilman of Leningrad's N. N. Petrov Research Institute of Oncology, pinpoints the hypothalamus as the probable suppressor of vital activities whose decline leads to aging and death, and he believes this hypothalamic activity is genetically programmed. But Dilman believes that the hypothalamus—and the pituitary, which it stimulates—does not so much act as *react* to information fed back from the body. When the biochemistry reaches a certain state of readiness for the next stage of the genetic program, it signals the hypothalamus to release its suppressors. Dilman's theory seems in no basic way to contradict Denckla's. If all this is proved to be correct, would a cellular clock of aging then be ruled out? Not at all—for the same reasons stated at the end of the last chapter.

We are ready now for a closer look at some further experiments that may help us move nearer to what I like to think of as a "unified field theory" of aging.

11

ACCELERATED AGING
IN NATURE

"MAY I have the slide? . . . What a splendid creature this salmon is, on its way to spawn! Next slide. And look at *this* forlorn hulk—a fish that has lately done so. Note the humped back, the hooked jaw, and the fungus mottling its skin. Soon it will be dead and drifting downstream. This is the fate of all five Pacific species of salmon." The speaker was Nobel virologist Peyton Rous, on the occasion of awarding the 1961 Kober Medal (of the Association of American Physicians) to British-born O. H. Robertson, who elucidated, for the first time, the mechanisms involved in the obscenely swift senescence of the Pacific salmon.

This "splendid creature," as seen in Peyton Rous's first slide, freely roams the vast sweeps of the Pacific Ocean for two or three years until one day the preset biological alarm goes off—the call to spawn, imperious, unrefusable. Swimming day and night, it heads like a torpedo for the coast from which it first came, guided by a fantastic inner navigational know-how that no human scientist can yet explain. Arthur D. Hasler of the University of Wisconsin believes the salmon may possess some means to take measurements from the sun, as navigational birds do. William Royce of the National Marine Fisheries Service thinks the information is genetic, imprinted in the chromosomes. At any rate, driven by whatever internal commands, the salmon moves upriver (see chapter 1) on an incredible journey to its inland spawning grounds*—perhaps the

* Because of the almost complete damming up of the Columbia River (only fifty miles of free-flowing water remain between Bonneville and Grand Coulee), the

very spawning grounds where it first came to life, almost literally over the dead bodies of its parents. The magnificent, condemned fish neither rests nor eats once it hits the fresh water of the river. And as soon as its reproductive function is achieved, it quickly turns into the soft-boned, rotten-fleshed "forlorn hulk" of slide two.

Some have speculated that the very act of coming in from the sea, the passage from salt water to fresh, somehow triggers the onset of senescence even as the salmon spends its last heroic energies running the obstacle course against gravity to its life-in-death rendezvous. More recent studies than Robertson's have been made in British Columbia by a multinational team of scientists aboard the *Alpha Helix*, the marvelously equipped research vessel of the Scripps Institution of Oceanography. These newer studies have shown that the totally preoccupied fish may quite literally starve to death, denying itself any nutritional refueling of its vanishing energies and at the same time rendering itself unable to produce the mucus that protects the gills, which filter its oxygen, so that it is deprived of oxygen as well as nutrients.

The change from salt water to fresh *could* be important in some varieties of salmon, inasmuch as such changes in environment do often trigger changes in biological activity, as Stewart Wolf points out. (Wolf, a research-oriented physician who now directs the Totts Gap Institute in Pennsylvania, was especially interested in the aging of the salmon during the period when he was director of the Marine Biomedical Institute at UTMB/Galveston.) As one example of the startling difference that a change of water salinity can make, Wolf cites the case of the shark, whose liver, under normal circumstances, resembles that of an alcoholic human's—cirrhotic and full of fat. It

---

salmon are finding it ever more difficult to get back upstream, even with the "fish ladders" the dam builders were required to construct as part of each project. "Salmon heading for their home streams in the upper part of the watershed must climb nine dams, each provided with fish ladders, with accumulated elevations of 612 feet," writes Anthony Netboy in *Esquire*. "Although the fish are said to have the stamina of racehorses, a goodly proportion do not make it to the spawning grounds. Those that spawn in the tributaries of the lower Snake may have to climb one or two additional hundred-foot barriers. The millions of smolts going downstream have to make the same journey: a large proportion are decimated going through the turbines at the powerhouses or over the spillways; others develop bubble disease from supersaturated nitrogen in the reservoirs and die."

does not manufacture any protein and contains a high concentration of urea, which would indicate advanced kidney failure in a human body. If that shark is moved from its customary salt-water habitat and put into fresh water, the urea levels quickly fall, and the shark's liver begins making albumin!

Nevertheless, O. H. Robertson dismissed the likelihood that the mere change from salt water to fresh could wholly account for the multitudinous, simultaneous biological transformations he observed taking place in the salmon. What made him dismiss the idea was the breed called kokanee—a dwarf blueback variety that lives in land-locked lakes. Though they spend their lives in fresh water and never get out to sea at all, they undergo the same rapid degeneration after spawning as the migratory varieties. For this very reason, the kokanee proved to be Robertson's favorite experimental animal; it was simply easier to keep track of throughout its life cycle.

Though Robertson's studies of the salmon probably represent the work for which he will be best remembered, he did not begin this research until his official retirement from the University of Chicago after a long and varied medical career in many parts of the world. On retiring, Robertson moved back to California, where he had spent a good part of his childhood (his Scottish parents moved there from England when he was two years old), to accept a lectureship at Stanford. It was from his new home base in the Santa Cruz mountains that he embarked on the salmon experiments, which were often as frustrating as they were painstaking. Once, after he had labored with the assistance of his friend the pediatric surgeon Clifford Sweet to perform some two hundred delicate laparotomies (surgical sections of the abdominal wall) on fingerlings in the Lake Tahoe hatchery, a hungry raccoon came along and devoured most of his experiment. But he persisted, working with several species of salmon, eliminating one possible cause after another—including sheer exhaustion or starvation—as the major explanation of the rapid aging phenomenon.

He eventually ruled out everything except endocrine dysfunction—some sort of drastic hormonal imbalance. And so it turned out to be. Robertson found that, in a process that probably began even before spawning, the salmon's adrenal cortex grew to many times its normal size while, at the same time, the pituitary also enlarged and its control capacities degenerated—resulting in an enormous overproduction of corticosteroids. As Peyton Rous (and

Stewart Wolf and Donner Denckla, among others) have noted, this strongly resembles what happens in Cushing's syndrome in human patients, where a great overbalance of glucocorticoids causes widespread and often severe symptoms. This violent hormonal disturbance could certainly account for the variegated senescent changes that ensue at such an accelerated pace in the salmon. The way Rous characterized the process is prophetic of Denckla's work: "death control, effected through an intrinsic mechanism"—an intrinsic hormonal mechanism, at that.

Denckla speculates that what happens in Cushing's syndrome and in the senescent Pacific salmon is similar to what may happen in individual human cells. As the organism ages, and the pituitary releases its death hormones, the cell is prevented from taking up thyroxine for its vital metabolic needs. Though the glucocorticoids within the cell do not increase in quantity, they are in sudden oversupply when the thyroid hormone is not there to counterbalance their effects. As a consequence, the cell is afflicted with a kind of Cushing's syndrome in miniature, which could result in a variety of aging changes, from free radicals and cross-linkages to somatic mutations and error catastrophes. This would occur throughout the body, though the deterioration, subtle at the start (in puberty) and growing more pronounced only with further releases of the "anti-thyroid" hormone later in life, would proceed at a statelier pace than in the salmon.*

Not that the salmon story can be considered as all told. Other scientists continue to study the Pacific varieties in more systematic ways than were available to Robertson. Among them are Andrew A. Benson and Walter Garey of the Scripps Institution in La Jolla, California, who were the leaders of the *Alpha Helix* expedition. The vessel's pioneering salmon-study voyage, which lasted through many months of 1968 and included some side projects at remote inland sites in British Columbia, was made by a team of thirty-seven scientists from Canada, the United States, Israel, and France. Igor Lobanov Rostovsky has written a beautiful account of the whole expedition, evoking its continuing sense of physical and intellectual adventure, in a magazine called *Oceans*.

"Not many of the men," writes Rostovsky, "had ever seen salmon

---

* For a stirringly evocative fictional biography of a Pacific salmon—with the non-fictional facts all meticulously researched—see *Sockeye* by Roger Caras.

except in a can or a fish market. Specialists in metabolism and human disorders (including ten doctors of medicine), their collective expertise encompassed: bone disease, milk protein, intestinal pathology (specializing in children), cell ultrastructure, brain diseases, glandular disorders, atherosclerosis and cardiovascular diseases." They studied four varieties of salmon: pink, chub, coho, and sockeye.

Their findings have already shed a great deal of light on the deteriorative events that hasten the salmon's demise—findings that should lead to many human applications. For instance, Don Puppione of the Donner Laboratory of Medical Physics in Berkeley was astounded to discover that, just before spawning, the salmon's bloodstream contained twenty times the amount of fatty compounds—including cholesterol—as are found in normal human blood; yet none of it seems to accumulate in the arteries! "From the salmon," says Puppione, "we may learn how to make a serum of lipoprotein that will not settle out in the human aorta. If we can find out how the fish holds his fat and protein together in serum lipoprotein, then perhaps we can learn how to feed a human being so that he makes this type of fat carrier in his blood."

Meanwhile, Douglas Copp of the University of British Columbia School of Medicine was studying a tiny gland, no bigger than a grain of rice. (The hormone it produces, incidentally, may prove useful in human bone and metabolic disorders.) "Situated behind the gills and in front of the heart," writes Rostovsky, "this minuscule, secreting organ is actually the *embryological precursor of the thyroid gland in humans*. Dr. Copp found that *this gland vanishes after the fish spawns*" (italics mine). This would seem to score another point for Denckla: the pituitary goes out of control and overproduces, while the thyroid component disappears.

In the salmon we seem to have occurring simultaneously the two diseases—both of them endocrine disorders—that most closely mimic aging in human patients: hypothyroidism (too little thyroid hormone) and hyperadrenocorticism (too much of the adrenal hormones, the corticosteroids, as in Cushing's syndrome). And both are, without much doubt, genetically programmed. As Rostovsky points out, "During a fortnight . . . the pink salmon's physiology runs through the steps of deterioration that may extend from 20 to 40 years in the life of a human being." Thus it makes an ideal model for gerontological study.

It was Eberhard G. Trams of the National Institute of Neurological Diseases and Stroke who especially concentrated on the brain and hormonal aspects of the salmon's senescence, and has continued to do so. He noted, as Robertson did but in more precise detail, the enlarged pituitary (three times as big in fresh water as in the ocean), the steroid overproduction, and other physiological changes. He also observed that the salmon died of "a complete metabolic shutdown," and that the increased production of adrenal steroids seemed to *inhibit antibodies*, thereby leaving the fish more vulnerable to infection: score points for Walford and Burnet. But also for Denckla again, especially since Trams said that the salmon's senescence "has the characteristics of a predestined bioprogramme," the expression, perhaps, of a "thanatotropic genetic imprint"—in other words, a genetically programmed impulse to die.

On the whole, the recent findings substantiate Robertson's in terms of hormonal causation, but it is now clearer that the process is already taking place during the entire time the salmon is journeying upriver. It could be that whatever impels the fish to undertake its amazing trip also triggers the decay processes—the compulsive behavior leading to the starvation leading to the glandular malfunctions in falling-domino fashion.

But perhaps not. Hear, for instance, one more fish story. The steelhead trout, like the salmon, comes in from the ocean and swims upriver to its spawning grounds, and also undergoes rapid degeneration. But Robert Van Citters of the University of Washington in Seattle discovered some years ago that the steelhead trout *do not all die*. Moreover, those that do survive and reach the ocean once more are somehow regenerated and rejuvenated! The terrible—presumably lethal—arterial lesions simply disappear. Using radioactive tracers, Van Citters ascertained that some of the trout were able to spawn, degenerate, and regenerate at least two or three times, apparently with no permanent damage. When he rediscovered Van Citters' neglected work, Stewart Wolf hoped, for a while, to do follow-up studies of the mechanisms that permit the trout's remarkable recovery. Can the trout teach us something about reversing human degenerative processes? Wolf pursued an ambitious plan that turned out to be impractical: to build an artificial trout stream at or near UTMB's Galveston campus in order to pursue these investigations.

Only Edwin W. House of the Idaho State University at Pocatello has continued to study the deteriorative processes in the steelhead trout. He and his associates have ascertained that the trout's atherosclerotic lesions do resemble those in human arteries. They have been able to induce atherosclerosis prematurely in young trout via injection of six hormones, both male and female, but have not yet found a means for reversing it. They have noted, too, that when juvenile steelhead are released by fisheries for migration to the ocean, about 10 to 20 percent of them do not make it; instead they mature sexually even before they become smolts and, developing all the signs of senescence, die within two months!

If the Pacific salmon and the steelhead trout represent nature's experiments—perhaps inadvertent—in accelerated aging processes,* there is a fortunately rare human disease which serves as a similar gerontological model for similar reasons. The disease is progeria—also known as the Hutchinson-Gilford syndrome, after the two British doctors who independently described it in the late nineteenth century—which the *Journal of the American Medical Association* once headlined as "Nature's Experiment in Unnatural Aging." According to Franklin L. DeBusk of the University of Florida, who undertook an exhaustive survey of the literature (reported in the *Journal of Pediatrics*), progeria occurs no more than once in eight million births, and he was able to find reports of only sixty cases worldwide as of April 1972.†

There cannot be many childhood diseases that are more tragic. The progeria victim appears, for a period of anywhere from six months to three years, to be perfectly normal in every respect, just as his height and weight were normal at birth. But then disquieting signs begin to appear. Growth is retarded, and the progeric child,

---

* Though the Pacific salmon and the steelhead trout are the best-known creatures who undergo this extremely rapid senescence after spawning (which has also been called "big-bang" reproductive physiology), other animals are also subject to it. The octopus, for instance, dies quickly after a single spawning episode—killed on program by a substance released from the optic gland. Merely removing the optic gland instantly after spawning gives the new parent a new lease on life. In the Australian marsupial mouse, *Antechinus*, all the males die, writes William Regelson, "following a one month hectic copulatory and male to male fighting period during female estrus. Males synchronously die within two weeks of the end of female estrus, and the only males surviving are those left in utero." As in senescing salmon, there is a Cushing-like overproduction of corticosteroid hormones.

† By now the figure has gone up to eighty or ninety cases, and the incidence is estimated to be twice as high.

if he survives through his teens, never gets to be any bigger than a normal three- to five-year-old. As soon as his telescoped childhood is over, other changes begin to take place. These have been described in several papers in the *Journal of the American Geriatrics Society* by William Reichel, director of the Family Medicine and Human Development Program at the Franklin Square Hospital in Baltimore, who has made the study of progeria (and the similar, later-appearing Werner's syndrome) his lifelong avocation.

The typical progeric child begins to look frail and old as early as the age of three or four. He may start experiencing cardiac troubles by the time he is five, though often not until ten or fifteen, and these troubles may include heart murmurs, atherosclerosis, elevated cholesterol levels, high blood pressure, angina pectoris, congestive heart failure, and finally the heart attack that is the most usual cause of death. The average life span of progerics is twelve to eighteen years, though some have died as young as five (DeBusk believes those who died between five and seven were really the victims of accidents, and that seven is the earliest death from "old age"), and some have survived to the age of twenty-seven. For the most part, though, it is an early–teen-age death, after a long period of steady and irreversible debilitation and deterioration. The progeric is a dwarf, but with a head that is of normal size and therefore looks larger than normal compared to the stunted body. The skin is wrinkled and parchmentlike, also almost transparent, with virtually no fat under the skin and with blood vessels showing prominently. The hair is gray and sparse—if any remains at all. The face is birdlike, the eyes protuberant, the nose hooked. In fact, progeria patients, as DeBusk points out, "bear an uncanny resemblance to one another." They are weak-limbed and stiff-jointed, and no medication or therapy has yet been found that will help them.

What perhaps renders their plight even more tragic, Reichel suggests, is the fact that they retain normal intelligence and hence are sensitive to the implications of their condition. "These children," DeBusk observes, "tended to be shy and aware of their unusual appearance. They were friendly, lively, witty and mischievous in the company of acquaintances, and they exhibited normal emotions, becoming happy, angry, and sad in the appropriate situations." Harvard's Dorothy B. Vallee adds, in *Pediatrics*, that "their major complaint is the social problems produced by the stigma of their appearance."

Though progeria undoubtedly *mimics* old age, its victims do not show *all* the signs of senescence (senile dementia is absent, for example), so there are reservations about viewing what happens as true aging. The similarities in symptoms *could* be sheer coincidence. Reichel asks: "Is it truly a disease of accelerated aging? Does it in fact represent a genetic error? If so, is there one genetic mechanism regulating man's normal life span? Or conversely: Is there a gene or group of genes whose purpose is to facilitate the incorporation of errors into a biological system? If so, does progeria represent an early activation of such a mechanism?" The questions must remain, for the moment, rhetorical.

Progeric children do not seem to have any gross chromosomal abnormalities. Though various studies have cast suspicion on the hormonal and immunological abnormalities of some progerics, the findings have not been consistent, and there exists no conclusive evidence that it is basically either a hormonal or an immunological disease. Reichel has found large accumulations of lipofuscin—the "aging pigment"—in the cells of progerics, as well as abnormalities in the connective tissue. As already mentioned, Samuel Goldstein of McMaster was able to coax only a few divisions out of progeric cells *in vitro*. Betty Shannon Danes of the New York Hospital–Cornell Medical Center has also reported, in *The Journal of Clinical Investigation*, that progeric cells have a lowered cloning efficiency as well as a diminished capacity to duplicate their DNA or to divide normally (all those deficiencies logically go together, of course). And a Harvard team has turned up suggestive evidence of faulty DNA-repair mechanisms in progeric cells.

No one group of people seem to be singled out as progeria victims: the cases are spread over many nations, and the disease seems to afflict blacks as readily as whites, males as readily as females. There are only three reports of more than one victim in a single family, and only one case that might have resulted from a consanguineous marriage.

Since the publication of *Prolongevity*, a progeria registry and cell bank have been set up by Dr. W. Ted Brown, head of the Human Genetics Unit at the New York Institute of Basic Research and Developmental Disability on Staten Island. William Reichel still maintains his interest in progeria, but says that Brown's center is now the recognized storehouse of reliable information. Brown knows of eleven living progerics in the United States, fourteen more in

other parts of North America, and another three or four abroad—
though he thinks there are probably more cases either undiagnosed
or unreported. One young woman victim has now lived to the
record-breaking age of twenty-eight; Brown suspects, however, that
she does not have true progeria but, rather, a related syndrome.
He believes increasingly that progeria is a dominant (as opposed to
recessive) genetic disease—though, of course, this has not been
provable, because progerics do not reproduce. In the parents of
progerics, the age spread between husband and wife (with the husband, on the average, six years older) is significantly greater than
in the rest of the population, but it is hard to know what to make
of this finding. A metabolic "marker" may have been found in
elevated levels of hyaluronic acid (an extracellular connective substance present throughout the body) in the urine of progerics—ten
to twenty times higher than normal. There is still no known effective
treatment or cure.

Progeria has received more public attention of late through a
series of happenstances. The Sunshine Foundation in Philadelphia,
an agency funded by the city police that tries to make dreams come
true for chronically ill children, learned of a progeric child in South
Africa whose dream was to go to Disneyland. The foundation made
the dream come true. While he was in this country, another progeric
child was identified in Texas, and the two were brought together,
with considerable fanfare. Previously, progerics had kept a low profile, and their families shunned publicity; to get a picture of a progeric for publication, for instance, was close to impossible. But that
has changed. The Sunshine Foundation has now supported two international get-togethers of progeria victims and their families at a
lodge in Pennsylvania's Pocono Mountains; and, thanks to the efforts of the foundation, Ted Brown, and a freelance New York
journalist named Cynthia Stevens, there have even been TV programs about progeria. The Sunshine Foundation helped Brown launch
his progeria registry and cell bank, and he now has a supplementary
grant from the American Foundation for Aging Research (AFAR),
an organization itself just in its infancy.

As of the present, then, progeria is increasingly suspected of being
a genetic disease, but much about it remains puzzling, and it has
certainly not yet been proved to be hereditary in origin. There is a
similar disease, however, which is known to be genetic—Werner's
syndrome. Its onset does not occur until somewhere between fif-

teen and twenty years of age, when most progeria victims are already dead. Some believe Werner's syndrome may be merely a later expression of progeria, as evidenced by some of the other names it goes by: *progeria adultorum, progeria à début tardif.* Werner's-syndrome victims also suffer from arrested growth, though not to the same extent as progerics. They are simply much shorter than average, and they, too, become prematurely gray and bald— as do some of their otherwise normal relatives. They are likely to succumb early to diseases ordinarily associated with aging, such as diabetes mellitus, atherosclerosis, heart disease, and cancer—especially cancer of the connective tissue. They die of what looks like old age in their forties and fifties. Though Werner's syndrome is also rare, it occurs about twice as frequently as progeria.*

What are we to learn from diseases such as these?

For one thing, whether we define them as "true" aging or not, there is no doubt that in both diseases widespread degenerative changes do take place at the level of both the individual cell and the total organism. Whatever occurs brings on degenerative changes much sooner than would happen in the normal course of events, suggesting strongly that the occurrences are not due to simple wear and tear. The probability appears high that some internal timing mechanism is at work, whether it is identical to the clock of aging or not, and that it affects the entire organism; and, further, that the mechanism is somehow built in to the individual's genetic information—perhaps as something added, perhaps as something missing, but in any event as something gone wrong. And the something wrong would seem to be in whatever mechanism regulates the onset and *rate* of deterioration. The defect could be in the molecular-genetic apparatus of the individual cell, passed on to all the body's cells by the original fertilized egg. Or it could be in the hypothalamic-pituitary controls of the endocrine system, which affect all cells.

In progeria, it is quite clear very early in life that something has gone radically wrong with the child's development. In Werner's

---

* Cockayne's syndrome is another genetic disease which, though not usually classified as one of the "progeroid" syndromes, exhibits the same kind of widespread degenerative changes. The same is true of Down's syndrome, which used to be called "Mongolism"—a disease which Walford believes may be the best model of all for studying the aging process.

syndrome, it is equally clear that the something-wrong has been postponed (if you compare it with progeria) *on program*. There are other devastating ailments, such as Huntington's disease, which are genetically triggered late in life; but in the case of Werner's, what is triggered is a whole cascade of degenerative, agelike changes. If these can be triggered genetically in Werner's-syndrome victims, they can be triggered in "normal" individuals at more advanced ages—giving added credence to all genetic-clock theories of aging. The hope in these diseases, as in true aging (which is also, in that case, a genetic disease), is that if a program can be accelerated by accident, it can be slowed down—or reversed—on purpose.

A brief return to the salmon, before we leave this chapter. The Soviet Union's V. N. Nikitin, long interested in what happens to DNA and its association with aging, has expressed a special fascination with some salmon experiments carried out separately by his Soviet colleagues G. D. Berdyshev and B. F. Vanyushin in the late 1960s. Before spawning and "premature death," as Nikitin calls it, the quantity of a nitrogenous base known as 5-MC (for 5-methyl-cytosine) in the salmon's DNA goes down considerably, perhaps by as much as half. This, by a chain of biologic reasoning, led Vanyushin to suspect "some previously non-functioning areas on the DNA molecule that may to some extent act as 'lethal genes' "—in a word, the programmed switching on of an aging-and-death mechanism.

12

DECELERATED AGING
IN THE LAB

NOW THAT we have looked at a few of nature's experiments in accelerated aging, it is time to examine a few human-designed experiments that have succeeded in *de*celerating the rate of aging—and, in some cases, perhaps, extending the life span—of laboratory animals by means of (1) parabiosis, (2) lowered temperature, and (3) restricted dietary intake—in ascending order of their possible application to people.

In the experimental technique called "parabiosis," an aging rat is hooked up to a young rat of the same carefully bred species so that they share a common blood circulation, like Siamese twins. They are joined tail to shoulder, which leaves them fairly free to move around. For the aging rat, parabiosis acts as a youth transfusion. In studies with more than five hundred parabiotic rats some years ago, Frederic C. Ludwig of the University of California at Irvine found that his older subjects lived significantly beyond their expected life span. Something in the blood of the younger rats enabled the older rats to live long after all their un-hooked-up littermates were dead. "When rats are joined parabiotically," says Zdanek Hruza of New York University, "remarkable biochemical changes take place." The older rats' cholesterol levels, for instance, go down "almost miraculously."

Several years earlier, at Baltimore's Gerontological Research Center (GRC), now part of NIA, Dietrich Bodenstein used parabiosis to create Siamese-twin cockroaches—again, young joined to old. Young cockroaches can regenerate lost limbs, but old roaches lose this capacity. In parabiotic union, however, the old roach recovered its regenerative powers. When Bodenstein lopped off a limb, it was promptly regrown. This renewal was attributed to the transference of the juvenile hormone from the young roach to its Siamese twin. Could something similar be happening to the rats? Hruza originally suspected the phenomenon to be hormonal in nature but finally concluded that, if a hormone is involved, it could not be any of the known hormones. What, then, is the nature of the "youth factor" that appears to circulate in the blood of a young rat and transfers its benefits to the senior partner? Could this factor be isolated and used to prolong life without the need for a troublesome parabiotic connection? And could the same be done for people?

It is possible, of course, that instead of contributing a mysterious "youth hormone" to the old rat, the young rat's blood merely helps to dilute and draw off some of the "death hormone" (DECO) circulating in the blood of the old rat. (Since DECO is a newly discovered hormone—and even now not yet purified—no one would have thought to try to measure its levels, or, for that matter, those of thymosin or DHEA.) If some of the deleterious substances are being thrown off into the bloodstreams of the younger rats, should this not expose their cells to the ravages of the death hormone sooner than would otherwise have been the case? They should therefore have grown old faster than *their* littermates. Did they? Unfortunately, the answers are not yet clear-cut. For a while, it appeared that this answer, and many more, would emerge from the research of Bar Harbor's David Harrison, who undertook, among his numerous other projects, an ambitious series of parabiotic mouse experiments. Effects did seem to flow in both directions, with the younger mice undergoing deteriorative changes—though inconsistently—and the older mice gaining certain advantages. For example, even when an older mouse was given, before the hookup was performed, a dose of radiation that would normally have been lethal, it was able to recover and thrive. The mice Harrison used were all of the same purebred genetic strain, so that the interchanged blood would not be rejected as foreign by the immune system of either host. Even so, the overall results were too erratic for him to arrive at any hard conclusions. Donner Denckla believes that the circumstances of parabiosis are so artificial, and probably so stressful for the participating mice, that a reliable analysis of the outcome would be difficult indeed—as it always is, even without parabiosis, where the exchange of hormones may be involved.

The same questions about the presence of a possible hormonal youth factor were raised by scientists like Finch in interpreting experiments such as Krohn's serial skin transplants. Though these do not strictly represent parabiosis, which normally applies to the joining of whole animals rather than the transplantation of cells, those cells are nevertheless nourished by the bloodstreams of their younger hosts, and their life spans consequently prolonged.

Parabiosis is a technique not likely to be applied to human subjects, even on an experimental basis. But the same is not necessarily true of the potential capacity to manipulate temperature to achieve prolongevity. It was known as early as 1917 that reducing body temperature slows the aging process, at least in cold-blooded animals. That year Jacques Loeb and John H. Northrop at the Rockefeller Institute discovered, in a series of now classic experiments, that they could significantly increase the life spans of fruit flies by keeping them at nineteen degrees Celsius instead of the usual twenty-five. Other researchers were quick to pursue and confirm their findings. More recently, Charles H. Barrows, Jr., of NIA's GRC/Baltimore, succeeded in doubling the life span of the rotifer—a pond-dwelling creature tinier than the period at the end of this sentence, but nevertheless a multicellular invertebrate organism—by lowering its water temperature from thirty-five degrees Celsius to twenty-five. Others have achieved similar results with fish. Roy Walford, for example, working with his UCLA colleague R. K. Liu, doubled the life span of the South American fish *Cynolebias belottii* by making the water colder by five or six degrees Celsius. Moreover, because they found a higher ratio of soluble to insoluble collagen in the colder fish than in control fish of the same age, they counted this as a further sign of retarded aging. (Collagen grows less soluble with advancing age.)

"In some cold-blooded animals," says Bernie Strehler, who has done temperature-aging studies of his own, "a tenfold increase in longevity has been achieved by lowering body temperature, without affecting body function." So-called cold-blooded creatures, or "poikilotherms," are—unlike warm-blooded animals ("homeotherms")—presumed to be unable to regulate their own temperatures internally, and thus their body temperature fluctuates with the temperature of their environment; but, as Walford has pointed out, this is not strictly true, since many creatures in this category, especially amphibians and reptiles, can exercise a fair degree of temperature regulation under certain circumstances. Nevertheless, they are certainly more susceptible to influence by their surrounding temperatures. Even in warm-blooded animals, however, the aging rate seems to be slowed by cooling. Robert Meyers of Purdue was able to cool monkeys a few degrees by direct manipulation of the "thermostat" in the hypothalamus and thereby increased their life spans. At Michigan State University, Barnett Rosenberg and Gabor Kemeny achieved similar results by using a drug that turns down the thermostat a few degrees in rats.

"There are no exceptions that I know of to the rule that animals live longer at lower temperatures," Strehler told a *Medical World News* interviewer. "The question is whether long-lived people have slightly lower-than-average body temperatures, because if you apply the same mathematical rule that applies to all the animal studies so far, then a few degrees Centigrade drop in body temperature could add something like 15 to 25 years to human life. And that could account for practically all the difference that one sees in human life span. This requires some study—it might be a good predictive index of longevity."

A number of scientists are now suggesting what science-fiction writers have been putting into their plots for a long time—that human life might be extended if people could be taught to hibernate, or put artificially into states of hibernation, like the astronauts in *2001: A Space Odyssey*.* To "hibernate" means literally to pass the *winter* in a state of sleeplike torpor, though it is used loosely to refer to any state of seasonal or periodic torpor. The bear is the best-known popular example of a hibernator. But some creatures "estivate"—that is, they "hibernate" during the summer instead. Others, such as the hummingbird, go into a state of torpor every night (I suppose one could say that they "noctivate") in order to get through their days. Animals can be tricked by various means into hibernating more than they normally would. "Among hibernating animals," Strehler observes, "those that are forced to hibernate more often tend to live longer." Walford looks at it from the op-

---

* The cryonics movement, to be discussed in chapter 20, advocates freezing rather than burial or cremation at death, against the day when future science can thaw and revive those now defined as "dead."

posite point of view: natural hibernators that are *prevented* from hibernating live a consequently shortened life span.

Now, gerontologists are not aiming to lengthen the life span by means of periods of hibernation without adding anything to the *waking* years of life. They do not seek to emulate Rip Van Winkle, who lasted a long time chronologically but whose conscious lifetime did not exceed that of other people.* Individuals who did this would be like Hayflick's deep-frozen WI-38 cells, which, when thawed, "remember" where they are: though they "live longer" chronologically, they go through the same number of doublings. What gerontologists seek in hibernation is some clue that would enable them to slow down the rate of aging—during sleep, during the waking hours, or both—in a way that would *add* a significant quantity of wide-awake, conscious, fully appreciated *living* time to life. Liu and Walford tried to achieve this sort of feat in rats—with only limited success—by using such compounds as the tranquilizer chlorpromazine and marijuana derivatives.

Most people—including many gerontologists—mistakenly believe that cooling automatically produces a lowered metabolic rate. But, as Liu and Walford wrote in *Gerontologia*, "To assume that lowering body temperature leads to a reduced metabolic rate is incorrect. The two do not necessarily go hand in hand, and the effect of temperature on life span cannot be explained in this simple fashion. . . . The metabolic rate is not necessarily decreased, and may in fact be increased. Certain metabolic pathways may be enhanced, others depressed." A great deal of confusion exists about the relationship betwen metabolic rate, temperature, and aging, and we will return to that topic shortly. But let one example suffice. The African lungfish *Protopterus aethiopicus* can, during estivation, lower its metabolic rate to 15 percent of normal without lowering its temperature at all. Under extreme drought conditions, the lungfish can remain in this suspended state for two years at a stretch, encased in hardened mud. Some years ago, Henry Swan—a former cardiovascular surgeon, now at Colorado State University, who first became interested in the phenomenon as a pioneer in the use of hy-

---

* Benjamin Franklin—who, by the way, predicted an eventual thousand-year human life span—thought it might be fun to drop in to visit the future. And John Hunter, the great eighteenth-century British anatomist and surgeon, anticipating *Brigadoon*, said he wouldn't mind coming back to spend a year every hundred years.

pothermia in open-heart surgery and blood-vessel grafting—imported some lungfish from Uganda, extracted and isolated a substance he called "antabalone," and injected it into some white rats. He thus induced a 40-percent reduction in their metabolic rate while lowering their temperature hardly at all.* Other investigators have meanwhile discovered a similarly acting substance called "HT" (for "hibernation trigger"), extracted from the blood of hibernating groundhogs. When it is injected into rhesus monkeys it induces the same kind of lethargy that Swan's lungfish antabalone induced in white rats. So there do appear to be non–species-specific chemicals that can transfer these effects from fish to rodents, and from rodents to primates. This is further evidence that universal torpidating agents, which could affect virtually all species, may exist.

To take advantage of the life-lengthening effects of low temperature, some gerontologists have seriously suggested that people might one day sleep in cooled bedrooms or on slightly chilled waterbeds. But though the principle of intermittent cooling is valid, these specific techniques would be of dubious benefit. Walford believes a cold environment without an actual lowering of body temperature would offer no advantage. Lowering the environmental temperature might make a difference in the case of poikilotherms, but, as Denckla points out, in homeotherms, such as human beings, any effective temperature lowering would have to be at the hypothalamic level— as was achieved by Meyers via direct manipulation and by Rosenberg and Kemeny via the drug route. Certainly more such drugs will be discovered, and this is the direction Strehler feels may be the most promising; but only as an interim measure, of course, while we are waiting to decipher the genetic on/off switching mechanisms. He warns, however, that "there is no way to predict the long-term side effects of artificially reduced temperature."

Some scientists are so concerned about the side effects that they have opposed any such experimentation at all. Clarence L. Hebert of NIH, for one, thought it would be most unwise to reduce body temperature artificially, even by two or three degrees, unless the

---

* Swan offers the terms "metabolic torpor" or "torpidation" to cover all forms of hibernation and estivation, including the daily "hibernation" of creatures like the bat and hummingbird. His lungfish studies drew him into total immersion in these phenomena, virtually a whole new career, resulting in his monumental *Thermoregulation and Bioenergetics: Patterns for Vertebrate Survival.*

individual were either sedated or anesthetized. He predicted that the subject would feel chilly and uncomfortable and would do a lot of shivering. Metabolism would, as a result, be sluggish, and so would intellectual processes. To keep someone's temperature thus lowered year in and year out would, in Hebert's opinion, result in earlier death rather than longer life. But in the view of Walford and Liu, the "induction of mild, chronic or intermittent hypothermia in the more thermostable homeotherms, such as man or the mouse, might significantly prolong lifespan without unfavorably influencing other functions." After surveying the literature, they conclude, "In the temperature range of mild hypothermia, bodily functions may not be depressed to any significant extent. On the whole, pronounced inhibition of metabolic processes are not observed until below 25°C." Meyer's experiments with monkeys do not seem to bear out Hebert's fears—at least not in the short run. And Kemeny and Rosenberg were able to reduce rat temperatures chemically without creating the effects described by Hebert. They, along with Walford and Liu, seem to agree with Strehler that slight reductions in temperature could probably be well tolerated over a hundred-year lifetime.

One final feature of these temperature-lowering experiments is worth special emphasis. Though cooling does seem to extend the life span, it does so only in the *later* stages of life. For instance, in the early investigations of *Drosophila* by Loeb and Northrop, cooling the larva had little effect on the rate of its aging (or, if you prefer, its development), but cooling the insect during its mature, imago state *did* slow its rate of aging. John Maynard Smith of Sussex demonstrated the phenomenon even more elegantly somewhat more recently. He kept one group of fruit flies at twenty-five degrees Celsius for the first half of their lives, then at twenty degrees for the last half. With another group he reversed the process, going from cool to hot. What he found was that the length of the first half of life, the developing period, was independent of temperature, while that of the second half, the maturing and aging period, was quite dependent on temperature—and could be considerably stretched out by cooling.

Liu and Walford did a similar experiment, but with an added twist, on their favorite tropical fish, *Cynolebias*. They kept careful track of four groups of fish. The first group spent their lives in water at twenty degrees Celsius. The second remained at fifteen degrees.

The third group started out at fifteen degrees but later were transferred to twenty degrees. The fourth started out at twenty degrees and were later moved to fifteen degrees. As might be expected, the shortest-lived fish were those that spent their whole lives in the warm water, and next in line were those who had moved from cooler to warmer water. But there was one big surprise: the fish who lived longest of all were not those who had spent their lives in cool water—but those who had started in warm water and only later moved to cool. Thus Liu and Walford ascertained to their satisfaction that spending the developing stage of life at a warm temperature enabled the fish to derive even greater benefit from the reduced temperature during the period of maturity and senescence.

Charles Barrows, too, working with his rotifers, found that cooling extended only the latter end of life. But he was eager to follow up another technique for life extension that Northrop had tried at Rockefeller with *Drosophila*: Northrop, experimenting with the effects of food restriction, discovered that periods of *reduced feeding* produced exactly the reverse result of cooling—that is, it stretched out the life span in the early, developmental, larval stages, whereas the same dietary deprivation had no such effect on the mature imago! The species of rotifer Barrows worked with had a normal life span of about eighteen days; his cooling techniques added an additional eighteen days. When he reduced the food supply by half, Barrows found he could add yet another eighteen days—this time to the early part of the rotifer's life. By combining temperature with diet control, then, he was able to *triple* the life span, adding another whole lifetime, as it were, at each end of life.

Clive M. McCay of Cornell, perhaps taking his cue from Northrop, began to experiment with underfeeding as a means of extending the life spans of rats. McCay's work, begun in the late 1920s, has also become classic, though it made its impact only slowly. One of McCay's initial motivations was to study the relationship of growth to aging. Some long-lived animals, such as the Galápagos tortoise and certain species of fish, grow slowly and continue to grow throughout their lives. McCay wondered if the pattern of aging in mammals might somehow be related to the fact that life begins with a rapid spurt of growth, then stops altogether when the organism is . . . well, full-grown. McCay started with two groups of very young rats. One group was fed a normal, well-balanced laboratory diet. The other group was also fed a balanced diet, with all the

necessary vitamins and minerals, but their caloric intake was drastically reduced, virtually to a semistarvation level (about one-third
of normal), in order to slow their growth. McCay did indeed slow
their growth and development; in some cases the control rats were
senile by the time the underfed rats had reached maturity, their
coats still glossy and youthful-looking. On the average, McCay had
come close to doubling the life spans of these rats. The Methuselah
of the batch on the normal diet lived only 969 days, whereas one
of the underfed lived 1,465 days. The slowed growth of the calorie-
restricted rats did not keep them from being normally active and
intelligent; and many were capable of resuming normal growth at
a later stage.

"McCay's 1,000-day-old retarded rats," wrote Robert Prehoda
in *Extended Youth*, "might be compared to a 90-year-old human
with the physical appearance of a teen-ager. . . . McCay disproved
the theory that the life-span is species-limited. Of even greater significance, he proved that the mammalian life-span can be doubled
and the period of youth as a percentage of the total life-span increased. Every responsible theory of aging must include an explanation of why McCay's retardation experiments were successful."

As an aside, the discovery that underfeeding can prolong life
made some investigators skeptical of Denham Harman when he
began reporting similar results through the administration of antioxidants: because the antioxidants he used were known to lower
the appetite, it was suspected that the longer lives of his mice might
be due simply to the fact that they were eating less! Comfort and
others went on to confirm Harman's results, as we now know; still,
although Harman undoubtedly enabled his animals to live longer
than they otherwise would have, it appears to have been the life
expectancy that he increased rather than the maximum life span.
But that story has already been told.

McCay's results have now been duplicated in mice, rats, and other
species by many scientists around the world—among them Comfort,
Strehler, Walford, Denckla, and Nikitin. Probably the most sophisticated veteran investigator in this vein has been Morris H. Ross
of the Institute for Cancer Research in Philadelphia. One important
truth (though this truth has now been modified, as we shall see) to
emerge from these experiments was that mammals—like fruit flies
and rotifers—could have their lives prolonged by calorie restriction
only if it was begun very early in life; not before weaning, of course—

not so early that it would result in damaging malnutrition—but certainly well before puberty. And the diet, though "restricted," could not be impoverished nutritionally but only calorically. At the same time, the life expectancy was also influenced by the composition of the diet. Ross emphasized the importance of the specific proportions of protein and carbohydrate in these restricted diets. Apart from the anti-aging benefits that result, and the slower growth, there is a considerably reduced incidence of tumors. "Rapid growth rates, structural or biochemical," Ross said in *Medical World News*, "are not commensurate with prolonged life span and reduced risk of age-associated diseases." Ross feels that the exact content of the restricted diet is important in determining how much an animal's life may be extended, but Edward Masoro of the University of Texas at San Antonio, another veteran researcher in this field, believes that the life span of lab animals can be prolonged by almost any healthy diet provided it *is* severely restricted.

Would calorie restriction have the same effect on people? A number of studies of long-lived people in regions of Asia, South America, and the Soviet Union have been made. The best known of these are probably the studies carried out by Harvard's Alexander Leaf—reported in *Hospital Practice* and the *National Geographic*, and, later and at greater length, in his book *Youth in Age*. There were only a few consistent features in the lives of these people. They were all relatively penurious and hard-working, and all ate a frugal diet throughout their lives, though the content varied from place to place. In that case, one might ask, why do poor people everywhere not live longer than others? Because they are *too* poor, and their diets lack vital nutritional ingredients. Though the populations studied by Leaf were far from affluent, they were not poverty-stricken to the point where they could not eat a proper diet. Neither malnourished nor undernourished, they were simply not sufficiently affluent to be able to afford to *over*eat. There are many stories of isolated tribes such as the Mabaan of the Sudan, studied by ear surgeon Samuel Rosen, who were practically free of deafness and cardiovascular disease at very advanced ages, but who, when they moved into Khartoum and began to share the diet and stress of city life, also began to acquire all the degenerative ailments of their new fellow citizens. And there are the instructive tales of wartime, such as the experience of those Scandinavian countries occupied by the Germans in World War II. When these populations were deprived of their usual high-calorie, high-fat diet, the death rate from heart attack went down sharply. When "good times" returned and they could resume their former eating habits, the heart-attack death rate also went back up to normal.

No one seriously considered trying McCay-style experiments on human beings. For one thing, gerontologists have little interest in merely prolonging the years of childhood and adolescence (though that might be interesting to study); what they want is an increase of the mature, vigorous years. To eat lightly but nutritiously, however, has generally been offered as good advice at any age, barring some special individual circumstances.

During the past few years, a new and exciting breakthrough has occurred: dietary restriction *starting in adulthood* can extend the years of life. It was Roy Walford again who led the way, demonstrating that, in rodents at least, it was not essential that the calorie restriction begin before puberty. By carefully manipulating the dietary changes—and especially the rate at which the diets were changed—he proved that the aging rate could be retarded. Barrows has also done pioneering experiments that confirm Walford's. These are the kind of results that can now begin to be tried on human subjects. Walford has been his own first volunteer subject, as he explains in *Maximum Life Span*. His personal calorie-restriction regime, including regular periods of fasting, will be spelled out in a later chapter.

There seem to be great similarities between the anti-aging effects of cooling and calorie restriction. In both cases, the rate of aging slows down. But the results are not necessarily equivalent in other respects. For instance, whereas McCay's underfed rats, though they lived longer, were undersized, Walford's cooled-down fish grew to larger-than-normal size. This difference could reflect merely the fact that some poikilotherms, such as carp and tortoises, *do* keep on growing as long as they live, and that homeotherms, such as rats and mice, do not. Thus, the *Cynolebias*, with more growing time, might be expected to end up bigger. The fish, after all, remain on their normal diets, whereas the rats may be getting so little food that they simply do not have the *substance* required to build the necessary tissue for added growth. The rats' growth rate in these circumstances was retarded despite the fact—as observed by V. M. Dilman of Leningrad—that during periods of starvation, the production of growth hormone is increased so that the organism can mobilize the fatty acids and convert them into usable energy.

Walford found that underfeeding and cooling both resulted in a definite suppression of the immune system, which seems to confirm that aging and immunity are indeed somehow related. But there is a built-in paradox here, because, in spite of the lowered immune response, these animals are *more resistant* to infection than control animals, and they get *fewer tumors*; as would be expected, however, they reject transplanted tissue less readily. Walford is confident that these apparent contradictions will be resolved as we gain ever-deeper insight into the complexities of our immune systems.

Prehoda believes—as he did in 1968, when he wrote *Extended Youth*—that Bjorksten's cross-linkage theory provides the best explanation of McCay's results. The underfed rats "had so little caloric food that it was quickly metabolized, with fewer cross-linking agents produced as intermediate products in food metabolism." But he also uses the same explanation to account for the immortality of Alexis Carrel's tissue cultures: "There is an almost total absence of cross-linking agents in the nutrient used to maintain tissue cultures." Now that Hayflick has proved that Carrel's cultures were not immortal after all, explanations must be sought elsewhere. This is not to fault Prehoda's original logic. At the time he wrote his book, just about everybody believed that Carrel's cultures *were* immortal. I am sure that some of the findings I describe with reasonably high confidence here will also be contradicted by subsequent investigation. In science, we can only work with the data that seem most reliable at a given moment.

For a long time, biomedical scientists believed that almost any slowdown in the rate of any of life's processes was accompanied by a slowdown in the metabolic rate. At least as far back as Max Rubner's publications in Germany early in this century, and those of his teacher, Karl von Voit, before him—or even back to Henri V. Regnault in France in 1849—it has been axiomatic that the life span is inversely proportional to the metabolic rate. And so it is, on a species basis. The shrew, with a high burning rate, lives only a year or two, whereas the Galápagos tortoise, with a very slow burn, goes on for a century or two. The hummingbird also has a very high metabolic rate, but it keeps itself going for ten or twelve years by "hibernating" every night—slowing its motor down to an idle, as it were. Bats have to do that for as much as twenty hours of the day in order to achieve a life span that ranges from five to twenty-five years, depending on species and locale. These maximum spans are known from long-term studies in the wild, says Richard Cutler, who believes that bats might well live even longer in captivity.

But this does not hold for individuals within a species. We have already heard Walford assure us that cooling does not necessarily produce a lowered metabolic rate. And Denckla, who has carefully reproduced McCay's experiments as well as other variations on the same theme, has ascertained beyond a reasonable doubt that in underfed rats whose growth is retarded, the metabolic rate is higher than in control animals of the same chronological age. Where individuals within a species are concerned, Denckla is convinced, and altogether convincing, on this point: we should abandon the notion that a higher metabolic rate symbolizes a faster burning up of an individual's living time. In experimental cooling or underfeeding, a higher metabolic rate may in fact be necessary to maintain the heat and energy the organism requires to compensate for lowered temperature and food supply. In many mammalian species, the metabolic rate goes *down* with aging. The same is true in human diseases that mimic aging, such as hypothyroidism. In such cases, previously held ideas would logically lead us to expect a rapidly rising metabolic rate to accompany accelerated aging processes. But the opposite is true. If, as Denckla hopes, we do discover or synthesize hormones that successfully *un*block the cells' ability to take up thyroxine—thus slowing, halting, or reversing the aging process—he fears that the beneficiaries may become uncomfortably warm as their metabolic rates rise. Presumably ways will be devised, by then, to counteract this side effect. The temperature-lowering drug of Rosenberg and Kemeny might be a possibility, though Denckla doubts that it would work. Perhaps, as an interim measure before a less cumbersome solution can be found, some sort of artificial cooling device, like the astronauts' air-conditioned space suits, would be necessary.

McCay's starved rats' metabolic rates remained higher, at every stage, than those of control rats of the same chronological age. In Denckla's view, the retardation of the rats' development through underfeeding simply delays the arrival of puberty, thus also delaying the triggering of death-hormone release by the hypothalamus and pituitary. This delay *permits* the metabolic rate to remain higher than in the unretarded controls, where thyroid blocking is already under way. Denckla's explanation also fits nicely with that of V. M. Dilman, who postulated that the hypothalamus is triggered into activity via signals fed back from the body when it reaches a given state of readiness; when the periods between those states are lengthened, hypothalamic triggering is to that extent postponed.

Among those who believe that the aging program and the early developmental program of life are probably part of a single program clocked by the hypothalamic-pituitary neuroendocrine system is Paola S. Timiras of the University of California at Berkeley. And she suspects—after performing a number of brain studies—that increasing quantities of serotonin, one of the major neurotransmitters, as the organism ages may have something to do with the feedback-triggering activity Dilman speaks of. Experiments performed in Timiras's lab by Paul E. Segall suggest that she may be right. Segall has been doing dietary-restriction experiments in the style of McCay and his followers—except that Segall has been focusing on a single element of the diet, the essential amino acid called tryptophan. He has found that tryptophan deprivation alone will often retard aging in some of the same ways as McCay's complete calorie-restriction diet. Because tryptophan is a precursor of serotonin biochemically, Segall and Timiras suspected that withholding tryptophan might also slow the production of serotonin; and so it turned out. It is possible, then, that the buildup of serotonin to a certain critical level is what triggers the hypothalamus to action. And if one can delay the critical serotonin buildup, then it makes sense, in Timiras's view, that one can "stop the clock." In 1982, Segall was able to demonstrate impressively the efficacy of tryptophan deprivation when a few of his female rats, long past the age when procreation would normally have been possible, gave birth to healthy offspring.

Suppose the hormonal triggers Dilman speaks of, perhaps induced by serotonin as Segall and Timiras suggest, lie in those genetic on/off regulatory switches in the DNA of a relatively few brain cells—the ones that signal the hypothalamus to send out "releasing factors" that in turn signal the pituitary to release the appropriate hormones. In that case, if those switches are subject to a strictly timed genetic program, how can they be influenced by outside factors, such as the restriction of calories? Why do they not turn on, no matter what, at the programmed moment? The probability is that such a genetic program would not be set according to the strict passage of time as measured by the mechanical clocks we have devised to coincide with the earth's movements around the sun, but, rather, according to the stages of the organism's own physiological development. These stages are timed events, to be sure, but the timing is sequential, not absolute. Should one not expect, then, that if a given stage of development can be artificially delayed, the signal that usually goes back to those critical brain cells to indicate the organism's readiness for the next stage would also be delayed?

13

GENES AND THE PROTEINS THAT SWITCH THEM ON AND OFF

FROM ALL the "experiments" described in the foregoing two chapters—nature's accelerations of aging in the Pacific salmon and in human progerics, and our own laboratory decelerations of aging via cooling, calorie restriction, and parabiosis—it is clear that (1) the rate of aging can be influenced by various circumstances, and (2) there is a constant, complex interplay between the aging of the cell and the aging of the whole organism. As we know, a cell in culture ages and dies in a different manner, and at a different pace, from the same cell when it is an integrated component of an organism.

Inasmuch as many-celled organisms are believed to have evolved from single-celled organisms, it is reasonable to expect each cell to retain, in some measure, the capacity for running through the life cycle that a cell possessed when it was a separate, independent entity. It also makes sense that the cell's capabilities, in the context of the larger body of which it has become a part, would be subordinate to that organism's central controls; otherwise how could the organism develop into what it needs to become? The central controls, usually hormonal or at least mediated by hormones, would in most cases prevail; but in the absence, or failure to function, of those controls, the cell would proceed with the program it never lost, modified though this program may have become in the course of its coevolution with the larger organism of which it became a part. This is what seems to occur *in vitro*, when cells are freed from their usual constraints.

In the insect-development experiments carried out by Joan Whitten at Northwestern, she demonstrated that the death of cells during the early part of the life cycle could come about either in response to hormonal command or as a result of "clocked" death mechanisms within the cell's nucleus. It does look more and more as if there might be at least two clocks of aging—the cell's own, carried somewhere in its nuclear molecular lattices, and the brain's hypothalamic-pituitary hormonal chronometer. Moreover, research in many places has now made it clear that hormones can act on individual cells at the nuclear level, where the genes reside, as readily as in the cytoplasm. One example cited by James H. Clark of the Baylor College of Medicine in Houston, based on his own research, is the fact that steroid hormones—e.g., estrogen, hydrocortisone—can act directly on the chromosomes to alter the nature and timing of gene transcription. In the absence of such interference, the cell follows its own internal clock. Thus, as already suggested, Hayflick and Denckla could both be right. It also appears that, whether the pattern of nuclear events (which express themselves as degenerative changes) is triggered by hormones, other kinds of death clocks, or no clocks at all, those nuclear events come to pass by virtue of the turning on and off of genetic switches, the repression and derepression of the pieces of information that govern all the cell's activities at any given moment in life.

The heart of the gerontological enterprise, then, may be to learn how these switches are turned on and off—and how to control them for our own benefit. This assumes, as discussed earlier, that the genetic information is not destroyed or damaged but, rather, masked, covered up, repressed, unavailable at the moment. For certain purposes we would like to know how to derepress it, to uncover it. At times it would of course be handy to know how to *re*-repress it as well—as in the runaway proliferation of cancer cells. In fact, before we ever arrived at any decision to derepress any genes artificially, we would want to be sure that we would be able to re-repress them in a reliable manner when we felt we had had enough of whatever activity we had turned on again—just as we would not want to build a nuclear reactor without knowing that we could turn it off if it threatened to "go critical."

In *Prolongevity*, I felt I had to go to painstaking lengths to describe some of the exciting preliminary experiments then in progress, in order to convince the reader that the transplantation of genes from one cell to another, from one organism to another, from one species to another, was not only a distinct possibility but had in fact already begun to happen. In these dizzying intervening years, the progress of genetics has astounded even the people who have been carrying out the work. "Recombinant DNA," a phrase hardly in use in 1976, began to appear in the headlines shortly thereafter. We have learned an enormous amount about the structure and function of genes, how they form coils and supercoils, how they ravel and unravel, how they repair themselves. We have created gene maps—often utilizing techniques that fuse cells of different species, such as man and mouse—by tracing hundreds of genes to their sites on specific chromosomes. We have learned about genes and groups of genes that jump from one place to another, about gene sequences that do not appear to have any function, about mysterious genes that, though many copies of them are present, never seem to be turned on. We can synthesize genes and proteins at unprecedented speeds, rendering obsolete the tedious prior methods. Moreover, we even have instruments to do these jobs for us, including "gene machines." We can deduce the code for a gene from the sequence of the protein that is its product, and vice versa. Genetic engineering is not merely a laboratory fact; it is a thriving industry ("biotech" firms by the hundreds have been formed in the last few years) with vast medical and agricultural implications, as well as a continuing moral and political issue. There is little doubt that gene therapy (the insertion, replacement, or turning on of faulty or missing genes) is in our reasonably near future, as is enzyme replacement therapy. At the moment, such therapies are discussed in terms of genetic disease, but there is no practical reason why the same techniques could not be applied in order to produce, or turn off the production of, any given genetic product. If our genes were to produce too much or too little of a given substance with advancing age, there should be no theoretical obstacle to turning their manufacture on or off, or modulating it at will, through genetic manipulation. And if there is indeed a genetic clock of aging in the nucleus, involving—as is generally believed (by those who believe it)—only a few genes, then we should be able to go in and map those genes, and then try to decide what we want to do with that knowledge. For all these reasons, I see no point now in burdening the reader of this new edition with laborious accounts of individual pieces of research, just to prove that genetic engineering is possible. We have now gone so far beyond those experiments I described as to make them seem ancient history.

In my discussions of genetic on/off switching—"gene expression" and "gene regulation" are now the favored ways of saying this—I have so far not sufficiently emphasized that the chromosomes are actually "nucleoproteins." That is, they are made up not only of DNA but also of associated proteins (though these proteins are originally manufactured in the cytoplasm) and, at times, some RNA as well. Our first real insights into the nature of genetic on/off switching was provided by the celebrated "operon theory" promulgated by the Nobel Prize team of Jacques Monod and François Jacob at the Pasteur Institute in Paris—though this terminology is hardly essential to the pursuit of our major themes. Research since then has of course brought a great deal of new understanding, especially of the role of the nucleoproteins in gene regulation. The knowledge acquired up to the mid-1970s was carefully spelled out in a 1975 *Scientific American* article by Gary S. Stein and Janet Swinehart Stein of the University of Florida, in collaboration with Lewis J. Klinesmith of the University of Michigan. In my most recent (1984) conversation with Gary Stein, he told me that, though the structure and function of these proteins are now understood in considerably more sophisticated detail, and the list of specific, known-for-sure proteins keeps growing, the general understanding of the nucleoproteins that scientists had arrived at in the 1970s still holds up very well.

The nucleoproteins known as "histones" have been identified —by James Bonner, Holger von Hahn, and others, notably Rockefeller University's Vincent G. Allfrey and Alfred E. Mirsky— as the main repressor proteins, the "off" switches. The histones literally cover the segments of DNA that contain the information meant to be off limits for the messenger-RNA molecules charged with the task of transcribing the information. In fact, when that information is repressed, the manufacture of the messenger-RNA molecules also comes to a halt, as added insurance that nothing will be messing around with the switches. Robert T. Simpson of NIH had speculated that it was the tightness of the histone bonds that kept the switched-off part of the DNA folded up like an accordion thus unable to make any music; the loosening up of the histones is what permitted the accordion to play again. But what loosens up the histones? Simpson's theory implied that the histones did it them-selves. But, as it turns out, they cannot do this without the assistance of the *nonhistone* nucleoproteins, which come in a profusion of varieties and possess enormous versatility. The nonhistones are now known to comprise the nuclear enzymes that carry out repair, rep-lication, and a host of other indispensable activities.

Histones do not, as originally thought, possess the ability to rec-ognize specific gene sites—as, say, an antibody recognizes an anti-gen, or a piece of transfer RNA recognizes an amino acid. They have, rather, a generalized ability to cover up any part of the DNA, just as a layer of putty can be slapped over any surface, regardless of its detailed configurations; or as a plastic barrier can deny access to a bookshelf without having to conform to the contours of the books or "know" anything about the books' contents or why they are not to be approached. The quantity of histones remains stable, too—just enough to cover up all the genetic information on all the DNA molecules in that particular chromosome.

The nonhistones, on the other hand, vary considerably in their presence at any given time—often depending on the number of genes that are turned on or off and the quantity of messenger-RNA molecules that are on hand. Some varieties of nonhistone protein unquestionably serve important roles in gene regulation, acting as if they were equipped with an intelligent understanding of the sched-uled details of the genetic program. At the appropriate time, and as if purposefully, they proceed to the segments of DNA that are ready to be derepressed; by loosening the histone bonds (peeling back the layer of putty, taking the plastic barrier off the bookshelf), they render the genetic information accessible for use again, allow-ing the messenger-RNA molecules to be made, and all the assigned RNAs to transcribe and transmit the information. Philip Lipetz of Ohio State University believes that the unintended loosening of the bonds that permit the "supercoiled" DNA to unravel, thus allowing the expression of genes at inappropriate times, is intimately related to the aging process.

In a series of experiments carried out by F. Marott Sinex and his associates at the Boston University School of Medicine, chromatin—which includes the DNA as well as the nuclear proteins—was sep-arated from the nuclei of mouse-brain cells of varying ages. First all irrelevant substances were meticulously eliminated from the mix. The insoluble residues that were left over indicated that more and more of the protein was bound to the DNA as the mice aged. Nikitin, using different techniques and different cells (liver cells from albino rats), reported three consistent sets of results with age: (1) the number of repressors (histones) goes up, (2) the number of derepressors (nonhistones) goes down, and (3) the making of chromatin RNA also goes down. This research by Sinex and Nikitin and others strongly suggests that many more genes are turned *off* as the cell ages.

The very active role played by the nonhistone proteins gives rise to an interesting speculation. In recent histories of the rise of molecular biology (all histories of such a new enterprise have to be recent; yet, so remarkably much has happened in this compressed period of time that histories by the score have been published), the historians like to point out how logical it was, in the beginning, to assume that the proteins were the chemicals of primary importance in the chromosomes. Proteins are so complex and versatile, having twenty different amino acids to draw upon and make into virtually infinite combinations and rearrangements, whereas the DNA, with its monotonous sequences and only a four-letter code, seemed to have many fewer possibilities.

Then came a whole series of discoveries: the truly epochal and late-to-be-appreciated experiments of Rockefeller's Oswald T. Avery—who somehow never got a Nobel—proving that it was DNA that contained the basic genetic information; the marvelous elucidation of the double helix by Crick and Watson; the insightful elaborations contributed by Monod and Jacob; the cracking of the genetic code by Marshall Nirenberg, Severo Ochoa, and others; and all the rest of the Book of Molecular Revelations. Now that everyone knows that DNA is the master molecule, we smile to think that we all once believed that protein was paramount.

Do we smile too soon? Consider: DNA does of course constitute the genetic manual of instructions, but does that make it the master? It is the library, but is it the librarian?

It would appear that the true intelligence in gene regulation lies in certain of the nonhistone proteins. If these are in fact the knowledgeable molecules charged with carrying out the genetic program, using a passive DNA as a convenient filing system or blueprint to be used only at the time and to the extent that such use is appropriate, then it is the protein that is paramount after all. Of course, there do exist regulator genes, including repressor genes, as well as genes that dictate the manufacture of the repressor proteins. But what turns the regulator genes on and off?

"It may not be long," the Steins and Kleinsmith predicted in their 1975 *Scientific American* article, "before proteins that regulate the expression of specific genes are isolated, introducing the possibility of a certain kind of genetic engineering: the proteins might be inserted into cells in order to modify abnormalities in gene transcription associated with development, differentiation and a broad spectrum of diseases, including cancer. Such a capability might revolutionize man's ability to deal with some profoundly destructive disorders." This does not seem an immodest prediction, in view of the developments in genetic engineering that have already revolutionized our potential for dealing with profoundly destructive disorders.

One of those profoundly destructive disorders—perhaps the ultimate among them—is old age itself. Our knowledge of the genes, and the proteins that turn them on and off, could empower us to put an end to it.

14

LAST BARRIER: THE AGING BRAIN

"PHYSICALLY I AM failing," wrote George Bernard Shaw, at eighty-nine, in the preface to *Back to Methuselah*. "My senses, my locomotive powers, my memory, are decaying at a rate which threatens to make a Struldbrug of me if I persist in living; yet my mind feels capable of growth; for my curiosity is keener than ever. My soul goes marching on; and if the Life Force would give me a body as durable as my mind . . ."

An intellect that remains buoyant can make up for a lot of physical failings. The beginning of wrinkle and sag may represent not much more than a cosmetic disappointment. Even the decline of physiological functions, barring some terrible disease, can be accepted with a certain degree of equanimity. But of all the deteriorative changes that go with advancing years, there is probably no prospect that people dread more than the dimming of the mind, for the mind not only is their principal vehicle for perceiving and communicating with their fellow human beings but also carries the stamp of their very identity and personhood.

Because the mind's major bodily instrument appears to be the brain, that is the main site of concern. This concern has been highlighted over these past few years by all the publicity given to the senile dementias, with their varied symptomatology of confusion, agitation, fear, depression, hyperactivity, memory loss, and other incapacities. Special attention has gone to Alzheimer's disease, and that grab bag of ailments billed loosely as "diseases of the Alzheimer's type." Deterioration of the brain, or some parts of it, does undoubtedly go with these diseases; and so, sometimes, do structural changes characterized by tangled fibrous knots within the nerve tissue. No one is yet certain which of these lesions and dysfunctions, if any, represent true aging, which may be genetic in origin, which may be the result of some insidious slow-virus infection, or which in fact may simply have been misdiagnosed. But even brains not thus affected, brains that are merely aging normally, are subject to irreversible deteriorative processes. For every mind that is still going strong, like Shaw's, at the age of eighty-nine, there are dozens of much younger minds whose capabilities are noticeably impaired. And long before any such problems have become apparent through the individual's overt behavior, brain cells have begun to die off in quantities that may or may not be alarming, depending upon which expert you consult.

Based on studies such as those of Harold Brody at the University of Minnesota in the early 1950s—and others as early as the 1920s— it has been estimated (an estimate now disputed, as we shall presently see) that the average woman or man, after the age of thirty-five, begins to lose something like 100,000 unreproducible neurons a day—every day of every ensuing year of life. That is hardly a negligible quantity, even considering that we start out with some ten billion neurons when the brain attains full growth. Some have speculated that the loss of neurons may itself considerably accelerate—or even be a major cause of—the rest of the body's aging. Others believe that brain-cell death is not so much programmed, or even the result of intrinsic wear-and-tear processes, as it is the consequence of increasing circulatory inefficiency with age. The brain, though it weighs only three pounds, utilizes about 20 percent of the oxygen circulating at any given time, so a cardiovascular difficulty serious enough to slow down circulation may condemn the cells in the brain, which are more dependent than most other cells on a plentiful, continuous supply of blood-borne oxygen, to die off in larger numbers than elsewhere.

Brain-cell death has been given a charmingly novel interpretation by zoologist Richard Dawkins of Oxford. "It is a widely deplored fact," he wrote in *Nature* in 1971, "that every day many thousands of our brain cells die and, unlike other types of cells, are never replaced. I suggest that this may not be a purely destructive process, as is normally supposed. . . ." Dawkins proposed that neuron death may be a *selective* process, nature's way of developing a most im-

portant mental function—the very "mechanism of information storage in the brain."

"One naturally thinks that the loss of elements from a system
must lead to its degradation, but," Dawkins reasoned, "this is not
necessarily so if the elimination is non-random. A sculptor changes
a homogeneous rock into a complex statue by subtraction, not addition, of material." In like manner, the shaping of the memory and
personality might *require* the discarding of substance not essential
to the design!

Though Dawkins went on to spell out the logic of his fascinating
conceit, his article drew a sharp, impatient response from Comfort,
who believes the concept of the daily demise of brain cells in mul-
timillenary quantities must be put in the category of "neuromythology," inasmuch as the original extrapolations had been made
from relatively skimpy data, and other laboratories had often failed
to corroborate the findings. (At Johns Hopkins, for example, Bruce
W. Konigsmark and Edmond A. Murphy counted the cells in small
brainstem samples from twenty-three autopsied cases, ranging in
age from newborn to ninety years, and could find no neuronal loss
with age in that particular area of the brainstem—though they readily admitted that losses might occur elsewhere.) Echoing Comfort's
sentiments was Joseph Tomasch of Iran's Pahlavi University at Shiraz,
whose own studies had failed to identify brain-cell deaths in anything
like the claimed quantities.

Harold Brody, the man whose early studies are among those
most often cited as evidence of hourly neuronal hecatombs, never
put forth any such specific figure as 100,000 cells a day; nor did he
ever claim that his findings—carried out in several areas that were
still, taken together, only a small fraction of the cerebral cortex—
necessarily constituted evidence of a brainwide phenomenon. He
feels today, as many gerontologists seem to, that neuron death occurs at varying rates in different parts of the aging brain, ranging
all the way from near zero in some areas to very large quantities in
others—some of them probably critical to the organism's overall
function. We have all heard the glib assurance that a human being
never utilizes more than a small fraction of his brain capacity over
a whole lifetime; unfortunately, however, there seem to be no physiological data on which to base that wishful-thinking cliché.

Among neuroscientists, at any rate, it is generally assumed that
the brain does lose cells, in regions of vital importance, at a rate

rapid enough to warrant concern—and that such dead cells are probably not resurrectable. According to NIA's Neal R. Cutler, brain weight drops by about 10 percent overall by the age of eighty—with a "neuronal dropout" in some areas as high as 25 percent—a loss often accompanied by a significant decline in various kinds of neurochemical activity. NYU's Harry Demopoulos, who, as a pathologist, has performed numerous autopsies, says the brain of a very old person may have shrunk by as much as a third, though a loss of overall bulk does not necessarily mean an equivalent loss in the number of cells. As noted earlier, the size of the spaces between neurons also shrink considerably.

If one believes in the possibility of retarding or even reversing the aging process—by means of, say, manipulating a genetic aging clock—then one can readily imagine a rejuvenated body with an irreversibly deteriorated brain, a horribly ironic joke to contemplate. Francis Otto Schmitt of MIT once suggested that brain cells might be taught to replace themselves by renewed division, just as the body's mitotic cells naturally do; and, if we remember the potential for carrying out such interventions via genes and nucleoproteins implied in the last chapter, Schmitt's notion no longer seems bizarre. But even if this were to become feasible, a number of gerontologists—Strehler among them—believe that renewed division of neurons might well result in the destruction of personality and of the individual's sense of identity and continuity, a cruel joke of another sort. What would be the fun of attaining great longevity if the lucky winner couldn't remember what had gone before? If one assumes that personal history—all memory, learning, and experience—is somehow stored in the molecular lattices of our neurons, then renewed mitosis would be expected to break up those patterns, shatter the individual historical record, and thus destroy identity.

One possible route to a longer-lasting brain record, and hence a more durable identity for future generations (though it offers no consolation to anyone already alive), would be to start out in life with a larger brain. "One cannot forget," as John Tyler Bonner comments in a *Scientific American* book review, "how different from all other animals man really is, and how all these differences seem to be associated with the extraordinary tumor-like growth of the brain starting only a few million years ago." Many students of human evolution have expressed amazement at this explosive enlargement of the brain—some think as much as a 50 percent increase in size since *Pithecanthropus* only a half million years ago. There is no reason to consider the current brain as a product finished forever, as large as it ever will be. Even if its growth were to continue, however, a rate that is deemed "explosive" or "tumor-like" on a geological time scale can be invisibly slow in terms of an individual human lifetime. And evolutionary development, by its very definition, operates in species over many generations, not in any single person's life span.

The always imaginative French biologist Jean Rostand once suggested that all it would take to double the size of the brain would be one additional division of the neurons in the course of development. If we could achieve this by deliberate genetic manipulation—postpone the turning off of the mitotic switches one division longer—we could presumably do it selectively, doubling the number of neurons in some regions (such as the cortex) while permitting other regions (such as the brainstem) to turn off on schedule. If this had to be done *in utero*, the fetus would be faced with the problem of how to get out, with a head so big. A Caesarean section might be one answer. Or, as Rostand further suggests, if the embryo-fetus-infant were to be developed *in vitro*, a potentially feasible engineering feat, the chamber opening could be made as large as necessary for a comfortable exit. On the other hand, the brain does continue to grow after birth, and it is conceivable that, if neurons need to double again only in limited critical areas of the cortex, such growth might still be contained within the existing cranium.

All this is much more in the realm of fancy, as far as we can at present judge, than some of the possibilities discussed earlier. Moreover, even if it suddenly became practical to carry out Rostand's fantasy, the dilemma posed by dying brain cells would only be postponed, not solved. Might there ever be a way to imprint upon *new* brain cells the patterns that existed earlier? This eventuality has been discussed in speculations about the cloning of new individuals from mature single cells. Though a clone would be an identical genetic twin of the person from whom the cell was taken, he would have a new brain and hence develop a totally different personality, shaped by environment and experience. A clone of an Einstein cell would not be likely to have thought of the theory of relativity, nor an artificial twin of Michelangelo to cope with the Sistine ceiling. So a person of wealth or eminence who wanted to clone himself and produce a reasonable replica of his own individual temperament and talents would be frustrated by this limitation, wouldn't he?

Not necessarily, says Strehler, ever the brave adventurer. Strehler has designed an elaborate machine (not yet built, but under development) by which he believes a person's essential personality patterns and memories could conceivably be recorded, stored, and imparted to a new brain. Looking over his as-yet-unpublished plans and patent applications, I was tempted to think of his device—too complex to explain here, even if I had his permission, and even if I properly understood it—as a kind of supercomputer. But it is not a computer at all, says Strehler; rather, it is a new invention, a series of interlocking data-processing devices capable of recognizing patterns of information whose importance is reflected by their redundancy, and possessing unprecedented capabilities of storage, manipulation, retrieval, and readout.

I have sat and stood and paced with Bernie Strehler literally for hours at a time as he freely discussed his machine—on one occasion in his living room at Malibu, the floor covered with spread-out rolls of computer data that he had brought down from the Veterans Administration lab in Martinez, California. He patiently explained the gadgetry and the theories supporting it. He produced microphotographs of layered brain tissue, drew circuit diagrams, and did a lot of hand-sculpturing in the air to emphasize his points. Drawing from neurobiology, electronics, cybernetics, molecular genetics, information theory, and solid-state physics, he dazzled me with expositions of how information is handled by the nervous system, in what ways it is analogous to molecular-genetic coder-decoder systems, which layers of neurons perform what kind of function, in what ways his theories and models depart from earlier assumptions. Each time I almost began to believe I understood. But later, looking over my notes and his doodles, and searching my own flawed memory, I would finally not be able to put the pieces together again. Yet, somehow, I was convinced that his idea—the kind of notion I would ordinarily consider unmitigatedly harebrained—was sound, and that his machine just might work. If the apparatus does someday perform as Strehler hopes, one could transfer, not all the *details*, certainly, but the essential *patterns* from an old brain to a new one, enabling the transferred identity to recognize itself as the same person! If he is right, then even the brain barrier may finally be overcome. Since *Prolongevity*, Strehler has continued to devote every spare hour to his brain project, giving it highest priority whenever his official research, teaching, writing, and editing duties allow. As 1984 drew to a close, Strehler told me he had worked out—at book length, on paper—a fully self-consistent model of the human brain, which he had shown to a number of neuroscientists. Though they were not in a position to confirm its validity, neither could they find any serious fault with it, and they agree, says Strehler, that if he is correct in his surmises, he will have revolutionized the way we think about the brain's organization, function, and purpose. And, if Strehler can work out so ingenious a machine so early in the game, surely he and others can do better later.

Meanwhile, though we must, for now, settle for the deteriorating brains we possess, we may draw hope from the knowledge that the exploratory study of what makes the brain age is only in its infancy. As the investigation continues apace, we may entertain a reasonable certainty that new understanding will suggest new ways—now unforeseeable in their specifics—to forestall or slow the rate of neuronal death and central-nervous-system degeneration. We may hope that by the time the gerontologists have devised effective means for slowing the body's aging, the neurogerontologists will have done as well by the brain.

As only one of the exciting possibilities in this direction that have arisen in the few years since the publication of *Prolongevity*, I point to the development of fetal brain-cell transplants. In research in both the United States and Sweden—sometimes collaborative between the two countries—such transplants to the brain have been successfully carried out. For instance, a Parkinson-like disease in rats was cured by transplanting fetal rat cells to the appropriate sites in the adult rat victims of the ailment.

What makes this such a fruitful avenue to pursue is the very special nature of the brain. Just as brain tissue has unique powers to keep out certain unwanted substances via the "blood-brain barrier," and just as the brain—though it is thought of as the very center of pain perception—does not itself feel any pain, so is the brain a "privileged site," immunologically speaking; it is much more favorably disposed to accept, and much less likely to reject, grafts of foreign tissue. Moreover, fetal tissue is much less likely to be rejected by any tissue, because it has not yet developed the necessary antigenic properties. So fetal brain grafts, especially when the tissue is from the same species as the adult donor, have a much higher probability of success than most other kinds of transplants.

Experiments have also shown that the brain will accept tissue from other parts of the same body—the adrenal glands, for example, when adrenal cells are required to secrete substances that part of the brain can no longer make itself. In Sweden, such an "autotransplant" was performed on a human patient; though it did no harm and seemed to benefit the patient somewhat, doctors are loath to do much in human patients—as indeed they should be—without a great deal of further experimentation in animals, including primates. But one of the great hopes in this new field of investigation, a hope already shown to be warranted by preliminary results, is that the brain can accept tissue not only from its own species but from other species as well, at least under certain circumstances. If this turns out to be possible, it will sidestep the sticky dilemma—for the large number of human patients who might benefit from such procedures—of where and how to obtain, ethically, the necessary quantities of fetal tissue. Another possible answer to this problem—an answer being actively pursued—is the growth of fetal cells in tissue culture in unlimited quantities.

In any case, such responsible scientists as Richard Greulich, who heads up NIA's research effort, and Richard Jed Wyatt of the National Institute of Mental Health, who has been a personal participant in some of these pioneering experiments, believe that cells and tissues transplanted to the ailing brain, including the ailing aging brain, may in the long run provide remedies for many mental disorders and deficiencies, and considerably prolong the optimal functional life of the human brain.

So the brain, sometimes billed as the last barrier to prolongevity, may not be an insuperable barrier after all. There of course remain many other barriers to overcome before we need face the particular "last barrier" which the death of irreplaceable neurons represents. Meanwhile, new research on the *healthy* aging brain (see chapter 17) suggests that, even without the breakthroughs to come, the neuronal news is not all bad.

15

A FRONTIER IN FLUX

ONE formidable barrier on the road to a proper scientific understanding—and thereby perhaps the abolition—of old age is not biological but, rather, psychological in nature. I am talking once more
about the credibility barrier. To help overcome it, I have given
myself license to go beyond mere reporting to employ what I think
of as creative integration. The research picture I have presented is
thus perhaps more coherent than the way most gerontologists see
it. It is not that I have deliberately exaggerated, distorted, or in any
way conveyed a fraudulent view of the state of gerontological research today; only that my view—though carefully and honestly
arrived at through extensive reading, visiting, and interviewing—
does not necessarily reflect the consensual view of gerontology itself.
Indeed, no such consensus exists.

I am aware that I have given entire areas of conventional, old-
fashioned gerontology short shrift in order to allow a fuller account
of some of the more recent avant-garde developments. I have simply
let the people and the events unfold as the narrative scheme developed in its own organic fashion. The result is a far from perfectly
balanced story. But the latter would in any case be impossible at
this stage of gerontological progress, when what might represent a
balanced view to one authority would seem a gross distortion to
another. It is futile to hope that I might please all gerontologists
and slight none; in fact, to slight none would automatically displease
others.

Each sortie into the frontier areas of aging research provides a reminder of how totally in flux those frontiers are. At the time I was putting the finishing touches on *Prolongevity*, I went to Boston to attend a meeting and took advantage of the opportunity to make a couple of last-minute calls on some gerontological sources. I wanted especially to touch base with F. Marott Sinex, whom I had not seen in some time. I always enjoy his sharp, skeptical mind, and I wanted to test a few of my evaluations against it. I was also curious to know his own current thinking, and I was, moreover, a bit uneasy about how little mention I had thus far made of his work although he was—and remains—a central figure in American gerontology.

One problem, from a storyteller's viewpoint, was that Sinex had not then—and still has not—developed any theory of his own, nor did he subscribe to any of the existing theories. "I hate theories," he readily admitted, tilting his chair back against the wall, his hands behind his head, grinning his wide, sudden grin. "I hate to talk about theories, and I wish other people wouldn't be so fond of them, either, especially in a science no more advanced than gerontology is right now." (I could see Strehler, had he been there, sitting bolt upright in protest.) "There are lots of observations," said Sinex, "lots of ideas, but nothing we should yet dignify with the designation 'theory.' " He nevertheless tolerated with good humor, as he continues to, my own discussion of various theories, which he punctuated with comments, some of them vehement, and an occasional chuckle.

At the mention of the somatic-mutation theory, whose popularity I had noted was on the wane, Sinex said, "Don't rule it out yet. New things are happening. I'm not at all sure I'm not a proponent of it myself—depending on how you describe it." So saying, he asked his secretary to give me a copy of the chapter he had just finished writing for *The Handbook of Aging*. "Read this and you'll see what I mean."

Discussing prospects for NIH's Institute on Aging, then brand-new, and speculating as to who might be chosen as its director, Sinex reflected that Hayflick might be a good candidate—one he could certainly approve personally, at any rate—though he doubted that Hayflick could afford to take the job. Just a few minutes later, however, he was speaking rather critically of Hayflick's experiments and theories. "If you think he's so wrong," I asked, "why do you consider him qualified to be director of the institute?"

"I didn't say Len was *wrong*," he replied, with a quick grin. "I just think some of the interpretations of his work are unwarranted at this stage of the game. That has nothing to do with my opinion of how good a director he'd make."*

If Sinex wasn't on Hayflick's side, theoretically speaking, how did he feel about Denckla, who, I knew, had been a recent visiting lecturer at Boston University? "Well, Donner is a very interesting fellow," he commented, cautiously. "He has a lot of fascinating ideas, but we have to reserve judgment. Too much remains to be proven."

Throughout our conversation, Sinex delighted in coming up with bits of information and names of people I knew little or nothing about, in spite of the quantity of research I had done; and he only pretended (or perhaps only half pretended) to be scandalized at each omission. What! I hadn't read Macfarlane Burnet's 1974 book, *Intrinsic Mutagenesis?* (I soon got it and read it.) What! I hadn't heard of Dick Cutler at Baylor, who'd been working on RNA transcription as it relates to aging? (I soon got to know Cutler, who has now for some time been at NIA's GRC/Baltimore, and he appears in several places in this edition.) What! I wasn't familiar with the investigation of the repair capabilities of DNA being carried out by Dick Setlow of Brookhaven and Ron Hart at Ohio State? Tsk, tsk.

The work of Setlow and Hart had shown that the capacity of DNA to repair itself was related to longevity. In a whole spectrum of mammalian species, those that lived longest were the ones with the best repair capacity. One example of what research in DNA repair can contribute to gerontology is a simple experiment carried out by Joan Smith-Sonneborn at the University of Wyoming. She used as her animal model the paramecium, a single-celled protozoan creature, whose rate of senescence is easily measurable. She started out by deliberately doing damage to the DNA of her paramecia by exposing them to ultraviolet radiation. Then she activated their DNA-repair mechanism—a known enzyme—merely by placing them in the dark for a measured period of time. (There are many kinds of DNA repair, utilizing many enzymes; this kind of "dark repair" is the simplest.)

---

* The director finally chosen was Robert N. Butler, more expert at the time in the psychosocial aspects, but soon fully appreciative of and knowledgeable about the biology of aging. He got NIA off to a flying start before he moved on, only recently, to set up a new department of geriatrics at New York's Mount Sinai Medical Center.

The startling part of the experiment was not that the DNA damage was repaired: that much was expected. But after undergoing repeated cycles of damage and repair, these organisms lived longer than paramecia that had never been damaged at all, by a full third of their expected life span! Smith-Sonneborn was able to pin this result to the fact that once the repair mechanisms had been activated, they were also able to repair other damage besides the damage that she had been responsible for. It would be as if your carburetor had conked out, and the mechanic decided that while he was repairing it he might as well do a lot of additional tuning and tightening up. Thus the car would emerge in much better condition and last longer than a similar car in which the carburetor had continued to function adequately and which had thus never received the mechanic's attention.

At one point during that 1975 visit with Sinex, in discussing the free-radical theory of aging, he asked if I had adequately considered that auto-oxidation of membranes is quite a different phenomenon from the action of what he called "superoxides"—or that antioxidant activity was not to be confused with the behavior of the natural scavengers of free radicals. I was forced to admit that I really was not aware of these distinctions. He again tsk-tsked at me and asked whether I knew the work of Irv Fridovich at Duke University on superoxides. To my distress, I did not. (I soon learned.) Though I had read everything I could get my hands on by the proponents of the free-radical theory at that time, including Denham Harman, Paul Gordon, Richard Passwater, Lester Packer, and Aloys L. Tappel, and had talked to many gerontologists about free radicals and antioxidants, I could not recall any mention of Fridovich or superoxides. "Well, those fellows are just behind the times, I guess," said Sinex, his grin very wide indeed. What to do? Back to square one and start over again?

Very shortly after that Boston trip, I had occasion to drive from Houston to Galveston with Donner Denckla. He, too, had new data to report, though his findings were then not yet publishable. Over the next couple of weeks David Harrison came down from Bar Harbor to visit, as did Strehler from California. Both of them updated me on their work and constantly evolving thoughts; Harrison, for example, was reconsidering his assessment of Hayflick. Strehler was in New York to attend a conference on the neurobiology of aging at New York University, which I also attended. The conference was full of new information and insights. As one example, Harold Brody, who had now moved to SUNY/Buffalo, discussed the notorious "aging" pigment, lipofuscin, the undisposed-of garbage that accumulates in aging nerve cells. He noted that, in parts of the brain where the cells contain large deposits of lipofuscin, the number of cells remains fairly constant throughout life; whereas in areas with little lipofuscin, cell deaths are much more numerous! This led someone in the audience to suggest that perhaps lipofuscin was *good* for cells. "Maybe we've been wrong about it all along. Wouldn't it be fascinating if it turns out that lipofuscin is a substance the cell produces to help it *fight off* the aging process?" It was a notion no one took very seriously, and the laughs were hearty. But no one pooh-poohed the idea, either, in view of Brody's surprising data.

It became clear—as it is now clear again, nine years later—that one could go on attending meetings, seeing people, reading, visiting laboratories, updating, and continue to return to the typewriter (these days it's the word processor) for further revisions. There is a dubious possibility that at some point one would finally reach the end of one's investigations. But by that time, one might have grown too old to write a book at all. And all that work would have been wasted.

I am truly conscious of how very much I have left out. (In self-defense, I defy any critic to point to a book or "comprehensive review" of aging that has not omitted a great deal.) I am troubled, for instance, about having said so little about GRC/Baltimore and all the programs that go on there, formerly under the directorship of Nathan Shock and now of Richard Greulich. In a different kind of aging book, GRC/Baltimore—and the NIA of which it is now a part—would deserve to be at center stage most of the time. I have never gone to visit a few of the important aging centers around the country—for example, those at Duke University and the University of Michigan—mainly because their work and interests seem more psychosocial than biological in orientation. At USC's busy gerontology center, I have spent real time only with Strehler and Finch. Even as I was in the midst of giving the manuscript of *Prolongevity II* a final reading before sending it to press, I ran into Carl R. Merril of the National Institute of Mental Health (preparing to move over to the NIH Clinical Center), who told me of research he and his colleagues have recently done (results not yet published) that strongly suggests (1) that not only can the error catastrophe theory of aging not be correct, but that very few error catastrophes actually occur, and (2) that free radical damage cannot be as extensive as some have theorized. Merril bases this interpretation on the analysis of electrophoretic studies of proteins in aging (Hayflick-type) fibroblast cells in culture. One would expect new kinds of protein configurations (brought about by presumed errors and damage) to appear in some significant quantities on the gels, but they in fact did not—at least in this initial series of experiments. If the results hold up, and if Merril is correct in his surmise, a new look will have to be taken at the data on which these aging theories are based. Merril was also working on some entirely new anti-aging substances (not new substances, but new in being perceived as having anti-aging effects), but he was unwilling to talk about them at so early a stage in the research. At about the same time, another investigator asked me if I had seen Jerry Williams's latest papers ("I mean his *latest* papers") on DNA repair. I hadn't, and realized that Williams was among the important people I had not so much as mentioned. Along with Edward Schneider. And Morris Rockstein. And no mention of extraordinary lay people such as Florence Mahoney, who has been so influential in getting aging legislation enacted in Washington; or of my friend Don Yarborough, that ebullient and enigmatic Texan, who, along with Senator Alan Cranston, was responsible for establishing FIBER and who has helped enhance the work of so many investigators, ranging from Allan Goldstein and Harry Demopoulos to Bill Regelson and Carl Merril; or of Paul Glenn, father of his small but important foundation. Et cetera. The same investigator who reminded me of Jerry Williams also told me that I really must look into some of the interesting new data coming in regarding coenzyme Q-10 (also known as CoQ and ubiquinone), which was one of many potentially anti-aging substances I had decided to omit, just because I had no plans to provide anything like encyclopedic coverage. Should I now hold things up for another look at CoQ? Obviously, as I've already said, one must arbitrarily declare a stopping point. There are all kinds of tidbits of gerontological data which, though less than world-shaking, have a real interest and charm of their own, and which I would have liked to find room for, but they simply didn't fall naturally anywhere in the framework of the narrative.

I have collected many technical papers from abroad—especially from Germany in German and from the Soviet Union in Russian—that I have not taken the time to have properly translated. Though I have touched on research in many nations, there are a number of nations (whose science I am sure is sufficiently sophisticated to be harboring some first-rate aging research) that have gone altogether unmentioned simply because I have not happened across any reference to them in my reasonably voluminous researches. But there is no point or profit in feeling guilty about not knowing everything.

Last time around, I admitted to guilt feelings about giving relatively scant attention to some of the mavericks outside the establishment of aging research. Among them were Benjamin Frank of New York City and Benjamin Schloss of Los Angeles, each with theories of aging and with ideas about how to counteract some of the ravages. Both have since died, and they will not have the chance to carry their work further, though others have pursued—and validated—a few pieces of it. Nor did I write about many other mavericks—such as the cellular therapists of Switzerland (especially the successors of the late Paul Niehans), the various rejuvenators (notably Ana Aslan of Rumania)—but they have all been written about extensively elsewhere, as, for instance, in Patrick M. McGrady, Jr.'s *The Youth Doctors*.

The reason I don't worry too much about these and other omissions is that they are not what this book is about. What I have been busy exploring here are the various theories, and some of the evidence supporting them, that suggest that human biomedical science may now feasibly hope to make old age obsolete—or at least to postpone it considerably and lessen its more unwelcome consequences—as well as, perhaps, to extend the maximum human life span.

The question raised by the title of part one of this book was: Can we do it? And the answer is: Quite probably, yes, we can.

Now let us see what we can do to put together the things we have been talking about into something like a unified theory of aging; and, moving on from there, to ask what this exercise suggests about ways in which we might intervene in behalf of the aging human organism.

16

PUTTING IT ALL TOGETHER: TOWARD UNIFICATION AND INTERVENTION

WE HAVE by now looked at a fair sampling of the extant theories of aging. Most of these have been of the sort I referred to as wear-and-tear theories. In the typical wear-and-tear theory, a scientist will select a particular kind of damage or deteriorative process as the critical factor in the body's overall senescent decline. The specific damaging event or mechanism selected will usually be the type that produces what Finch has called a "cascade effect"; that is, its consequences will tend to generate further consequences, in accordance with Brash and Hart's "principle of propagation" along the body's "senescent pathways." Thus Bjorksten observes cross-linkage, deduces how widespread its effects could be throughout the entire organism over a lifetime, and offers the cross-linkage theory of aging. And thus Orgel sees how easily—in the chain of genetic expression from DNA via RNA and enzymes to protein manufacture—a single crucial error could set off an explosive multiplicative process in the living cell, and comes up with the error-catastrophe theory. Some of the other theories we have noted are lipofuscin accumulation, somatic mutation, free-radical damage, the stiffening of collagen and connective tissue, the loss or dimming of genetic information (decline in DNA repair capacity, or in the expression or regulation of genes), autoimmunity, and the failure of immune protection.

The second major category of aging theory is the "genetic clock" theory—the idea that aging is simply the latter part of our built-in developmental program; just as the genes dictate the sequence of our fetal development, infancy, childhood, adolescence, and entry into adulthood, so do they dictate the nature and sequence of our aging process. Such a clock would govern our overall aging. The question arises: if there is such a clock, where is it? And we have seen that there are two major answers being offered. One is that the clock is right there in the DNA, in the nucleus of each living cell. The other is that the clock is in the brain, in particular in the hypothalamus and pituitary, and that its orders are carried out by hormonal messengers.

If pressed to pick my own favorite among the wear-and-tear theories, I would probably fall back on the principle of parsimony and ask: which of the phenomena at the heart of which theory might create the kind of cascade effects that could explain all the other kinds of damage and thus encompass all the other theories? And the resulting answer leads me, as of this moment, to cast a tentative vote for the free-radical theory. Free radicals can cause cross-linkage as well as lipofuscin accumulation. They do damage to all cells (including the white cells that make up the immune system); they do damage anywhere in the cell (membrane, nucleus, or cytoplasm) or outside the cell (connective tissue); and they do damage to any kind of molecule (including DNA, RNA, enzymes, hormones, and all other proteins). They can thus account for somatic mutations, error catastrophes, lost or faulty capacity to express and regulate genes, diminished or erratic immune function, and virtually all the other individual signs of aging. Free radicals have, moreover, been implicated in damage to the brain and central nervous system, in injury to the heart and cardiovascular system, and in the causation of cancer. So the free radical appears to me to be the likeliest candidate for the trigger that can set off the greatest cascades of virtually *all* the kinds of damaging and deteriorative events we have been talking about.

My problem with it as a truly unifying theory is that I fail to see how any single wear-and-tear type of damage, or even all of them taken together, can account for the fact that, unless we are cut down prematurely by accident or disease, we all age in roughly the same sequence and at roughly the same rate. Individuals who age much earlier than average probably do so because of some genetic failing or predisposition (the extreme examples being progeria, Werner's syndrome, Down's syndrome, Huntington's disease, and the like), or an unusually stressful life style—but even in the latter case, the ability to cope may well be influenced by the individual's genetic heritage.

The existence of species-specific life spans throughout the animal kingdom also militates against wear and tear as the principal instrument of aging. As I argued in an earlier chapter, if it were purely a matter of wear and tear, would we not expect, at least every now and then, to see a Galápagos tortoise die of old age at one and a half, as the shrew does, and to see a shrew go on living to be 150 or more, as the tortoise does? And would we not expect to see cancer cells in tissue culture, exposed to the same laboratory environment—the same culture ingredients, the identical conditions of wear and tear—age and die at roughly the same rate as do normal cells, instead of retaining their apparent immortality?

So my final, tentative vote goes against wear and tear and for the genetic clock as the primary theory of aging. Which of the two genetic clocks—the hormonal, brain clock or the cellular, DNA clock? I say both. This answer is not a hedge. I would guess that the basic, controlling program is in the hypothalamo-pituitary area of the brain, operating by means of a hormone or a family of hormones such as Denckla's DECO. One can see that—by inhibiting the action of thyroid hormone (and perhaps other hormones, too—the thymosins and DHEA, for example), which is the major rate-controlling hormone for both the immune and the cardiovascular systems as well as for the metabolism of individual cells—all varieties of wear-and-tear damage can be considerably accelerated on program. Hormones, as we know, can operate at any level of the cell, from the membrane to the nucleus, and can generate cascades of molecular events both inside and outside the cell (see chapters 7 and 8). It is worth a reminder that even if the main clock is a hormonal, brain program, it would still have to be turned on by the critical genes in the critical brain cells responsible for releasing the critical hormones at the appropriate times. So, just as surely as in an individual cellular clock, the carrying out of the task would be instigated by specific stretches of DNA.

The auxiliary genetic clock is the one in the nucleus of each cell, as shown by Hayflick. A cellular clock would make sense for at least two reasons. One is that, if our evolutionary theories are correct, organisms evolved from the individual cells that have become their components, however modified; and one would expect that these cells would still retain their own built-in clocks, though now under the restraints of the central control. The other reason is that a cellular clock would supplement nature's design—if nature's design it be—to age us and kill us off reasonably on schedule; a redundant, built-in, fail-safe mechanism, a backup system to do the job in case the primary system failed, should not be a surprising feature of any genetic aging program. Going beyond mere logic, however: how else would one explain how those WI-38 cells in Hayflick cultures age and die at such a consistent rate? To me the WI-38 phenomenon represents the carrying out of the cellular genetic program once it is turned loose from the restraints of the organism's primary hormonal controls.

If one assumes the existence of a genetic clock, perhaps two-phased, it is easier to understand how techniques such as cooling or calorie restriction might be able to slow down all aging damage by slowing down the program itself.

Now, how does all this unify things? Does it mean that wear-and-tear damage is illusory, that without dictation from the genes there would be none? There would, of course, be wear and tear, from both intrinsic and extrinsic causes, without any genetic program. But it would probably proceed at a much slower pace, and our body's repair systems would probably continue to be able to fix the damage for a much longer time. If the scheme I have outlined is anywhere near the truth, cross-linkage and lipofuscin accumulation and all the rest would occur without the need for free-radical bombardment, merely through encounters, over a lifetime, with the world's complexity. But free radicals probably serve as the main amplifier, multiplier, and accelerator of other kinds of wear and tear. And free radicals would continue to be generated, and free-radical damage to occur, even without the persistent goading of the aging clock, though probably not with anything like the same frequency and vehemence.

None of the theories of aging is really wrong, then. The designated events do undoubtedly occur, and they are usually responsible, to some degree, for other kinds of damage. Hence, as Alex Comfort pointed out, the ease of parlaying almost any such event or process into a reasonable theory of aging: if it were to go on long enough, the event or process could eventually do us in. If the free-radical theory unifies all the wear-and-tear theories, it does so by encompassing them in a manner that can explain the claims of each.

But what is not explained, to me at least, is how the relative consistency of aging rates and species-specific life spans could come about through purely random events. Hence, a larger unification is required. This can be achieved by hypothesizing—and adducing some evidence for—a genetically programmed aging, the built-in clock mechanism, which satisfies the intellect and explains the observed sequences of events in ways that wear-and-tear theories (all of which are themselves successfully encompassed in the clock theory) do not. Such is my own personal opinion, at any rate.

What all this tells us is that even if we were to discover and bring under our control the clocks of aging, we would—over the longer haul—still have wear-and-tear damage to deal with. Meanwhile, if we learned to deal with some of those ravages of wear and tear any time soon, we could surely improve the quality of our later years—and probably add to their number as well—without having to wait for a genetic aging program to be identified. The whole aging process as we now perceive it suggests many possible interventions along many possible pathways. Some of them will be spelled out in part two of this book.

But just to sketch out some idea of the potential anti-aging remedies that might be available to us:

To solve the puzzle of the brain's hormonal clock, let us suppose that Denckla is right. We would need to purify DECO and then devise an anti-DECO, or, better still, find DECO's natural inhibitor. Most pituitary hormones are assumed to have natural inhibitors, as well as "releasing factors," both made by the hypothalamus. In the absence of the inhibitor, it might still be easier to try to block DECO's releasing factor—which would be a much smaller molecule—than to block DECO itself.

As for the nuclear genetic clock in the individual cell, this should be manageable through genetic manipulation. A number of investigators believe that a genetic aging clock should be concentrated into a very few genes, perhaps a single "supergene" such as the major histocompatibility complex on a single chromosome.

Genetic-engineering techniques will also be used, of course, to heal injuries of the wear-and-tear type: to enhance DNA repair systems, for example, to shore up faltering gene expression or gene regulating capacities, to fix or replace missing or malfunctioning genes, to tighten up DNA supercoils that may have begun to unravel, to *loosen* DNA coils in some instances so as to let in "healing" information molecules. Genetic techniques might also be employed to shore up and regenerate various organs and systems.

Research on encapsulating and delivering enzymes to cells where certain enzymes are either absent or not working has already shown some early promise. It should be possible to find ways to replace or repair not only enzymes and hormones, but practically any other kinds of protein as well; or to rebuild them from their constituent components, perhaps under the direction of new or renovated genes.

We already have on hand a number of substances—antioxidants and free-radical scavengers—to deal with free-radical damage. More will surely surface, and we will learn much more precisely how to employ them effectively and safely. Among the other remedies suggested—and in some cases already tried—have been anti–cross-link substances and cross-link preventives, lipofuscin scavengers, membrane stabilizers, cell "eustatants" (stabilizers of coordinated functioning), DHEA, the anti-Parkinson drug L-dopa, memory enhancers, coolants, immune boosters such as thymosin.

The aging programs themselves may be slowed down by dietary measures—as simple as the careful and intelligent restriction of calorie intake which Roy Walford, for instance, is testing on his lab animals and on himself.

As our knowledge of body and mind grows ever more detailed and more sophisticated—and I am talking about knowledge at the molecular and even at the subatomic, quantum level on the one hand, as well as at the holistic level on the other—our interventions can grow both more precise and more intelligent.

It seems increasingly evident that we are, physiologically and biochemically speaking, unique individuals. Most of our knowledge so far has tended to be general, and so has our medical practice. But in the future, as our detailed knowledge of individuals grows along with our computerized capacity to store and to utilize that knowledge, one can envision the emergence of a new breed of health professional who will be practicing a much more individually tailored kind of prevention and therapy.

I recently heard Lewis Branscomb, chief scientist of IBM, talking about people's fears that computerization will mean ever-greater homogenization, with everything becoming increasingly alike; but Branscomb, citing shoes for an example, pointed out that whereas most of us now need to wear shoes that fit us only approximately, computerized manufacture will make it possible for all of us to have shoes that exactly fit our own unique, individual feet (even our left and right feet are not symmetrical, as we know from experience). The same kind of prospect might apply to future medicine. We have been learning to map our genes, tracing them to their sites on specific chromosomes. We have also begun—especially through techniques such as two-dimensional electrophoresis and high-pressure liquid chromatography—to make indexes of our proteins. Many scientists are confident that one day we will have mapped all our genes and indexed all our proteins—found ways, in fact, to do it on an individual basis, since no two of us are identical. All this information, or any part of it, could be called up on computer screens or readouts, along with our unique biochemical pathways and other individualized information, so that the health practitioner of the future could draw on this knowledge not merely to treat diseases but to maintain us in an optimal state of health for a much longer time.

I will be discussing, in part two, when we might expect some of the remedies and breakthroughs to occur, and how we might meanwhile, as individuals, devise practical individual prolongevity programs.

Can we do anything about aging? We surely can.

PART TWO

ENTERING THE AGE
OF PROLONGEVITY

Few people know how to be old.

> —Duc François de La Rochefoucauld
> *Maxims*

> *. . . I ceaselessly keep repeating, Live,*
> *live, that you may*
> *become better servants of God!*

They do not pause to consider what immense importance ten years more of life, and especially of healthy life, possess when we have reached mature age, the time, indeed, at which men appear to the best advantage in learning and virtue—two things which can never reach their perfection except with time.

> —Luigi Cornaro
> *Discorsi della vita sobria*

The universe that suckled us is a monster that does not care if we live or die—does not care if it itself grinds to a halt. It is fixed and blind, a robot programmed to kill. We are free and seeing; we can only try to outwit it at every turn to save our skins.

> —Annie Dillard
> *Pilgrim at Tinker Creek*

17

GOOD NEWS—WITHOUT BREAKTHROUGHS

NEARLY all descriptive accounts of the aging process—including most of what you have read so far in this book—emphasize the steady decline of virtually all powers and functions as the years go by. But it is time to pause for a reminder that this dismal picture, especially as applied to the healthy rather than the sickly older person, is somewhat exaggerated when one considers the total experience of living. For example, there is a fairly steady diminution of most of the body's capacities between the ages of, say, thirty and fifty. Yet the body has an enormous amount of built-in redundancy; we are like the car designed to go 150 miles an hour though we don't intend to drive it at more than 70. The fifty-year-old does not do as well under stressful circumstances as he did at thirty, nor does he recover as quickly from the effects of stress. But unless the stress is extreme, he may hardly notice the difference; under normal circumstances, he can do just about anything he did at thirty, and do it just about as well. Besides, some functions hardly ever decline at all, and some not until very close to the end of life.

If we look at the gastrointestinal processes in a healthy older person, as one example, we note that the secretion of hydrochloric acid in the stomach diminishes with age. So do the quantities of certain digestive enzymes in the stomach and elsewhere. We note, too, that a few substances, such as fat, iron, and calcium, are not so well absorbed as they once were. There also appears to be some liver atrophy. On the other hand, most proteins, sugars, vitamins, and minerals are absorbed without difficulty, and liver problems—

barring specific illness—seldom become serious, or, when they do, not until really advanced ages. And the simple truth is that the overall gastrointestinal functions are not noticeably impaired in healthy old people.

For what it's worth, and I guess some will consider it worth a lot, the healthy body's ability to metabolize alcohol remains constant throughout life.

The overall volume of blood in circulation—again, barring specific cardiovascular disease—hardly diminishes before eighty. Nor do circulating levels of the male hormone, testosterone, drop significantly until men reach their fifties or later, though sexual drive may be lowered for other reasons.

Until recently it was believed that the number of taste buds on the papillae of the tongue decreased significantly with age, but recent studies show that there is no such loss. The sense of smell does lessen, however, and this can affect taste sensations. So can certain other changes, such as an increased tendency for the mouth to dry out as its membranes produce less mucus.

Only a generation or two back, it was assumed that just about anyone who lived past the middle years would wind up with a full set of dentures. No longer. True, the tooth's surface enamel wears away somewhat, and decay or accident may account for a certain amount of tooth loss; by age thirty, most people have already begun to lose some teeth. Yet, with good dental care, a set of teeth may now remain perfectly serviceable throughout a long lifetime. The major dental problem associated with aging now seems to be periodontal disease, in which a loosening of tissue at the gumline opens up "pockets" between tooth and gum. In these spaces, well out of toothbrush reach, bacteria can take hold and make sometimes irreversible inroads, leading to bone and tooth loss. But new treatments now in the works may make it unnecessary, in another decade or two, to worry about such problems at all.

The lens of the eye tends to harden and thicken as we grow older, a tendency that, because it interferes with the eye's focusing efficiency, is rated as an impairment. But the accuracy of that definition depends on what your vision problems may be. The thickening of the lens can and often does reach a point where it actually cures farsightedness, and reading glasses can be discarded.

There are other incidental benefits as we grow older. We sweat less; we also hurt less, simply because our tolerance for pain goes up, especially as we move into the sixties. Some of our pituitary's functions improve, too. For instance, it does a better job of maintaining the body's water balance, perhaps as a tradeoff for declining kidney function.

We have heard a great deal about the hazards of obesity—and rightly so. At almost any age, a lot of extra poundage does indeed constitute a health problem. The heart works harder as we lug around all that excess baggage. The risk of heart disease goes up, as does the severity of other ailments, such as high blood pressure and diabetes. Being overweight, especially if it is the result of a diet high in fats, can also heighten the risk of developing certain types of cancer. Most of our lives, then, we are better off staying fit and trim. Yet for those who tend to be overweight there is, surprisingly, some good news.

As we reach, say our mid-sixties, a newly recognized and still mysterious factor comes into play. At these later ages, moderate overweight—ten to fifteen pounds, or even a bit (but only a bit) more—may actually enhance the odds of living longer. This startling—and still far from universally accepted—finding emerges from the work of NIA's Reubin Andres, who has for years been one of the major researchers conducting a massive "longitudinal study" (that is, observing the same people over a period of many years) at GRC/Baltimore. Basing his average desirable weight on the standard Metropolitan Life Insurance tables, Andres found that those who are somewhat overweight, though not grossly obese, in their sixties are more likely to be around in their eighties and nineties than are those whose weight is "just right" or under the average.

Intrigued by his findings and still skeptical because the results flew in the face of all medical wisdom, including his own, Andres sought out other statistical studies to see what correlations might exist between weight and longevity. He was able to find more than twenty studies in the world literature (several in the United States, others in the United Kingdom, Australia, Finland, and Japan), and though no single one of these studies is statistically ideal for Andres's purposes, in *no* study were the moderately overweight shown to die earlier than those who weighed less. Most of the studies demonstrated that the moderately overweight, on the average, did live longer.

We are still usually advised to "maintain ideal weight," but the definition of "ideal" is less clear in the light of Andres's findings.

There could be other explanations for the results, however, and other interpretations of them, so until a lot more, and more careful, research can be carried out, Andres warns that it is premature to tell anyone that extra weight in the later years is *good* for him, especially if he's diabetic. But he thinks it is safe to assure moderately overweight older people that they are probably no worse off than their skinnier contemporaries in terms of longevity.

The Andres results are especially puzzling in view of a seemingly contradictory ten-year study of 855 Swedish men carried out in Göteborg by Bo Larsson. Larsson's data suggest that for a man of fifty, being even moderately overweight increases his risk of developing hypertension, clinical diabetes, kidney stones, and gallstones by the time he is sixty! So "ideal weight" does seem important at fifty. What makes the difference as this same individual goes into his sixties and seventies? Or is this pattern not true for the same individual, but only for the "average" person?

We know that there is appreciable loss of lean body tissue with age, but this is more than compensated for by an increased *percentage* of fat. It could well be that old people, with their lowered immunity and diminished overall functioning, have greater need of emergency fat reserves, especially in winter. Besides, in our society, many old people either can't afford to eat properly or aren't motivated to do so. Excessive leanness, often equated with healthy slenderness, may actually be a sign of illness or malnutrition. When all these factors have been considered, however, Andres believes that the good news in terms of prolongevity for the somewhat overweight elderly is likely to hold up.

As already mentioned, sexual drive does seem to diminish as we age, but no one is sure how much of this is due to physiological aging and how much to psychological factors—the pressures of a career, overfamiliarity with a long-time partner, the effect of the perceptions and expectations of others, and what may be the current norms in regard to appropriate desires and behavior for older people. Whatever the reasons, we have known, at least since Kinsey (and, anecdotally, long before Kinsey), that the frequency of sex does decline. The pioneering work of Masters and Johnson has shown, however, that an individual of almost any age can function adequately as long as an interested and interesting partner is available. There are of course some physiological conditions that can render a person of either gender less interested in sexual activity, or less capable of carrying out such desires as exist. But as often as not, anxiety about performance is the precipitating cause, especially for the male who fails to realize that an occasional absence of desire or response doesn't mean his sex life is over, any more than his failure to want dinner on a given evening means that his appetite is gone forever. In general, there is no reason why healthy older people cannot continue to enjoy sex until almost the very end. A man, despite a lowered sperm count, is still capable of fathering children even into his eighties—though a woman's child-bearing days have ended long before that age.

Men tend to worry more than women do about the possible decline of sexual capacity, perhaps because "failure" is more visible, and such concerns are nurtured by the macho traditions of our culture. Apart from apprehension about prostate problems—surely a legitimate concern for every aging male (most men past eighty will have lost theirs through surgery), though such problems do not necessarily affect sexual functioning—the observant male may notice that his testes tend to sag and that his penis, as the years go by, erects more slowly and at a less upstanding angle. He also tends to take more time building up to orgasm and does not feel the need to ejaculate on every sexual occasion.* Despite all this, the older man may actually enjoy a distinct sexual advantage over younger men. What if the penis is slower to respond and slower to ejaculate? One hears much testimony that this only makes intercourse more pleasurable and satisfying for both parties. In a private enterprise as leisurely as lovemaking, why should endurance not be prized above speed? Experience counts, too. The same is true, of course, for women. Young men who prefer older women are not just being kind—except, perhaps, to themselves.

One of the more surprising recent findings in gerontology is that people can remain in perfect cardiovascular health up to ripe old ages. And when they do, their hearts can pump as much blood during vigorous exercise as those of the very young! This discovery arises from a series of intensive studies of sixty-one subjects—forty-seven men and fourteen women, ranging in age from twenty-five to seventy-nine—who were carefully selected from among the people

---

* A team of German researchers, late in 1984, reported a study of grandfathers in which healthy older males were shown to retain a sperm count and a degree of sperm motility not much different from those of younger men.

in NIA's ongoing longitudinal-study group. They were subjected to all the most rigorous and sophisticated tests known to cardiology in order to make sure that they were as free as possible from any hint of cardiovascular disease; those eliminated by these preliminary tests were still extraordinarily healthy specimens.

The finally selected "supernormals"—as they are called by NIA's Richard Greulich—were studied by Myron L. Weisfeldt, Gary Gerstenblith, and their heart-specialist colleagues at Johns Hopkins University, including Edward G. Lakatta, formerly of NIA. At the end of their study, they commented that, though "it has been generally accepted as a 'fact' of gerontology that a diminution in resting and exercise cardiac output is a manifestation of the adult aging process," on the basis of their data they concluded "that aging per se does not limit cardiac output either in subjects at rest or during vigorous exercise." Even under the most stressful tests—on stationary bicycles in the lab, for instance, where the subjects "rode" without letup as hard as they could until totally exhausted—those in their sixties and seventies maintained essentially the same cardiac output as those in their twenties and thirties. There was an important difference in how the bodies of the older people did the job, however: the heart rate did not increase nearly so much as that of the younger subjects, but the stroke volume—the amount of blood pumped with each heartbeat—increased, to compensate for the slower rate. The Johns Hopkins researchers think they have begun to understand the mechanisms of this change. But the fact remains that the seventy-nine-year-old could exercise with the same vigor, and with the same cardiac output, as the twenty-five-year-old. Though these supernormals constitute a distinct minority of the elderly population, it is clear that there are many people who, though they fall short of the "super" state, still remain healthy and disease-free, and can work and play with much of their former stamina.

Greulich, who heads the research program at NIA, says there is new interest in collecting groups of superhealthy older people, who are not only free of heart problems but who seem to have lost few of their energies or faculties over the years. He notes that, contrary to our stereotyped view of the aged as a group merging into a homogenized gray sameness, people actually get more and more different as they age—especially if they are healthy. Greulich believes that too much of our "knowledge" of the elderly emerges from our studies of pathology, and that we have not really paid much attention to health in old age.

Where this new interest in looking at the nonpathological aspects of aging—an interest that has grown up in the few years since *Prolongevity*—has paid off even more than in cardiology is in our changing views of mental function in old age. It was already understood that healthy older people undergo very little mental impairment;* that, though they learn new things more slowly, they learn them just as well as when they were younger; and that signs often interpreted as symptoms of senility are in fact due to the effects of, say, drugs or depression, and hence reversible. But the new publicity lavished on the senile dementias, especially Alzheimer's disease, has brought on new worries. At the first sign of memory loss, people wonder: Is this the beginning? They fear that any perceived lessening of their mental faculties is the start of a steep and steady decline. But, in the absence of real disease or brain damage, chances are that the decline is minor and not progressive. It usually does not keep getting worse. Like other investigators, Barry Riesberg of New York University has found that most of these worries are groundless; that, in fact, the worriers are the ones who usually don't have to worry—the elderly person who really has a mental problem probably isn't aware of it.

In chapter 14, I spoke of brain-cell loss with aging. And there seems little doubt that the brain does shrink. By the time the average individual moves into his sixties, Harvard's Marjorie LeMay estimates, his brain has lost about three ounces of its original three pounds of substance. Again, however, if there is no disease or damage, this may not mean much more than, say, the loss or graying of hair. We noted earlier that the brain not only lost some of its neuronal tissue, but also underwent a number of changes in its neurochemical processes. But this need not be interpreted, as it traditionally has been, in terms of functional decline; the brain may simply be carrying out its work via another route, as the healthy heart seems to. Long-term studies at the University of Southern

---

* John S. Thompson and his collaborators at the University of Kentucky, studying a group of centenarians, concluded that about a third of those who pass the age of 100 remain mentally alert—as well as physically active and free of major illnesses, perhaps because their immune systems remain surprisingly efficient.

California have demonstrated that healthy people tend to retain most of their intellectual capacities, and some even do better than ever in standard testing as they enter their seventies and eighties!

The most encouraging and exciting of the newer studies are those that have been able to take imaginative advantage of advanced techniques to probe what happens—and what can happen—in the cells and tissues of the aging brain. Scientists whose specialty is the early part of life have for years used what they call the "enriched environment" as a means of studying the impact of extra "stimulus nutrition" on young, developing brains. One of the pioneering investigators in this area was the late David Krech of the University of California at Berkeley. He and his collaborators built a complicated nursery school for young rats, a veritable Disneyland of toys, games, mazes, swings, slides, and other challenges and entertainments. Rats raised in these surroundings were much more alert and intelligent than those who went through the standard, ho-hum routines in the lab. Moreover, their brains were heavier and contained a much greater number not only of neurons but of their supporting glial cells as well; and they were characterized by much more intricate neural networks. Any number of variations on these methods by many investigators led to the enthusiastic use of enriched environments and stimulus nutrition for the improved development of human infants and children.

Now another Berkeley scientist, Marian Diamond, has hit upon the brilliant idea of applying these techniques—for the first time, as far as I can find out—to the study of aging rats, and with equally startling results. Like Krech's young rats, Diamond's elderly ones also look forward to the excitement of their playgroundlike environments and to the special care and attention they receive; they are brighter, and more exploratory in their behavior; their brains get bigger (tissues seem to be added especially to the cerebral cortex) and presumably better. These are two- and three-year-old rats, well qualified for senior citizenship in this breed of rodents—and they not only keep learning and continue to function well, but often live up to 30 percent longer than would otherwise be expected. All of which upholds the long-standing observations that older human beings who maintain a diversity of interests and enthusiasms, and who keep up their supportive social networks, tend to stay healthier and live longer than those who choose to sit around listlessly waiting for the end.

In earlier chapters we discussed accelerated aging in nature. In the case of the Pacific salmon, we saw that the fish's rapid senescence after spawning was due, as in the human Cushing's syndrome, to an overproduction of cortisonelike steroid hormones. And we speculated that this is what could happen in human cells as a result of Denckla's aging hormone, DECO. Recently Phillip Landfield and his associates at North Carolina's Bowman-Gray School of Medicine have succeeded in changing the rate of aging—or at least the signs that are interpreted as aging—in rat brains by manipulating the levels of these steroid hormones. When excess steroids were injected, brain aging was speeded up; when the adrenal glands were surgically removed, thus cutting off the main supply of steroids, brain aging was slowed down. These preliminary results suggest some fascinating future possibilities for adding to the gerontological repertoire yet another means of hormonal manipulation to modulate senescent changes in the brain.

You may recall from chapter 14 the charming notion put forth by Dawkins that the loss of neurons in the brain might be likened to the chipping away of excess stone by a sculptor in order to reveal the finished piece of art—the mature human brain. Marian Diamond's experiments certainly imply that the more the brain is stimulated, even in advanced age, the more tissue there is to keep stimulating. Now Paul Coleman of the University of Rochester, through autopsies of healthy human brains (the cause of death was elsewhere, in each case), has shown that even in the later years, from the sixties through the nineties, the neurons' "dendritic trees," those complex, many-branched extensions that make up the intricately interconnected networks through which the brain cells interact, keep growing longer and continue to make new connections. Could this be the sculpturing that Dawkins's fancy suggested? I like to think that those ever-more-enmeshing neuronal webs represent the special kind of knowledge and understanding that can come only with seasoning, with the experience of being in the world over an extended period of time. In other words, the very stuff that wisdom is made of.

Perhaps the most astonishing of the hopeful good-news items about the brain applies with certainty, so far, only to the brains of songbirds. Entrenched with the force of dogma (and I have been passing this dogma along to you intact up to this point) is the fact that brain cells do not regenerate. Once the adult brain is formed, no new neurons are ever again born, and once dead they are dead to stay. They are among those postmitotic cells that just last as long as they last. The only known exception to this rule has been the growth of new neurons in fish—not particularly surprising, since both the bodies and brains of fish do continue to grow in adulthood. But in 1984 Fernando Nottebohm and his collaborators at Rockefeller University discovered that, in the forebrains of songbirds (canaries are the most studied thus far), hosts of neurons die, and hosts of others are born, not once, but again and again—and the phenomenon occurs *after* sexual maturity. There is a very clearly specified part of the bird's forebrain that governs singing behavior, and it is mostly (though not entirely) in this area that the neuronal turnover occurs. The birds sing through the breeding season in spring, and stop singing in late summer. Then, in the fall, they start learning the songs they will need for the following year's breeding season. With the new learning process, new neurons are formed—at times, as many as 20,000 a day! There is plenty of room for the new neurons only because, after the most recent breeding season ended, the critical forebrain areas had lost nearly 40 percent of their old neurons.

This finding, says Nottebohm (quoted by Gina Kolata in *Science*), "is so contrary to anything we anticipated that we are not yet prepared to sound intelligent when we talk about it." Nevertheless, he does risk talking about it, in this same article. Asked about the possibility that new neurons might grow in human brains, he replied, "From all we know of nervous systems, we get the impression that principles of function are widespread across taxonomic phyla. We ought to apply ourselves to see if adult neurogenesis occurs in humans. And if it is not found, we should ask, Why not? What is preventing it? Can it be induced?"

In some earlier experiments, there were reports that new neurons had appeared in the adult brains of rodents, but these results were not taken seriously because it is tremendously difficult to prove that new neurons really are new neurons. Nottebohm, faced with the same problem, enlisted the support of a Rockefeller colleague, John A. Paton, and between them they went through a series of tedious and painstaking experiments that finally proved to their satisfaction that there could be no mistake about what they had discovered. In light of their findings, and with newly developed techniques to employ, someone is no doubt already repeating the experiments with rodents. If one kind of mammalian brain can produce new neurons, why can't the brain of another species do the same? So we have the hope that the human brain, too, may be replacing some of its dead neurons, after all.

Even if it turns out that the no-new-neurons dogma holds up for the human brain, we may still learn some practical tricks from the birds. The regeneration of their neurons seems to be under some kind of hormonal control. Nottebohm obviously does not deem it ridiculous to hope that once we learn the mechanism of how the bird brains grow new cells we can use that knowledge to induce our brains to do likewise—especially to replace cells lost through injury or stroke—without having to carry out the kind of fetal brain transplants discussed in chapter 14. It would meanwhile be very interesting, of course, to know whether those very healthy, supernormal elderly adults are in fact able to keep producing new brain cells while they are at the same time increasing the complexity of their circuitry.

Though most of us—even those who are lucky enough to avoid the serious ailments that so often afflict the later years—could never qualify for the select groups of the supernormal elderly that Greulich speaks of, all these new explorations do offer us the hope that we can grow old with a modicum of grace and vigor. Each of us may be able to take advantage of the good news, without waiting for the gerontological breakthroughs. For those of us whose heritage includes genetic susceptibilities or predispositions to various ailments, the task is more difficult. But it now becomes feasible to examine how we live, and ask what we might change in order to enhance our personal chances for prolongevity.

The small population of supernormals seem to have achieved one of gerontology's major goals—abolishing "old age" as we have always known it. They maintain superior health even through their ripest years, and the rest of us may look forward eagerly to what we can learn from studying them. Chances are that good fortune and good genetics play a key role in the maintenance of their phenomenal staying power. But even those less blessed may pick up some useful insights that can be applied to their own lives. Meanwhile, the very existence of these supernormals among us makes it easier to believe that gerontological success can do as much, or more, for all of us.

18

STRATEGIES AND FORECASTS

JUST ABOUT the time I was arriving at roughly this point in *Prolongevity*, and trying to look ahead a few chapters, I wrote to a doctor who, I had been given to understand, concerned himself officially with the social consequences of longevity on behalf of one of the state departments of health. I asked him if he might help me speculate about the consequences of an increased human life span. His reply was thoughtful and useful within the scope of longevity problems as currently defined—those created mainly by the fact that an ever-growing proportion of the population are reaching old age. But he readily admitted, "I have not dealt with the hypothesis you raise, that in fact longevity will be increased," which he regarded as an "unlikely event." He went on even more explicitly: "While speculation on the effects that increasing life span would have is fascinating, you will realize that most physicians believe it is in the realm of science fiction, rather than practical possibility." He was neither chiding nor chastising me, but simply pointing out, in a gentle, kindly way, a fact I might not be aware of.

His attitude, of course, did, and still does, prevail within the medical community—and, for that matter, among the majority of mainstream gerontologists. But we really have reached a point in our understanding when such complete skepticism, however justified it may have been in the past, is becoming untenable. I do hope that by now I have offered sufficiently persuasive evidence and arguments to convince you that the possibility of an extended human life span has moved out of the realm of science fiction.

It would be fatuous to forecast a precise timetable of developments in the field of prolongevity. Too much depends on the availability of research funds, the motivations and creative limitations of individual investigators, good luck or bad luck, unforeseen obstacles. Especially baffling to the nonscientific observer of research in the biomedical sciences is the way promising work may suddenly be dropped—perhaps because the investigator didn't get his renewal grant for that project but did get money for something else, or because he moved to another lab or university to become department head and no longer had time for research, or for any one of a variety of reasons, personal or professional. And the work may be picked up by someone else, or it may not be.

(In fields like cancer and heart disease, promising research is much less likely to be abandoned, because the goals are more clearly defined and the commitment to arrive at solutions—at therapies, cures, or preventive measures—has been made by large numbers of dedicated investigators in the scientific mainstream, who are supported by large amounts of money. In the field of aging, there does not yet exist a real belief in many quarters that anything much can be done about the aging process, even though one can often see in gerontology the directions in which research might fruitfully progress—not always the case in areas such as cancer and heart disease.)

In writing *Prolongevity II*, for instance, I have had the not uncommon experience of calling a researcher's former university or institution—where he seemed to be moving full-speed-ahead eight years ago, at the time of *Prolongevity*—and find that no one in his department seems to remember him or knows where he is now working. And, in terms of trying to forecast timetables, what does one make of a turnabout such as that of Donner Denckla, who has lost not only his research funds but also his inclination to proceed, since he thinks the world is not yet mature enough to handle the power to control the clock of aging in a sensible fashion? Meanwhile, one must scout around to see who else is pursuing a particular line of research, and with what kind of vigor, and with what chances of success—and then try to guess if and when that success might arrive.

We may reasonably hope, nevertheless, that with a bit of good luck and not too much bad luck, modest breakthroughs will begin to occur within a few decades, well within the lifetimes of many now living. It could begin to happen sooner—or later. We have to be honest about our lack of predictive evidence. Strehler has guessed that we might know the essential answers to the aging process before the century is out, whereas Hayflick believes that, in view of the skimpy resources being devoted to gerontology compared with the enormous sums going to other areas of research, it is overoptimistic to think we'll have answers of real substance before some time into the next century. More will agree with Hayflick than with Strehler (though Walford is among those who have lately joined Strehler), but almost everyone agrees that we do not have to wait until we know everything about aging in order to take practical advantage of what we do know. Edward Jenner, after all, developed his small-pox vaccination without ever understanding much about why or how it worked. We do not yet altogether understand the precise mechanisms of many common medications and therapies that have been in everyday use for a long time. It is only recently, with the discovery of the prostaglandins, that we have acquired some real insight into how aspirin works.

Because research will proceed on many fronts and at many levels simultaneously, it is doubtful that practical applications will come in any orderly, step-by-step sequence. For an indefinite period, while gerontologists seek the more comprehensive solutions, we will continue to do what medicine has sought to do all along—to cure or prevent diseases or palliate their symptoms; to combat or hold off the ravages of wear and tear in whatever piecemeal fashion presents itself.

Conventional biomedical scientists still look to the conquest of the major killer diseases as our most realistic route to an increased life expectancy. But, as we have already seen, crash programs dedicated to the one-by-one elimination of these ailments offer no guarantees of solution. A more sensible and more economical way to attack the remaining degenerative diseases might be to seek the key to the aging process itself. Most of the major diseases seem to come in two varieties, a childhood (early-onset) and an adult (late-onset) form. Thus we have the childhood cancers, juvenile diabetes, juvenile arthritis, the early-onset heart diseases, the early varieties of mental retardation, and the like. These constitute a relatively small percentage (though a large number) of the victims of the diseases in question, and they are generally believed to be mainly genetic in nature. The vast majority of such ailments come late in life and are viewed by many as inevitable accompaniments of the aging process itself, though genetics may still play an important role in terms of individual susceptibility. (A Pittsburgh cancer investigator recently said to me: "You want to cut the cancer rate by much more than ninety percent? Just arrange to have everybody die at the age of forty.") This does not mean that I think we should trim our commitment to these other very necessary avenues of research, only that we should put a bit more into aging research—enough more to make a difference.

Much of our aging research today is concentrated on the care of the elderly ill—and that, too, is necessary, because those who have present needs cannot wait for future developments. The care of those elderly today, even though that "care" often amounts to not much more than warehousing them in nursing homes while they wait to die, costs enormous sums of money; it's been estimated that, within a decade or so, the appropriations for such care will rival those of our defense budget. If we are mainly looking for ways to help these patients be more comfortable, to adjust better, to achieve small increments of improved health and well-being, we will be behaving as, say, the March of Dimes might have done had it chosen to spend all its polio money on improved iron lungs and better rehabilitation techniques instead of seeking, and finding, preventive vaccines.

The gerontological equivalent of the polio vaccine would be some inhibitor of the basic aging process. But even if we were to push ahead successfully to such a solution, there would still be the problem of wear and tear. If we had at hand right now the control mechanisms for all the genetic clocks, and could effectively employ those controls, our bodies and the individual cells within them would still be subject to the hazards that go with mere existence in the world. To be sure—as already pointed out—if we had the secret on/off switches at our command, we could hope to keep our self-repair systems operating for essentially indefinite time spans; thus wear and tear would proceed at a much statelier pace. Even so, we might have to find external methods of coping with some types of damage and erosion. The fortunate paradox is that wear and tear, which might be one of the last aging problems we overcome, is one of the first we can begin to take effective measures against.

Biomedical scientists of all persuasions will of course continue to seek new surgeries, new medications, new treatments, new vaccines, new theoretical approaches. To replace worn-out parts, transplantation techniques will be perfected and the immunological barrier overcome; and ever more sophisticated replacements will be devised. A concomitant hope is that the human body can be taught to regenerate its own missing or malfunctioning parts, as some other creatures do, though this kind of achievement may also (though not necessarily) require a detailed understanding of the genetic controls. As for specific anti-aging therapies, a number of promising drugs—and suggestions for changes in life style—are already with us. Several are undergoing animal testing; others, limited human testing.

One of the most interesting developments since *Prolongevity*, in terms of possible rapid human self-application, is the finding that the steadfast restriction of calories—carried out so that good nutrition is maintained throughout—can increase the life spans of animals even when begun in adulthood. This work and its consequences are best spelled out in Roy Walford's book *Maximum Life Span*. (Remember that, in 1976, all of us, including Walford, believed that calorie restriction could extend life only if begun before puberty, thus holding little practical value for individuals who have reached the age of competence to decide whether or not they wish to use themselves as experimental subjects.) As mentioned earlier, Walford has begun to carry out his dietary techniques on himself as part of his own personal prolongevity program. What he does will be described in the next chapter.

An example of the search for piecemeal remedies is the study of lipofuscin. You will recall that this is the dark, fatty, probably heterogeneous "old-age pigment" that represents the gradual accumulation, over the years, of unsatisfactorily disposed-of cellular garbage. Lipofuscin is to be found most plentifully, as might be expected, in nerve and muscle cells, which do not renew themselves after maturity and do not have the advantage of the cells that go on dividing; in the mitotic cells of the skin and gut, for instance, waste matter is continually being diffused throughout the constantly self-renewing cellular bodies.

Though few investigators look upon lipofuscin as a cause of aging, most believe it is certainly a symptom of aging—probably harmless through most of life. As the wastes take up more and more of the cells' spaces, however, particularly in neurons, they may well interfere with cellular functions, and therefore with overall activity—including mental activity, where brain cells are involved. Can the wastes be cleared away, or prevented from forming at all?

There is no common agreement yet as to what causes lipofuscin to arise, though more and more gerontologists are convinced that it must be the result of oxidation reactions, which turn loose free radicals to do their various kinds of damage, including the cross-linking of molecules inside the cell as well as outside it—for example, in the connective tissue's collagen molecules. In that case, anything that might combat or correct free-radical damage, or mop up free radicals before they can wreak their mischief, might reasonably be expected to reduce lipofuscin accumulations as well. This would only be one of many—and certainly not the most important—of the wear-and-tear processes that might be considerably reduced if not eliminated by the use of antioxidant substances (see next chapter).

To stay with lipofuscin for a while, though, much of it seems to accumulate in the membranes of the cell's mitochondria, but a lot may also end up in the organelles known as lysosomes; among other functions, they serve as the cells' garbage-disposal units. When lysosomal membranes are damaged, harmful substances leaking through them may be responsible for many deteriorative changes. This has been the view, for instance, of Richard Hochschild, who, in addition to carrying out his own continuing private research in Corona del Mar, California, acts as scientific director of the Glenn Foundation for Medical Research, whose main interest is aging. Acting on what was at first only a hunch, Hochschild decided to try a natural substance called DMAE (for dimethylaminoethanol) as a possible retarder of senescence, because DMAE was known to be a lysosome-membrane stabilizer. By adding DMAE to the drinking water of mice, Hochschild was able to increase their life span significantly. A closely related derivative of DMAE was actually marketed for some years by a pharmaceutical house under the trade name of Deaner, but not for the uses Hochschild envisioned (though at least a few physicians—among them Richmond's William Regelson—did employ it with some success in relieving symptoms of senility). It has now been taken off the market, because not enough of it was being sold, though it has recently become easily available from health-food stores. But the research that would be required to validate it as a treatment for the mental problems of aging has never been, and may never be, done. Thus our knowledge remains sadly incomplete. To use on a casual basis any substance that affects the brain and central nervous system is never advisable. (NYU's Harry Demopoulos, for instance, believes that DMAE could cause convulsions in susceptible individuals.) The frustrating experience with DMAE—whose efficacy, I would have guessed, in 1975, would be either proved or disproved by now—serves as a good example of the difficulties inherent in trying to make accurate time predictions.

Other investigators, notably Kalidas Nandy, have successfully employed a synthetic compound derived in part from DMAE—centrophenoxine—to retard the formation of lipofuscin in the brains of guinea pigs. In France, where centrophenoxine was first synthesized and shown to have almost no toxic side effects, the drug has been used with apparent success to improve the impaired mental capacities of senile human patients. Paul Gordon, then at Northwestern, was truly intrigued by the action of centrophenoxine. Its "apparent reversal of lipofuscin deposition," he wrote at the time, "is fascinating, and indicates that latent lipofuscin scavenging mechanisms may be activated, to the advantage of the aging organism." Just as he believed that centrophenoxine might be triggering the cell's own latent capacities rather than attacking lipofuscin as a direct garbage-cleanup agent, so did Gordon believe that Hochschild's DMAE might simply be activating or enhancing the cell's own self-repair mechanisms rather than itself plugging the leaks in the lysosomal membranes. Gordon had been personally experimenting with yet another drug related to DMAE—isoprinosine—and found that it "partially reverses the deteriorated brain functioning of aging rats."

Centrophenoxine, however, ran into unfortunate troubles in the United States—and this again underlines the built-in difficulties of forecasting. In the American clinical trials, which Nandy still maintains were faulty studies, poorly conceived and poorly carried out, a couple of the elderly subjects died of heart attacks while taking centrophenoxine. Thus heart attacks were presumed to be one of the hazardous side effects of the drug, and it never won FDA approval. But Nandy claims that no other experiments, either in this country or abroad, showed any such side effects, that there is no logical or biochemical reason why centrophenoxine should cause any cardiovascular problems, and that in fact in any experimental group of elderly patients, already ill, one would expect a couple to die of heart attacks over a period of time, even if they were on no medication at all; but, says Nandy, the experimental design simply did not take this into account.

Nevertheless, the damage was done. No one else was willing to invest the resources necessary to pursue the drug's potential beneficial uses, and the French company finally gave up trying to market it in the United States. Now the patent has run out, and the likelihood that any pharmaceutical house will make the investment is dim indeed. There ought to be some channel through which the requisite research can be carried out on such promising substances; and, if warranted, they should be placed in the pharmacopeia for the benefit of all the physicians who have become aware of the increasingly widespread nature of the senile dementias, especially Alzheimer's disease. Chances are that the NIH or some other federal agency will take up the challenge, but when that might happen is anybody's guess.

Meanwhile, a variety of substances are being pursued for the same ends—the enhancement of failing memory and other mental and intellectual deficiencies of aging. They are in various stages of experimentation, and most investigators predict that it will take a few years to get them on the market. There do exist drugs such as Hydergine (already available by prescription, it could be much more effective, a few physicians contend, if given in larger dosages— perhaps three times as high as currently recommended—a regimen they have tried, with apparent safety and success, but only on a few of their patients) and Gerovital (H3), the well-publicized drug developed by Ana Aslan of the Bucharest Geriatric Institute; but the Rumanian doctor's claims remain highly controversial, and Gerovital (really just a 2-percent novocaine injection) has failed to gain acceptance in the United States.

Previous chapters have already emphasized the effectiveness of a number of antioxidant substances in counteracting free-radical damage. Jaime Miquel of NASA's Ames Research Center has increased the life spans of fruit flies and mice with antioxidants, and numerous others—among them Harman and Tappel—have had similar success with animals. Demopoulos has moved on to testing antioxidants in fairly large dosages on human volunteer subjects, and, having satisfied himself as to their safety, has been pleased enough with the results to start marketing some of them on his own. Walford is another investigator who has allowed his laboratory enterprise to spill over into a commercial enterprise. Meanwhile, Robert Kohn in Cleveland and Bjorksten in Madison have been testing, with some preliminary success, agents that appear to undo collagen damage and combat cross-linkage.

There is already available, then, a diverse array of potentially useful substances, and this account does not begin to represent anything like a complete sampling of the catalogue of lipofuscin inhibitors, anti–cross-link chemicals, antioxidants, immunoregulators (including the interferons), hormones (including the thymosins as well as DHEA and its derivatives), coolants, enzymes, and other agents that offer real hope of alleviating or retarding, in some measure and at least temporarily, many of the deleterious effects of aging. A number of pharmaceutical houses are of course following these experiments; some are actively engaged in them.

At least a few of the experimental substances will clearly be testable in the almost immediate future. It could certainly be established with reasonable speed—as Comfort, Harman, Hayflick, and others have pointed out—whether or not antioxidants are truly effective as anti-aging therapy and which antioxidants are the safest and most potent. Such research would not have to wait for any new basic information to come in. One problem is that most of the known antioxidant substances that seem safe enough for human use (vitamins C and E, some of the B vitamins, beta-carotene, glutathione, selenium, and the like) are not patentable. Thus no one is going to go to the considerable trouble and expense necessary to prove their efficacy. Meanwhile, they are readily salable in health-food stores everywhere as long as no specific health claims are made for them, so there is little motivation for those who sell them to carry out the research that would prove or disprove their true value.

Many experimental drugs, such as the unnamed compound used by Barnett Rosenberg and Gabor Kemeny to lower temperature, have had such erratic side effects that they will undoubtedly require a long period of testing in animals before anyone is willing to try them on people. Centrophenoxine could be tried again on human patients, but the obstacles to that have already been described; it may turn out, however, that antioxidants (assuming they prove to be effective) will also prove to be good lipofuscin inhibitors, since free radicals are believed to generate the cascades of events that end up in lipofuscin formation. The family of thymosins, already undergoing human testing in cancer, autoimmune, and immunodeficiency diseases, is another likely candidate for anti-aging trials. Its importance will depend on how vital the maintenance of a high level of cell-mediated immunity is to the aging organism.

In studying the proportions of numerous neurotransmitters present in the brain at any given time, Paola Timiras and Paul Segall at Berkeley discovered rising levels of serotonin with age, but they also discovered that levels of dopamine go *down*. And, indeed, the late George Cotzias and his associates at Brookhaven used L-dopa (developed as a medication for Parkinsonism), which stimulates dopamine production, to retard aging in laboratory animals. So L-dopa may be added to the list of potential anti-aging drugs.*

Some purely dietary therapies, now outside the boundaries of conventional scientific interest, may as time goes on earn more attention from the geriatric/gerontological community. These include the regimen suggested by the late Benjamin Frank and carried on, with her own modifications, by his former assistant Carmen Fusco, now associated with the New York Medical College in Valhalla. At Chebotarev's institute in Kiev, gerontologists have been much readier than American scientists to test the possible efficacy of unorthodox remedies, among them that highly nutritious secretion of the honeybee's pharyngeal glands known as "royal jelly" (because it is fed to all queen larvae); Ana Aslan's Gerovital; and Academician V. P. Filatov's "tissue therapy"—which, with its use of placental tissue, is somewhat reminiscent of Swiss cellular therapy. The Kiev group have also concocted a number of experimental mixtures of their own, including a multivitamin complex they have named Decamevit (already in wide use in the Soviet Union) and a hormonal preparation called Nerobol. In addition, I. I. Brekham, a physiologist at the Institute of Marine Biology in Vladivostok, has found merit in extracts of the wild plant *Eleutherococcus senticosus*, which, because of its family relationship to ginseng—source of the time-honored Chinese and Korean tonic—is known in the United States as "Siberian ginseng."

Though the Russian researchers have reported good results in terms of improving the health and mental capacities of the aged with a number of these preparations, they are cautious about their indiscriminate use until they are better understood. In Chebotarev's own words: "It should be stressed . . . that there is as yet no sufficiently explicit, objective information pertaining to the pharmacodynamics of these agents, to their indication for use in the treatment of the aged." Nevertheless, in view of the number of

---

* Soviet scientists, too, have claimed anti-aging effects for L-dopa, as well as for other commonly used drugs, among them the antidiabetic, phenformin, and the anticonvulsant, dilantin.

drugs now being prescribed—from digitalis to reserpine—which were originally folk remedies, science should not hesitate to investigate thoroughly substances that do seem to do some good.

A vast amount of data has been accumulated on the biochemical consequences of aging. Kanungo, for example, in a long review article in *Biochemical Reviews*, lists dozens of such changes; since that survey was done in 1970, the list would have grown much longer. Enzyme levels may be especially important as indicators of the aging process. The quantity and activity of hundreds of different kinds of enzymes change with age. If it becomes known with certainty that the absence or lowered activity of identifiable enzymes is responsible for the loss of function, then perhaps those enzymes, or enzyme activators, can be supplied artificially, either orally or by injection. If, on the other hand, functional loss is invariably associated with an increase in either the quantity or the activity of various other enzymes, then perhaps specific inhibitors can be found for *those* enzymes. Thus one can envision a kind of enzyme and antienzyme cocktail mix or injection as an anti-aging treatment—though each ingredient would have to be added with great care, with sure knowledge of its role in aging. An indiscriminate mixture of enzymes might supply some that were already in oversupply and thus accelerate aging. It should be emphasized here that getting enzymes to specific cells where they are needed—especially to brain and nerve cells— is no easy matter, but scientists working in the field of enzyme replacement therapy are confident that someone will figure out a way to do it.

Obviously, if one is able to treat successfully the specific consequences of the aging process, one would wish to target those consequences that have other consequences, those that cause what Finch has called "cascade effects." These effects were worked out mathematically some years ago by Strehler and A. S. Mildvan in a well-known but complex theory that predicts the decline in an organism's "viability index," based on the total impact of all the aging factors that influence it. Thus, if properly targeted, some purely symptomatic treatments could result in keeping the viability index much higher for much longer periods of time.

In the end, though, no matter how many antidotes we may find for specific kinds of wear and tear, no matter how many diseases we cure or prevent, if we do nothing about the basic aging process, then we still die when our genetic program runs out. Hayflick envisions people who had not even been ill suddenly dropping dead at the age of, say, a hundred—going all at once, like "the wonderful one-hoss shay." He considers this a laudable outcome, however— as did the late René Dubos. Dubos had some doubts about the wisdom, or even the morality, of extending the human life span, but felt it would be an unmitigated good to keep people in the best of health through all the years for which they had been programmed. To keep people fully functional and in possession of all their faculties until the very end has been the noncontroversial goal of gerontology, conforming with the stated aim of the Gerontological Society to add life to years rather than years to life.

Nevertheless, many gerontologists, and many of the citizens who support their work, will not want to stop there. And it may be unreasonable as well as undesirable, as knowledge accumulates, to expect them to stop there. A major goal—despite its controversial aspects—is still the real extension of the maximum human life span, for significant periods of time.

If Denckla is right about a hormonal, brain-based clock of aging, then that hormonal quest (no longer his for now, since, as stated previously, he has indefinitely postponed his participation in it), if crowned with success, certainly moves us toward that goal. Denckla's plan, as of the mid-1970s, was first to isolate and synthesize DECO, then to create an anti-DECO that would destroy the death hormone and counteract its influence—a tedious business at best, even if findings were to fit theories. It would still be tedious with today's considerably easier and speedier methods for synthesizing all proteins, including hormones.

There could have been—and may yet be—a shortcut, however. Once DECO, the death hormone, is better identified and defined, we will be better able to identify the releasing factor by which the hypothalamus presumably instructs the pituitary to produce the hormone. There appears to be a separate releasing factor (RF) for every pituitary hormone. The RFs thus far discovered, principally by Roger Guillemin and his colleagues, are much smaller and simpler molecules than the pituitary hormones they control. Thus, instead of having to synthesize a complex hormone and create an equally complex antihormone, we could hope to work with DECO's own RF and construct a substance that inhibits *its* release by the hypothalamus. This would enormously simplify the task—though it still could not be called anything like a simple task.

Even better than this scenario is an alternate—and a feasible—one. Just as the hypothalamus seems to produce and release, at the appropriate times, the RFs that trigger hormone secretion by the pituitary, so does the hypothalamus know how to produce *natural inhibitors* to each of the pituitary hormones (though some of these substances may also be made elsewhere in the body). We already have both the RF and the inhibitor for growth hormone, for example. If we had DECO, perhaps we could do as well by it. Then all we would need to do is isolate and synthesize the inhibitor. (One of the newer birth-control pills works on exactly this principle—using a synthesized inhibitor to block the hormone.) In either case, the hoped-for result would be the inhibition of DECO release by the pituitary. Thus the programmed blockade of thyroid hormone—and whatever other events DECO caused—would not come to pass, and cells would not age, except for the overlay of wear-and-tear damage—which, by then, might have been largely overcome.

If we were able to abort the hormonal clock in this manner, that would be one genetic program down—but perhaps still one to go: the cell's own nuclear, genetic clock. To affect this in any substantial way, one would of course first have to identify and locate it; then, depending on how many genes or how many chromosomes were involved, the techniques of genetic engineering would have to be applied. We are not yet anywhere near this kind of gene-manipulating ability; but, considering how much further we have come with genetic technology in the past decade than we would have dared dream we could, it would be foolish to rule out the possibility that, by the time we locate the genetic clock, we could slow it down, or even set it back.

In these discussions about what might happen and when, I have so far been ignoring one thorny problem. Let us now suppose that we already have at hand anti-aging chemicals, enzyme cocktails, "pacemaker" hormones and their inhibitors to regulate the rate of aging, or genetic-engineering clock-fixing capabilities, or any combination of these—thoroughly tested in the laboratory and found to possess no serious side effects. The question is this: how can we test these therapies on people and, within a reasonable period of time, prove that the aging process has really been interfered with, that the subjects' lives are really being prolonged, or the rate of aging slowed down?

It would seem that we would have to wait an entire lifetime to see if a given individual died on schedule or not. And the criteria by which we could fix an arbitrary figure for anyone's "scheduled" demise would be difficult indeed to establish. True, if enough people in a given population, all taking the therapy, began to live far longer than members of the same population who were not on the anti-aging regimen, then we could begin to feel some confidence that the therapy was working. But it would surely require statistically significant quantities of people over several generations—not just a few hardy individuals here and there putting new life-span limits in the *Guinness Book of Records*—to prove both efficacy and safety. This means that the gerontologists who started the project would probably not live to see the end of it (though they might well be tempted to try, by making use of their own treatments or elixirs, tested or not). And would the next generation of gerontologists care? Would the money continue to come forth to meet the expenses of such a large-scale undertaking over so long a time—especially if it were dependent upon the vagaries of governmental appropriations? Exactly such considerations have often in the past discouraged biologists from entering this field of research. Investigators like to see the end results of their work; hence their preference for short-lived, quick-turnover species—*E. coli*, rotifers, nematodes, *Drosophila*, rodents.

Such obstacles pose formidable difficulties even for the dauntless. Fortunately, some realistic shortcuts may exist. Their success would depend on our ability to establish reliable measurements to determine an individual's rate of aging over relatively short periods of time. We might then test a given remedy's effectiveness by monitoring the significant aging factors to see if their rate was indeed slowing down.

Such a battery of tests to determine aging changes in the short run was proposed by Alex Comfort in 1969. Because individual human beings do tend to age in different ways at different rates when specific functions are measured, it would be important, in devising an array of tests, to select functions that could be counted on to change steadily and irreversibly with age in virtually all individuals. Measurements of such variables as serum-cholesterol levels or blood pressure would not do because, although these are factors usually associated with aging and degenerative diseases, they do not decline steadily; they tend, rather, to go up and down somewhat erratically during any given time. The chosen functions would also have to diminish in clearly measurable increments over relatively short periods—say, three to five years—so that meaningful experiments could be carried out within that kind of time span.

Comfort suggested that the subjects be around fifty years old at the start, and that they be men in order to "avoid further statistical breakdown and complications associated with differences in age of menopause, which affects some variables."

A great deal of data on the decline of physiological functions with aging has been massed over the years in a number of longitudinal studies, most notably the continuing study (it celebrated its twenty-fifth continuous year in 1984) of hundreds of the same men, with some women added in recent years, carried out at GRC/Baltimore. In fact, back in 1960, the director of GRC and of that particular project, Nathan Shock, tentatively listed half a dozen or so measurements that might serve as a starter toward the kind of test battery Comfort was later to suggest. The longitudinal studies have continued to provide valuable measurements that are being constantly refined. The Strehler-Mildvan "viability index" mentioned earlier in this chapter could be another useful tool in assessing overall physiological age. The same is true of an ingenious and highly mathematical (but soundly based in physiology) "multiple regression analysis" worked out by Toshiyuki Furukawa and his associates at Japan's Osaka University Medical School.

Though Comfort's original suggestion for the test battery was spelled out in a detailed technical article in *The Lancet*, he later explained his idea more briefly and simply in *Playboy*. Because we now better understand the nature of aging changes, he said, and moreover have automated methods and equipment at our command, we can now hope to measure the *rate* of aging over short periods of time instead of having to wait whole lifetimes. The new strategy: to select a battery of biochemical, physical, and behavioral measurements that, taken together, could constitute a reasonably valid index of overall aging; then get about five hundred volunteers—say, a group of fifty-year-old men—who could be monitored regularly for a period of three to five years. This would be no larger or more difficult than many medical experiments already being done. "We could start human experiments next week," he said, "measuring such things as hair graying, skin elasticity, change in body chemicals, hearing and mental agility as indexes of the speed at which aging is progressing."

Much more information has been coming in at an ever increasing rate since Comfort made that suggestion, and investigators have been looking harder for a set of "biomarkers" by which a standard "aging profile" could be established. As an example of what might serve as a biomarker: The protein known as transferrin is mainly responsible for transporting iron through the bloodstream to wherever it is needed in the body. Clinical observations in males ranging in age from sixty to ninety have suggested that transferrin levels in the blood go down steadily during those years. To get a more precise fix on the decline of transferrin levels, John Papaconstantinou and his colleagues at UTMB/Galveston carried out a series of controlled studies on mice and found that the amount of transferrin circulating in the bloodstream goes down, at a fairly uniform rate, by almost half during the latter part of life. Further research revealed that although there was no appreciable reduction in the manufacture of transferrin with aging, the kidney cells were able to release it into the bloodstream only in steadily diminishing quantities. Because this decline in kidney-cell secretory capacity can be precisely measured, Papaconstantinou believes that the drop in blood levels of transferrin (which plays a role in regulating cell division as well, a process that Papaconstantinou is also studying) might well serve as a reliable biomarker for aging.

As another example, the neurotransmitter dopamine, which is critical for a number of brain (and therefore body) functions, and has been implicated in such disorders as Parkinsonism and schizophrenia, also declines with age. The dopamine system and its association with these mental disorders is being intensively studied by another UTMB investigator, Creed Abell. The functional losses—as in the case of Parkinsonism, for instance—are attributed to the loss of receptor proteins on critical brain cells, a loss that prevents dopamine from reaching its normal destinations. The whole process can now be measured with great precision, and also manipulated by drugs (though only for short periods of time). Because of this aspect of the work, carried out largely by NIA's George Roth, and by Caleb Finch in collaboration with Raymond T. Bartus at the Lederle Laboratories in Pearl River, New York, Finch expressed his strong conviction—as of late 1984—that this age-related loss of dopamine receptors was the likeliest candidate to serve as a general mammalian biomarker.

The most thorough and up-to-date account of the search for biomarkers in aging is Regelson's long opening chapter of *Intervention in the Aging Process*, published in 1983. It is an exhaustive catalogue of aging changes in all the body's cellular processes, intracellular realms, organs, systems, behavior patterns, mental functions—from the molecular level to the total organism—including a description of measurement techniques and assay systems. Regelson concludes that "biomarker studies will lead to an understanding of aging as a defined syndrome that will be subject to rational measures that will improve the quality and length of our survival through direct responsible intervention." He stresses, however, the need for automated systems for monitoring differences brought on by aging, and laments the passing (through untimely budget cuts) of what might have been an ideal system: an elaborate, computerized, TV-monitored tissue-culture system that provided continuous three-dimensional surveillance of tissue-culture growth patterns, developed by Don Glaser and his colleagues at Berkeley.

At the time I was finishing *Prolongevity*, the late Benjamin Schloss of Los Angeles was waxing enthusiastic about a patented device of his own. Hundreds, perhaps thousands, of substances change in their quantity and quality as the body ages. According to Schloss at the time, an instant interpretation of these changes could probably be made from a computer readout of a single blood sample. There do, of course, exist automated blood analyzers that, requiring only a drop of blood, routinely carry out about a dozen blood tests simultaneously and return the answers in a minute or two (and anyone who had predicted such a capacity would, at one time, have been thought a fool). Schloss was sure that one could get such instant readings on hundreds of different substances in the same manner, thus making it possible to monitor hundreds of biochemical changes associated with aging in a single individual over time. Schloss, whose training was more in bioengineering than in gerontology *per se*, did in fact obtain a patent on just such a device, though he never reached the point of constructing a prototype before he died. He had insisted that the device was amazingly simple in its operational principles. The patent still exists; it's in the possession of Major Ward Dean, now in the U.S. Army, a former associate of Schloss's who, in the absence of any designated heir, became caretaker for a lot of Schloss's material. Not too long ago, I was able to get this patent from Dean and submit it to a company that specializes in evaluating such devices; it was sent back with the disappointing word that, because so little time remained before the patent would run out, it was not worth looking into. Sad. Yet there it is for the taking by some enterprising soul—or even by one of those "soulless" corporations.*

* Just as this book goes to press, I received word from another company I sent the patent to that Schloss's device, though cleverly conceived, probably would not work.

Another device aimed at achieving similar feats—that is, offering instant readouts on a multitude of substances from a single blood sample—this one based on ultraviolet spectroscopy, is still being pursued by Frank J. G. Van den Bosch at SUNY's Downstate Medical Center in Brooklyn. Meanwhile, Charles Sweeley and his collaborators at Michigan State University, using computer-coupled mass spectrometers, have worked out a system that enables them to identify speedily—as well as to quantify—hundreds of substances in a single drop of urine. The metabolic profile that results makes it possible to identify forty-or-so-genetic disorders in newborns and, the researchers believe, may help diagnose—among other diseases—Alzheimer's and some forms of cancer.

One of Schloss's never-realized designs was an elaborate "interaction chamber" designed to record—and process instantaneously—enormous quantities of data about an individual's physiological condition. The subject, lying comfortably inside the machine, would be fitted with a face mask and hooked up to a variety of sensors and other instrumentation attached to a computer. This setup, Schloss believed, would enable him to measure the decrease in the functional capacities and response times of the whole body as well as its various organs, tissues, and even individual cells. His "short-range" objectives, he said, were (1) to determine "the nature of the deterioration by identifying those changes that are responsible for each type of deterioration," and (2) to apply "corrective measures by introducing substances that compensate for the observed changes."

Schloss's schemes still intrigue me, but a much less ambitious device for measuring aging has been devised by the ever-ingenious Hochschild. He calls it H-SCAN. It is practical, it is now in everyday use on an experimental basis, and it will soon be made available to a wider public. Though it may not yet serve as *the* individual profile of aging biomarkers sought by Regelson for large-scale testing, it is surely a start in that direction. What Hochschild gets from his machine is what he calls IDBA—"instrument-defined biological age." Building on the prior efforts of scientists and engineers in the United States, Japan, and the Netherlands, Hochschild put together fourteen age-dependent tests in a single instrument that looks something like an offbeat video-arcade game. H-SCAN has a screen, half a dozen pushbuttons, earphones, a breathing tube, and other appurtenances, and it fits on a tabletop. Though it is driven by a computer, it is so simple that it doesn't require an operator. This feature, apart from economy and efficiency, removes an element that often provided a nagging worry in other lab testing of this type: that the human operators conducting the test might impose their own varying styles—without knowing it, of course—on the subjects in a way that might affect the results.

Sitting at the H-SCAN, the subject—after recording his name, height, and age—is taken through the fourteen tests, step by step, and at the end of about forty-five minutes he learns what his individual IDBA turned out to be, and gets a copy of the printout for himself. (Equivalent tests used to take half a day, and were much more cumbersome.) The averages are based on data accumulated on fourteen hundred people tested so far; as the number grows, the average IDBA profile may be modified. But the important factor is not so much whether the individual's IDBA is truly average but, rather, that he now knows his own IDBA accurately (it may take more than one go-round to give him this confidence) and should thenceforward be able to tell if something he is doing, or taking, brings improvement.

In addition to lung function—and especially vital capacity, considered by many to be the most reliable aging biomarker, and predictor of longevity—there are memory exercises, tests for the highest-pitched sound that can be heard, the auditory reaction time, visual reaction time, speed of various kinds of motion and touch sensitivity, and more. Hochschild, in a collaborative project with the Glenn Foundation and San Diego State University, has started to use H-SCAN to test whether regular vigorous exercise has an impact on aging rates. He has in mind many other uses for his machine. Meanwhile, he keeps modifying it as new data come in and new techniques arise, and he feels confident that, were there an effective anti-aging remedy at hand right now, H-SCAN could help evaluate it. In fact, there is a project afoot—secret as of this writing, but no longer so by the time this book is published—in which Hochschild, wearing his Glenn Foundation hat, plans to test various specific pharmacological agents, including some of those we have been talking about, employing the H-SCAN along with a battery of blood and urine tests.

Speaking of assays, the importance of having in the lab—in many labs—species of organisms that can themselves serve as bioassays should not be overlooked. Such organisms may be thought of as bioassays because they can serve as preliminary screening devices to determine whether given substances or techniques are worth trying out on human subjects. Let me take just one example to show you what I mean: the paramecium bioassay developed at the University of Wyoming by Joan Smith-Sonneborn.

Paramecia work well as a model system because they have short, predictable life spans (the species Smith-Sonneborn works with lives from forty to sixty days, or two hundred cell doublings) and have a certain advantage even over human cells in culture. A paramecium is not just a cell but also an entire organism in itself. Bacteria and paramecia are both single-celled organisms, but bacteria are *plants* and "prokaryotes"—that is, they contain no mitochondria and their DNA is unprotected by any separate membrane; whereas paramecia are *animals* and "eukaryotes" with mitochondria and a limiting membrane surrounding the genetic material. Moreover, paramecia undergo sexual mating of a sort, and their aging is measurable. There is a definable process of senescence, and you can tell whether you have interfered with it successfully. One of Smith-Sonneborn's more striking experiments, in which she used "dark repair" of DNA to extend the life span of her paramecia, was described in chapter 15.

Philip Lipetz, who worked with Ronald Hart at Ohio State, has been collaborating with Smith-Sonneborn, using her protozoal bioassay to test some of his own aging theories. He specializes in the very complex ways in which DNA coils itself into tightly wound "superhelixes" that may represent whole clusters of genetic instructions, controlling diverse cellular (and therefore bodily) functions or even regulating other genes or groups of genes. Lipetz believes that these supercoils, as they tighten or loosen or become somewhat disorganized, may interfere with the carrying out of genetic instructions, thus bringing on much of the deterioration we recognize as aging. His early experiments with Smith-Sonneborn suggest that he may be right. Other investigators could similarly use bioassays like that provided by the paramecia to screen their own ideas about what causes aging—and to get some clue as to whether suggested remedies will work or not.

It is clear, then, that we are not, even at this stage, at a loss for various means (and I have cited only a few) to screen, measure, and evaluate anti-aging agents as they emerge; and this capacity is likely to increase rapidly. So the pessimism over the feasibility of testing prolongevity strategies without having to wait a lifetime is clearly giving way to a more hopeful outlook. When the medications and pacemaker substances are ready for human trials, so should the technical capacities be for ascertaining their value, or lack of it, within reasonable time spans.

To go back once more to our original question about timetables, let me summarize briefly:

First, some possible remedies are already at hand. These include the new calorie-restriction discoveries that can now begin to be applied cautiously to human adults; the use of at least a few of the antioxidant, free-radical–fighting compounds, even though all the evidence is not in; for certain limited usage, drugs like Hydergine that might hold back the decline of mental functions; and, of course, important changes in life style and attitude.

Somewhere not too far down the line, a matter of years rather than decades, we may hope to see other subsances come onto the market—perhaps immune boosters such as the thymosins, protective hormones such as the derivatives of DHEA, and a number of the wear-and-tear remedies we have talked about, including some that might blunt the ravages of diseases like Alzheimer's and restore mental and intellectual deficits. There is no need to recatalogue all these possibilities here; this is just a reminder that numerous substances are being actively tested to combat the various kinds of damage that accumulate with long life, and it would be surprising if some of them did not become available within, perhaps, a decade, thus significantly improving the quality of our later years.

As for the larger breakthroughs—the discovery and manipulation of the clocks of aging, for instance—it seems probable that we will have to wait until the next century, perhaps well into the next century, before we achieve them. With good luck (though some people would consider it bad luck, as we will discuss in part three), these advances might occur much sooner than now appears possible—as has already occurred throughout the incredible realm of genetic engineering. Suppose, for instance, Denckla were to change his mind and return vigorously to the quest for DECO, and receive all the support he required, and hit the kind of lucky streak that gamblers and scientists sometimes do; then he might come up with his hormone and its inhibitor in record time. The same could be true of the cellular genetic clock. If, as Walford suspects, it could be identified in a few segments of the MHC "supergene," the barriers for our new breed of genetic engineers would surely not be insurmountable.

In Robert Heinlein's novels about long-lived individuals who thrive through many lifetimes on many planets—especially his durable hero, Lazarus Long, of *Methuselah's Children* and *Time Enough for Love*—rejuvenation, even in the star-trekking future, is a complex and time-consuming business, requiring the cloning and regrowth of the individual's deteriorating parts, among other arcane procedures. But if some of the gerontologists whose theories we have been discussing turn out to be right, rejuvenation should be a much simpler matter. It should not be too different from undergoing treatment for any other degenerative ailment; it might be a lot easier than most.

Another assumption frequently made by novelists who enjoy exploring these themes—like Fred Mustard Stewart in *The Methuselah Enzyme*—is that rejuvenating therapies will be available only to the very wealthy, and dispensed by secretive and unsavory doctors in isolated Swiss sanatoria. But Alex Comfort sees no reason why anti-aging substances, once they are discovered, synthesized, tested, and put on the market, should not be just as universally available as any other drug or medical treatment (which is precisely what worries some people, as I will explain in part three). They may, in fact, be cheaper and more accessible than many of today's heroic but high-cost biomedical technologies.

If such pacemaker substances as a DECO inhibitor were to become available to us, would they really be able to reach and affect cells everywhere in our bodies, and all our major organs and systems? It is not unreasonable to imagine so. At least, they might well exert beneficial effects on every tissue reached by the bloodstream. Might skin wrinkles, then, be unwrinkled, old muscles made supple, and gray hair turned to brown or red or blond? It is all possible. The tissues of the female reproductive tract certainly rejuvenate with hormonal treatment.

But what about the parts of the eye, for example, that the blood circulation doesn't reach? And what about the teeth? How far can even the most sophisticated dentistry carry us? These are problems that may of course require separate solutions. And though they seem simpler than the overall aging problem, they could take longer to work out—just as one can imagine a cure or preventive for cancer coming into existence while we continue to be afflicted with the common cold. (We have suddenly begun to live in an era, however, where such wildly versatile substances as the interferons are being tested on both cancer *and* the common cold.)

19

MEANWHILE, TOWARD A PERSONAL PROLONGEVITY PROGRAM

THERE was no real how-to chapter in *Prolongevity*, an omission that gave rise to some criticism. The fact is that I was extremely hesitant, given the state of our scientific knowledge, to offer any simple checklist of tips for Staying Younger Longer. I have not lost my wariness, especially when I read Gerald Gruman's descriptions of the various regimens of "prolongevity hygiene"—as he calls it—which have been enthusiastically and authoritatively offered throughout history, from ancient times to the turn of this century. Not that all these programs were harebrained. Some of the traditional advice has remained fairly consistent and still holds up well today. Advocacy of frugality in eating and moderation in life style, for instance, are common, recurrent themes. Besides, in the last decade just enough additional knowledge has accumulated—knowledge about free radicals and antioxidants, for instance, and about the effects of dietary restriction—to make me feel more confident now than in the mid-1970s in offering a few necessarily tentative and nonauthoritative guidelines. The past few years have, after all, seen the publication of books like Roy Walford's *Maximum Life Span*, in which he, as an impeccably credentialed gerontologist, does not hesitate to provide personal advice and specific recommendations; Kenneth R. Pelletier's *Longevity* (though it is more reportage and philosophy than how-to advice); and the bestselling *Life Extension* (and now the *Life Extension Companion*) by Durk Pearson and Sandy Shaw, who are by far the most hopeful and exuberant (some think excessively so) in regard to what might be done with what we already know. By the time *Prolongevity II* appears, Saul Kent, author of *The Life Extension Revolution*, will have come out with another book containing his own recommended life extension program. Sheldon S. Hendler's *Complete Guide to Anti-Aging Nutrients* will also have arrived by then—along with, I'm sure, other books I haven't yet heard about.

It needs to be underscored at the outset that virtually no substance, technique, or treatment has been accepted and validated as a guaranteed anti-aging remedy, backed up by the kind of thoroughgoing research demanded by the scientific community. What follows will be no more than a distillation of probabilities—based on some evidence (sometimes quite a bit) and logical extensions of that evidence—that a given practice ought to help and ought not to do any harm. In short, this is what I've been willing to accept as my own personal prolongevity program. It is based on extensive reading, the research of others, the changing enthusiasms of the investigators I know best, and the subjective testimony of those who have tried it (never the most reliable evidence), all spiced with roughly equal measures of reason and intuition.

What I do—or, rather, what I advise myself to do and intend to do (though I keep backsliding)—I don't necessarily recommend for everyone. Those of us who make up such personal programs for ourselves—and this includes many gerontologists—are self-appointed volunteer experimental subjects, willing to take the not-altogether-understood risks for the presumed-but-still-unproved benefits. Even authors who hand out this kind of advice with unabashed glibness still feel constrained, as a rule, to surround it with qualifiers, and finally to tell the reader: Ask your own doctor for advice. I can tell you in advance that your doctor, unless he or she is a most unusual individual, will say that much of the offered advice is nonsense. This does not mean that your doctor really knows best. It could merely mean that he has not kept up with the literature—or that, even if he has, he understandably elects to play it safe in your behalf. When you join the prolongevity game, you're on your own—though some of the elements of the game are entirely noncontroversial.

The program's components are essentially:

What you eat and drink.

What you do to supplement what you eat and drink.
What you do with your body.*
What you do with your mind.

Let's look first at what you eat and drink, noting as we do that most diet/nutrition advisers seem to forget all about drink. Nutrition is still a primitive science, as was abundantly evident in the 1980 discussions and pronouncements of a joint task force of experts gathered by the Department of Agriculture and the department that was then still called Health, Education and Welfare. "We've got to remain humble," said NIH's Robert Edleman at the time, "and admit that we don't know very much about nutrition right now." But there was pressure from Congress to issue guidelines, so a twenty-page pamphlet called *Nutrition and Your Health: Dietary Guidelines for Americans* finally emerged from the deliberations. It contained a few safe, qualified recommendations, which will be easily encompassed here, remarkable mainly for their unadventurousness. "What's curious about the arrival of this document," wrote science critic Dan S. Greenberg in the *New England Journal of Medicine*, "is that though it could have been issued 10 years ago and contains no surprises, it was released with the fanfare of Moses unveiling the tablets." The guidelines were even more watered down than necessary. Though the USDA has come around in recent years to an accommodation of sorts with consumerism, nevertheless, as Greenberg pointed out, "the political *raison d'être* for the Depart-

---

* Because I have been frequently asked about the possible life-prolonging benefits of "chelation therapy," I feel obliged to say a word about it. This therapy usually employs a substance called EDTA (for ethylenediaminetetraacetic acid) which, as it is slowly introduced into the bloodstream to circulate through the body, binds to (chelates) calcium. The chelated calcium is excreted, apparently forcing the body to pick up calcium from the unwanted plaques covering the artery walls, thus renewing the blood's calcium supply while breaking up the atherosclerotic buildup and reducing the risk of heart trouble. The treatment is also supposed to result in dramatic improvement in some cases of rheumatoid arthritis. Mainstream physicians worry about the possibly toxic side effects, including a dearth of blood calcium, the inadvertent chelation of other needed minerals, and potential kidney damage—not to mention the dangerous postponement of useful therapies and the worsening of the disease while waiting to see if chelation works or not—and thus shy away from it. Those physicians who use chelation therapy, and there are quite a few, swear by its benefits, and claim side effects are readily controllable. I don't know enough about it to recommend either for or against it, for cardiovascular disease or arthritis, but I certainly would not choose to undergo chelation therapy as a prophylactic or life-prolonging measure in the absence of disease symptoms.

ment of Agriculture is to make it easier for farmers to make money. And that purpose is not well served," he added, by permitting NIH people to "run loose on such politically sensitive matters as red meat, butter and eggs."

As Kenneth Pelletier put it, the controversies arise "not necessarily out of objective disagreement but due to the fact that nutrition is an emotionally charged subject and is inextricably linked to social, political and economic considerations." With such considerations on the one hand and a dearth of sure knowledge on the other, you can see why I hesitate to adopt an authoritative stance on this topic. When all disclaimers have been made, however, there does remain a fair amount of knowledge, imprecise though it may be. I have picked up, over the years, a set of convictions (tentative and ready to be scrapped with the arrival of better information) that govern my own eating and drinking habits. When I eat, I try to eat not just for today or for this week, but with the long haul in mind.

Before I launch into my personal dietary notions, some words need to be said about Roy Walford's "undernutrition" program. In earlier chapters we saw that one of the first effective ways scientists found to extend the life span of laboratory animals was to cut their intake of calories rather drastically while feeding them a nutritionally balanced diet. The trouble was that you apparently had to start doing this before puberty; begun in adulthood, it simply didn't work. Thus there seemed no prospect of applying this technique to humans, even on an experimental basis. But Walford, among his other achievements, made a significant breakthrough that changed the prospects. Working with his UCLA colleague Richard Weindruch, he was able to show that dietary restriction begun in adulthood could extend the life span after all, though perhaps not as impressively. Earlier investigators had simply not hit upon the right way to do it; they had been starting the restrictions too suddenly instead of introducing them gradually over a period of time. Once it was clearly proved that a later start could be effective, and the proof was confirmed by others, Walford felt confident enough not just to embark on his own restricted-diet program but to recommend it, with due caution, to others. He has worked out what he deems to be a supernutritious diet (low in fat and proteins but relatively high in complex carbohydrates) on 1,500 to 2,000 calories a day—though he personally prefers to fast on two successive days, then eat a bit less unrestrictedly (2,140 calories) for the remaining five days of the week. He spells all this out, including his rationale for it, in *Maximum Life Span*, which also contains detailed tables of nutrients as well as recipes and daily menus. Walford is more disciplined than I am inclined to be, but I strongly recommend that you have a good look at what this man, who lives on the front lines of gerontological research, has to say.

It certainly seems clear that what we eat can have a lot to do with how many years we live and how fully lived those years may be. Take, for instance, those celebrated, long-lived highland folks in the Andes, in Russian Georgia, and in the Western Himalayas. Though researchers have now found their life spans to have been exaggerated, these people did live—and still do—in large numbers, to ripe and vigorous old ages. All the studies of them emphasized their long-range adherence to frugal though nutritious diets.* When it comes to food and drink in relation to longevity, both quantity and quality count.

"We are drowning in information," as John Naisbitt reminds us in *Megatrends*, "but starved for knowledge." This is as true in nutrition as elsewhere. Out of the welter of information and misinformation (and who can always tell the difference?) that assails us, I have tried to formulate a few rough principles that make sense to me. I don't invariably abide by them, of course—but, then, my first principle is to be relaxed and nonfanatical about the other principles.

Each of us is a unique, individual human being, and what works for one doesn't always for another. If you have food allergies, genetic dietary impediments or disturbances, or any condition that requires rigid adherence to, or avoidance of, specific foods, then you really must let your doctor be your guide. There are some general principles, though, that I think most of the rest of us are well advised to follow.

The first is: stay away from fad diets, especially the "crash" variety. There have been critiques by the score of Stillman, Atkins, Scarsdale, and the rest. I don't plan to deal with any of them in any detail. The fact is that most of them do "work"—for some people, at least, and for short periods of time—in that the devout dieter does lose weight, perhaps even dramatically. The problem is that

---

* The Japanese peoples now boast the highest life expectancy in the world. Among these peoples, the longest-lived are the Okinawans, who, according to Walford, eat the fewest calories and the smallest amounts of sugar and salt.

the benefits don't last because you can't really stay with the diet for long, and pretty soon the weight is regained and you backslide into your former habits. Nathan Pritikin has succeeded better than most diet gurus in this respect by insisting that his clients undergo a weeks-long period of total immersion in the program at the very onset. To win the long-range benefits of sensible eating, you must eat in a way that you know you can trust yourself to continue all your life, through the exercise of no more than reasonable self-discipline.

One disadvantage of nearly all fad diets is the relative sameness of the fare. It's not only boring but in some cases dangerous, because of nutrients left out for long periods of time. Virtually everyone agrees on the importance of variety, even if you are eating a diet that appears nutritionally sound. I had this drummed into me some years back when, as managing editor of *Family Health* magazine, I frequently saw Harvard's Jean Mayer (now president of Tufts University), who was our nutrition columnist and indisputably one of the world's leading authorities on the subject. I can still hear Mayer's voice ringing out, "Variety! Variety!" He believed that, precisely because of the large gaps that remain in our knowledge, we should avail ourselves of the diversity of nutritional opportunities accessible to us in our culture. Water chestnuts and bamboo shoots might supply ingredients that we don't get from carrots and peas—and that we might not even know we need.

Another good reason for a varied diet is that foods interact with one another in potentially hazardous ways. We are just beginning to learn what a few of these interactions are. For instance, raw legumes, such as dried beans, peas, and peanuts, can block enzymes that help digest proteins. Cabbage and Brussels sprouts can keep the thyroid gland from getting all the iodine it needs. Spinach and rhubarb contain substances that can render certain minerals and other nutrients unabsorbable. Tea and red wine can interfere with the body's use of iron and vitamin B-12. And so on. If you are not eating the same diet all the time, you are much less likely to get enough of any of these foods to interfere seriously with the others.

A lot of variety is not to be confused with a large quantity. How much should we eat? Throughout most of our lives, the simple answer is: *not too much*. The right amount may vary for different people, depending on body build, inheritance, energy expended in work or play, and individual metabolism. But in a relatively affluent society, most of us who can afford to, do in fact eat a lot more than we need. I won't repeat all the sermons you've heard about junk-food snacks gobbled during coffee breaks and at bedtime. But even if we just stick to meals, the average restaurant meal, like the old-fashioned many-course meal at home, is too much to eat at one sitting. You should not get up from the table feeling too bloated to move any farther than the nearest couch. Because obesity does remain one of the nation's major health problems, you are better off, most of your life, staying as trim as possible without starving yourself into a state resembling anorexia. This means simply that, if your metabolism is reasonably normal, you content yourself with smaller portions than customary—perhaps *much* smaller portions, depending upon your custom. When you have really had enough to eat but can't bear to leave the rest on your plate, remember the dictum enunciated by my late mother-in-law: "Don't turn your stomach into a garbage pail."

You will recall the recent NIA research suggesting that in the mid-sixties and later in life *moderate* "overweight" (as heretofore defined in actuarial tables) may actually enhance your chances of living longer. Remember, too, however, that this principle is still far from being universally accepted.

Prior to the mid-sixties, even moderate overweight does seem to be almost universally regarded as a disadvantage. And no one, to my knowledge, has a good word to say for gross overweight at any age as a longevity enhancer. Most animal studies also support the idea that overeating and overweight shorten life. As a general rule, for most of our adult lives, less is better.

So much for quantity. And though I have already recommended variety, and the need for a balanced diet, one word more is called for. A well-balanced diet does not mean that every meal—or even every day's meals—must be precisely balanced. (If that were the case, Walford's partial-fasting regimen would quickly do him in.) It is probably good enough, according to the National Academy of Sciences, to ensure that within the span of a few days—perhaps as much as a week—you don't leave out anything essential. *Continuing* deprivation of any critical ingredient can cause problems. Such ingredients number in the dozens, but all are included in the five main categories of nutrients—proteins, fats, carbohydrates, minerals, and vitamins.

When we think of proteins, we are usually thinking of *whole* proteins, those containing all the essential amino acids. There are some twenty-plus amino acids, but only eight are officially classified as essential because they are the ones the body cannot manufacture; they must be taken in as food. We get our whole proteins mostly from meats of all kinds (including fish and fowl) and from dairy products. Many vegetables are also high in protein, but usually one or more amino acids are missing. Fortunately, the amino acids missing in one vegetable are not the same ones missing in others, so such vegetables as rice and beans can be mixed and eaten together to serve as complete proteins. The Tarahumara Indians of Mexico, who live long, healthy lives and are famous for their feats of vigor and endurance, subsist on a low-protein, low-fat diet whose main staples are beans, corn, and squash. Whole books have been devoted solely to the topic of educating the public about proteins, the most popular probably being Frankie Moore Lappé's *Diet for a Small Planet.*

We do of course need proteins no matter what age we are, to rebuild the very substance of our bodies. But as we grow older, our substance diminishes, and we generally use less energy as well, so we don't need enormous quantities of protein food. If we eat a lot more protein than we need, in fact, our bodies may not be able to handle it efficiently, resulting perhaps in a kind of cellular-garbage glut and a heavy burden on the kidneys. Too much protein can also force the body to excrete more calcium than is good for us. The solution is simply to eat smaller portions.

As soon as we start to list protein foods in any order of preference, we have to take into consideration their fat content. So let's put that off for a moment while we have a hard look at fats.

One bit of advice on fats that everyone agrees with is: go easy. Much emphasis has been deservedly placed on saturated animal fats, the kind that may send up your blood cholesterol level, thus increasing your risk of heart troubles. We have been exhorted to switch to polyunsaturated fats. My own recommendation is that we go easy on polyunsaturated fats as well. An increasing number of gerontologists, as we have noted, believe that free radicals cause aging damage—including an increased risk of cancer. Because polyunsaturated fats increase the cell's oxidation reactions, they create more free radicals, hence probably causing aging changes as well as other kinds of injury. It would be ironic indeed if, in switching to polyunsaturates in order to lengthen our lives by lessening our chances of heart disease, we were actually shortening our lives by prematurely aging (or rendering malignant) our cells. Nobody can yet be said to know this for sure, but the compelling logic of the matter and the accumulating evidence make me sufficiently uneasy to say: go easy on *all* fats.

Myron Winick of Columbia, an outstanding nutrition authority whose knowledge I esteem—though he would not approve of all I am saying here—recommends that we restrict our fat intake to no more than 25 to 30 percent of our total diet. We should remember, too, that the body tends to store any unused energy—from sugars, for instance—in the form of fat, adding to the dangers of obesity and hence of cardiovascular disease and diabetes. Moreover, as we increase our use of ready-cooked, processed foods, we consume even more fat (as well as more sugar and salt). Winick warns that high-fat diets have been implicated in cancer of the breast (probably because they cause hormonal imbalances) and colon (probably because they have a complex series of effects on intestinal bacteria)—and, to a lesser extent, in cancer of the ovaries and prostate. All this underlines the desirability of a low-fat (not, of course, a no-fat) regimen.

Now, proteins again. With an understanding of fats, we should have an easier time figuring out our preferences. Of the major meats, beef, lamb, pork, and ham, being the fattiest, are the least desirable. Pick the leanest cuts and trim off the fat wherever possible. Veal is somewhat better. Better still are chicken and turkey; but don't eat the skin, and don't hesitate to trim fat here, either, if the bird is hefty. Fish contains even less fat, so it goes high on the preferred list, though some low-fat shellfish, such as shrimp, are nevertheless high in cholesterol. As for dairy products, eggs are high in cholesterol; so are the hard cheeses, the creamy cheeses, butter, and whole milk. Obvious advice is to cut down on eggs and switch to low-fat, non-creamy cheese and skim milk. Yogurt is reputed to reduce cholesterol levels. I would also, while cutting down on butter, cut down on margarine, too, for reasons already stated: as a polyunsaturate, it is a free-radical generator.

And whatever you eat, eat it any way but fried. Any other means of cooking—steamed, boiled, broiled, baked, poached—is better.

Now that I have passed along all these dire warnings, it may seem contradictory if I tell you I don't want to be an alarmist. When I say, "Go easy," I mean merely that. I don't intend to be fanatical or rigid, either in my advice or my personal practice. Unless you're under doctor's orders to the contrary, or have some familial condition that dictates special care, there's no reason why you can't allow yourself an occasional treat without feeling guilty. I'm a firm believer in enjoying food. And, on no scientific evidence whatsoever, I often feel that food that I'm not enjoying isn't really doing me much good. Which doesn't mean that if you're on a salt-free diet because of hypertension you should foolishly decide to reach for the salt shaker on the grounds that enjoying it will do you more good. (As an added precaution, you should know that rats, given a large smorgasbord of foods to choose from, tend to select foods that shorten their lives!)

There's an additional reason why—though I'm careful about my own intake of fats—I stop short of being rigid about it. The whole cholesterol story, even though it keeps being reconfirmed by more and more (especially epidemiological) evidence, is at the same time getting more complicated, and in some ways fuzzier with each acquisition of new knowledge. (For instance, our cells *need* a certain amount of cholesterol, and even if we were on a diet totally free of cholesterol, the liver would still make some itself.) I suspect that the cholesterol dangers are going to turn out to apply mainly to a minority of the population, perhaps 20 percent, whose genetics render them somehow less able to metabolize fats normally. If that turns out to be true, and if we can identify those at risk (which we are already able to do in some cases), then the rest of us may be able to relax on that score. Meanwhile, though, we'd better keep our guard up.

There are times, of course, when you have all too little control over your diet. Most dietary advice is offered as if you had unlimited access at all times to any kinds of food you wanted—as well as unlimited funds to acquire them. In many places, stores don't stock what you're looking for. If you're somebody's guest for dinner, the host and hostess may not appreciate your disdaining the gourmet offerings over which they have labored long and lovingly (how tough you can be about this depends on your own temperament, of course). Restaurant menus often give you no choice between sinning and abstinence, especially short-order roadside eateries, a necessary evil when you're on the move and in a hurry. With the best of intentions, you may wind up with a cheeseburger and french fries. Or, heaven forfend, a hot dog. (Most frankfurters, along with luncheon meats and cold cuts in general, are to be avoided even more devoutly than hamburgers.)* Anyway, all you can do is the best you can do.

The best, however, is often better than you think, especially if you're willing to exercise a little determination. More and more restaurants are becoming sufficiently nutrition-conscious (albeit grudgingly so) to include offbeat items, even vegetarian dishes, on their menus. You can always ask the waiter to leave off the gravy or the mayonnaise, or to put the salad dressing on the side. And if you're a male, you really don't have to order bacon and eggs and home fries just because all the other guys do. Be secure enough, if your good sense so guides you, to order bran flakes with sliced bananas and skim milk.

Bran flakes bring us to the subject of fiber. Americans have traditionally eaten a low-fiber diet, which is now considered inadvisable for a number of good reasons. It can, according to Winick, cause chronic constipation and diverticulitis, and probably increases the risk of gall-bladder disease and even appendicitis. Moreover, some types of fiber—such as bran and pectin—are believed to reduce blood cholesterol levels. Most important, perhaps, is that a low-fiber diet elevates the risk of colon cancer, especially when the diet is also high in fat. The reasons for this are not clear, but it's suspected that a higher fiber content speeds the food along through the intestine, requiring less effort from the intestinal muscles to push it along, and leaving less time for potentially carcinogenic substances to stay in contact with any specific areas of the intestinal walls.

As a result of all this, it's suggested that we eat foods rich in fiber. Meats and dairy products contain hardly any. But whole-wheat bread and a variety of fruits, vegetables, nuts, and grains are fiber-rich. As a general rule, incidentally, it's OK to eat all the fruits, vegetables, and grain you want. Even potatoes and pasta (virtually fat-free until you add butter, sour cream, parmesan cheese, and the like) are among the starchy carbohydrates being more freely recommended these days—and in the government guidelines, too. Fruits are fine, even though sweet; their sugar, fructose, is better for you

---

* Even as I put the book to press, a report has appeared claiming that *fried* (and only fried) beef contains a substance that may protect against cancer! Though the investigators involved caution against changing dietary habits based on their preliminary data, this does illustrate the hazards of offering "authoritative" advice.

than the sucrose contained in sugar bowls. Fruits and vegetables should be fresh whenever possible; frozen is the next choice; canned and prepared last. Fiber is lost in processing, as is much of the vitamin content, not to mention flavor; besides, sugar, salt, fat, and other perhaps unwanted ingredients may be added. (Always read labels!)

As you increase your intake of fiber-rich foods, remember that here, too, it's possible to overdo. You don't need *massive* quantities of fiber—heaping bowls of whole bran, for example. The habitual intake of too much fiber can interfere with the absorption of vital minerals such as iron, zinc, and calcium. As elsewhere, a relaxed, balanced, sensible approach is called for.

Other items to go easy on, as already implied, are sugar and salt. We have a national addiction to both substances, far beyond the body's need for them. Sugar, especially white refined sugar, is one substance we could probably do without altogether. It's an empty-calorie carbohydrate; that is, it can't be converted into anything but energy—but *that*, as we know, can be converted into fat. We know that sugar is bad for the teeth. It probably makes us more susceptible to diabetes as we grow older. It may be able to send up cholesterol levels and increase heart-disease risks (though this is now generally believed to be true only for certain predisposed people, who can be identified by an easy test). Richard Bucala of Rockefeller University recently discovered that glucose can damage—and perhaps cross-link—protein molecules, including those that make up the connective tissue. Glucose also seems able to accumulate along the DNA chains. Though Bucala hesitates to speculate about the long-range health hazards implicit in his findings, I find in his results an additional reason to be sparing with sugar.

Our passion for sweets is responsible for much of our obesity problem; and even if sugar doesn't cause heart problems directly, it certainly leads us to increase our fat intake considerably via ice cream, pies, cakes, cookies, doughnuts, and other nonnourishing temptations. We don't eat those things so much for the fat as for the sugar. So, again, go easy! Satisfy your sweet tooth with fresh fruits when you can get them.

It's been claimed that children in our society become sugar junkies and find it difficult to kick the habit when they are adults. Studies suggest, however, that this is not true. Sugar is not addictive, though we often act as if it is. Older people need to understand that they are at special risk—because of impaired taste buds—of overdoing on sugar as well as salt.

Salt is condemned as a villainous substance mainly in hypertension, and hypertension's being so common, and still so little understood, would be reason enough for us to go easy on salt. According to Winick, we consume from ten to thirty-five times as much salt as our body could conceivably need, adding to our water-retention problems and placing an unnecessarily heavy load on the kidneys. If we never again reached for a salt shaker, there would be no danger that we wouldn't get more than enough salt from our unsalted foods. What makes it so difficult to cut down to reasonable quantities— we should halve our intake, at least—is, again, our increased dependence on processed foods, in which both sugar and salt are virtually ubiquitous. Again—read labels.

What about taking extra vitamins and minerals, not to mention other "food supplements"? Well, that is one of the more controversial questions in nutrition today. The standard answer we get from official sources is that if we eat a normal, balanced diet, we don't need any supplements—except in special circumstances or if a given individual suffers from a known deficiency. That is one answer I can't accept, however; obviously, lots of other people can't, either, or the health-food stores would not continue to thrive and proliferate. What with depleted soils—and soils that have widely divergent mineral content, depending on geography—and the losses that accompany food handling and processing, the least I'd recommend is a one-a-day, all-purpose vitamin-mineral tablet.

For the rest, I hesitate to serve even as your unofficial, nonexpert guide—though I will keep my promise to outline what I do myself. But first I think it's worth saying one more time that those of us who megadose on vitamins and other substances are carrying out mass experiments on ourselves. There exists no long-term study of, in fact no precedent for, large populations of people taking these substances in quantity over significant stretches of time. Harry Demopoulos wonders if it will now ever be possible to carry out such a scientific study in the United States, partly because it would be difficult to identify a control group of people who had not already been taking vitamins and minerals, either on their own or inadvertently via food additives. It is a delusion to think that just because a substance is thought of as "natural"—no matter how manufactured it might really be—we can safely take unlimited quantities of it.

OK, I am among the legion of self-appointed guinea pigs, and so are many scientists and doctors of my acquaintance—who cannot in all conscience, however, advise either their patients or the general public to follow their lead. I take, for instance, much more than the RDAs (the official Recommended Daily Allowances) of most (though not all) vitamins and minerals. A number of scientists—Harry Demopoulos is one—do not like the term "vitamins" at all, and especially not "megavitamins." "The trouble is," says Demopoulos, "that vitamins are defined in terms of deficiency states rather than in terms of optimal health. I think we should start employing some new term, such as 'micronutrients,' to describe what we take to enhance health." Demopoulos, who has been observing self-megadosers in large numbers over long periods of time, is convinced that the supplementation has no harmful side effects *if the material is free of impurities*, which is often not the case. As for the efficacy of megadosing as preventive maintenance, the faith in it is largely based on anecdotal, subjective testimony. And there is certainly no unanimity among the champions of micronutrient supplementation as to which of the micronutrients—and how much—we ought to take.

A journalist trying to cover this field is continually reminded of the lack of consensus among even his favored experts. Let's take, as one example, Harry Demopoulos, who, with the young and enthusiastic team he has gathered at NYU, has done some pioneering research into the nature of free radicals, the kinds of damage they do, and ways to combat them. Back when I was writing *Prolongevity*, I knew that certain antioxidants—vitamins C and E, for example—were reputed to enhance one another's effectiveness. But it turns out that this enhancement is not merely additive. Rather, it's a case, says Demopoulos, of each antioxidant's having a specific free-radical target that it goes after (though there is some overlap). Hence, vitamin C will pick off certain radicals that E misses, and vice versa. There are many kinds of free radicals and many kinds of antioxidants that work in different ways; some, for instance, scavenge already existing free radicals, while others prevent their formation. Berkeley's Lester Packer believes that, when the necessary research has been done, antioxidants may be classed as essential dietary ingredients.

Demopoulos is now convinced that antioxidants not only are important protective substances, but also must be taken in fairly high doses, and in combination: there's a much better chance of preventing or lessening free-radical damage if a number of antioxidants are at work simultaneously. This advice is given partly because of the diversity of free radicals, and partly because the antioxidants themselves cause cascades of further reactions in which free radicals may be generated, so each serves to mop up the possibly adverse side effects created by the other. I soon shared his conviction, and since Demopoulos made available to me the ultrapure products he was using in his research, I have been taking them for some time with some regularity. One of these products is a large golden-yellow capsule that contains 800 milligrams of vitamin C (about thirteen times the RDA), along with half a dozen of the B vitamins: B-1 (thiamine, in the hydrochloride form), 40 milligrams, about twenty-five times the RDA; B-2 (riboflavin), 4 milligrams, more than twenty times the RDA; B-3 (Demopoulos prefers the niacin rather than the niacinamide form), 20 milligrams, which is merely the RDA; B-5 (pantothenic acid, though Demopoulos prefers the calcium pantothenate form), 120 milligrams, twelve times the RDA; B-6 (pyridoxine), 40 milligrams, or twenty times the RDA; B-12, 200 *micro*grams, about thirty-three times the RDA.

In my mind, C is clearly a good vitamin. I take about 2,000 milligrams (or 2 grams) a day, sometimes more. Billed as an antistress and immunity-boosting vitamin, it has a number of interesting side benefits. For example, it helps the body absorb iron, and it prevents nitrates from being converted to potentially cancer-causing nitrosamines in the gut. Despite Linus Pauling's labors in its behalf, however, there is still no accepted proof that C prevents or cures colds—though some people swear it works for them. Some authorities believe that, taken in megadoses over long periods, C can precipitate kidney stones; others scoff at this. There are a few studies suggesting that, in order to handle the abnormally large quantities of C that come with megadosing, the body has to rev up its metabolic machinery in such a way as to build up an actual dependency on C. Then, if the large doses are suddenly stopped, a full-blown case of scurvy may result, even though amounts of C that would formerly have been considered normal are still present! If I need to go off C for any reason, then I'll be sure to withdraw *gradually*. A similar dependency could occur with excessive quantities of other vitamins. All in all, however, Demopoulos tends to agree that megadosing with C is safe. Though he also offers a good biochemical rationale for taking large quantities of the B vitamins he packages along with C—they help the body make optimal use of the C while carrying out their other beneficial functions—I shy away from taking as many of these capsules as some people in his subject population do. On the other hand, Demopoulos deliberately leaves out of his capsules several of the substances that are normally included by others in their B-complex preparations—among them folic acid, PABA (para-amino-benzoic acid), inositol, biotin, and choline. He does not feel that these are safe in large quantities, or even that they are needed as supplements at all, except in special cases of known deficiency. (Choline, because it is a precursor of the neurotransmitter acetylcholine—important in memory and learning—was touted for a while as a potential therapy for Alzheimer's disease; but experimental results so far have been disappointing.) Yet, others disagree with Demopoulos sufficiently to convince me that now and then I need to take a B-complex capsule that includes these. At any rate, water-soluble vitamins such as C and those in the B group are for the most part excreted harmlessly. (A and D, which are fat-soluble, tend to be stored in the body in ways that enable them to build up to toxic quantities. E, too, is fat-soluble and may be stored, but very large quantities indeed must be present before it is considered hazardous.)

Among Demopoulos's other antioxidant preparations, I take a small white capsule (sometimes more than one, but, again, never as many as some people take) containing 50 milligrams of glutathione, which is itself an antioxidant and is, moreover, a necessary component of one of the body's own natural antioxidant enzymes, glutathione peroxidase. I also take one or two, usually two, of his tiny orange-brown soft-gel capsules of beta-carotene (15 milligrams each), because there has been some good, suggestive biochemical as well as epidemiological evidence that beta-carotene is an effective antioxidant that also affords some protection against cancer. Not only is beta-carotene an antioxidant in its own right, but each molecule of it can be broken down by the body into two vitamin-A molecules. Thus Demopoulos includes no vitamin A in his formulas because, he says, the presence of plenty of beta-carotene assures a continuing, adequate supply of A, and there is no danger of A toxicity because the body breaks it down from beta-carotene only as needed. Finally, I also take, in droplet form, somewhere between 400 and 800 units of his pure liquid vitamin E. Some people take more than 2,000 units a day, a dosage Demopoulos considers safe. Other antioxidant experts, such as Denham Harman, worry that an overkill effect might damp some of the oxidative processes the body needs to keep going. Richard Cutler's research leads him to suspect that too much E, taken regularly, might cause the cells to cut back their own normal production of their native antioxidant enzyme, superoxide dismutase.

The only one of Demopoulos's capsules I hardly ever take is a combination of calcium and vitamin D, mainly because I have been convinced (as Demopoulos has not) by the work of, among others, Mildred Seelig of NYU's Goldwater Hospital, that D is the one vitamin where the RDA (400 units, or about 10 micrograms) is probably more than most people need, the one that I feel I get plenty of from dairy products and exposure to the sun.

I also depart from Demopoulos's advice in the matter of minerals. He does not include any minerals (except routine quantities of calcium) in his capsules, because he feels they might well have cumulative deleterious effects and that the body's digestive system is superbly efficient at utilizing minerals. But here I go along with those who feel that the positive benefits outweigh the slight (in their view) risks. I take 50 to 100 micrograms of selenium, which, besides being a good antioxidant in its own right, is also reputed to enhance the antioxidant activity of both C and E, and without which the antioxidant enzyme glutathione peroxidase cannot perform its job. I also take 50 milligrams of zinc, because so many of the body's enzymes are zinc-dependent, zinc deficiency is suspected as a factor in so many diseases, and so much zinc is lost in food processing. (Some of the health-food literature exhorts men to take zinc as protection for the prostate, but the evidence for this claim is very tenuous.) I do try to keep a close eye on the literature here, for I know that zinc can interact in tricky ways, especially with other minerals; in an individual with a borderline copper deficiency, for instance, excess zinc can tip the balance in the wrong direction. Too little is known for sure about these complex mineral interactions* (even such "supernutrition" enthusiasts as Richard Passwater and Carl C. Pfeiffer advise caution here), and, for the most part, I make do with the contents of a standard, one-a-day multiple-purpose pill. Another exception I make, though, is magne-

---

* In fact, Jane Brody warns, in one of her *New York Times* "Personal Health" columns: "Perhaps the most dangerous of all food-nutrient interactions is often self-induced by people who take megadoses of micronutrients—the vitamins and minerals the body needs in very small amounts." I have tried to take these interactions into account in planning my own personal regimen, and have been helped in these efforts by the generosity of people like Steve Blechman, head of research at Twin Laboratories, Inc., who has given me the benefit of the company's computerized access to the vast literature on the topic.

sium, of which I take at least 200 milligrams a day. I have become convinced, through the work of Mildred Seelig and others, notably that of Burton and Bella Altura at SUNY's Downstate Medical Center in Brooklyn, that most of our population tends to be magnesium-deficient. The more we include in our diets such substances as fat, sugar, salt, phosphates (as in carbonated soft drinks), fiber, and calcium, the more magnesium we need. The evidence, still not widely known or accepted, is that magnesium deficiency is not good for cardiovascular health.

All this talk about minerals started partly to make the point that one can and does depart from the advice of one's favorite experts, in this case Demopoulos. On the other hand, I have tended to follow his hunches in avoiding substances recommended by other of my favorite experts. Walford, for example, recommends, and takes, some supplementary DMAE and BHT, substances also recommended by Pearson and Shaw, among others. DMAE, you may recall, was used by Hochschild as a lysosomal-membrane stabilizer, and by others as a lipofuscin scavenger; it also seems to be some sort of brain stimulant. Demopoulos is bothered by some evidence that DMAE may cause convulsions, though others—including Walford, Hochschild, Nandy, and Regelson—insist that this is an unfounded fear; the convulsive hazard, they say, is restricted to those who are already predisposed to epilepsy. As for BHT (butylated hydroxytoluene, used widely to prevent food rancidification), it is known to be an effective antioxidant, yet Demopoulos does not like its potential side effects—though others regard these as exaggerated. It is hard to say what makes a given expert's advice prevail, in any given instance, over that of others equally respected.

To summarize the supplementation I myself take—as of now—apart from a standard one-a-day, all-purpose vitamin-mineral pill, it consists of considerably above RDA doses of C, E, and most of the B vitamins, as well as the antioxidants glutathione and beta-carotene and, among the minerals, zinc, selenium, and magnesium.*

---

* There are also substances I try to avoid—often, again, without too much hard scientific evidence. For example, I mentioned in chapter 6 the concern expressed by Bjorksten and others regarding the possible connection between aluminum and Alzheimer's disease. This kind of report tends to change my habits, unfair as it may turn out to be to the makers of aluminum. I avoid, whenever possible, aluminum-based antacids (which is to say most antacids). It's also hard to find deodorants that don't contain aluminum, but I now use one that doesn't.

These are the supplements I tend to take on a regular basis, but I am always experimenting, for short periods, with other things I hear about that seem intriguing; for instance, I am at the moment of this writing cautiously trying out a whole new class of "eustatants," which are supposed to supply the cell with all the biochemical "information" it needs to function optimally, on the theory that the cell can select what it needs and leave the rest. (Efficacious or not, eustatants do seem as harmless as chicken soup.) New substances will keep coming along, as often as not unpredictably, that will be worth watching—quite apart from those discussed in earlier chapters. They are not likely to get to the basic cause of aging, in the very near future, but they could still prolong the good years of life through symptom relief. If a drug were to appear that could do no more than un-cross-link collagen molecules in the connective tissue outside the cells, for instance, the benefits could be considerable.

Collagen, after all, makes up some 30 to 40 percent of the body's protein. Its ubiquitous presence in the body's framework is what has led scientists of Robert Kohn's stature to suggest that the aging of collagen could be a primary factor in the overall aging of the organism. Nutrients going from the bloodstream to the cells must pass through collagen in order to get there, as must waste materials being carried in the other direction. If collagen becomes dense and rigid, it also becomes less permeable (perhaps even impassable in some cases); hence the cells have a harder time getting their food and getting rid of their wastes, and heart and lungs have to work correspondingly harder. Changes in collagen molecules, just like changes in any other protein molecules,could also invite autoimmune attack. So it is clear that the loosening up of collagen via un-cross-linking (or by preventing cross-linkage in the first place) could help keep the body younger longer. This would probably be true of appearance as well, since much of the skin's aging and wrinkling might be due to collagen changes.* It is even conceivable, as Hochschild has suggested, that it could slow down the graying and thinning

---

* One thing I've recently started to do for my skin is to spray on it a substance called Na-PCA (the sodium salt of pyrrolidone carboxylic acid). Na-PCA is not really a cosmetic. It is a moisturizing compound normally found in the skin, but old skin contains only about half the amount present in young skin; hence it makes sense to me to add it as a corrective supplement. Na-PCA has no odor and feels just like water. The particular brand I use has aloe vera added. Na-PCA is available in health-food stores.

of hair. There is still no accepted way to do that. Dermatologist-gerontologist Norman Orentreich of New York, among others, has been performing hair transplants for many years, which has certainly helped at least some people in some circumstances. Now, late in 1984, comes a report in *Nature* out of Scotland's University of Dundee that holds out greater hope. In healthy hair, cells called papillae nestle at the bottom of the hair follicles to nourish the hair roots and stimulate growth. The Dundee researchers grew papillae in the lab, implanted them (in rats) at the base of nonworking follicles, and thus stimulated hairs to grow that otherwise almost certainly would not have. The major obstacle to follow-up so far has been the difficulty in growing papillae in lab cultures; they seem to lose their stimulative ability after four cell divisions. But the investigators are looking for ways around this impasse, and are encouraged by the new opportunities to do something about baldness, or, at the least, to enhance the quality and ease of hair transplantation.

It may pay you, then, to keep a weather eye out for news of substances and procedures that might, from time to time, be added to your personal prolongevity program.

Though I have discussed at length food and supplementation, I still owe you a few words about drink. First off, *water* is a vital nutrient, also necessary for internal cleansing and flushing purposes. A prevalent myth holds that water with meals hinders digestion; in fact, water helps both the digestion and absorption of food. Most of us do not drink nearly enough water: we should get down several glasses a day. Too often, when thirsty, we reach instead for a Coke or a beer. It's true that water, in many places, is not too palatable; but a little lemon or ice can make it go down more easily. Another inhibiting factor is that, in many workplaces and public places, water fountains are few and far between. (Not long ago, I tried to help an old woman find a water fountain in New York's Penn Station, and we never did find one. The man at the information desk didn't think there were any. Scandalous.) Besides, it takes forever to get a satisfying drink out of most water fountains; usually we wet our lips and throat with a sip or two, and let it go at that. So getting enough water to drink (for the good of your blood, your kidneys, and the general hydration of your body) can be a problem, but you can usually overcome it by deciding it's important enough to make the effort.

What of other beverages?

Milk? Yes, unless you have digestive problems with it. And make it skim, preferably. You can use the calcium for your bones, which have a habit of gradually, insidiously shedding their substance as we grow older, more so in women than in men. In fact, women especially should in their middle years increase their intake of calcium. Good calcium sources besides milk are sardines and green leafy vegetables, but if I did not drink milk—at least with my breakfast cereal—I would certainly consider taking a calcium supplement, and then vitamin D, which is needed to process calcium properly (though the kind of natural D that sunshine induces your body to make is a little different, and a little better, than the synthetic variety). I wouldn't take calcium and D, though, without taking some extra magnesium as well. It is worth noting here that major inhibitors of both calcium and magnesium absorption are phosphates, which we get mostly from meat and soft drinks.

This brings us to carbonated beverages, which we swill by the gallon, especially in summer. The public has already become so conscious of the caffeine and sugar content of so many soft drinks that their manufacturers have been obliged to put out special versions of their products that are free of caffeine and/or sugar. But what the public has not yet realized is the need to cut down on phosphates themselves (there is no carbonation without them).

As I just suggested, caffeine is another go-easy item. Our hearts simply do not need all that artificial stimulation all the time, especially as the years go by; we'd do better to increase our heart rate through exercise instead. So I would urge a drastic cutback on coffee and cola drinks (and the less sugar in your coffee, the better). Tea and other beverages are somewhat lesser offenders.

Which brings us to alcohol. Current wisdom—and it seems convincing—is that light to moderate drinking (say, a couple of drinks a day, which could be beer, wine, or heavier stuff) won't hurt us, unless we are allergic to alcohol or have a tendency to alcoholism. In fact, it appears even to be good for us; statistics suggest that light drinking decreases our long-range risk of heart attacks. Teetotalers don't seem to do much better than heavy drinkers in that respect, though this *could* be due to the special temperament it must require to remain a teetotaler in our society. Chronic heavy drinking is discouraged on all counts. It can lead to chronic gastrointestinal malfunction as well as extensive organ damage—to liver, pancreas, heart, brain.

I have now spent quite a bit of time talking about the first two aspects of my prolongevity program: what you eat and drink, and what you do to supplement what you eat and drink. I will be much briefer about the last two aspects: what you do with your body, and what you do with your mind. Of course, what you eat and drink, and the supplements you take, are all part of what you do with your body (and sometimes with your mind as well). But here I'll be talking more about what you do with your body in terms of exercise (and what you do *to* your body in terms of other habits); and what you do with your mind in terms of behavior and attitudes—the psychosocial ingredients of any prolongevity program. What I'm talking about, in short, is *life style*.

Though the discussion of life style will take up much less space than the earlier parts of the chapter (this is, after all, a book mainly about the *biology* of aging), it does not mean that I rate it as any less important than nutrition and supplementation. Kenneth Pelletier insists, in fact, that your psychosocial adjustment counts more in promoting longevity than any biological factors, including your genetics. You can eat and drink all the right things, refrain from eating and drinking all the wrong things, take all the right supplements, and still not thrive—if, for instance, you smoke, never fasten the seat belt in your car, lead a totally sedentary life, are depressed and pessimistic, have no friends or social support network, are bored, have nothing and no one you care very much about—need I go on?

A word first about smoking: don't! I can't offhand think of a favorable thing to say about the habit. The evidence, though not absolutely conclusive in the eyes of those who don't want to believe it, is fairly overwhelming that smoking—cigarettes in particular—substantially increases the risk of lung cancer as well as other kinds of cancer, of emphysema and other respiratory ailments, of virtually every variety of cardiovascular problem. I won't belabor this, because everyone sufficiently interested in science and health to be reading this book has surely already heard it all; and is meanwhile hearing it again and again from the Surgeon General's office, from the American Cancer Society, the American Heart Association, the American Lung Association, and any number of other sources. My simple advice—and not casual advice this time—is: Listen. Do what they tell you. If you don't smoke, don't start. If you do, quit. It's clearly not an easy task, or there would surely be many fewer smokers. Many people are probably so blessed and protected by their genetic immunity to various kinds of damage that they will live long lives and, no matter what they do, won't ever get cancer. But there is no way at this point to tell whether you are one of those so blessed or not. If you care about your longevity, or even in some cases about your relatively short-term health prospects, or even about the health of those around you who are forced to breathe your tobacco smoke, you will make special efforts to desist.

I have already briefly discussed alcohol. Taken lightly or moderately, it is merely something to drink, and, as already suggested, may even confer benefits. But taken excessively, it moves into the category of "abused" substances, the main difference being that it is not illegal.

The illegal drugs scarcely need discussion—marijuana, cocaine, heroin, and the like. They're all considered bad for us, though heroin is regarded as the most toxic and addictive, as well as the most menacing to other members of society, while of those mentioned marijuana is the least harmful. We don't know nearly as much about these substances as we should. Anyone who has used them, or seriously considered it (and there seem to be myriads of Americans who have at least tried, or who regularly use, the "lighter" drugs) is probably aware of the hazards and the ambiguities. I'll simply remind you that the use of any of these drugs is still against the law. So the least you risk is getting caught and being punished. And jail is bad for your health.

What of exercise?

You might not believe that the benefits of exercise still remain a matter of controversy. Many scientific purists insist that there is no clear-cut and universally acceptable *proof* that exercise prolongs life— or even that it surely does us any good. And the value of exercise is not easy to prove beyond all doubt; it is easier to prove that exercising inappropriately can be hurtful. But most scientists and physicians are content to settle for less than irrefutable, rock-hard data, and we all "know" intuitively that it has to be good for us, even though the lazy among us would rather believe in the wisdom of the man who said: When I feel the urge to exercise, I lie down until it goes away.

The evidence at hand—and I could fill many pages merely citing the people and the places who have done the work—is quite convincing enough for me. It suggests that exercise can hold off many of the functional failings of aging—the loss of bone strength and muscle mass, for example. Overall energy, stamina, agility, aerobic and cardiac capacity remain higher in exercisers than in the sedentary; the same advantage seems to hold for healthy levels of blood pressure, sugar,and cholesterol, not to mention mental outlook. As confirmatory evidence, just about every study of every one of those pockets of longevity around the world consistently shows that these hardy oldsters, in addition to eating frugally though nutritiously, remain physically active all their lives. For people who do not participate routinely in vigorous athletics, I urge that they find some congenial way to get a moderate amount of exercise *regularly*. An occasional spurt of hard exercise or physical work that may be unavoidable—such as shoveling snow, or pushing a stalled car, or running to catch a train while carrying a heavy suitcase—can be very dangerous if you haven't been doing anything else for a while. The weekend athlete is a notorious example of someone courting heart trouble.

If you have allowed yourself to get really out of condition, it is advisable to get a thorough physical examination and let your doctor work out some safe regimen to get you started. Exercise, if not every day, should occupy a little of your time at least three times a week. It should be not so strenuous as to tax you unduly, but strenuous enough to keep you reasonably fit. Some stretching and twisting and reaching are probably called for, and exercises that challenge the strength and mobility of every part of your body. With a little ingenuity, in almost any occupation you can find an excuse, a couple of times a day, to indulge in a little spurt of vigorous movement apart from your regular activities.

Here, too, books and exercise systems (from aerobics to yoga) abound; almost any of them is better than nothing. In addition to whatever you do at home or at work, you ought to do something outdoors,* something fairly easy and enjoyable but preferably some-

---

* Part of the reason for taking some time out-of-doors, in all seasons—apart from the benefits of fresh air (if you're lucky enough to live someplace where it still exists)— is that the human body, including the human eye, needs a certain amount of exposure to the full spectrum of natural light. The light that enters the eye plays a role in the cyclic production of the hormone melatonin, by the pineal gland, and a growing number of investigators believe that natural light is important to various aspects of health, mood, and behavior—too long a story to tell here. Sunlight has lately been perceived mostly as something to protect oneself against with sunscreens in order to avoid burns and, in the long run, skin cancer; and indeed these warnings should be heeded. But sunlight also activates a substance in the skin that helps produce natural vitamin D (not quite the same as synthetic D), which the body needs for the health of its bones. Even in winter, don't cover up every inch of skin with gloves, ski masks, and the like, as defense against the cold. Leave some skin exposed, on the face, at least, for periods of time. And, while eyes require protection, there's no need to wear sunglasses every minute of your stay outdoors.

thing that exercises your whole body—bicycling, swimming, jogging, skating, dancing (this one is mostly indoors, of course), or even just taking long and not-too-leisurely walks. Any of these activities ought to take up a half hour, at least; but, again, anything is better than nothing. We have placed great emphasis in our society on labor-saving devices, all the way from pushbutton garage doors to golf carts. Saving labor is fine if you're really physically overworked or handicapped or just plain exhausted. Otherwise it doesn't save a thing. It costs.

Because there has been no mainstream research to validate it, I have made no mention so far, but now feel I must, of certain body-movement systems that go far beyond any of the standard athletic or purely "exercise" systems in their scope and intent. There is, for instance, the Alexander Method, worked out by the late F. Mathias Alexander in Great Britain, and the "awareness through movement" system elaborated over many years by Israel's Moshe Feldenkrais, which seeks to integrate mind and body through the subtle and complex coordination of muscle and brain. They are better known to those in the performing arts than in the health community. Now Robert Masters of the Foundation for Mind Research, building on Alexander and Feldenkrais, has orchestrated their concepts and methods into an overarching system he calls "psychophysical re-education." In my view, it has great, even revolutionary, potential for human health, and probably for the retardation of physical aging, and is worth a major research effort. But until that comes to pass, I can only recommend that you look into it on your own if you're curious about it—in which case you might, for openers, read *Listening to the Body*, coauthored by Masters and his wife, Jean Houston (director of the Foundation for Mind Research).

In any case, the human body is a magnificently dynamic organism, designed for motion. Move it!

So much for the physical aspects of contending with aging. Let us now take a brief look at its psychosocial aspects. What that phrase means to me here is simply what the individual's mind, psyche, soul, spirit, call it what you will—and this encompasses his overall attitude and outlook, his personal philosophy—can do to help him thrive; coupled with how well he manages to flow in his social context. In the long-lived societies I have mentioned several times earlier, one of the reasons the old folks can glory in their state is that with it comes *status* as well. They are fully participating citizens of their communities. And this could have at least as much to do with their good health as their vigorous exercise and frugal diets. In some parts of the Orient and in many tribal societies, just reaching a certain age can bring the elderly individual automatic veneration, or at least respect. We know this is not the case in the United States (or in much of the Western world) today. True, a certain number of older people gain and retain a certain measure of respect through their wealth, their fame, their undeniable continuing achievements. But for the most part, worries abound that a diminishing work force of younger people will have to shoulder the ever-mounting burden of supporting an indecently proliferating population of the idle and infirm in their latter decades. So we cannot count, when we age, on the social supports that are taken for granted in some other cultures. Though we may hope that people's views will grow more supportive, experts believe they detect a growing "ageism," at best a somewhat testy tolerance of the aged.* If the attitude and mood of older people have a lot to do with their state of health, these frequently mirror society's negative attitudes toward *them*. Thus, when we talk—in terms of any personal prolongevity program— about psychosocial aspects, our emphasis has to be on the psyche. We'd best expect to make it on our own.

"Keep up your spirits," advised Ben Franklin at eighty, "and that will keep up your bodies." In fact, *if you don't keep up your spirits, all the purely bodily remedies you can muster will not do the job*. (This may be true at any age.) We know from countless scientific studies as well as from our own experience that body and mind are intimately interlocked. We know, for example, that the arrival of a piece of very good news, or very bad news, can spread shock waves from the brain throughout the body, triggering a whole battery of hormonal activities, drastically changing the biochemistry, affecting virtually every organ and system and billions of their constituent cells—and all this without anything *physical* having happened. So Ben Franklin's advice is amply supported by all current evidence. But it was certainly easier for Franklin, as an internationally venerated old man, to keep up his personal spirits than it

---

* Thomas R. Cole believes that ageism may be fostered by some of those who most deplore it. For example, advocates of prolongevity, in their eagerness to overcome the ravages of senescence, may, he thinks, succeed in making old age sound so ugly and undesirable as actually to arouse antipathy toward the elderly.

is for many of us more ordinary folks. Spirits can be hard to keep up under some circumstances, particularly under the often anxious and troublesome conditions of aging—and enforced retirement—today.

It's well accepted that our self-esteem, even our well-being, often depends on how we are perceived—or think we are—by others. This has always been true, in most cultures. Jerome Frank of Johns Hopkins wrote in *Persuasion and Healing* of a northern-Australian tribe known as the Murngin. Among them, "when the theft of a man's soul becomes general knowledge, he and his tribe collaborate in hastening his demise. Having lost his soul, he is already 'half dead.' " Other tribe members perform mourning ceremonies and make clear what they expect. The victim's efforts, under the circumstances, are geared not to living but to dying. Before we dismiss the Murngin rites as barbarous, should we not look to ourselves, perhaps substituting "retirement ceremonies" for "mourning ceremonies"—to which they bear a striking similarity as anticipatory events? When we force a still-vigorous individual to retire, do we not, in a sense, steal his soul? The more fool he, of course, for having permitted his employment to *become* his soul, to be so easily stolen.

To keep up the spirits, then, to hang on to one's soul, may be more difficult for old people—and those approaching old age (and who is not, every day of his life?)—in our society today than it has been at most times in most places. Yet a much greater proportion of old people come through with hardy psyches than is generally revealed in all those gloomy stories about "the graying of America." This point has been convincingly documented by such authorities as Robert N. Butler, USC's James E. Birren, and the University of Chicago's Bernice L. Neugarten.

Though this book is not primarily for the aged but, rather, for the aging (that is, the entire population), I have been concentrating for the moment on the retirement syndrome because it highlights for me the difference between success and failure in following Ben Franklin's advice. Out of myriad cases one could choose from, there's one that Herbert Klemme of the Menninger Foundation handled of a happy and successful man suddenly faced with retirement. Despite strong family ties—usually a powerful counterforce to such feelings—Mr. Jensen (the name is fictitious but not the patient) was "agitatedly seeking release from the pain he is experiencing. Because of the severity of his distress, I referred him to the very competent psychiatric facilities available in his local community. He is severely depressed and . . . suicide is a definite possibility. . . . In my opinion he is also a prime candidate for a severe debilitating physical illness: stroke, acute coronary heart disease, cancer. . . ."

Unfortunately, many people, in real life, commit suicide for no greater reason, as the fictional Willy Loman did under somewhat similar circumstances in *Death of a Salesman*. Depression, like stress (depression *is*, of course, a form of stress), has a striking effect on brain chemistry. Indispensable to the proper functioning of brain and mind are the substances known as "neurotransmitters" (notably the catecholamines). Stress in rats can lower levels of a critical neurotransmitter to the point where the animal is simply no longer able to organize itself to act self-protectively in a threatening situation; the chemicals necessary to transmit the messages across the nerve synapses—and hence evoke the motivation to survive—are just not there, at least not in sufficient quantities to do the job. The same kind of deprivation could be taking place in those afflicted with the retirement syndrome. But these exaggerated cases are, like the mourned-in-advance Murngin, people who have left their souls out unguarded, up for grabs.

Most of those who fail to thrive in retirement do not of course commit suicide; they simply go downhill fairly rapidly. The tragedy is that the decline is avoidable—or would have been, with some advance thought and preparation; there is nothing automatic about the decline of either mental or physical health after retirement.

Most people, in fact, seem to become happier, even healthier, after retirement than before—especially those who did not care all *that* much about their jobs anyway and who have other interests they have always wanted more time to pursue. A retiree often has more opportunity to take care of himself, to eat and exercise properly, to get enough rest, to enjoy play and leisure without guilt and still derive much satisfaction from continuing to work fruitfully in some less competitive way. Most long-lived people do continue to work at something, whether physical, mental, or both. Some people find themselves working even harder after retirement than before. Their attitude toward what they do is all-important. Mark Twain used to insist that he never worked, only played. Challenged by friends who knew how many hours he spent at his desk, he would reply that writing was not work.

Just as the distinction between work and play is often a matter of attitude, so is the distinction between stress and challenge. We all need just enough stress in our lives to keep us interested; only when it gets beyond our coping capacity and is *perceived* as stress can it properly be so described. One individual's stress is another's marvelous opportunity.

Despite the continuing decline of the human organism with age, many people in their later years are able to slow down that decline considerably by taking up sports and other vigorous activities they never tried before, developing new skills, new muscular strength and physical endurance, new powers of coordination. Even sexual powers, though gradually diminishing, are still present—as emphasized earlier—and employable essentially throughout life. In many cultures, as Jean Houston likes to point out, old people are *expected* to excel in all kinds of accomplishment—and so they do! Remember the difference it made to the brains of Marian Diamond's aging rodents to live in a stimulating environment?

Old talents can continue to sparkle well into the late decades (Arthur Rubinstein at the piano), and new talents can flourish (Grandma Moses at the easel). Perhaps most important, new powers of mind may be developed late in life—the ability to concentrate, to meditate, to expand awareness and consciousness. In our society, Robert Butler has written, "we rarely find anyone paying . . . attention to the growth of wisdom in the individual" with age. Considering what we now know about the continued growth and integration of our brain's neuronal networks with age, we should not be too surprised if the wisdom of the elders turns out to be biologically based and not merely a polite cultural recognition (which our own culture in any case denies) for past services rendered.

After exhorting you—sometimes with an exclamation point—to do so many things, I now want to say something with at least an implied exclamation point. My purpose has not been to give you orders in the hope that you'll follow them, but, rather, to point out a few directions among many in which you might go, instead of just sitting around despondently waiting for decrepitude to eat you up. The point is not for you to do anything in particular; in fact, with the tenure you've earned merely by growing old comes the right just to *be;* Colin Turnbull has nicely spelled out, in *The Human Cycle*, how creative just being can be, and how useful to yourself and to others (as is recognized in many other cultures, though not in ours). Another important thing to remember, especially as you grow older, is that, as Gay Gaer Luce points out in *Your Second Life*, "Each person is unique and will unfold in his or her own way." And its noncompetitive corollary: "Nobody can be compared with anyone else." In fact, it was Luce and her collaborators who established the remarkable Project Sage in California's Bay Area, which has served as a beautiful demonstration of what can be done by older people once they understand how they can combine various insights and aspects of body and mind to begin to grow again in surprising and pleasing new ways.

A positive, optimistic, interested, engaged outlook on life, then— in the absence of any chronic organic disease—surely can have a positive effect on the aging individual's physical and mental functioning. Such an outlook usually includes maintaining friendships and family relationships—or renewing them, or seeking them out— and making use of whatever social support networks are at hand (one does not have to stand in lone, independent splendor, though one may choose to).* It usually also includes a continuing curiosity and caring about the world—its small things and its large things, its joys and its problems—and the people in it. After studying long-lived people in a diversity of cultures, David Gutmann of the University of Michigan concluded that "active mastery . . . is the ego state most clearly associated with longevity." Not power over others, but a sense of being master of one's own life and circumstances. In another study of longevity, Robert Samp of the University of Wisconsin noted that a vital ingredient was *a continuing interest in the future*. This does not mean a continuing ambition to get ahead personally. In fact, among 1,200 men and women a hundred years old or older who were interviewed by the Social Security Administration—a project described by Osborn Segerberg, Jr., in *Living to Be 100*—it was clear that, though these individuals worked hard and enjoyed their work, there was a marked lack of high ambition. They had tended to live relatively quiet and independent lives, were generally happy with their jobs, their families, and their religion, and had few regrets. Nearly all expressed a strong will to live, and a high appreciation for the simple experiences and pleasures of life.

---

* In a study of 5,000 men and women in Alameda County, California, carried out by Lester Breslow and his associates at UCLA, recurring themes were the importance of social connections and general "life satisfaction."

Keeping up the spirit, the whole human spirit, engages all our available capacities, all our lives. Or it does when we allow it to, or when other people or just plain rotten luck do not deny us access. One example of the kind of bad luck that can befall us is a polluted environment. I guess there is not much you or I can do about that personally, except to avoid undue exposure to hazards and contaminants when possible; and, for everyone's good, to refrain from doing anything to add to that polluton—or to the social pollution (including negative views of old age) that puts such a burden on individual psyches.

A personal prolongevity program initiated now will, in some people's eyes, amount to buying time in anticipation of the larger anti-aging breakthroughs to come. In regard to the specific possibilities outlined earlier, keep an eye out for further developments. They will surely appear and be publicized in the media. If you should volunteer to serve as an experimental subject for any of these potential remedies, just be sure that the consent you give is truly informed.

Finally, you can do your utmost to influence, by whatever means may be at your command, those responsible for biomedical research policy, to see that gerontology is adequately encouraged and financed.

That is, if you think it should be.

And whether it should be or not is the next question we must come to grips with.

PART THREE

BUT SHOULD WE DO IT?

D. *Our first question has to do with immortality.*
R. *Why immortality?*
D. *Only because it is the most personal matter, literally, that can engage the human mind.*

—Norman Cousins
The Celebration of Life

[Roger] Bacon deduced that, if, after the Fall, men [Methuselah and the other antediluvian patriarchs] still were able to live almost a thousand years, then the short life span of his own times might be the result not of the will of God but of the ignorance of man.

—Gerald W. Gruman
A History of Ideas About the Prolongation of Life

Here, then, is the greatest of all opportunities for medical science: the improvement of the human condition in the final years of life. . . . But most of all, if we hope to ward off demographic disaster—a pile-up of the feeble and the infirm—we need research, good, old-fashioned, obsessive, reductionist science.

—Lewis Thomas
"Medicine's New Role," *Discover*

20

THE IMMORTALISTS

GILGAMESH, the legendary king of Uruk, mighty in war and daring in peace, extravagantly endowed with all the juices of life, gave little thought to the prospect that his prodigious energies might one day fail. He had seen death frequently and had not hesitated to inflict it; but, as we might say today, he didn't relate to it personally. Then death took his closest comrade, Enkidu. Gilgamesh was outraged. He wanted Enkidu's company, and he was used to having what he wanted. But he finally had to concede that he could no more call Enkidu back than King Canute, later, could command the tides. Dismayed at the irrevocability of Enkidu's departure from the world, he was haunted now by the suspicion that his own everlasting survival wasn't guaranteed either. He grew so obsessed with the fear of death, however far off it might be, that he found no further joy in living. As Ionesco has asked, in our own time, "Why was I born if it wasn't for ever?" Or, as Unamuno put it in *The Tragic Sense of Life*, "If consciousness is . . . nothing more than a flash of light between two eternities of darkness, then there is nothing more execrable than existence."

Gilgamesh was able to shake off his despondency only by resolving that he would live forever. *His* light would not be engulfed by those dark eternities. Reaching for immortality, he traveled far to seek out the advice of the wisest, and there was no recipe that he disdained. But finally, understanding that he was human and mortal, he decided to enjoy what he could and accept the inevitable.

The Gilgamesh epic, reconstructed by scholars from millennia-old clay tablets, has reverberations for us today. There, as one example, stands Bernie Strehler, comparing death to Moby Dick and vowing, "We'll get him yet!" Psychiatrist Robert Jay Lifton of Yale, student and chronicler of death in Hiroshima and Vietnam, has evolved a theory in which human extinction displaces sex (Freud's candidate) as the human psyche's central concern. Lifton believes that the modern individual is torn by his awareness of death and his suppression of that awareness; he is oppressed by his mortality, and by his yearning for immortality.* Lifton discerns in each of us "a compelling universal urge to maintain an inner sense of continuous symbolic relationship, over time and space, with the various elements of life . . . a *sense* of immortality . . . a symbolization of his ties with both his biological fellows and his history, past and future."

Tolstoy's Ivan Ilyich, as he lies dying prematurely of a baffling illness, typifies these contradictory aspects of the human condition. Ivan always "knew" he would have to die, as everyone does; yet, faced with death's imminence, he refuses to accept it. He desperately wants to go on living, but knows that, where immortality is concerned, the reach for it is as unacceptable as the grasp of it is unattainable.

We do of course need to accept death, but also to accept—and honor—that sense of our immortality (even the yearning for it, futile though it might be) that Lifton speaks of. But all our cultural traditions militate against our allowing these feelings about immortality to surface—or, if they do surface, acknowledging them as legitimate rather than deriding them, as we customarily do. This could represent a failure of the psyche, perhaps even our species's psyche, of which Jung, for one, was always so aware and which he was at such pains to point out to the rest of us. Yet Jung could write: "As a physician, I am convinced that it is hygienic to discover death as a goal toward which one can strive; and that shrinking away from it is something unhealthy and abnormal."

These days it has become especially fashionable—in large part

---

* A similar thesis was expounded by Ernest Becker in his brilliant book-length essay, *The Denial of Death*, much admired by Lifton. Joachim E. Meyer of the University of Göttingen, in *Death and Neurosis*, also gives primacy to the fear of death, rating it as much more central in its effects than, say, separation anxiety or the fear of castration.

through the rise of thanatology and the movement to establish hospices for the terminally ill—to encourage the acceptance of approaching death. The thanatologists, those whose professional specialty is to think about the nature of death and to help prepare people for it, know that there is a period when the dying person "practices denial." Part of the thanatologist's job is to facilitate the passage from denial to acceptance.

Side by side with this trend has been the growth of a small immortalist movement, whose advocates hold out the hope of abolishing, or at least indefinitely postponing, death. They feel that human beings already think too much, not too little, about death; that we have actually been too accepting of it; that in fact it might be healthier for us to practice some of the denial that the thanatologists are trying to educate us out of. "It is precisely this orientation to death which hinders us from launching a global crash movement to overcome mortality," writes F. M. Esfandiary in *Up-Wingers: A Futurist Manifesto*. "Humans are still too death-oriented too guilt-ridden too submissive and fatalistic to demand immortality. To even hope for it."

There are scientists, such as Strehler, who talk of defeating death. What they really intend, however, is merely the further postponement of death, the extension of the human life span beyond (perhaps well beyond) its present limits. But people like Strehler do not qualify as true immortalists: immortalists aim not to die at all. When they speak of immortality, they are not referring to a vicarious or metaphorical immortality, the sort conferred by, say, creating works of art that will live on in posterity's esteem, or by remaining alive as memories in the minds and hearts of loved ones. They are aware that books can be burned, that the loved ones who remember will also die in their turn, that buildings are destroyed and cities covered with sand, that even pyramids erode away in the fullness of time. What immortalists want is to be here in person, if not for eternal life, at least for indefinite life. Nor will a repeatedly incarnated life satisfy their yearning; the life must be continuous, with the same consciousness remaining aware of itself and its own history through time.

When, in a fictional dialogue in Norman Cousins's *The Celebration of Life*, the Docent asks, "Can you conceive of immortality without continuity of personal memory?," the Respondent answers: "No. How can I be expected to contemplate the meaning of immortality if my immortal self would not know who my mortal self was? If I am deprived of the continuity of memory, how would I know I was immortal? Obviously, I would have to know later who I am now. And I want to know now that I shall know this later."

The novelist Alan Harrington sounded the central theme in the opening sentence of *The Immortalist*, published in 1969: "Death is an imposition on the human race, and no longer acceptable." His epigraph was Unamuno's "All or nothing! . . . Eternity, eternity! . . . that is the supreme desire!" By then, Robert C. W. Ettinger had already published *The Prospect of Immortality*, which launched the cryonics movement. What Ettinger and the cryonicists advocate is the freezing of dead bodies rather than their burial or cremation, to preserve them in as intact a condition as possible against the day when the infinitely more knowledgeable medical science of the future could thaw them back to renewed life. The cryonics movement (its catchphrase: "freeze-wait-reanimate") is an integral part of the immortalist movement. Though all cryonicists are immortalists, all immortalists are not necessarily cryonicists. Nevertheless, if the origin of the current immortalist movement can be traced to a single event, it was probably the publication of Ettinger's prophetic and evangelistic book. Despite the unlikely nature of his proposals, Ettinger, a professor of physics, writes with intelligence, clarity, and good humor.

I devoted considerably more space to cryonics (and immortalism in general) in *Prolongevity* than in *Prolongevity II*. Because they are not central to the main topic of this book—the progress of aging research—the details I have provided are skimpier than last time. Yet I could not in all conscience omit these movements altogether. They are related to gerontology, and readers deserve to know that they exist as phenomena on the contemporary scene. If you are curious to know more about cryonics, I suggest that you read *The Prospect of Immortality* as well as Ettinger's later book, *Man Into Superman*. A subscription to the Cryonics Society's lively mimeographed newsletter, *The Immortalist*, is a good way to keep up with cryonic goings-on.

Some immortalists feel a bit uneasy about being too closely identified with the cryonics movement, because, for one thing, immortalism is not dependent upon cryonics, and, for another, they fear that some people who might otherwise be attracted to the immortalist philosophy may be put off by the cryonic idea. Cryonicists

themselves certainly do not tout their way of thinking as the One
True Path to Immortality; they simply regard it—in the absence of
any practical alternative—as the only way that anyone currently
dying (which means anyone now alive) can hope to win a long-shot
gamble on a renewed stretch of life. They hope, of course, that
accelerated research in cryobiology will increase the odds. Hence
Ettinger's basic advice: "Try to stay alive a little longer."

Thus, even to Ettinger and his followers, cryonic interment is
merely a stopgap measure, something to do while waiting for the
larger gerontological breakthroughs to occur. They look for the day
when it will no longer be necessary to freeze anyone, because all
illness will be curable and no one will grow senescent or die except
by some catastrophic accident that destroys the body beyond hope
of retrieval—though what constitutes "beyond hope of retrieval"
will also change with time.

"Immortality," says Esfandiary in *Optimism One*, "is only another phase in evolution. It is no more spectacular than the evolution
of the upright position or the attainment of speech. Certainly it is
far less spectacular than the emergence of life from matter." And
in *Up-Wingers:* "Immortality is now a question of how and when—
not if." Esfandiary's sentiments are echoed in *The Immortality Factor*, by Osborn Segerberg, Jr., and by Jerome Tuccile in *Here Comes
Immortality*. In *Man Against Mortality*, Dean F. Juniper, of the
University of Reading in England, sums up:

> Life itself is, on the best evidence, not immortal. It is also very
> clearly not the same thing as inanimate matter, which is slowly
> simplifying. Life is constantly renewing itself, striving to keep
> itself going in a world of steady simplification by taking inanimate
> matter and using it to maintain itself, in a kind of fluctuating
> battle, the skirmishes of which are births and deaths.
>
> And it is surely not too fanciful to suggest that if there is a
> battle, life may eventually triumph—not in the precarious sense
> in which we see it at present, but in a total, unconditional victory.
> In this war man may be life's ultimate weapon. *He may be de-
> signed to make himself and life immortal, the necessary skills and
> motivations having been built into him.* If this is the case then all
> his myths and fantasies of immortality may be in the nature of
> necessary rehearsals for an as yet unrealistic, but eventually to
> be realized, ultimate transformation. [Italics mine.]

Gilgamesh, then, may merely have been born out of time.

The best single source of information about the immortalist movement used to be A. Stuart Otto of San Marcos, California, who has
lately discontinued his newsletters. His own basic immortalist book
(written under his adopted name, "Friend Stuart") is *How to Conquer Physical Death*. His essentially Christian-metaphysical thesis
is curiously similar to that of George Bernard Shaw's Franklyn Barnabas in *Back to Methuselah*: you achieve continued life by *willing*
it. Shaw himself, that supreme rationalist and intellectualizer, seemed
in his later years to have developed the belief that evolution may
have come about through a kind of intense protoplasmic yearning
for it. His character Dr. Barnabas tells the politicans: "Do not
mistake mere idle fancies for the tremendous miracle-working force
of Will nerved to creation by a conviction of Necessity. . . . They
will live three hundred years . . . because the soul deep down in
them will know that they must, if the world is to be saved." Friend
Stuart does not of course stop at three hundred years. He believes
there might well already exist beings among us who have lived many
lifetimes—who are in fact immortals—and who would not be likely
to reveal this to the rest of us in the current state of our development.

In mid-1975, Otto spearheaded the organization of the Committee for the Elimination of Death, whose members included Tuccile
and Esfandiary. Its central tenet, as first expressed, was "that immortality here and now, rather than hereafter, is both possible and
worth striving for."

The hard core of immortalists strive for literal immortality—living
forever—or at least, as Dean Juniper puts it, "the amount of time
that any man might wish to live supposing that he had the power
to do so"; in other words, "a state of absolute choice." But people
like Ettinger and Alan Harrington will settle for less. They know
that the eternity Unamuno demanded is a long time. As Harrington
has written:

What must be eliminated from the human situation is the inevitability of death as a result and natural end of the aging process.
I am speaking of the inescapable parabolic arching from birth to
death. But we must clearly understand that any given unit of
life—my individual existence and yours—can never be guaranteed eternity.

Until such time as duplications of individual nervous systems can be grown in tissue cultures (at this point no one knows "whose" consciousness they would have), our special identities will always be subject to being hit by a truck or dying in a plane crash. A sudden virus or heart seizure, even in the body's youth, may carry us off. . . . But the distress felt by men and women today does not arise from the fear of such hazards. Rather, it comes from the certainty of aging and physical degeneration leading to death. It is the fear of losing our powers and being left alone, or in the hands of indifferent nurses, and knowing that the moment must come when we will not see the people we love any more, and every thing will go black. . . .

In our conception immortality is *being alive now, ungoverned by span, cycle or inevitability.**

Harrington discusses various symbolic ways of "defeating" death, but is tough about insisting that "the struggle against real death requires training, and must be fought out industrially and in the laboratory." His faith, unlike Friend Stuart Otto's, is altogether nonmetaphysical. But he makes clear his conviction—again, so much like that of Shaw's Dr. Barnabas—that we must either succeed in this endeavor or watch civilization go down the drain.

The immortalist movement is small in terms of membership, and its scientific proponents are few indeed. But its existence, and the vigor and enthusiasm of its adherents, suggest that many people have strong yearnings in this direction—for longer life, if not for the whole immortalist package. ("We don't crave immortality," said Pindar, in the fifth century B.C., "but we must reach out to the limits of what is possible for mankind.") Hence my feeling of certainty that, once the capacities for extending human life are at hand, there will be plenty of volunteers for the benefits that so many others still rate as dubious.

Henceforth I will be talking not about immortalists but about advocates of prolongevity, those who would wish for longer, healthier, more vigorous lives than are now the norm—those who would welcome the discoveries enabling us to live out our current life spans

* In the late eighteenth century, Condorcet had a similar vision of a day "when death will be nothing more than the effect either of extraordinary accidents, or of the slow and gradual decay of the vital powers; and that the duration of the interval between the birth of man and his decay will have itself no assignable limit."

in the best possible health (a relatively, but not altogether, noncontroversial goal), but who would also favor (or even just assume that one event would follow from the other) an additional stretch of good years, an extended life span. How extended? Well, if one learns to extend the life span, presumably by altering one or more of the genetic clocks, one can only use the word "indefinite." This does not mean forever, or even a substantial stretch of years. On the other hand, one simply cannot say. If the span can be extended to 120, why not to 150? And at what number can one draw the line? So it becomes theoretically possible to think about Methuselan ages in the real future.

There is no doubt that the mere contemplation of a designed immortality, or a contrived prolongevity (though what aspect of our improved longevity thus far has not been contrived?), raises strong misgivings in the breasts and brains of many thinking, feeling people, who worry about the human consequences of even a fractional gerontological success in extending the life span.

21

CONSEQUENCES

IN W. W. Jacob's famous short story "The Monkey's Paw" an elderly British couple comes into possession of an ancient, shriveled monkey's paw. Its owner, they are told, is entitled to make three wishes. But the previous owner of the paw warns the old man: "It had a spell put on it by an old fakir, a very holy man. He wanted to show that fate ruled people's lives, and that those who interfered with it did so to their sorrow." Properly cautious, the old man decides to make a safe, modest wish: He wishes for two hundred pounds. Exactly that sum of money does arrive the next day, but in the form of a compensation payment for the death of their son in a horrible accident. The second and third wishes do nothing to retrieve the situation.

There must be few human cultures whose literature and folklore do not contain such cautionary tales. Our most deep-seated Jungian natures seem to harbor large suspicions as to the advisability of tampering with the "natural" order of events, even when we have the opportunity to do so for our own benefit (*especially* if we do so for our own benefit). We are convinced that even the smallest and most innocent request will cost us more than it is worth. It will be misunderstood, misinterpreted, misapplied; it will, somehow, back-fire on us. There is always a catch to the gift request. As in the case of Faust—or the owner of Stevenson's Bottle Imp—a pact must be made with the devil, who implacably extracts his due.

In the brash scientific era, our Faustian Western civilization has been cavalier about interfering with the natural order of events, sometimes on an impressive scale. But the consequences—in terms of pollution, overpopulation, ever-more-destructive weaponry, social and personal stress—seem to confirm our soul-felt fears about the hazards of such tampering. Where medicine is concerned, it does not really surprise us that every medication, every therapy comes with a built-in likelihood of adverse side effects, from mild to lethal. Even medical measures that have had an undeniably curative or life-prolonging effect—where the benefits plainly outweigh the risks for the ailing individual patient—are not without their controversial aspects. When therapies are discovered that keep alive the victims of various hereditary (or partly hereditary) afflictions, people who would otherwise have died at earlier ages—and keep them alive long enough to marry and have children of their own— we applaud the medical victory. Some geneticists nevertheless grumble that such practices may have deleterious effects on the human gene pool. When the malarial swamps of a poverty-stricken, heavily peopled area are sprayed with DDT, the mosquitoes are destroyed and countless human lives saved, and there are cheers all around. But the population then spurts rapidly beyond the region's food resources, and soon just as many people are dying of starvation as formerly died of malaria; and who knows in which vital organs of the area's noninsect inhabitants the DDT may have settled? In recent years, the same kind of concerns have been aroused by the increasingly favorable prospects of genetic engineering.

Despite such caveats, few people have any real qualms about applying medications, surgery, or any biotechnology that might cure, prevent, or ameliorate the suffering and discomfort of the sick and injured. There is much more hesitation, however, over the notion of tampering with the human life span, for is it not right that a person should die at his appointed hour?* Even gerontologists like

---

* Gruman calls this kind of thinking "apologism." He explains: "Where meliorism implies that human effort can and should be applied to improving the world, apologism condemns any attempt by human action basically to alter earthly conditions . . . within the framework of this study [on prolongevity], apologism may be defined as the belief that prolongevity is neither possible nor desirable. . . . To be classified as an apologist, it is not sufficient for someone to assert blankly that the prolongation of life is not possible; he must, so to speak, take the offensive and claim that, moreover, it is not desirable." Gruman's catalogue of apologists goes all the way back to Aristotle, Lucretius, and Cicero.

Apologism is not too far from what Freeman Dyson, in *Disturbing the Universe*, calls the "cult of evanescence," which, he says, "is nothing new. It is strong in

to cite the story of Tithonus, out of Greek mythology. Tithonus, prince of Troy, was loved by the goddess Aurora, who persuaded Jupiter to grant him immortality. The catch was that she forgot to specify youth and strength to go with the added years. Though godlike in his immortality, Tithonus was as subject to senescence as any mortal. He grew old, feeble, utterly miserable, wishing for death but condemned to go on living. It was for him that Tennyson wrote the lines: "And after many a summer dies the swan. / Me only cruel immortality / Consumes. . . ." (Aurora finally turned Tithonus into a grasshopper—which was, I guess, a solution of sorts.)

Searching for the roots of human despair, Kierkegaard, in *Sickness unto Death*, virtually equated it with a revulsion against the obviously dismaying—to him—possibility that the individual might be condemned to eternal existence, with no end and no escape. Certainly the eternal wheel of existence in the ancient Oriental doctrine of metempsychosis, with each soul engaged in an unending series of reincarnations, evoked despair in the breasts of millions of the miserable throughout the generations; and the promise of escape from that wheel through the attainment of nirvana must have been one of the great attractions of Buddhism.

The theme of immortality-as-curse is carried on through the centuries, as evidenced, for example, in the eternally senile Struldbrugs encountered by Gulliver on Luggnagg, or, today, in Robert Silverberg's *A Matter of Life and Death*. Gerontologists have no interest, of course, in turning us into a race of Tithonuses or Struldbrugs. What they seek to extend is not the period of senility, but the good vigorous years of life. Whenever people have succeeded in doing this—in literature—what they have achieved is usually made to seem wrong, even sinful. The central character of Karel Čapek's 1922 play, *The Makropoulos Secret*, is a woman who has been able to keep herself alive and relatively young for some three hundred years by the use of a secret formula. She has lived several lives under several names. A small group of people who have learned the truth

Homer's *Iliad* and in the apocryphal book *Ecclesiasticus* of the Hebrew Bible. The essence of it is a profound sense of the nobility and beauty of short-lived creatures, a beauty made more intense by the fact of their evanescence. The cult is made up of joy and grief inextricably mingled. In Stapledon's vision of the future, the cult of evanescence keeps mankind in balance and in contact with the natural world. It holds in check our tendency to unify and homogenize ourselves. It keeps us forever humble before nature's prodigality."

about her gather in a room. One man, Gregor, taking the stance of a prosecuting attorney, intones: "The accused, Emilia Marty, a singer. She is accused before God and us of fraud and falsification of papers for her own selfish purposes. And furthermore and in addition, she has transgressed against all trust and decency—against life itself! That does not belong to human judgment. She will have to answer for it in a higher court."

Such a view may seem extreme to us in the mid-1980s, but I believe it accurately reflects the disquiet people often feel about prolongevity. Some years ago, I participated in the Committee for the Future's first SYNCON (for "synergistic convergence") at Southern Illinois University at Carbondale. The SYNCON was a rather complex kind of conference, about a week long, in which various "task forces"—each with its own "coordinator," each assigned a particular area of human concern—met in the separate, walled-off rooms of a large, circular structure out of whose hub the leaders operated. The assignment for Carbondale was grandiose by necessity: to set, for the next twenty years, goals and a program by which the human species could move toward solving some of its pressing global problems. During the conference, some walls were removed here and there so that different task forces in related fields could interact. Toward the end of the week, *all* the walls came down so that everyone could come together in a large confrontation and sharing. At this time each coordinator was to reveal to the assemblage the goals his own task force had set; then we would see what kind of consensual program we might arrive at. As coordinator of the biological task force, I was called on early. One of the high-priority goals we had set, I said, was a program directed toward the conquest of old age and the addition of a number of good years to the human life span.

Hands went up all over the place.

The first to speak was a clergyman who was coordinator of one of the other task forces. "I would think," he said firmly, "that extending the human life span would be one of our *lowest*-priority goals—if indeed we should undertake it at all at this time in our history. Many of my parishioners are bored with life at forty. I spend a lot of my counseling time trying to give people a reason for getting up the next morning and just making it through the day. Now, until we can make it worth people's while to live for seventy years, it seems pointless to try for a hundred and seventy!"

Applause.

The next person to object was the coordinator of the environmental task force. She, too, thought that an anti-aging program should be last on our list rather than first. Considering the problems of pollution, overpopulation, diminishing resources (indeed, much of the SYNCON's attention had been focused on the "Limits to Growth" thesis) that already plagued us, she was horrified that we would even tolerate the idea of keeping people around longer, thus aggravating all our afflictions.

More applause. And other speakers took their turns, voicing one objection after another, ranging all the way from the very personal to the global, cosmic, and evolutionary.

It is clear that the idea of living longer does not win anything like automatic or universal assent. Many people are downright hostile to the idea. This was especially brought home to me during the many lectures and TV and radio appearances (the broadcasts were often with live or call-in audiences) that I undertook after the publication of *Prolongevity*.

The immortalists argue that many harbor negative feelings about prolongevity out of conditioning and habit, and because they believe they have no choice anyway; but that, if there did exist a real and believable option to live out a longer span of good years, a number would change their minds and vote the other way. I think this is probably true. Nevertheless, I believe a great many individuals—even given the choice—would still elect to let nature bring life to its current culmination. (The assumption, of course, is that no one would be forced to take advantage of the option to live longer, which would simply be available for those who chose it.) And their reservations are not merely the unthinking expressions of antiprogressive bias. Rather, they bespeak a valid concern, deeply felt in both brain and belly, that our most prized human values may be in danger.

"Perhaps the biggest threat to the human race at the moment," wrote Kenneth Boulding in the *Bulletin of the Atomic Scientists* in 1970, "is not so much the nuclear weapon as the possibility of eliminating the aging process. If we could rearrange the human genetic structure to program death at the age of 1,000 [thirty-one years older than Methuselah] rather than at 70 . . . the human race would face the biggest crisis of its existence, a crisis which I illustrate easily to an academic audience by asking them who wants to be an assistant professor for 500 years."

Prolongevity does have consequences. And the consequences if, starting tomorrow, we were all to live a thousand years would be overwhelming. It is not that Boulding believes anyone is likely to chance upon the kind of breakthrough that would permit individuals now alive to enjoy the millennial life spans of the biblical antediluvians. Gerontological success, when it begins to be achieved, will probably arrive in much more modest increments. Yet, in the long run, of course, the problems created by increased longevity will be so far-reaching as to exceed our present ability to imagine them.

Not that we are trying very hard to imagine them. Robert Heilbroner has noted that human beings, despite protestations to the contrary, do not truly care about posterity. They cannot relate to it in a personal way, the individual welfare of their children, yes, or even their grandchildren; but beyond these limited familial responsibilities, the future (even fifty or a hundred years off) is somewhere Out There, too remote to warrant much of today's worry energy. Later generations, with their more highly developed science and technology—we tell ourselves—will surely figure it all out when the time comes. Meanwhile, like Candide and Cunegonde, we must hoe our gardens.

"However altruistic we may be," says Dean Juniper, "we are usually capable of stifling our anxieties about those of our acts whose consequences will affect our descendants. We tend to talk in rather lofty ways about building for the future, but those plans do not carry the flavor of anxiety with them."

Those who have most energetically tried to imagine what human beings might be like if they were to live indefinitely are, as might be expected, the science-fiction writers. And their writings do usually carry "the flavor of anxiety" that Juniper finds missing in the rest of us. This anxiety shows through even in the imaginings of fairly optimistic writers like Robert Heinlein, who has succeeded in conjuring up a number of tolerably livable futures. Typical is Alan E. Nourse's short story "The Martyr," in which many of the long-lived characters seem to have a hard time getting anything accomplished. Under the euphoric influence of knowing that they always have plenty of time, they never feel any need to hurry. The members of a research team preparing to launch a large spaceship seem to be constantly on the verge of completing the project; but then someone sees a way to make the ship, and the mission, a little more perfect, and—since there is plenty of time—why not? So they keep tearing everything apart and starting all over again, until it becomes apparent to newly arrived observers from another planet that they are never going to get the ship launched at all.

Some writers have, in fact, imagined scenarios in which the human race becomes much less adventurous; in which that long stretch of life becomes so precious that its beneficiaries are obsessed with mere survival. Perhaps the ultimate story in this genre is Stephen Leacock's "The Man in the Asbestos Suit," from *Afternoons in Utopia*. Leacock envisions a once-great city, several centuries hence, where no one ever dies of anything but accident or injury. All the inhabitants go about encased in protective asbestos suits, spending all their time being careful, concentrating every attention on not having an accident.

Would longer-lived individuals really lose their sense of adventure, their zest for engaging in risk-taking enterprises? If so, society would stagnate—which, of course, it could not afford to do. A civilization inhabited by people wholly concerned with their personal survival at all costs would end up rendering impossible its own survival; for civilizations require high technology, and the taking of risks to cope with change, in order to sustain themselves. I suppose we might one day arrive at a point where we could turn the whole global enterprise over to a giant computer, though presumably it would still require some human repair, monitoring, and reprogramming capabilities.

If people lived longer, would they really be more easily bored—or less so? Would they be happier, more creative, more "human" (whatever we think that means)? Would we prize our lives and those of others more, or less? Would we be readier to go when death eventually arrived, or would we fight it more bitterly? Would our natures be kinder, or more ruthless? Obviously, our feelings about life and death would—then as now—be individual and conflicting. As the Cambridge philosopher Bernard Williams points out in *Problems of the Self*, "Death is said by some to not be an evil because it is not the end, and by others, because it is. . . ." Williams himself declares that immortality would be intolerable, but he does concede that it might be nicer to live longer. How much longer? He would elect to die "shortly before the horrors of not doing so became evident." It is likely that much of our character and temperament,

our social attitudes and ethical standards, would be heavily dependent upon the overall context in which we lived. And, at any given
time in the future, the quality of that context would in turn depend
upon how satisfactorily we managed the population problem.*

"It has been calculated," writes Juniper in *Man Against Mortality*,
"and this gives us an idea of the extraordinary capacity of geo-
metrical increase, that if life had been unnegated from the beginning, that is, if it had not been accompanied by death, we should
now be part of a solid ball of flesh expanding into the universe at
a speed approaching that of light." And even this, he adds, is "a
fantastically qualified speculation." He then goes on to make some
scary extrapolations.

It is clear that, if people stay around for longer periods of time
instead of dying off on the old schedules, they will fail to make room
for new arrivals. Thus, whatever birth ratios make for zero population growth in the 1980s will not hold for the ensuing decades and
centuries. People who remained alive and vigorous longer would
continue to consume the earth's resources through all those added
years, and therefore—based on present technologies—use them up
at an accelerated rate. They would also continue to add their wastes
and garbage and the emanations of their machines and appliances,
thus also accelerating the rate of planetary pollution.

Moreover, inasmuch as we are assuming that the new breed of
long-livers will remain physiologically younger for considerably extended periods of time (there may be no menopause), we may also
assume that their reproductive periods will be lengthened, so that
couples (or single women) can and may well want to go on having
children far beyond the usual cutoff point. Gilbert W. Kliman, a
psychiatrist in White Plains, New York, has observed that some
women seem happily secure only when they are pregnant; and that
this is, unfortunately, often especially true of disturbed or retarded
women. Though they lose interest in the children once infancy is
past, they like to go on having babies. If people were to remarry
again and again—an increasing likelihood as lives grow longer—and
still had energetic years of life to look forward to, they might choose

---

* Concern about overpopulation was a major factor in Lucretius's opposition to the
idea of prolongevity. (Yes, it was already being discussed in ancient times, though
not by that name.) At a later date, in England, the same was true—as might be
expected—of Malthus.

to have new families with their new spouses. Few parents seem to feel they did a good enough job; many might opt to see if they could do better next time around.

Yet, having a family at all may become a special privilege. As time goes on, the probability clearly grows that governments may have to intervene in traditionally sacrosanct personal and familial areas. As Juniper puts it, "We can deduce a strict control of immortalist men and women, in terms of a sophisticated, fool-proof, psychopath-proof system of ensuring that the option of immortality also entails sterility." The day might well arrive when would-be parents were required to apply for a license to have a child—and, in order to do so, would have to wait for a vacancy.* (Since they would have a lot of time, they might not mind the wait so much.) Enforcing such a requirement, especially making it as foolproof as Juniper suggests, would of course be fraught with difficulties.

As soon as a state begins to require licensing for any activity, those authorized to issue the licenses also feel authorized—indeed, duty-bound—to inquire into the qualifications of (in this case) the potential parents, not to mention the quality of the potential off-spring. Thus the family becomes ever more politicized. After all, if a society is going to admit to its membership only a few new children in each generation, its leaders will want to be very selective. Under these conditions, children should be especially prized individuals, well cared for, nurtured, and educated under the benevolent sur-veillance, not merely of their own parents, but of the entire society. Yet the very concept of strict, compulsory birth limitation implies the total disqualification, and perhaps the enforced sterilization, of many people adjudged (by whom?) to be "unfit," or merely insuf-ficiently perfect. It further implies compulsory genetic counseling, compulsory prenatal diagnosis, and, any time the outcome looks doubtful, compulsory abortion. Most of us alive today might fail the admission requirements to such a society.

As foreshadowed by Anthony Burgess's *The Wanting Seed*, in order to achieve population control homosexuality might be encouraged, heterosexual coupling discouraged, and "mother" be-

* Boulding once suggested, more than half seriously, a "green-stamp" plan, in which each young person in a given society would be awarded a certain number of stamps entitling him to, say, 1.3 children, or 0.8 children—which he could barter for other privileges (or vice versa).

come a dirty word not only in jokes about psychoanalysts. (Remember the gay male "mother" in *La Cage aux Folles*, who—on hearing that his adopted son is going to be married—asks, scandalized, "Married? To a *girl?*") The decisionmakers—the brave new society's equivalent of Huxley's Predestinators—may well decide that sexual intercourse is no longer the ideal civilized means for human propagation. They may opt for *in vitro* fertilization of selected donor eggs and sperm, perhaps prefrozen, the cloning of cells taken from preselected individuals, and the use of other advanced procreative biotechnologies. The late Nobel geneticist Hermann Muller was a vocal advocate of "adoptive parenthood" rather than old-style genetic parenthood, where people selfishly choose to perpetuate their own names and images rather than to have children with more suitable genetics. In an era when the genetic program for aging is under human control, the capacity should also be at hand for genetically programming most individuals to be infertile, if we so choose. In what form would the family survive? Would children be reared by the state or the community rather than by individual parents? How would this affect the character of the citizens that resulted? Which human qualities might be lost, and which gained? All these speculations—and they do not begin to exhaust even the obvious possibilities—reverberate with worrisome overtones.

To cryonicists and immortalists like Ettinger, Esfandiary, and Saul Kent (author of *Future Sex* and *The Life Extension Revolution*),* such worries are not taken too seriously. A major motif that runs through many of their arguments is that human nature, as well as the human social context, will have undergone such great changes that any extrapolations from present standards are simply meaningless. Indeed, when we consider how radically our standards have changed in the last few decades *without* the application of any advanced biotechnology (unless one puts the Pill in that category) or any widespread immortalist hopes or beliefs—and, further, how rapidly the new standards (or lack of them) have been accepted—it would seem foolhardy to brush aside too summarily the case for much more drastic transformations ahead. Such science-fiction seers as Arthur C. Clarke, Isaac Asimov, and Olaf Stapledon have imag-

---

* Kent also puts out *Anti-Aging News* and runs the Life Extension Foundation in Hollywood, Florida.

ined futures whose highly evolved, star-trekking inhabitants are hardly recognizable as their former human selves.

To think seriously about the implications of an extended life span, however, one does not have to project one's scenarios into the scarcely imaginable future, or even to global concerns closer to us in time such as pollution and overpopulation. On an immediate personal, community, and national level, extended life would have a profound impact. We are hardly aware of how much of our thinking, our life patterns, and our social institutions depend on the assumed immutability of the human life span. One need only take a superficial look at some built-in assumptions of our economy to get a quick idea of the magnitude of the consequences.

Suppose only a modest number of vigorous years have been added to the average person's life. Think what might happen to Social Security programs, retirement benefits, insurance commitments. All such plans are predicated on making payments for a strictly limited number of years. Think of the Veterans Administration budget if war veterans did not die off but went on expecting a continuation of their compensatory payments for unlimited periods of time. Think of a city like New York, already reeling from the financial burden of paying lifetime retirement benefits to its still-young retirees after twenty years of service, making payments to those same people long after one would have expected to attend their funerals, though they may look and feel as young as ever. Each working generation would be supporting several generations of retired people simultaneously. Obviously adjustments and revisions would have to be made. The same would be true of all insurance contracts. If life expectancies go way up, should insurance premiums not come way down? Would long-lived, healthy people feel the need for insurance at all, except for special circumstances? Upper limits would of course have to be set on long-term loans, with interest piling on interest over the years. All our economic programs might need extensive overhauling, if not complete redrafting.

In a society where old people not only lived longer but remained in such well-preserved condition as to be hardly distinguishable from the young in vigor and appearance, unfamiliar attitudes and relationships would evolve, new hopes and opportunities would arise, as well as new frustrations and resentments. Young people, even those who love and respect their elders, look to the day when those elders will step down from their positions, retire from active competition, die. They wait their turn, not always too patiently, for jobs, status, inheritance.

If a man or woman at sixty-five expected to remain vigorous and healthy for, say, another sixty-five or more years, current retirement policies would be mightily resisted and probably have to be changed. (It is possible this dilemma might be partly solved by "retiring" people into other careers, though there can be no assurance that openings would be more plentiful in other fields unless this was a built-in part of the package.) Healthy old people might be as unwilling to give up possessions as positions, and the longer they lived, the less willing they might be. The power and wealth they could accumulate over a long lifetime would be formidable.

At present the old can give up their jobs and their status with a modicum of grace and good cheer because they know they cannot hope to do those jobs or take advantage of benefits for much longer anyway. They can leave fortunes to their heirs and to charitable institutions because they know that "you can't take it with you." They generally cherish the young—or at least the young to whom they are personally related, especially their own children. But how much of this feeling is based on insecurity, on the knowledge that they will grow decrepit and need filial care and attention (although they can't realistically expect too much of that these days)? And how much is based, too, on the desire to see their names and images carried on in the next generation?

These feelings are bound to undergo some changes with increased longevity. If people begin more and more to think of themselves as their own heirs, relatively speaking, how will it affect their attitudes toward their children—and vice versa? If people no longer needed to worry about the early decline of health and strength, would they continue to cherish and cultivate those who, they hope, will be their future caretakers? And if they can carry on their own names and images indefinitely in person would they still care as much whether others carry them vicariously? It may be, of course, that no matter how long life lasts, people will still worry about the end of it, will still want the assurance of closely related and caring people—though some futurists insist that all humankind should exercise the same kind of caring concern for all its members without the need for "blood" ties or genetic relationships.

It would be a puzzling experience indeed for young people to live in a world where old people did not age. At present, young people at least have the advantage of their youthful looks and energies. They can overwhelm their elders in almost any sport, in any contest of physical strength or endurance, and, usually though not invariably, in any competition for the sexual favors of attractive partners. If older people retained their own youthful exuberance, these compensatory advantages might all evaporate. And if the old had youth as well as wealth and power, displacing them might be almost beyond competitive hope. The young would increasingly resent and abhor the presence of these perpetually youthful monopolists—unless the latter could figure out a means of sharing their benefits without threatening their own welfare. If prolongevity did not come about too suddenly—as is probable—there might be time for everyone to change basic attitudes and values. Young people, for instance, knowing that they too will reap the benefits of longer life, could make plans accordingly. Wise leaders could facilitate new and mutually rewarding accommodations.

Juniper suggests that a person who lived on and on "might not be allowed to amass wealth beyond a set figure or after a certain time. He might be required to hand back to a central property pool, or make over to a common fund, wealth he had accumulated beyond a given limit." I suppose this idea is simply an extension of the precedents established by income and inheritance taxes. It is even likely that a limit might be placed on life spans, or, at least, on the length of time a given individual would be permitted to spend on earth. In that event, death control would go hand in hand with birth control. As population pressures, among other pressures, mounted to a critical point, an upper limit of, say, two or three hundred years might be set, after which the lucky winner might have a choice of going to live in orbit (or another planet or asteroid), if space were available out there, or else . . .

Would people be any readier to depart after two or three centuries of life than they now are after three score and ten years? Or would they hold life more dear than ever? We have no way of knowing, though here again there would probably be a spectrum of individual reactions. As we have seen, visionaries all the way from Pindar to Condorcet to Alan Harrington have assumed a new serenity in our attitudes if we were no longer condemned to a fixed life span. But Ernest Becker quotes Jacques Choron to the contrary: "Postponement of death is not a solution to the problem of the fear

of death. . . . . There still will remain the fear of dying prematurely."
And Becker himself, in *The Denial of Death*, says: "The smallest
virus or the stupidest accident would deprive a man not of 90 years
but of 900—and would be then 10 times more absurd. Condorcet's
failure to understand psychodynamics was forgivable, but not
Harrington's today. If something is 10 times more absurd it is
10 times more threatening. In other words, death would be 'hyper-
fetishized' as a source of danger, and men in the utopia of longevity would be even less expansive and peaceful than they are
today!"

For those reluctant to go, would there be an automatic death
sentence? Would we be willing to institute capital punishment for
the crime of having lived too long? Might there be special circumstances for requesting extensions? Would a trial be necessary? Might
there be a thriving black market in false birth records? Wouldn't it
be hard to keep track of people who were highly mobile for a couple
of centuries, and prove their correct ages? Could we in any case
really bring ourselves to carry out the death penalty when the
condemned individuals had done no wrong, were still in the productive prime of life, still very much wanted to live, and had
the support of others who loved them and also wanted them to
live? Perhaps there could be a lesser penalty—an interruption
rather than a termination of life via an indefinite stretch of hibernation.

For people ready to die, there would be no difficulty. They
would simply commit suicide by some approved method, on
schedule, as envisioned in some of the science-fictional futures—
Heinlein's, for example. In a world where the life span had
been extended, we would in any case perhaps be obliged to
change our rigid views on the act of suicide. It would probably no
longer be considered either an immoral or a criminal act. My
assumption is that if it becomes possible to medicate or manipulate our bodies to enable ourselves to live longer, no one will
require us to take advantage of the opportunity. We will be
allowed to age and die in peace, as of yore, if that is our personal
choice.

Some strange relationships might develop between the short-lived
and the long-lived. And there might be objections to permitting
people to age and die in the old way on the grounds that they would
thus be unproductive and, moreover, represent an unfair drain on

society's medical and custodial resources.* In such a society, would people turn away from "ugly old people" even more than they do now? Now, at least, we see in old people our future selves and should therefore look upon them with greater sympathy. Or is it perhaps precisely because we see in them our future selves that we turn away from them, not wanting to be reminded of our fate? Among the more melancholy people in all of history may be those old people who are still around when gerontological help arrives but are themselves too far gone to be helped, the last generation condemned to age irreversibly and die as heretofore. The most optimistic gerontologists hope, of course, that once answers are arrived at, progress may be swift enough to help everyone who wants to be helped.

Even now, there is much debate concerning a patient's right to die if he wishes to, rather than to accept heroic biotechnological measures to keep him alive from one day to the next to the next when there is no real hope that he can pull through. In a few responsible quarters there is even some support for the idea that any person, ill or not, who simply decides he does not feel like living any longer should—after all efforts to revive his interest in life, including religious and psychiatric counseling, have failed—be not only permitted to end his life, but actually helped to make his exit in as tranquil and merciful a fashion as possible.

This is the view, for instance, of German-born Nobel laureate Max Delbrück, one of the physicists who made such important contributions to molecular biology. In an interview for the American Medical Association publication *Prism*, Irving S. Bengelsdorf asked Delbrück, "Would you then say that we cannot avoid using science and technology to control the termination of life?"

"Yes," Delbrück replied. "Further, I would suggest that our

* This is exactly the kind of argument used to justify the passage by New York State in 1984 of a law making it mandatory for drivers and front-seat passengers to wear seat belts or face a fifty-dollar fine each time they are caught unbelted. Some protested that the law was an unconstitutional interference with an individual's freedom of choice, an abuse of state power. But one of the bill's staunch advocates, the Automobile Club of New York, included among its arguments: "Injuries associated with non-use of seat belts increase the demands being made upon medical and rehabilitative services that are in limited supply, increasing governmental costs for such services . . . as well as consumers' costs for both automobile and health insurance."

society provide 'suicide education' as it now provides birth control information. . . . Society must have free access to information about forms of suicide that are not too repulsive.

"The present thrust of our society," he continued, "is to prolong life as long as possible. But there is no inherent biological or cultural necessity for such an attitude. The taking of one's life should be a matter of maturity as it was during the last hours of Socrates, as so wonderfully described by Plato."

He cites the case of the Nobel physicist Percy W. Bridgman, who, at the age of eighty, terminally ill with cancer, shot himself and left behind a note that read: "It isn't decent for society to make a man do this thing himself."

Delbrück went on to discuss how and when such education might be carried out. In high school or college? No, that is perhaps too soon. "I would suppose that suicide education should be given to people at an age when the person begins to realize that his stay on earth is finite. I don't think you can talk seriously to people about how to leave a party when they are just getting there and they think it's going to be a great party."

Whether or not we think life is going to be a "great party" does of course have a lot to do with our desire to stay or leave. Just accepting life as a tolerably good party is usually enough. The suicidal person has, as a rule, come either to look upon life's party as a dismal bore not to be tolerated or to feel that his own condition renders the party no longer enjoyable—as in the case of Bridgman or, say, Hemingway, neither of whom found his life boring. There is every reason to believe that life in an age of prolongevity would be a very interesting party indeed; I'll come back to that in a moment. But note Delbrück's emphasis on realizing that one's stay on earth is finite. If death were postponable and life's quality remained high, would he still advocate suicide education? Delbrück clearly does not have much faith in the promise of gerontology. In an earlier portion of the same interview, Delbrück does flatly say, "We are mortal and will remain so. What we accomplish by medical research is merely to shift the statistics in the causes of death."

In the case of an artificially extended life span, individuals would probably have a much clearer right to opt out when they felt they had lived long enough. It might simply be a matter of deciding to go off the life-prolonging medications or techniques—in which case the individuals would not shrivel into instant decrepitude, like the long-lived heroine of H. Rider Haggard's *She* when the fire of the Pillar of Life was withdrawn; rather, the remainder of life might follow its natural course. Or perhaps the genetic aging clock might be reset and the leave-taker could meanwhile keep himself going full-swing until the day the clock stopped. If cessation of medication were to entail a long-drawn-out period—especially a long-drawn-out period of deterioration and debility—he might look for a quicker exit, and perhaps society would feel he was entitled to it. It may even be that if aging had been programmed out of the genes, the "fail-safe mechanism" removed, growing old would be very difficult even if desired. In either case, the only way to die rapidly might be to commit suicide. Ideally, perhaps, people should be able to live as long as they want, even indefinitely, but go gracefully when they choose (as Bernard Williams suggested), with society's blessing. Thinking such thoughts is a difficult and distasteful pastime currently; but in an age when the planet had become overcrowded and potential parents were waiting for vacancies so they could have children, perhaps we could face the willing deaths of people who had lived as long as they pleased much more easily than we now cope with the pain-filled departures of loved ones who would wish to stay with us longer—and whose added years might enrich the world and all that dwell therein.

If we were to permit the deliberate ending of the lives even of healthy people in full possession of their faculties, one wonders how we might begin to feel, on a planet of finite size with limited resources, about the retarded, the crippled, those who by some official designation were deemed defective or imperfect. Might we find ourselves thinking more and more in "eugenic" terms and want to put these unfortunates "out of their misery" and not permit them to be "burdens to society"? Many people have already demonstrated their attraction to this kind of thinking, and we would do well to be on guard against it. Preventing hypothetical people from being conceived and born is not the same as putting existing individuals to death; and we place our humanity in jeopardy when we contemplate such measures. There is no reason why we should ever do less than our best for every individual born into the world—unless, perhaps, his life entails intolerable anguish—and at least let him live out his natural span of years as pleasantly as possible.

Considerations such as these are in large part what led Donner Denckla to put his DECO research on indefinite hold. Suppose

DECO does turn out to be the clock of aging, or one of the clocks. And suppose, further, that we had in hand right now a DECO antidote, a simple, inexpensive white powder. Would we really want to give it to everybody? The profoundly retarded forty-five-year-old in a mental institution, still wearing diapers, will live out his allotted time—but would we really want to extend *that* existence indefinitely? Denckla wonders if, in the face of such prospects, powerful institutions could really maintain their adamant opposition to birth control or birth prevention. And what of seemingly intractable criminals, already sentenced to spend their lives in prison—do we extend those lives, too? Denckla has been deeply disturbed by what he considers society's overreadiness to treat. For instance, he feels that many of the techniques being rushed into use to save premature newborns, even those with serious birth defects, do not constitute therapy at all, but, rather, experimentation on babies. "An experiment by its very nature may be defined as possessing zero data on which to forecast the outcome," he insists. "And zero data is what is often possessed on some of these 'therapies.' " He says he would like to see more careful and mature thought enter the arena of medical morality (and he recognizes that such thought is increasingly being brought to bear, but believes that political considerations too often get in the way) before he is ready to help speed the advent of an extended life span.

Denckla feels certain that when faced with the reality of such dilemmas nearly everyone will agree that there must be some limitation on who gets the DECO antidote (or any other sweeping life-extension invention). And he foresees, in that case, the development of a sizable black-market traffic in it. One remembers Alan Harrington's novel *Paradise I*, in which the masses of people get wind of the fact that there is an anti-aging remedy being given selectively to a hand-picked group of people, and riots break out in major cities, the have-nots demanding their equal right to prolongevity. Denckla believes it could be even wilder than the novelist imagines, even close to civil war if the circumstances warranted. And what of all the world's billions everywhere on earth—would they not also want it? Not all people in all cultures would want it, of course, but surely those who did would add up to impressive numbers. And wouldn't many of their rulers, especially the dictatorial types jealous of their powers and prerogatives, be almost certain to deny anti-DECO to their own masses? And wouldn't the resulting black market be more profitable than dealing in narcotics? Would the underworld control its distribution? And would there be mass migrations from those nations where the white powder was not available to those where it was? (Immigration barriers have never been very effective in keeping out people who were determined to get in.)

Let us return, for a moment, to the kind of "party" life might be in the event that gerontology achieves its major goals. A prolongevity society would surely pose new identity crises for its citizens. It would also require revised definitions of life and death, of youth and age. All human relationships would undergo change or at least reappraisal, including working arrangements, personal friendships, doctor-patient relationships, political associations, religious affiliations, sexual and romantic relationships, marriage and parenthood. We know that all change is stressful, and we can count on many more changes coming about through new biotechnological options—many of which were spelled out in my book *The Second Genesis*. We will possess a variety of interim biomedical strategies for delaying death, such as the successful transplantation of donor organs, the implantation of artificial parts, perhaps the growth of organs *in vitro* and their regeneration *in vivo*, and surely the control of immunological disorders, cancer, and the degenerative diseases— and ultimately for overcoming senescence and prolonging the life span. We are likely, too, to develop a large measure of control over our brains and minds, enlarging their capacities enormously—through, for instance, biofeedback, cybernetics, and brain-computer communications—and considerably ameliorating those aspects of "mental illness" contributed by faulty physiology and biochemistry. We will have at our command, as already indicated, an armamentarium of procreative biotechnologies, each with its accompanying risks and benefits: prenatal diagnosis and therapy, and the whole range of birth-control techniques—control of both fertility and infertility, artificial insemination, artificial enovulation, frozen egg and sperm banks, ova and ovary transplantation, parthenogenesis, androgenesis, superovulation, *in vitro* fertilization and *in vitro* gestation, cloning, genetic engineering, gene transplants, and gene therapy. We may well be in control of all the basic mechanisms of all life's processes, and thus trustees of our own future evolution.

Are we ready to take on such awesome responsibilities? Can we really hope to maintain our human qualities in a much longer-lived world? And do we know what we mean by human qualities? It is clear to Donner Denckla that we do not know what we mean. In fact, one of the things that bothers him most is that we have no consensus whatever among ourselves as to how we define a human being. Is anything that emerges alive from the womb of a human female, he asks, automatically entitled to human status? And therefore to the full range of human rights and benefits, including the indefinite extension of his life, no matter what its quality? Do we not need a constant infusion of "fresh blood" and young minds to help us cope with the challenge of changing circumstances? Would we not all become rigid, stultified, "set in our ways," desirous of preserving what makes us comfortable? Would we cease to be creative and thus be incapable of social evolution?

And what of our biological evolution? Could it proceed if death were indefinitely postponable and the turnover of generations (with fewer members in each) were to slow down? What of Denckla's fail-safe mechanism? How could the species continue to evolve, or even to survive, in the face of environmental modifications if there were insufficient replacement of individuals to allow genetic mutations to take place, and to be passed on?

In this chapter I have sought merely to offer a quick, provocative, impressionistic first sketch of the nature and extent of the consequences implicit in indefinite prolongevity. I am somewhat dismayed to report that in the interim since a very similar chapter was written for *Prolongevity*, no one has done much better! Very few people in government have taken the matter seriously. One of the exceptions is Senator Alan Cranston of California. Another is Greulich; but though he is worried about the consequences, he admits he has not devoted much substantive thought to the issues at the source of that worry, perhaps because he knows that in his position as director of NIA research he is expected to push ahead on all fronts (though in my view NIA doesn't really do that). In industry, too, there has been a dearth of concern about these matters, though a rare few, such as Wilfred Kraegel, recently retired from the Northwestern Mutual Life Insurance Company, have been urging that attention be paid. Academia has not done much better, though there have been a few attempts, such as that of Bernice Neugarten at Chicago, and one getting under way at UTMB/Galveston's Institute for the Medical Humanities, where Thomas R. Cole is spearheading some exploratory projects. A few projects—one, for example, a joint effort of the Hastings Center and the Futures Group, another a team led by Bernice Neugarten and Robert Havighurst under the auspices of the National Science Foundation—have given attention to a few of these issues. But, by and large, most demographers go on making their futuristic extrapolations directly from present trends, on the assumption that nothing much in the field of gerontology is going to happen to change matters. Some scientists are of course paying attention, such as Roy Walford and especially Donner Denckla, who has been doing some highly original thinking about the consequences of gerontological success. Even a superficial look at the dilemmas, however, is enough to make many people hold their heads in alarm and holler: "Good heavens, haven't we got enough problems already? Let's not do it!"

Should we not?

22

NEVERTHELESS . . .

BY NOW you have undoubtedly surmised my own strong advocacy of gerontological research—not necessarily of the immortalist, or even what Gruman calls the prolongevitist, philosophy, but of the quest for ways to add good years to the human life span. My advocacy is based on the belief that the thrust in this direction is (a) probably inevitable and (b) certainly desirable. I shall try, in this last brief chapter, to explain why I harbor these convictions despite my concern about the consequences we have just been discussing. I do share many of the qualms and misgivings of those less enthusiastic about pushing ahead with an anti-aging program. The "flavor of anxiety" is certainly not absent from my own musings about the future, as the previous chapter demonstrates. But that should be true of anyone's musings about the future—even without any considerations of gerontology or prolongevity. We are pressed upon from all sides by a multiplicity of dilemmas, all perplexing and all demanding simultaneous solutions. For the relatively foreseeable future, small increases in the number of good years of individual lives will surely not add more than a few percentage points of aggravation to such overriding concerns as, say, worldwide pollution and overpopulation. These concerns are of such magnitude, and such immediacy, that they will have to be dealt with and, to some reasonable degree, solved long before the gerontologists have stirred their ingredients into the mix.

Moreover, it would be a mistake to assume that all the ingredients will necessarily be troublesome to society. Some may, indeed, provide substantial side benefits. One ingredient that longevity could well add to the mix—an ingredient that, though neither tangible nor measurable, might help energize us for the more rapid resolution of our dilemmas—is *motivation*. Earlier I mentioned, for instance, the pessimism some people feel about the prospect of motivating ourselves to care about what happens to posterity. "We may worry about our children and perhaps our grandchildren," as the prince tells his priest in Giuseppe di Lampedusa's *The Leopard*, "but beyond what we can hope to stroke with these hands of ours we have no obligation." We might, however, suddenly find it much easier to relate to the future if we ourselves were to *become* posterity.

If individual human beings have a good chance of finding themselves still personally on the scene to suffer the consequences of pollution, overpopulation, and bungled statesmanship, they will be more likely to devote some attention to avoiding those consequences, just as many individuals (though not all) might consider changing their diets, habits, or life styles in order to add a few healthy years to their lives under present circumstances. It is an old truism that proprietors, or even long-term tenants, take much better care of their houses and apartments than transient occupants of the same premises. Even those whose minds are centered on industrial or personal profits might take a different view of pollutants shooting up from smokestacks, or effluents being discharged into rivers, of oceanic oil spills, of pesticide-poisoned wildlife, and assorted associated blights; and might even take independent initiative toward speeding ameliorative and prophylactic measures without needing to be goaded by militant environmentalists and conservationists. It would, after all, be their own supplies of breathable air, of drinking water, of food, of resources, of all the appurtenances of health, comfort, and convenience that were being endangered. In such a case, as Juniper again observes, "for the first time man will have the power to be himself, to make his own evaluation of life, and the effect may be to create between him and earth a new non-clinging, non-changing bond. This will be a relationship of equals, and the result may be that man may develop an entirely new sense of personal commitment to earth—a brother-earth philosophy of deep and abiding dimension." This would be a fulfillment of René Dubos's dream of us as the responsible, benevolent custodians of our planet. The extension of one's own life into the indefinite future, together with the possibility of identifying personally with posterity, might go a long way toward motivating us to a new impatience with delays and dawdling—the exact opposite of Nourse's eternal pro- crastinators.

Any forecast of how human beings are likely to behave in an imagined set of future circumstances is, by its very nature, prob- lematical. But I would guess that Stephen Leacock's man in the asbestos suit represents an unwarrantedly gloomy forecast of how long-lived individuals will behave. It seems doubtful to me that men and women will become so lackadaisical, even if allowed to indulge themselves without limit, as to lose their sense of adventure entirely. At any time, under any conditions, only a minority of the population are inclined to take unusual risks, but they are a consistent and substantial minority. Many young women and men of, say, twenty or twenty-five quite willingly lay their lives, or at least their limbs, on the line, not only in the service of good humanitarian causes or even for selfish gains, but often for the sheer sport of it, for the intrinsic thrill of taking the risk. To people so young, the fifty or sixty years of leftover life they are risking must seem like long stretches of life indeed; if it were longer, they would probably still risk it. Older people, too, risk portions of their lives that may grow increasingly precious to them. I believe we will always be trying things just because the ideas happened to occur to us, that we will always climb mountains just because They Are There.

My intuitive feelings about these matters, of course, can in no way be documented, or justified through *a priori* analysis, and could turn out to be badly mistaken. We know that the malleability of human nature, though not infinite, renders all predictions about it untrustworthy. (Of course, it also provides hope against the pessi- mism of those who insist, "You can't change human nature.") Nevertheless, we will be well advised to imagine what scenarios we can, to guess at the spectrum of human options implied, and to assign probability values—where we can—to the attitudes we deem most likely to prevail under various circumstances.

I am convinced that most of today's human values, our traditional sense of what is right and good versus what we feel to be wrong and evil, will still serve us well in most of the futuristic scenarios we can envision—those scenarios, at least, that do not imply a to- talitarian social fabric. Such a conviction may of course say more about my own programming than about future realities. And the human values I speak of are in any case, at any given time, more honored than practiced. But we should certainly exercise care, as we learn increasingly to manipulate our minds and characters, that we do not program ourselves out of the qualities we most wish to keep.

Some future-watchers have emphasized the unboundedly hedonistic opportunities ahead, the royal play. But a narcissistic preoccupation with the self cannot dominate the characters of those who populate the future; they will have to possess a good measure of altruistic concern for their fellow beings, and for their still generously endowed, though finite, planetary abode in the universe. It is only in the last instant of geological time that we have discovered the finiteness of our planet, and the fact that we have not yet, in that instant, solved the dilemmas the discovery has raised is hardly an adequate reason for pessimism.

We have lived through a period of bewildering change, and there is every evidence that change in the future will be constant and often radical. Change, as we know, is painful, or at least stressful—even change for the good, change we all applaud. "The leader who denies the pain of change," says George Leonard, "is fooling his followers or, what is worse, himself." We will be constantly readjusting to these changes and helping others, who are perhaps less able to cope, do likewise. The well-functioning individual must be neither too selfish nor too selfless. He should have a healthy ego and a great appetite for joy, but also a compassionate sensitivity to the needs of others. Some of his joy should be generated by the very exhilaration of meeting the challenges of change—and of freedom.

The new era could bring us totally unprecedented freedoms, but freedom often turns out to be among the more unwelcome of human gifts. Our enemy is whoever gives us the means really to do what we want to do—which forces us to decide what we want to do. Despite our vocal celebrations of freedom, we tend to run from it. We prefer to have decisions made for us, to feel the security of a known order. I have elsewhere (in a series of articles in *Modern Medicine*) suggested a new definition of a healthy person: one who is exhilarated by the challenge of freedom. Such healthy people— and, with luck, that will include most of us—can find solutions to our problems, or devise ways to move us confidently into the future, with the sense of purpose that will provide a firm flow of stability against a backdrop of change—especially if they live long enough. In our current pessimism, we tend to overlook the probability that some of our seemingly insoluble problems may become obsolete or irrelevant as, possessed of new knowledge and capacities, we enter new human situations. (Consider one homely example: if we succeeded in harnessing new and plentiful energies, there would never again be an "oil crisis.")

I said a moment ago that I consider it virtually inevitable that anti-aging research programs will proceed, and that they will succeed. We will almost surely pursue the necessary lines of research, for all the usual scientific and medical reasons. We do not know nearly enough about either the organism we inhabit or the diseases and impairments that afflict it: cancer, heart disease, stroke, arthritis, diabetes, genetic defects, immunological disorders, "mental" illness, a variety of still-prevalent infectious diseases. It is therefore unlikely that we will abandon promising avenues of biomedical research while so many millions of our fellow creatures continue to suffer from these ailments—one or more of which will, as likely as not, strike us down personally sooner or later. It is unthinkable that we would settle for what we now know, and for our present treatments. In the absence of better alternatives, we blast the afflicted with lethal doses of radiation, pickle them in large quantities of poisonous drugs, perform surgery that is complex, expensive, time-consuming, and often mutilative. Many disease victims are increasingly dependent for their lives on unwieldy machinery and heroic intensive care. Sometimes—as in the case of some birth defects and the senile dementias—the care can be no more than custodial and ends only at death. Enormous effort is often expended for a tiny gain in added life that may be of dubious quality.

To declare a moratorium on all biomedical research (which no one I know of is seriously proposing) would be to condemn us permanently to medical conditions that are intended only as an interim holding action. Would we really be willing to forgo the discovery of causes, cures, and preventive measures that would render these therapeutic extravaganzas obsolete? To attain the longer-range goals will be not only infinitely less costly in cash but infinitely more rewarding by any human criterion. The people who would have been victims will be producing, earning, spending, instead of costing so much. Instead of needing to be cared for, they will be able to take care of, and provide for, others—and certainly for themselves. Many of our social goals are muddied by a conflict of values; what is good for society may be bad for the individual, and vice versa. But in this instance the desired outcome would serve both individual happiness and the good of the species.

For many good reasons, then, we will doubtless pursue the kinds of research we have been describing in this book. Alex Comfort told me in 1984 that he believes the best way to achieve prolongevity may be to let it just come about, by simply pursuing biomedical research as usual—rather than to go after it as a stated goal. The bundle of biological information that we need in order to understand life, to cure genetic diseases and defects, to discover the cause and cure of cancer and the secrets of immunology, to overcome the major degenerative disorders, is the same bundle of information that will reveal the mechanisms of the aging process.* I disagree with Comfort; I think we might as well accelerate success by deliberately seeking the gerontological answers. (It is my view, incidentally, that biological controls will also provide us with hitherto unknown methods of generating energy, recycling wastes, and creating substantial new sources of food supply.)

I guess what I am trying to say here—after devoting the entire previous chapter to the consequences of success in achieving prolongevity—is that a decision *not* to go ahead with research on aging would also have its profound consequences. The resulting situation in times of stress, when people tend to get meaner toward their fellow beings, could tempt those so inclined to find excuses for hurrying the "useless" elderly out of the world.

A good many of our current human values, in fact, would have to undergo examination, and no doubt confusion, if we were to decide against all attempts at prolongevity. For example, we now consider death to be a tragedy in most circumstances, and we weep for our loved ones who are about to die. Yet, if we vote *against* prolonging their lives (in good health, mind you), are we not in the same position as someone who fails to throw a readily available lifeline to a drowning person? In such circumstances, any tears we might shed for the dying would seem the epitome of hypocrisy. What we would be saying, in effect, is not that death is a tragedy but that permitting the person to go on living is the tragedy! Must

---

* Herman T. Blumenthal of Washington University in St. Louis, for instance, has done studies suggesting that atherosclerosis and certain kinds of central nervous system deterioration are part of the aging process rather than disease states distinct from it.

we, then, greet the good news of someone's passing with laughter and applause? We do of course accept the death of loved ones for the greater good of the nation or society, yet grieve for the individual tragedies those deaths represent. We could learn to adopt the same attitude toward those we permit to die in order to avoid problems for the species, or for civilization.

But that is a slippery slope indeed. If we start thinking that way, perhaps we could soon begin to accept the death (while mourning them individually, of course) of all kinds of people—the severely handicapped, the infirm elderly—for the greater good of society, and would find ourselves in the midst of an inadvertent eugenics program. In a curious way, by extension, a vehemently anti-prolongevity stance is tantamount to an advocacy of eugenics.

Right now, in all our emotion-laden bioethical discussions about whether or not to treat certain patients, the disputants tend to land with both feet on anyone who lets "quality-of-life" considerations influence his judgment. But if we were to decide that prolongevity would change the quality of our lives in ways that would make it too difficult for us to cope, and therefore vote no, would we not have let quality-of-life considerations govern our decision?

Once the knowledge is at hand, nevertheless, there will certainly be those who will want to use it to extend their lives and postpone their deaths. Many may protest that they would never make use of it for themselves under any circumstances. Some may feel strongly, in fact, that no one else should be permitted to employ it for pro-longevity purposes, either. But when it becomes clear that the end result really will be not merely an ever-growing population of the old and enfeebled but, rather, a group of elderly men and women like none who have preceded them, living for many years in the vigorous possession of their powers—I believe that more and more people will wish this outcome for themselves and for those they love. And the arguments for preventing others from taking advantage of this knowledge to this end will grow steadily thinner.

Consider how we spend our lives (those of us who are not handicapped by being either chronically ill or poverty-stricken). In our early lives, our development is generally directed by others. They "educate" us. If we are lucky, they help us develop in directions that are in harmony with what seem to be our natural inclinations; they prepare us to become creative citizens, to make whatever contributions we may be capable of making to the world. Then, typically, when we have reached the stage where we are considered educated, mature, ready for adulthood, we marry and begin to sire, bear, and rear the next generation—whose education and development we then undertake as our major responsibility. We may, during these energetic years, fulfill ourselves in terms of a career, but for most people that career turns out to be only a job, because if we are to consider ourselves responsible citizens, our first concern is to earn a living, pay the rent, buy the baby a new pair of shoes. All that has its own undeniable rewards, of course, but during these "best years of our lives" we may—male and female alike—be forced to forgo many pleasures, postpone many activities and ambitions. To what end? To raise our children to *their* adulthood so they can go and do likewise.

Finally, our responsibilities are taken care of. We have seen our children through college, say, and we are able to turn our attention to ourselves (if we have not, by then, forgotten what we wanted to do, what those marvelous contributions were that we secretly hoped we might achieve to justify the time we spent on earth), to indulge ourselves somewhat with minimal guilt, to start using some of the creative capacities that our education and experience have prepared us for. (As Epicurus remarked long ago, most people spend their lives preparing to live it.) We have finally acquired a modicum of seasoning and of wisdom. And we realize that our health and vigor are not what they once were. We see the signs that the organism has begun to deteriorate irreversibly. Just when we could best make use of a generous stretch of time, we become acutely aware of how little time is left us—and that awareness colors everything we think and do. We begin to be haunted by the specter of a decline into relative helplessness, a fear confirmed by what we see on all sides when we look at the plight of the elderly; and we are saddened by the tragedy of lost human potential.

In Čapek's *The Makropoulos Secret*, one of the characters finally feels a great surge of sympathy for what Emilia Marty has done and, far from condemning her, he advocates the same longevity for all:

VITEK (*Standing up and coming to the center of the group*): We'll make the Makropoulos secret public.
KOLONATY: Oh, no! Not that!
VITEK: We'll give it to everybody! We'll give it to the people.

Everyone—everyone has the same right to life. We live for such a short time. How insignificant! God! How insignificant it is to be a human being.

KOLONATY: Rubbish!

VITEK: No, gentlemen, it does mean something! Just consider— the human soul, brains, work, love—everything. Good God, what can a man do in sixty years! What does he enjoy? What does he learn? He doesn't even enjoy the fruit of the tree he has planted; he doesn't learn all that his predecessors knew; he doesn't finish his work; he dies, and he hasn't lived. Ah, God, but we live so insignificantly!

KOLONATY: Well, Vitek—

VITEK: And he hasn't had time for gladness, and he hasn't had time to think, and he hasn't had time for anything except a desire for bread. He hasn't done anything, and he hasn't known anything. No, not even himself. Why have you lived? Has it been worth the trouble?

KOLONATY: Do you want to make me cry?

VITEK: We die like animals. What else is immortality of the soul but a protest against the shortness of life? A human being is something more than a turtle or a raven; a man needs more time to live. Sixty years—it's not right. It's weakness, it's ignorance, and it's animal-like.

HAUK-SENDORF: Oh, my, and I am already seventy-six!

VITEK: Let's give everyone a three-hundred-year life. It will be the biggest event since the creation of man; it will be the liberating and creating anew of man! God, what man will be able to do in three hundred years! To be a child and pupil for fifty years; fifty years to understand the world and its ways, and to see everything there is; and a hundred years to work in; and then a hundred years, when we have understood everything, to live in wisdom, to teach, and to give example. How valuable human life would be if it lasted for three hundred years! There would be no fear, no selfishness. Everyone would be wise and dignified. (*Wringing his hands.*) Give people life! Give them full human life!

In like manner, Shaw's Dr. Conrad Barnabas, in *Back to Methuselah*, propagandizes for an extended life span. (Curiously, he, too, fixes on three hundred years as the ideal figure.) In trying to urge his prolongevity program on a couple of eminent politicians, he says: "We're not blaming you: you hadnt* lived long enough. No more had we. Cant you see that three-score-and-ten, though it may be long enough for a very crude sort of village life, isnt long enough for a complicated civilization like ours? Flinders Petrie has counted nine attempts at civilization made by people exactly like us; and every one of them failed just as ours is failing. They failed because the citizens and statesmen died of old age or overeating before they had grown out of schoolboy games and savage sports and cigars and champagne."

In his preface to the long and seldom-performed play, Shaw himself had this to say:

Men do not live long enough; they are, for the purposes of high civilization, mere children when they die. . . . Life has lengthened considerably since I was born; and there is no reason why it should not lengthen ten times as much after my death.

This possibility came to me when history and experience had convinced me that the social problems raised by millionfold national populations are far beyond the political capacity attainable in three score and ten years of life by slowgrowing mankind. On all hands as I write the cry is that our statesmen are too old, and that Leagues of Youth must be formed everywhere to save civilization from them. But despairing ancient pioneers tell me that the statesmen are not old enough for their jobs. . . . We have no sages old enough and wise enough to make a synthesis of these reactions, and to develop the magnetic awe-inspiring force which must replace the policeman's baton as the instrument of authority.

Are we talking here about prolonged life only for leaders, or potential leaders, selected as a special elite? Of course we are talking about a longer life for everyone. But this idea seems to offend some who at first are attracted to the idea of life extension. Here again, the two plays from which I have just been quoting offer some interesting parallels.

When Čapek's Vitek once again says, "We must prolong the life of all," Prus replies, "No, only the life of the strong. The life of

* Among his other linguistic quirks, Shaw didn't believe in using apostrophes in contractions such as "hadnt," "cant," "isnt."

the most talented. For the common herd this short life is good enough." Vitek remonstrates, but Prus brushes him aside:

PRUS: Please, I do not want to argue. The ordinary, small, stupid one surely does not die. He is everlasting. Littleness multiplies without ceasing, like flies and mice. Only greatness dies. Only strength and talent die—and cannot be replaced. We ought to keep it in our own hands. We can prolong the life of the aristocracy.
VITEK: Aristocracy! Do you hear that? Privilege on life!
PRUS: Only the best are important in life. Only the chief, fertile and executive men. I am not mentioning women, but there are in this world about ten or twenty, perhaps a thousand, men who are irreplaceable. We can keep them. We can develop in them superhuman reason and supernatural power. We can breed ten, a hundred or a thousand supermen—masters and creators. So, I say, select those who have the right to unlimited life.

Similarly, when Shaw's Franklyn Barnabas (Conrad's brother) starts to explain, "When we get matured statesmen and citizens—" the politician Lubin stops short and exclaims, "Citizens! Oh! Are the citizens to live three hundred years as well as the statesmen?" Conrad says, "Of course," and Lubin replies, "I confess that had not occurred to me." ("*He sits down abruptly*," the dramatist's stage instructions read, "*evidently very unfavourably affected by this new light*.") The other politician, Burge, finally says, after some calculation, "It's out of the question. We must keep the actual secret to ourselves."

Most fiction that deals with the prolongevity theme does go on the assumption that the life-prolonging or rejuvenation therapies and medications will be difficult and expensive, and accessible therefore only to the wealthy or privileged few. In *Bug Jack Barron* by Norman Spinrad, rejuvenation depends on the transplantation of glands from a child—who is killed by the operation. There is only a black market for the glands, and only rich old men to buy them. Fred Mustard Stewart's *The Methuselah Enzyme* features a Swiss surgeon in an out-of-the-way sanatorium, and wealthy old people whose added years are robbed from younger people. In fact, there is no reason why whatever drugs and treatments flow out of gerontological research should not, as Comfort believes, be as universally available as any other drug or treatment, and they could be considerably less expensive than many now in use.

The case that Vitek and Conrad Barnabas make for an extended life span is not a ridiculous one. For individuals who enjoy life, aging and death are authentic tragedies. And these can be society's tragedies as well—for, as already discussed, just when women and men reach a point in life where their wisdom and experience equip them to begin giving their best to the world, just when they have completed their family duties and are free to pursue their creative inclinations, this is when their energies fail, and body and brain begin to degenerate.

But suppose their bodies remained strong and their intellects sharp?

Most of the varieties of biological control we have discussed involve the manipulation of ourselves from the outside, or at least with outside assistance. But, biotechnics aside, we should not overlook the many new opportunities that already exist for consciousness-expanding and life-enriching experiences from within ourselves. These lie in a heightened awareness of our own relatively untapped inner resources, as represented by the more worthwhile aspects of the still rather amorphous "human potential" and "new consciousness" and "holistic" movements, which go by various names. Many techniques have been employed to bring about the desired results: drugs, altered states of consciousness, physical and spiritual exercises, meditation, the Oriental martial arts, biofeedback, sensory deprivation, psychedelic environments, the cultivation of psychic (with a small *p*) capacities—and the plain, straightforward opening up of people's awareness that can take place when unsuspected realities and potentials are pointed out to them. Writing about these experiments in the *Saturday Review*, Jean Houston (who, with her collaborator-husband Robert Masters, heads the Foundation for Mind Research) proposes a "psychenaut program,"* the aim of which would be "to put the first man on earth." The psychenaut program would be an "exploration of inner space." It would "map the mind and tap its unrealized capacities. It would acquaint the psychenauts with the phenomenal contents of their own beings—their mind-body systems (with more emphasis on the body than is

---

* In 1969, in his presidential address to the American Psychopathological Association, Joel Elkes of Johns Hopkins University, a pioneer psychopharmacologist, proposed a quite similar "intronaut program," stressing the need for "inner space laboratories" soundly grounded in psychobiological research.

customary in Western culture)—and teach them to employ and to enjoy the multiplicity of human qualities that seem almost unattainable on first encounter. Through intensive training, psychenauts would have new control over their creative energies, their health, their experience of time and space, heat and cold, pain and pleasure.

"This exploration of the farther reaches of human consciousness," Houston continues, "typifies a new kind of mind research, already well begun."

She also makes clear that the psychenauts she is referring to will not be an elite handful of superpeople; they will, rather, be masses of ordinary women and men, but aware and awakened in an unprecedented manner. Thus future life could feasibly be not merely as enjoyable as present life, but much more so.

As George Leonard agrees, in *The Transformation*, "Any decisive outward movement of human consciousness requires an equal and opposite movement to greater depths. In the long run, there can be no successful outer trip without an inner trip." One revelation of the inner trip: "We are strange and radiant creatures, flesh of the sun's flesh, most favored visible heirs of the primal consciousness." In this book of Leonard's, and those that preceded and followed it—*Education and Ecstasy* and *The Ultimate Athlete*—he offers some of the most luminously lyrical depictions of the "great party," to borrow Delbrück's phrase, that life can be. Leonard describes a diversity of transcendental experiences, which, he emphasizes—as do Masters and Houston—are for the masses of people, and thus democratic rather than aristocratic. Moreover, he insists, "There can be the same sort of awareness in every daily situation. Walking can become an exercise in blending with the motion and stillness, the fields, of all surrounding objects. Every human interaction can partake of the essence of being. Each chore can be totally involving. Under these conditions, what we call 'boredom' is impossible."

Even without "the immortality factor," as Osborn Segerberg calls it, the potential splendors of the upcoming era have been delineated in shimmering terms by recent philosophers and sages all the way from Teilhard de Chardin to Sri Aurobindo. Leonard has called this period just ahead The Transformation; I have called it The Second Genesis; Boulding—in *The Meaning of the Twentieth Century*—labeled it "post-civilization" (to be inhabited, perhaps, by Sir Julian Huxley's "trans-humans"); Jonas Salk has given it a name that may have the best chance of sticking—Epoch B (in contrast with Epoch A, denoting all of human history until now)—and has, in *The Survival of the Wisest* and *The Anatomy of Reason*, supplied us with some guidance as to how to make it come about. The promise of space—orbital space, the moon, the planets, and beyond—has provided a heady set of goals for many, among them Wernher von Braun and Neil Armstrong, Krafft Ehricke and Gerard O'Neil, Earl and Barbara Hubbard.*

Even without dreaming of extraterrestrial travel or colonization, without seeking the enhanced turn-ons to be provided by the new expansions of consciousness, many people would quite happily settle for more of the same, especially if endowed with reasonably good health and adequate means. To have time to travel everywhere, and go back again and again to favorite places. To go on learning—new skills, new sports, new languages, new musical instruments. To undertake a variety of careers and a diversity of relationships; for some, perhaps, a diversity of marriages. To read everything you want to read. To listen to all the music. To look at all the pictures, and even paint a few. To savor and resavor experience and arrive, not at boredom, but at new levels of appreciation. To be around long enough to use your talents to make some contribution to the world.

But what of the consequences, expressed earlier, of an insufficiency of "fresh blood"—and therefore of fresh thinking—as a discouragement of creativity? The prolongevitist hope is that people who live longer will become wiser, that their continued vigor will keep them thinking freshly and creatively, that the mature individual—no longer prey to energy-draining anxiety over his failing powers—will save his anxiety for the future of his species (especially since he will be the personal sharer of that future). The definition of that species, as Leonard suggests, might be expanded to include all life on earth—at least, until life is discovered elsewhere. Moreover, children would continue to be born, though in diminished numbers; and it is assumed that, rather than being looked upon as new-arriving upstarts and competitors, they would be especially nourished, cherished, and encouraged to develop, in mind and body,

* Each of the Hubbards is now pursuing similar goals along separate routes—Earl as the lone artist-philosopher writing his prophetic books, Barbara through the vehicle of the Committee for the Future and, later, Futures Network.

their maximum human potential in the most congenial possible educational milieu. Thus, fresh thinking *would* continue to arrive, the quantity lessened but the quality perhaps improved. "Up to now," writes Leonard, "death has served as a primary mechanism of evolution, from the lower organisms up through humankind in society. ... When the time comes—as it may well be coming—that individual human organisms can truly change and go on changing in ways that now seem hardly possible, when they can create and go on creating ever-changing cultures, then death will have lost its function where human evolution is concerned." Leonard, whose attention has not been particularly centered on aging or immortality, goes on to add: "Realizing and questioning its [death's] utility, we should not be caught by surprise when we find that aging can be greatly slowed or even stopped."

Dean Juniper, too, questions whether "the youth-versus-age combination is vital in keeping up a flow of new ideas. Flexibility of contact between creative individuals and creative groups does seem to be essential. But given the fact that all creative persons would retain their physical and intellectual powers indefinitely it would seem immaterial how continuous cross-fertilization came about, provided it came about. Thus an immortalist society which deliberately set out being creative might end up more creative by design than it might ever have been by natural accident."

As for biological evolution, we know that most mutations are deleterious and only a minority contribute to positive evolution; and in following nature's clumsy trial-and-error method, individuals sicken, suffer, and die in large numbers in order that the species may adapt and survive through the vicissitudes of environmental change. In the age of prolongevity, with genetic engineering at our service, perhaps we could create our own mutations with greater efficiency and incalculably less human misery (though of course we could cause incalculably more if we used our knowledge foolishly). Hence we would have no further need of the built-in fail-safe mechanisms we have called aging and programmed death.

There is no telling what a woman or a man might become or achieve in a significant number of extra years. It is not just that an individual who lived for a very long time could learn more facts and more skills, but that she could consolidate and synthesize her learning in altogether new ways. She could go back over her varied and ever-expanding knowledge and continue to make new connections.

She could resynthesize, in collaboration with similar long-livers, whole new systems of thought, bringing together mathematics, physics, astronomy, cosmology, geology, meteorology, chemistry, paleontology, archeology, biology, psychology, medicine, anthropology, sociology, economics, history, politics, art, literature, drama, poetry, music, theology, law, philosophy—the entire catalogue of human disciplines and indisciplines, plus others yet to be created; the grand union of simultaneous-multitudinous connectedness that Hesse could only hint at in the intricate "glass bead game" of *Magister Ludi.*

One of the highest talents of such an individual might be creative mythologizing. We are in constant need of myths to live by, as Joseph Campbell, among others, has tirelessly emphasized. And by "myth" I do not mean a fanciful story or framework which we must accept purely on faith (though I don't downgrade faith), with no evidence to support it, but, rather, a *likely* myth which works for us because we believe in it. And we believe in it because it fits the knowledge we possess at any given time—or at least does not contradict that knowledge in a way that grossly affronts our intelligence. Much of our knowledge, though certainly not all of it, may be acquired through science. Because such knowledge must remain incomplete, at least for any time ahead that we can foresee, it can seldom if ever be absolute in nature; it must remain to some extent tentative, subject to revision on the arrival of new insights or more reliable data. But our knowledge could still have high probability value as pragmatic truth to live by, within a creatively structured mythological context that could answer our deeply felt spiritual longings and permit us to maintain hope, self-esteem, and a sense of purpose. The kind of long-lived individual I have just been hypothesizing, armed with an understanding of probabilistic reasoning as well as a due respect for the irrational in our natures, might be ideally equipped to create such vital myths for us. It is not unreasonable to hope that such human seers (by current standards) might even provide us with viable social and political solutions to which our present limitations blind us.

There could arise a new breed of human being who, merely by virtue of his prolongevity, through the acquisition of a steadily maturing wisdom and a steadily expanding awareness, could finally become exactly the kind of gifted individual we need to help take our species into a challenging and expanded future—a being to whom we might entrust the decisions that go with controlling the mechanisms of life, a being worthy to be the trustee of our further evolution to a destiny of our own choosing.

What has always prevented any serious, widespread consideration of such questions is the long-standing and continuing lack of credibility that such questions would ever truly *become* serious. As Shaw's Lubin finally says to Franklyn Barnabas: "I grant you that if we could live three hundred years we should all be, perhaps wiser, certainly older. You will grant me in return, I hope, that if the sky fell we should all catch larks."

It is difficult to consider seriously a proposal that is impossible of attainment. And everybody except a few cranks and crackpots has always "known" that extending the human life span is and always will be a pipe dream. That is why I have devoted the major space in this book to spelling out the research and theories that suddenly transform the pipe dream into at least a feasible fantasy, and perhaps a reality we can plan for. Unlike Shaw's Barnabas, who was relying on the sheer power of wishful thinking to bring about his extended life span, we may soon have in our hands the biological tools to create, in a practical manner, the long-sought elixir of life, in one form or another. Old age will be a disease you can go see your doctor about, if, indeed, prophylactic measures do not virtually eradicate it.

Our species is at a critical transition point in its history on this planet. To fear the consequences of further knowledge—and thus decide to halt further research—would be the surest road to a non-solution of our problems, and thus to disaster. We do not begin to know all that we need to know. Why not take up, with some anticipatory exhilaration, the challenge of pursuing whatever path may bring us to our full humanhood?

The fact that we must work with incomplete knowledge should not deter us from moving ahead with high spirits—always tempered, to be sure, by a reasonable caution. To the basic question of epistemology, we must answer that the knowledge we possess or can realistically hope to acquire has its limitations. But we do not begin to know what those limitations are, and we may properly assume that, in the next phase of our evolution (perhaps increasingly self-directed), and the next, the scope of our understanding will continue to be enlarged. With this enlargement there may emerge startlingly different views of reality, of the way we perceive the universe and ourselves.

To the basic question of teleology, we must admit that we do not know with any certainty if there is purpose in the universe (unless we accept it as given via any of our religions); or, if so, what that purpose is; or where we fit into it either as a species or as individuals. Nevertheless, those philosophers who adduce impeccable arguments to prove that there definitely is *not* any purpose in this random, entropic universe, or any meaning to human life beyond an existential imperative to survive without illusions,* I find most unconvincing. They are, at the least, arriving at premature conclusions based on the skimpiest of data. (I am thinking, for instance, of Jacques Monod's beautifully written and elegantly reasoned *Chance and Necessity*.) The teleological question must remain open. Meanwhile, it is not fatuous to believe that there is a purposeful thrust to what is happening—something akin to what Earl Hubbard calls "the creative intention"—even though we are not (at least not yet) equipped to discern it. I like to think that one of life's purposes is to divine life's purpose.

I have talked somewhat glibly about controlling our own destiny and moving on to the next stage of evolution, to L. L. Whyte's "next development in man." But I would certainly prefer to see us postpone any hasty moves to that next evolutionary phase, which we can at best only dimly perceive, until we have firmly consolidated our present phase. We must learn to be truly human before we can aspire to be trans-human, or even to understand with any clarity what that means. To become truly human, however, will still require that we transcend our present selves in ways that will demand all the courage, compassion, imagination, good sense, and good cheer that we can muster. And the mustering of those resources would, I think, be considerably enhanced by the addition of good years to good lives.

---

* It should be noted that I do not equate "illusion" with "myth" as I defined it earlier. Even if an existential view were warranted, I do not think it would inevitably lead us to either total absurdity or total despair—but that is another whole book.

BIBLIOGRAPHY

ABELSON, PHILIP, "Dietary Carcinogens," *Science*, Sept. 23, 1983.

ADELMAN, RICHARD C., personal communications.

——, "Enzyme Adaptation in Aging," presented at American Association for the Advancement of Science, San Francisco, 1974.

——, "Impaired Hormonal Regulation of Enzyme Activity During Aging," prepublication manuscript for *Federation Proceedings*, 1974.

——, and Britton, Gary W., "The Impaired Capability for Biochemical Adaptation During Aging," *BioScience*, Oct. 1975.

—— et al., "Endocrine Regulation of Enzyme Activity in Aging Animals of Different Genotypes," in Bergsma and Harrison, *op. cit.*, 1978.

ADLER, WILLIAM H., "An 'Autoimmune' Theory of Aging," in Rockstein, Sussman, and Chesky, *op. cit.*, 1974.

——, "Aging and Immune Function," *BioScience*, Oct. 1975.

AJL, SAMUEL J., personal communications.

ALDRICH, ROBERT A., personal communications.

ALTMAN, LAWRENCE K., "Syndromes That Age the Young Are Studied for Clues to Aid the Old," *New York Times*, July 10, 1984.

AMES, BRUCE, "Dietary Carcinogens and Anticarcinogens: Oxygen Radicals and Degenerative Diseases," *Science*, Sept. 23, 1983.

ANDERSON, ALUN, "Ageing Japan: Riches Make for Longevity," *Nature*, July 12, 1984.

ANDRES, REUBIN, personal communications.

——, "The Normality of Aging: The Baltimore Longitudinal Study," summary presentation at NIA/GRC, Baltimore, Oct. 1976.

——, "Defining and Evaluating the Myriad Influences on Human Aging," *Geriatrics*, March 1975.

——, "The Study of Aging in Man: Practical and Theoretical Considerations," in Rockstein, Sussman, and Chesky, *op. cit.*, 1974.

ANDRON, LEO A., II, and STREHLER, BERNARD L., "Recent Evidence on tRNA and tRNA Acylase-Mediated Cellular Control Mechanisms: A Review," *Mechanisms of Ageing and Development*, Vol. 2, 1973.

Anti-Aging News (Kent, Saul, Ed.), newsletter published by the Life Extension Foundation, Hollywood, Florida.

APPLEZWEIG, NORMAN, personal communications.

ARA, GULSHAN; RITCHIE, DAVID; and PAPACONSTANTINOU, JOHN, "Age-Related Alteration in Transferrin Secretion," presented at American Aging Association, Oct. 1983.

ASTLE, CLINTON M., and HARRISON, DAVID E., "Effects of Marrow Donor and Recipient Age on Immune Responses," *Journal of Immunology*, Feb. 1984.

ATLAN, HENRI; MIQUEL, JAIME; and BINNARD, ROSEMARIE, "Differences Between Radiation-Induced Life Shortening and Natural Aging in *Drosophila Melanogaster*," *Journal of Gerontology*, Jan. 1969.

BALAZS, A. "Organismal Differentiation, Ageing and Rejuvenation," *Experimental Gerontology*, Oct. 1970.

BANERJI, T. K.; PARKENING, T. A.; and COLLINS, T. J., "Adrenomedullary Dopamine-Beta-Hydroxylase (DBH) Activity Is Increased with Age in Male Rodents," presented at American Aging Association, Oct. 1983.

BARROWS, CHARLES H., JR., personal communications.

———, "The Challenge—Mechanisms of Biological Aging," *Gerontologist*, Spring 1971.

———, "Ecology of Aging and of the Aging Process—Biological Parameters," *Gerontologist*, Summer 1968.

BATTEN, MARY, "Life Spans," *Science Digest*, Feb. 1984.

BECKER, ERNEST, *The Denial of Death*. New York: The Free Press (Macmillan), 1973.

BEHNKE, JOHN A.; FINCH, CALEB E.; and MOMENT, GAIRDNER B. (Eds.), *The Biology of Aging*. New York: Plenum Press, 1978.

BENDER, A. D.; KORMENDY, C. G.; and POWELL, R., "Pharmacological Control of Aging," *Experimental Gerontology*, Vol. 5, 1970.

BENET, SULA, *How to Live to Be 100: The Life-Style of the People of the Caucasus*. New York: Dial Press, 1976.

BENSON, ANDREW A., personal communications.

BERGSMA, DANIEL, and HARRISON, DAVID E. (Eds.), *Genetic Effects on Aging*. March of Dimes Original Article Series on Birth Defects, Vol. XIV, No. 1. New York: Alan R. Liss, 1978.

BEVERLEY, E. VIRGINIA, "Exploring the Many-Faceted Mysteries of Aging." *Geriatrics*, March 1975.

BILDER, GLENDA E., and DENCKLA, W. DONNER, "Restoration of Juvenile Competence in Immune and RE Systems After Hypophysectomy of Adult Rats," *Mechanisms of Ageing and Development*, Vol. 6, 1977.

BIRREN, JAMES E., personal communications.

—— (Ed.), *The Relations of Development and Aging*. Springfield, Ill.: Charles C. Thomas, 1964.

——, *Handbook of Aging and the Individual, Psychological and Biological Aspects*. Chicago: University of Chicago Press, 1959.

——, "Research on Aging: A Frontier of Science and Social Gain," presented to U.S. Senate Subcommittee on Government Research, Oct. 24, 1966.

BJORKSTEN, JOHAN, personal communications.

——, *Thirteen-Year Report (1952–1965) of the Studies on Aging*. Bjorksten Research Foundation.

——, "Aluminum as a Cause of Senile Dementia," *Comprehensive Therapy*, May 1982.

——, "The Crosslinkage Theory of Aging as a Predictive Indicator," *Rejuvenation VIII*, Vol. 3, 1980.

——, "Pathways to the Decisive Extension of the Human Specific Lifespan," *Journal of the American Geriatrics Society*, Vol. XXV, 1977.

——, "Crosslinkage and the Aging Process," in Rockstein, Sussman, and Chesky, *op. cit.*, 1974.

——, "Approaches and Prospects for the Control of Age-Dependent Deterioration," *Annals of the New York Academy of Sciences*, June 7, 1971.

——, "The Crosslinkage Theory of Aging," *Finska Kemists. Medd.*, Vol. 80, No. 2, 1971.

——, "Study of Low Molecular Weight Proteolytic Enzymes," *Finska Kemists. Medd.*, Vol. 80, No. 4, 1971.

——, "The Crosslinkage Theory of Aging," *Journal of the American Geriatrics Society*, April 1968.

——, "Enzymes and Aging," in *Enzymes in Mental Health* (Martin, Gustav J., and Kisch, Bruno, Eds.). Philadelphia: J. B. Lippincott, 1966.

——, "Why Grow Old?," *Chemistry*, June 1964.

——, "Aging, Primary Mechanism," *Gerontologia*, Vol. 8, 1963.

——, "Aging: Present Status of Our Chemical Knowledge," *Journal of the American Geriatrics Society*, Feb. 1962.

——, "A Common Molecular Basis for the Aging Syndrome," *Journal of the American Geriatrics Society*, Oct. 1958.

BLUMENTHAL, HERMAN T., "Immunological Aspects of the Aging Brain," in *Neurobiology of Aging* (Terry, Robert D., and Gershon, Samuel, Eds.). New York: Raven Press, 1976.

————, "Athero-Arteriosclerosis as an Aging Process," in *Physiology and Pathology of Human Aging*. New York: Academic Press, 1975.

————, and Alex, M., "Special Issue on Athero-Arteriosclerosis: An Iconoclastic View of Current Concepts Concerning Genesis, Prevention, and Control," *Gerontologia*, Vol. 21, No. 3, 1975.

BOLLA, ROBERT, personal communications.

————, and Denckla, W. Donner, "Effect of Hypophysectomy on Liver Nuclear Ribonucleic Acid Synthesis in Aging Rats," *Journal of Biochemistry*, Vol. 184, 1979.

BONDAREFF, WILLIAM, and NAROTZKY, ROBERT, "Age Changes in the Neuronal Microenvironment," *Science*, June 9, 1972.

BONNER, JAMES, personal communications.

————, *The Molecular Biology of Development*. New York and Oxford: Oxford University Press, 1965.

————, "tRNA and Ageing," *Nature*, Sept. 20, 1974.

BORTZ, EDWARD L., *Creative Aging*. New York: Macmillan, 1963.

————, and Bortz, Walter M., II, "Major Issues of Aging," *GP*, July 1959.

BOULDING, KENNETH, "Is Science Reaching the Point of a Diminishing Return?," *International Herald Tribune*, Sept. 7, 1970.

BRASH, DOUGLAS E., and HART, RONALD W., "Molecular Biology of Aging," in Behnke, Finch, and Moment, *op. cit.*, 1978.

BRODY, JANE E., *Jane Brody's The New York Times Guide to Personal Health*. New York: Times Books, 1982.

————, *Jane Brody's Nutrition Book*. New York: W. W. Norton, 1981.

————, "Personal Health: Compensating for the Lack of Sunlight in Winter, Which Can Affect the Body and Emotions," *New York Times*, Nov. 14, 1984.

————, "Surprising Health Impact Discovered for Light," *New York Times*, Nov. 13, 1984.

————, "Personal Health: Food-Nutrient Interactions: New Dietary Preferences Underline Their Importance," *New York Times*, Nov. 7, 1984.

————, "Hope Grows for Vigorous Old Age," *New York Times*, Oct. 2, 1984.

BRODY, HAROLD, personal communication.

————, "A Study of Aging in the Human Cerebral Cortex," *Journal of Comparative Neurology*, Vol. 102, 1955.

BROWN, W. TED, personal communication.

————, "Werner's Syndrome," in *Chromosome Mutation and Neoplasia*. New York: Alan R. Liss, 1983.

————, "Human Mutations Affecting Aging—A Review," *Mechanisms of Ageing and Development*, Vol. 9, 1979.

————, and Darlington, Gretchen J., "Thermolabile Enzymes in Progeria and Werner Syndrome: Evidence Contrary to the Protein Error

Hypothesis," *American Journal of Human Genetics*, Vol. 32, 1980.

———; Epstein, J.; and Little, J. B., "Progeria Cells are Stimulated to Repair DNA by Co-Cultivation with Normal Cells," *Experimental Cell Research*, Vol. 97, 1976.

———; Ford, John P.; and Gershey, Edward L., "Variation of DNA Repair Capacity in Progeria Cells Unrelated to Growth Conditions," *Biochemical and Biophysical Research Communications*, Nov. 17, 1980.

———, and Wisniewski, Henryk M., "Genetics of Human Aging," *Review of Biological Research in Aging*, 1983.

———, et al., "Detection of HLA Antigens on Progeria Syndrome Fibroblasts," *Clinical Genetics*, Vol. 17, 1980.

———, et al., "DNA Repair Defect in Progeric Cells," in *Birth Defects: Original Article Series*, Vol. XIV, No. 1, The National Foundation–March of Dimes, 1978.

BUCALA, RICHARD, personal communication.

———; Model, Peter; and Cerami, Anthony, "The Chemical Reaction of DNA with Sugars: A Possible Mechanism for Nucleic Acid Aging and Age-Related Dysfunction in Gene Expression," presented at American Aging Association, Oct. 1983.

BUCHER, N. L. R.; SCOTT, J. F.; and AUB, J. C. "Regeneration of Liver in Parabiotic Rats," *Cancer Research*, Vol. 10, 1950.

BULLOUGH, W. S., "Ageing of Mammals," *Nature*, Vol. 229, 1971.

BUNZEL, JOSEPH H. "Recognition, Relevance and Deactivation of Gerontophobia: Theoretical Essay," *Journal of the American Geriatrics Society*, Vol. 21, No. 2, 1973.

BURNET, SIR F. MACFARLANE, *Intrinsic Mutagenesis: A Genetic Approach to Aging*. New York: John Wiley & Sons, 1974.

———, *Genes, Dreams and Realities*. London: Pelican Books, 1973.

———, "A Genetic Interpretation of Ageing," *Lancet*, Sept. 1, 1973.

BURON, G. W., and INGOLD, K. U., "Beta-Carotene: An Unusual Type of Lipid Antioxidant," *Science*, May 11, 1984.

BUTLER, ROBERT N., personal communications.

———, *Why Survive?—Being Old in America*. New York: Harper & Row, 1975.

———, "Latest on Extending the Human Life Span," interview in *U.S. News & World Report*, Aug. 24, 1981.

———, "New Directions for Research and Health Care of the Aged," *Medical Communications*, Winter 1977 / Spring 1978.

———, "Medicine and Aging: An Assessment of Opportunities and Neglect," testimony before U.S. Senate Special Committee on Aging, Oct. 13, 1976.

———, "Age: The Life Review," *Psychology Today*, Dec. 1971.

——— (Ed.), "Symposium on Mental Health and Aging: Life Cycle Perspectives," special issue of *Geriatrics*, Nov. 1974.

CALLOWAY, NATHANIEL O., "Nutrition in Aging," paper presented to American Association for the Advancement of Science, San Francisco, 1974.

ČAPEK, KAREL, *The Makropoulos Secret*. Boston: International Pocket Library, 1925.

CAPLAN, ARTHUR L., "Is Aging a Disease?," in *Vitalizing Long-Term Care* (Spicker, Stuart, and Ingman, Stanley, Eds.). New York: Springer, 1984.

——, "The 'Unnaturalness' of Aging—A Sickness Unto Death?," in *Concepts of Health and Disease: Interdisciplinary Perspectives* (Caplan, Arthur L.; Engelhardt, H. Tristram, Jr.; and McCartney, James J., Eds.). Reading, Mass.: Addison-Wesley, 1981.

CARAS, ROGER, *Sockeye: The Life of a Pacific Salmon*. New York: Dial Press, 1975.

CARPENTER, DONALD, personal communications.

——, "Correction of Biological Aging," *Rejuvenation*, June 1980.

CARREL, ALEXIS, "On the Permanent Life of Tissues Outside of the Organisms," *Journal of Experimental Medicine*, Vol. 15, 1912.

CHEBOTAREV, D. F., personal communications.

—— (Ed.), *The Main Problems of Soviet Gerontology*. Kiev, 1972.

——, "Biological Active Agents ('Geriatrics') in Prevention and Treatment of Premature Aging," in Chebotarev (Ed.), *op. cit.*, 1972.

—— (Ed.), "Longevous People (Physio-Clinical and Socio-Hygienic Research)," *Journal of the International Association on the Artificial Prolongation of the Human Specific Lifespan*, Vol. 1, No. 1, 1973.

CHEN, JENN C.; WARSHAW, JOSEPH B.; and SANADI, D. RAO, "Regulation of Mitochondrial Respiration in Senescence," *Journal of Cellular Physiology*, Aug. 1972.

CHERKIN, ARTHUR, and FLOOD, JAMES F., "Remarkable Potentiation Among Memory-Enhancing Cholinergic Drugs in Mice," in Regelson and Sinex, *op. cit.*, 1983.

CHERRY, RONA, and CHERRY, LAURENCE, "Slowing the Clock of Age," *New York Times Magazine*, May 12, 1974.

CHOWN, SHEILA M. (Ed.), *Human Ageing (Selected Readings)*. London: Penguin Books, 1972.

CLARKE, ARTHUR C., *Profiles of the Future: An Inquiry into the Limits of the Possible*. New York: Harper & Row, 1962.

CLEMENS, J. A., and MEITES, J., "Neuroendocrine Status of Old Constant-Estrous Rats," *Neuroendocrinology*, Vol. 7, 1971.

COLE, THOMAS R., personal communications.

——, "Prolongevity and the Assault on Old Age in America, 1880–1925," presented at annual meeting of American Association for the History of Medicine, May 1984.

——, "The 'Enlightened' View of Aging," *Hastings Center Report*, June 1983.

COLEMAN, DOUGLAS L., personal communications.

——; Schwizer, R. W.; and Leiter, E. H., "Effect of Genetic Background on the Therapeutic Effects of Dehydroepiandrosterone (DHEA) in Diabetes-Obesity Mutants and in Aged Normal Mice," *Diabetes*, in press, 1984.

COLON, E. J., "The Elderly Brain: A Quantitative Analysis in the Cerebral Cortex of Two Cases," *Psychiatria, Neurologia, Neurochirurgia*, Vol. 75, 1972.

COMFORT, ALEX, personal communications.

——, *The Biology of Senescence*. New York: Elsevier, 1979 (3rd ed.).

——, *The Nature of Human Nature*. New York: Harper & Row, 1966.

——, "To Be Continued," *Playboy*, November 1971.

——, "The Position of Aging Studies," *Mechanisms of Ageing and Development*, Vol. 3, 1974.

——, "So You Want to Live Longer," *Observer Magazine*, Sept. 23, 1973.

——, "Neuromythology?," *Nature*, Jan. 22, 1971.

——, "The Biological Basis for Increasing Longevity," *Medical Opinion & Review*, April 1970.

——, "The Prospects for Living Even Longer," interview in *Time*, Aug. 3, 1970.

——, "Test-Battery to Measure Ageing-Rate in Man," *Lancet*, Dec. 27, 1969.

——, "The Prevention of Ageing in Cells," *Lancet*, Dec. 17, 1966.

——, "Longevity of Man and His Tissues," in *Man and His Future*. Boston: Little, Brown, 1963.

COSTANZI, JOHN J., and GOLDSTEIN, ALLAN L., "Immunotherapy: New Hope for the Cancer Patient," *Family Physician*, Vol. 8, 1973.

COTZIAS, GEORGE C., et al., "Levodopa, Fertility and Longevity," *Science*, April 29, 1977.

COUSINS, NORMAN, personal communications.

——, *The Healing Heart*, New York: W. W. Norton, 1983.

——, *Anatomy of an Illness*, New York: Bantam Books, 1981.

——, *The Celebration of Life*. New York: Harper & Row, 1974.

COWDRY, E. V., *Aging Better*. Springfield, Ill.: Charles C. Thomas, 1972.

CRANSTON, ALAN, personal communications.

——, "Science Slows Aging," *Runner's World*, May 1981.

——, "Coming: Longer Life Spans," *Reader's Digest*, Jan. 1979.

CRISTOFALO, VINCENT J., and STANULIS, BETZABE M., "Cell Aging: A Model System Approach," in Behnke, Finch, and Moment, *op. cit.*, 1978.

———, et al., "Modulation of Proliferation Capacity as a Probe of the Mechanism of Senescence," in Regelson and Sinex, *op. cit.*, 1983.

CURTIN, SHARON R., *Nobody Ever Died of Old Age*. Boston: Little, Brown, 1972.

CURTIS, HOWARD J., *Biological Mechanisms of Aging*. Springfield, Ill.: Charles C. Thomas, 1966.

CUTLER, RICHARD G., personal communications.

———, "Carotenoids and Retinol: Their Possible Importance in Determining Longevity of Primate Species," *Proceedings of the National Academy of Sciences*, Dec. 1984.

———, "Antioxidants, Aging and Longevity," in *Free Radicals in Biology*, Vol. 6 (Pryor, W. A., Ed.). New York: Academic Press, 1983.

———, "Evolutionary Biology of Aging and Longevity in Mammalian Species," in *Aging and Cell Structure*, Vol. 2 (Johnson, J. E., Ed.). New York: Plenum Press, 1983.

———, "Species Probes, Longevity, and Aging," in Regelson and Sinex, *op. cit.*, 1983.

———, "The Dysdifferentiative Hypothesis of Mammalian Aging and Longevity," in *The Aging Brain: Cellular and Molecular Mechanisms of Aging in the Nervous System* (Giacobini, E., et al., Eds.). New York: Raven Press, 1982.

———, "Evolutionary Biology of Senescence," in Behnke, Finch, and Moment, *op. cit.*, 1978.

———, "Evolution of Longevity in Primates," *Journal of Human Evolution*, Vol. 5, 1976.

———, "Evolution of Human Longevity and the Genetic Complexity Governing Aging Rate," *Proceedings of the National Academy of Sciences*, Nov. 1975.

DANES, B. SHANNON, "Progeria: A Cell Culture Study on Aging," *Journal of Clinical Investigation*, Vol. 50, 1971.

DANIELLI, JAMES F., personal communications.

———, and Muggleton, Audrey, "Some Alternative States of Amoeba, with Special Reference to Life Span," *Gerontologia*, Vol. 3, 1959.

DAVIES, DAVID, "A Shangri-la in Ecuador," *New Scientist*, Feb. 1, 1973.

DAWKINS, RICHARD, "Selective Neurone Death as a Possible Memory Mechanism," *Nature*, Jan. 8, 1971.

DE BEAUVOIR, SIMONE, *The Coming of Age*. New York: Putnam's, 1972.

DeBUSK, FRANKLIN L., "The Hutchinson-Gilford Progeria Syndrome," *Journal of Pediatrics*, April 1972.

deDUVE, CHRISTIAN, "Lysosomes and Aging," paper presented to American Association for the Advancement of Science, San Francisco, 1974.

DELBRÜCK, MAX, "Education for Suicide," interview in *Prism*, Nov. 1974.

DEMOPOULOS, HARRY B., personal communications.

————, "Progress in Free Radical Pathology, Antioxidants, Aging and the Age Associated Disorders," presented to Foundation for Integrative Biomedical Research (FIBER) Symposium, Nov. 1982.

————, "The Basis of Free Radical Pathology," *Federation Proceedings*, Vol. 32, 1973.

————, "Control of Free Radicals in Biologic Systems," *Federation Proceedings*, Vol. 32, 1973.

————; Pietronigro, Dennis D.; and Seligman, Myron L., "The Development of Secondary Pathology with Free Radical Reactions as a Threshold Mechanism," *Journal of the American College of Toxicology*, Vol. 2, No. 3, 1983.

————, et al., "Further Studies on Free Radical Pathology in the Major Central Nervous System Disorders," *Canadian Journal of Physiological Pharmacology*, Vol. 60, 1982.

————, et al., "Oxygen Free Radicals in Central Nervous System Trauma," in *Pathology of Oxygen* (Autor, A. P., Ed.). New York: Academic Press, 1982.

————, et al., "The Possible Role of Free Radical Reactions in Carcinogenesis," *Journal of Environmental Pathology and Toxicology*, Vol. 3, No. 4, 1980.

DENCKLA, W. DONNER, personal communications.

————, *The Physician and Man's Fate* (brochure).

————, interview in *Omni*, Nov. 1981.

————, "Ions, Energy and Aging," prepublication manuscript.

————, "Searching for the 'Death' Hormone," interview in *Anti-Aging News*, Oct. 1981.

————, "Is There a Biological Aging Clock?," interview in *Anti-Aging News*, Sept. 1981.

————, "Interactions Between Age and the Neuroendocrine and Immune Systems," *Federation Proceedings*, Vol. 37, 1978.

————, "Systems Analysis of Possible Mechanisms of Mammalian Aging," *Mechanisms of Ageing and Development*, Vol. 6, 1977.

————, "Role of the Pituitary and Thyroid Glands in the Decline of Minimal O_2 Consumption with Age," *Journal of Clinical Investigation*, Feb. 1974.

————, "A Time to Die," *Life Sciences*, Vol. 16, 1974.

————, "Minimal O_2 Consumption as an Index of Thyroid Status: Standardization of Method," *Endocrinology*, July 1973.

————, "A New Interpretation of the VO_2 max," *Journal of Applied Physiology*, July 1971.

————, "Minimal Oxygen Consumption in the Female Rat: Some New Definitions and Measurements," *Journal of Applied Physiology*, Aug. 1970.

DEROPP, ROBERT S., *The New Prometheans*. New York: Dell, 1972.

———, *Man Against Aging*. New York: St. Martin's Press, 1960.

DIAMOND, MARIAN C., "A Love Affair with the Brain," interview in *Psychology Today*, Nov. 1984.

———, et al., "An Enriched Environment Altered the Cerebral Cortex of 900-Day Old Rats," presented at American Aging Association, Oct. 1983.

DILMAN, VLADIMIR M., *The Law of Deviation of Homeostasis and Diseases of Aging*. London: John Wright–PSG, 1981.

———, "Age-Associated Elevation of Hypothalamic Threshold to Feedback Control, and Its Role in Development, Ageing, and Disease," *Lancet*, June 12, 1971.

DOBZHANSKY, THEODOSIUS, personal communications.

———, *The Biology of Ultimate Concern*. New York: World Publishing, 1969.

———, *Mankind Evolving: The Evolution of the Human Species*. New Haven, Conn.: Yale University Press, 1962.

DONALDSON, THOMAS, "Therapies to Improve Memory," *Anti-Aging News*, Feb. 1984.

DOOLEY, MARGARET M., and PRYOR, WILLIAM A., "Free Radical Pathology: Inactivation of Human Alpha-l-proteinase Inhibitor by Products from the Reaction of Nitrogen Dioxide with Hydrogen Peroxide and the Etiology of Emphysema," *Biochemical and Biophysical Research Communications*, June 15, 1982.

DUBOS, RENÉ, personal communications.

———, *Beast or Angel? Choices That Make Us Human*. New York: Scribner's, 1974.

———, *A God Within*. New York: Scribner's, 1972.

———, *So Human an Animal*. New York: Scribner's, 1968.

———, *Man Adapting*. New Haven, Conn.: Yale University Press, 1965.

DYKHUIZEN, DANIEL, "Evolution of Cell Senescence, Atherosclerosis and Benign Tumors," *Nature*, Oct. 18, 1974.

EFFROS, RITA B., and WALFORD, ROY L., "T Cell Cultures and the Hayflick Limit," *Human Immunology*, Vol. 9, 1984.

ELGIN, SARAH C. R., and WEINTRAUB, HAROLD, "Chromosomal Proteins and Chromatin Structure," *Annual Reviews of Biochemistry*, 1975.

ELKES, JOEL A., personal communications.

ELLIOTT, JOHN, "Experts Clash on Nutrition Policy," *Journal of the American Medical Association*, Dec. 14, 1979.

EPSTEIN, J.; WILLIAMS, JERRY R.; and LITTLE, JOHN B., "Deficient DNA Repair in Human Progeroid Cells," *Proceedings of the National Academy of Sciences*, April 1973.

ERLANGER, M., and GERSHON, D., "Studies on Aging in Nematodes—II. Studies of the Activities of Several Enzymes as a Function of Age," *Experimental Gerontology*, March 1970.

ESFANDIARY, F. M., personal communications.
———, *Optimism One*. New York: Popular Library, 1978.
———, *Up-Wingers: A Futurist Manifesto*. New York: Crowell, 1973.
ETTINGER, ROBERT C. W., personal communications.
———, *Man into Superman*. New York: St. Martin's Press, 1972.
———, *The Prospect of Immortality*. New York: Doubleday, 1964.
———, "Cryonics and the Purpose of Life," *Christian Century*, Oct. 4, 1967.
FABRICANT, J. D., et al., "Reproductive Studies in Young and Old CBA Mice Following Orthotopic Ovarian Transplants," presented at American Aging Association, 1982.
FABRIS, N; PIERPAOLI, W.; and SORKIN E., "Lymphocytes, Hormones and Ageing," *Nature*, Dec. 29, 1972.
FEINBERG, GERALD, personal communications.
———, *The Prometheus Project*. New York: Doubleday, 1968.
———, "Can We and Should We Do Anything to Prolong Youth?," presented at Donnell Library Center, New York, Jan. 11, 1971.
FINCH, CALEB, personal communications.
———, "The Regulation of Physiological Changes During Aging: A Hypothesis," prepublication manuscript.
———, "Comparative Biology of Senescence: Evolutionary and Developmental Considerations," prepublication manuscript.
———, "A Progress Report on Neurochemical and Neuroendocrine Regulation in Normal and Pathological Aging," in *Aging 2000—Our Health Care Destiny*, Vol. 1 (Samorajski, T., Ed.). New York: Springer Verlag, in press, 1985.
———, "The Relationships of Aging Changes in the Basal Ganglia to Manifestations of Huntington's Chorea," *Annals of Neurology*, 1980.
———, "Neuroendocrine Mechanisms and Aging," *Federation Proceedings*, Vol. 38, 1979.
———, "The Brain and Aging," in Behnke, Finch, and Moment, *op. cit.*, 1978.
———, "Neuroendocrinology of Aging: A View of an Emerging Area," *BioScience*, Oct. 1975.
———, "Hormones and Mammalian Ageing: A Synopsis," prepared for Conference on Nutrition and Aging Processes, Seattle, 1973.
———, and Landfield, Philip W., "Neuroendocrine and Autonomic Function in Aging Mammals," in *Handbook of the Biology of Aging* (Finch, Caleb E., and Schneider, E. L., Eds.). New York: Van Nostrand, in press, 1985 (2nd ed.).
———, et al., "Ovarian and Steroidal Influences on Neuroendocrine Aging Process in Female Rodents," *Endocrine Reviews*, Vol. 5, 1984.
———, "Studies on Ovarian-Hypothalamic-Pituitary Interactions During

Reproductive Aging in C57BL/6J Mice," *Peptides*, Vol. 1, Suppl. 1, 1980.

FOLKERS, KARL, "Enzyme Cofactors and Aging," in Regelson and Sinex, *op.cit.*, 1983.

————, and Yamamura, Y. (Eds.), *Biomedical and Clinical Aspects of Coenzyme Q*. New York: Elsevier, 1977.

FRANK, BENJAMIN S., personal interviews and communications.

————, *Nucleic Acid Therapy in Aging and Degenerative Disease*. New York: Psychological Library Publishers, 1968.

———— (with Miele, Philip, *Dr. Frank's No-Aging Diet*, New York: Dial Press, 1976. Reprinted as *No-Aging Diet*, Baton Rouge, La.: The B of A Communications, 1981.

FRANKS, L. M., "Cellular Aspects of Ageing," *Experimental Gerontology*, Oct. 1970.

FRIDOVICH, IRWIN, "Superoxide Dismutases," *Annual Reviews of Biochemistry*, 1975.

FRIEDMAN, D.; KEISER, V.; and GLOBERSON, A. "Reactivation of Immunocompetence in Spleen Cells of Aged Mice," *Nature*, Oct. 11, 1974.

FROLKIS, V. V., "Acetylcholine Metabolism and Cholinergic Regulation of Functions in Aging," *Gerontologia*, Vol. 19, 1973.

————, "Functions of Cells and Biosynthesis of Protein in Aging," *Gerontologia*, Vol. 19, 1973.

————, "Regulation and Adaptation Processes in Aging," in *The Main Problems of Soviet Gerontology*. Kiev, 1972.

————, "Catecholamines in the Metabolism and Functions Regulation in Aging," *Gerontologia*, Vol. 16, 1970.

————, "The Autonomic Nervous System in the Aging Organism," *Triangle*, Vol. 8, 1968.

————, et al., "The Hypothalamus in Aging," *Experimental Gerontology*, Vol. 7, 1972.

FURUKAWA, TOSHIYUKI; MICHITOSHI, INOUE; et al., "Assessment of Biological Age by Multiple Regression Analysis," *Journal of Gerontology*, Vol. 30, No. 4, 1975.

FUSCO, CARMEN L., personal communications.

————, columns in *Anti-Aging News*.

GALTON, LAWRENCE, *Don't Give Up on an Aging Parent*. New York: Crown Publishers, 1975.

GARDNER, E., "Decrease in Human Neurones with Age," *Anatomical Record*, Vol. 77, 1940.

GARDNER, FRANK H., and BASS, EMMANUEL C., "Physiologic Mechanisms and the Hematopoietic Effects of the Androstanes and Their Derivatives," *Current Topics in Hematology*, Vol. 4, 1983.

GAREY, WALTER (Project Manager), *R/V Alpha Helix Bering Sea Expe-*

dition, Feb.–Oct. 1968, and *Alpha Helix Research Program, 1972–1974.* Reports of the Scripps Institution of Oceanography, University of California at San Diego.

GARFIELD, EUGENE, "Current Comments: The Dilemma of Prolongevity Research—Must We Die Before We Die, or If We Don't, Will We?," *Current Contents,* April 11, 1983.

GELFANT, SEYMOUR, and SMITH, J. GRAHAM, JR., "Aging: Noncycling Cells, an Explanation," *Science,* Oct. 27, 1972.

GERSHON, DAVID, "Detection of Inactive Enzyme Molecules in Ageing Organisms," *Nature,* Sept. 19, 1970.

———, "Studies on Aging in Nematodes—I. The Nematode as a Model Organism for Aging Research," *Experimental Gerontology,* March 1970.

GERSHON, HARRIET, and GERSHON, DAVID, "Inactive Enzyme Molecules in Aging Mice: Liver Aldolase," *Proceedings of the National Academy of Science,* March 1973.

GIBSON, MARIE J., et al., "Mating and Pregnancy Can Occur in Genetically Hypogonadal Mice with Preoptic Area Brain Grafts," *Science,* Aug. 31, 1984.

GLADE, PHILIP R., and HIRSCHHORN, KURT, "Products of Lymphoid Cells in Continuous Culture," *American Journal of Pathology,* Vol. 60, 1970.

GLASS, H. BENTLEY, personal communications.

———, "Genetics of Aging," in *Aging: Some Social and Biological Aspects* (N. W. Shock, Ed.). American Association for the Advancement of Science, 1960.

GOLD, MICHAEL, "The Cells That Would Not Die," *Science/81,* April 1981.

GOLDSTEIN, ALLAN L., personal communications.

———, statement (at hearing on "Longevity and the Lifestyle of the Older Individual") to U.S. Senate Subcommittee on Aging, Sept. 24, 1984.

———, "Update on Thymosin, the Immunity Hormone," interview in *Anti-Aging News,* Sept. 1984.

———, "The Thymus Gland: Experimental and Clinical Studies of Its Role in the Development and Expression of Immune Functions," in *Advances in Metabolic Disorders,* Vol. 5. New York: Academic Press, 1971.

———, and White, Abraham, "Thymosin and Other Thymic Hormones: Their Nature and Roles in the Thymic Dependency of Immunological Phenomena," in *Contemporary Topics in Immunology.* New York: Plenum Press, 1973.

———, et al., "Thymosin: Can It Retard Aging by Boosting Immune Capacity?," in Regelson and Sinex, *op. cit.,* 1983.

GOLDSTEIN, SAMUEL, personal communication.

——, "Aging in Vitro: Growth of Cultured Cells from the Galápagos Tortoise," *Experimental Cell Research*, Vol. 83, 1974.

——, "Biological Aging: An Essentially Normal Process," *Journal of the American Medical Association*, Dec. 23–30, 1974.

——, "The Biology of Aging," *New England Journal of Medicine*, Nov. 11, 1971.

——, and Moerman, Elena, "Heat-Labile Enzymes in Skin Fibroblasts from Subjects with Progeria," *New England Journal of Medicine*, June 19, 1975.

——, and Moerman, E. J., "Heat-Labile Enzymes in Werner's Syndrome Fibroblasts," *Nature*, May 8, 1975.

——, and Singal, D. P., "Alteration of Fibroblast Gene Products in Vitro from a Subject with Werner's Syndrome," *Nature*, Oct. 25, 1974.

GOOD, PHILLIP, and MACIERA-COELHO, A., "Ageing Cell Cultures," letter to *Nature*, Nov. 8, 1974.

GORDON, PAUL, "Free Radicals and the Aging Process," in *Theoretical Aspects of Aging* (Rockstein, M., Ed.). New York: Academic Press, 1974.

GREENBERG, DANIEL S., "Nutrition: A Long Wait for a Little Advice," *New England Journal of Medicine*, Feb. 29, 1980.

GREULICH, RICHARD, personal communications.

GRUMAN, GERALD J., personal communications.

——, "A History of Ideas About the Prolongation of Life: The Evolution of Prolongevity Hypotheses to 1800," in *Transactions of the American Philosophical Society*, Dec. 1966. New York: Arno Press, 1977.

——, "The Rise and Fall of Prolongevity Hygiene, 1558–1873," *Bulletin of the History of Medicine*, May–June, 1961.

——, "An Introduction to the Literature on the History of Gerontology," *Bulletin of the History of Medicine*, Jan.–Feb., 1957.

GUILLEMIN, ROGER, personal communications.

——, "Synthetic Hypothalamic Releasing Factors," interview in *Reproductive Endocrinology*, 1973.

——, and Burgus, Roger, "The Hormones of the Hypothalamus," *Scientific American*, Nov. 1972.

GUTMAN, E., "Nervous and Hormonal Mechanisms in the Aging Process," *Experimental Gerontology*, Oct. 1970.

HABER, BERNARD, personal communications.

HALSELL, GRACE, *Los Viejos: Secrets of Long Life from the Sacred Valley*. Emmaus, Pa.: Rodale Press, 1976.

HALL, KATHLEEN Y., et al., "Correlation Between Ultraviolet-Induced DNA Repair in Primate Lymphocytes and Fibroblasts and Species Maximum Achievable Life Span," *Mechanisms of Ageing and Development*, Vol. 24, 1984.

HARMAN, DENHAM, personal communications.

———, "Free Radicals and the Origination, Evolution and Present Status of the Free Radical Theory of Aging," prepublication manuscript, 1984.

———, "Free Radicals in Perspective," presented at American Aging Association, Oct. 1983.

———, "Statement of Dr. Denham Harman, President, American Aging Association," before congressional subcommittee hearing testimony on establishing a National Institute on Aging, March 16, 1973.

———, "Free Radical Theory of Aging: Effect of Vitamin E on Tumor Incidence," presented to Gerontological Society, Puerto Rico, 1972.

———, "Free Radical Theory of Aging: Dietary Implications," *American Journal of Clinical Nutrition*, Aug. 1972.

———, "The Biologic Clock: The Mitochondria?," *Journal of the American Geriatric Society*, April 1972.

———, "Free Radical Theory of Aging: Effect of the Amount and Degree of Unsaturation of Dietary Fat on Mortality Rate," *Journal of Gerontology*, Vol. 26, No. 4, 1971.

———, "Prolongation of Life: Role of Free Radical Reactions in Aging," *Journal of the American Geriatrics Society*, Aug. 1969.

———, "Free Radical Theory of Aging: Effect of Free Radical Reaction Inhibitors on the Mortality Rate of Male LAF Mice," *Journal of Gerontology*, Oct. 1968.

———, "Atherosclerosis: Possible Ill Effects of the Use of Highly Unsaturated Fats to Lower Serum-Cholesterol Levels," *Lancet*, Nov. 30, 1957.

———, as told to James C. G. Conniff, "How to Live to a Healthy 105," *Bell Telephone Magazine*, May–June 1969.

HARRINGTON, ALAN, *The Immortalist*. New York: Random House, 1969.

HARRIS, MORGAN, *Cell Culture and Somatic Variation*. New York: Holt, Rinehart & Winston, 1964.

HARRISON, DAVID E., personal communications.

———, "Experience with Developing Assays of Physiological Age," in *Biological Markers of Aging* (Reff, M. E., and Schneider, E. L., Eds.). Bethesda, Md.: National Institutes of Health, 1982.

———, "Must We Grow Old?," *Biology Digest*, Feb. 1982.

———, "Is Limited Cell Proliferation the Clock That Times Aging?," in Behnke, Finch, and Moment, *op. cit.*, 1978.

———, "Defective Erythropoietic Responses of Aged Mice Not Improved by Young Marrow," *Journal of Gerontology*, Vol. 30, No. 3, 1975.

———, "Normal Function of Transplanted Marrow Cell Lines from Aged Mice," *Journal of Gerontology*, Vol. 30, No. 3, 1975.

302 | *Bibliography*

——, "Normal Production of Erythrocytes by Mouse Marrow Continuous for 73 Months," *Proceedings of the National Academy of Sciences*, Nov. 1973.

——, "Normal Function of Transplanted Mouse Erythrocyte Precursors for 21 Months Beyond Donor Life Span," *Nature New Biology*, June 16, 1972.

——; Archer, Jonathan R.; and Astle, Clinton M., "Use of the Mouse in Bioassays for Aging," in Regelson and Sinex, *op. cit.*, 1983.

——, and Doubleday, John W., "Normal Function of Immunologic Stem Cells from Aged Mice," *Journal of Immunology*, April 1975.

HASLAM, RICHARD J., and GOLDSTEIN, SAMUEL, "Adenosine 3':5'—Cyclic Monophosphate in Young and Senescent Human Fibroblasts During Growth and Stationary Phase in Vitro," *Journal of Biochemistry*, Vol. 144, 1974.

HAYFLICK, LEONARD, personal communications.

——, "The Coming of Age of WI-38," in *Advances in Cell Research* (Maramorosch, Karl, Ed.). New York: Academic Press, 1983.

——, "The Biology of Human Aging," *Plastic and Reconstructive Surgery*, April 1981.

——, "Recent Advances in the Cell Biology of Aging," *Mechanisms of Ageing and Development*, Vol. 14, 1980.

——, "Future Directions in Aging Research," *Proceedings of the Society for Experimental Biology and Medicine*, Vol. 165, 1980.

——, "Cell Biology of Aging," *BioScience*, Oct. 1975.

——, "Current Theories of Biological Aging," *Federation Proceedings*, Jan. 1975.

——, "Cytogerontology," in Rockstein, Sussman, and Chesky, *op. cit.*, 1974.

——, "The Longevity of Cultured Human Cells," *Journal of the American Geriatrics Society*, Vol. XXII, No. 1, 1974.

——, "The Strategy of Senescence," *Gerontologist*, Feb. 1974.

——, "Aging Human Cells," *Triangle*, Vol. 12, No. 4, 1973.

——, "The Biology of Human Aging," *American Journal of the Medical Sciences*, Vol. 265, No. 6, 1973.

——, "Cell Senescence and Cell Differentiation In Vitro," in *Altern und Entwicklung*. Stuttgart: F. K. Schattauer Verlag, 1972.

——, "Aging Under Glass," *Experimental Gerontology*, Dec. 1970.

——, "Human Cells and Aging," *Scientific American*, March 1968.

HEDGECOCK, EDWARD M.; SULSTON, JOHN E.; and THOMSON, J. NICHOL, "Mutations Affecting Programmed Cell Deaths in the Nematode *Caenorhabditis elegans*," *Science*, June 17, 1983.

HEINLEIN, ROBERT A., *Time Enough for Love*. New York: Putnam's, 1973.

——, *Methuselah's Children*. New York: New American Library (Signet), 1968.

HEW, statement of Dr. Charles C. Edwards, Assistant Secretary of Health, before U.S. Senate Special Committee on Aging, Aug. 1, 1974.

HEW News, release on Robert T. Simpson, Oct. 2, 1974.

HIROKAWA, KATSUIKU, and MAKINODAN, TAKASHI, "Thymic Involution: Effect on T-Cell Differentiation," *Journal of Immunology*, June 1974.

HIRSCH, GERALD P., and STREHLER, BERNARD L., "Cross-Tissue Translational Capacities: I. The Adequacy of tRNAs from Heterologous Tissues in the Translation of Hemoglobin Message. II. Relative Effectiveness of Heterologous Synthetases (and Other Supernatant Factors) in the Translation of Hemoglobin Message," *Mechanisms of Ageing and Development*, Vol. 2, 1973.

HOCHSCHILD, RICHARD, personal communications.

———, "Prospects for the Control of Human Aging," prepublication manuscript.

———, "Clinical Trials of Effects of Selected Pharmacological Agents on Biomarkers of Aging," information for Glenn Foundation Investigators, Oct. 3, 1983.

———, "The H-Scan: An Instrument for the Automatic Measurement of Physiological Markers of Aging," in Regelson and Sinex, *op. cit.*, 1983.

———, "Effect of Dimethylaminoethanol on the Life Span of Senile Male A/J Rats," *Experimental Gerontology*, Vol. 8, 1973.

———, "Effect of Dimethylaminoethyl p-Chlorophenoxyacetate on the Life Span of Male Swiss Webster Albino Mice," *Experimental Gerontology*, Vol. 8, 1973.

———, "Effects of Various Additives on In Vitro Survival Time of Human Fibroblasts," *Journal of Gerontology*, Vol. 28, No. 4, 1973.

———, "Effects of Various Additives on In Vitro Survival Time of Mouse Macrophages," *Journal of Gerontology*, Vol. 28, No. 4, 1973.

———, "Effects of Various Drugs on Longevity in Female C57BL/6J Mice," *Gerontologia*, Vol. 19, 1973.

———, "Effects of Membrane Stabilizing Drugs on Mortality in Drosophila Melanogaster," *Experimental Gerontology*, Vol. 6, 1971.

HOLLANDER, C. F. "Functional and Cellular Aspects of Organ Ageing," *Experimental Gerontology*, Oct. 1970.

HOLLIDAY, ROBIN, "Errors in Protein Synthesis and Clonal Senescence in Fungi," *Nature*, March 29, 1969.

———; Porterfield, J. S.; and Gibbs, D. D., "Premature Ageing and Occurrence of Altered Enzyme in Werner's Syndrome Fibroblasts," *Nature*, April 26, 1974.

HOPSON, JANET L., interview with Marian Diamond, *Psychology Today*, Nov. 1984.

HOUSE, EDWIN W., personal communications.

———, and Benditt, Earl P., "Ultrastructure of Spontaneous Coronary Arterial Lesions in Steelhead Trout, *Salmo gairdneri*," prepublication manuscript.

———, Dornauer, R. J., and Van Lenten, B. J., "Production of Coronary Arteriosclerosis with Sex Hormones and Human Chorionic Gonadotropin (HCG) in Juvenile Steelhead and Rainbow Trout, *Salmo gairdneri*," *Atherosclerosis*, Vol. 34, 1979.

HOUSTON, JEAN, personal communications.

———, "Putting the First Man on Earth," *Saturday Review*, Feb. 22, 1975.

HRUZA, ZDANEK, personal communication.

Human Behavior, "Aging," Dec. 1974.

HUYCK, MARGARET H. *Growing Older*. Englewood Cliffs, N.J.: Prentice-Hall, 1974.

Immortalist (Junod, Mae A., Ed.), newsletter published by the Cryonics Association, Oak Park, Michigan.

INGRAM, C. ROBERT; PHEGAN, KATHRYN J.; and BLUMENTHAL, HERMAN T., "Significance of an Aging-Linked Neuron Binding Gamma Globulin Fraction of Human Sera," *Journal of Gerontology*, Vol. 29, No. 1, 1974.

INGRAM, DONALD K.; ARCHER, JONATHAN R.; and HARRISON, DAVID E., "Physiological and Behavioral Correlates of Lifespan in Aged C57BL/6J Mice," *Experimental Gerontology*, Vol. 17, 1982.

IVY, G. O., et al., "Inhibitors of Lysosomal Enzymes: Accumulation of Lipofuscin-like Dense Bodies in the Brain," *Science*, Nov. 23, 1984.

JACOB, FRANÇOIS, and MONOD, JACQUES, "Genetic Regulatory Mechanisms in the Synthesis of Proteins," *Journal of Molecular Biology*, Vol. 3, 1961.

jax, "Sooner or Later, Everyone Begins to Think About Growing Old," Fall 1972.

JOHNSON, ROGER; CHRISP, CLARENCE; and STREHLER, BERNARD, "Selective Loss of Ribosomal RNA Genes during the Aging of Post-Mitotic Tissues," *Mechanisms of Ageing and Devlopment*, Vol. 1, 1972.

JUNIPER, DEAN, *Man Against Mortality*. New York: Scribner's, 1973.

KANUNGO, M. S., "Biochemistry of Aging," *Biochemical Reviews*, Vol. 41, 1970.

———; Koul, Omanand; and Reddy, K. R., "Concomitant Studies on RNA Protein Synthesis in Tissues of Rats of Various Ages," *Experimental Gerontology*, Sept. 1970.

KASTENBAUM, ROBERT, "Age: Getting There Ahead of Time," *Psychology Today*, Dec. 1971.

KATO, RYUCHI, and TAKANAKA, AKIRA, "Metabolism of Drugs in Old Rats," *Japanese Journal of Pharmacology*, Dec. 1968.

KEMENY, GABOR, and ROSENBERG, BARNETT, "Compensation Law in Thermodynamics and Thermal Death," *Nature*, June 15, 1973.

KENT, SAUL, personal communications.

——, *The Life Extension Revolution*. New York: William Morrow, 1980.

——, "Clinical Use of Thymus Hormones," *Anti-Aging News*, Sept. 1984.

——, "Genetic Engineering & Lifespan Extension," *Anti-Aging News*, March 1984.

KISHIMOTO, SUSUMU; SHIGEMOTO, SHOZO; and YAMAMURA, YUICHI, "Immune Response in Aged Mice: Change of Cell-Mediated Immunity with Ageing," *Transplantation*, Vol. 15, No. 5, 1973.

——, and YAMAMURA, YUICHI, "Immune Responses in Aged Mice: Changes of Antibody-Forming Cell Precursors and Antigen-Reactive Cells with Ageing," *Clin. exp. Immunol.*, Vol. 8, 1971.

KLEMME, HERBERT, "The Later Years—Are You Ready?," *Menninger Perspective*, Fall 1974.

KOHN, ROBERT R., personal communication.

——, *Principles of Mammalian Aging*. Englewood Cliffs, N.J.: Prentice-Hall, 1971.

——, "Aging and Cell Division," letter to *Science*, April 18, 1975.

KOLATA, GINA, "New Neurons Form in Adulthood," *Science*, June 22, 1984.

KONIGSMARK, BRUCE W., and MURPHY, EDMOND A., "Neuronal Populations in the Human Brain," *Nature*, Dec. 26, 1970.

KORMENDY, CHARLES G., and BENDER, A. DOUGLAS, "Chemical Interference with Aging," *Gerontologia*, 1971.

——, "Experimental Modification of the Chemistry and Biology of the Aging Process," *Journal of Pharmaceutical Science*, Feb. 1971.

KRAEGEL, WILFRED A., "Implications of Extended Life Spans," presented at American Council of Life Insurance, Oct. 1982.

——, "Mortality: Probabilities, Problems and Prospects (A Scenario in 1992)," presented at Middle Atlantic Life Insurance Medical Directors Club, April 1982.

——, "Implications of Future Mortality Trends," presented at Society of Actuaries, Oct. 1980.

KROHN, P. L., "Review Lectures on Senescence. II: Heterochronic Transplantation in the Study of Ageing," *Proceedings of the Royal Society*, Vol. 157, Dec. 18, 1962.

LAMBERT, DARWIN, "Bristlecone Harmonics," *National Parks & Conservation Magazine*, March 1972.

LANG, CALVIN A., "Biological Age: A Key Parameter in Aging Research," presented at AAAS meeting, San Francisco, 1974.

——, "Macromolecular Changes During the Life-Span of the Mosquito," *Journal of Gerontology*, Oct. 1967.

LANGONE, JOHN, *Long Life*. Boston: Little, Brown, 1978.

LANSING, A. L., "A Transmissible, Cumulative and Reversible Factor in Aging," *Journal of Gerontology*, Vol. 2, No. 3, 1974.

LAPPÉ, MARC, and MORRISON, ROBERT S., *Ethical and Scientific Issues Posed by Human Uses of Molecular Genetics*. New York Academy of Sciences, 1976.

LARDNER, JAMES, "If the Life Extenders Get Their Way, Living Could Go On Forever," *Washington Post*, May 15, 1983.

LAZARUS, GERALD S., "Mechanisms of Connective Tissue Degradation," *Science*, Nov. 15, 1974.

LEAF, ALEXANDER, personal communication.

———, *Youth in Old Age*. New York: McGraw-Hill, 1975.

———, "Unusual Longevity: The Common Denominators," *Hospital Practice*, Oct. 1973.

———, "The Peaks of Old Age," *Observer Magazine*, Sept. 30, 1973.

———, "Where Life Begins at 100," *National Geographic*, Jan. 1973.

LEDERBERG, JOSHUA, "Biomedical Frontiers: Genetics," in *The Challenge of Life* (Roche Anniversary Symposium). Basel, Switzerland: Birkäuser Verlag, 1972.

———, "Biological Future of Man," in *Man and His Future* (Wolstenholme, Gordon, Ed.), a Ciba symposium. Boston: Little, Brown, 1963.

LEHMAN, HARVEY C., *Age and Achievement*. Princeton: Princeton University Press, 1953.

LEONARD, GEORGE, *The Transformation*. New York: Dell Publishing Co., 1972.

LEOPOLD, A. C., "Aging, Senescence and Turnover in Plants," *BioScience*, Oct. 1975.

LEVEILLE, P. J., et al., "Dietary Restriction Retards Age-Related Loss of Gamma Crystallins in the Mouse Lens," *Science*, June 13, 1984.

LEWIN, ROGER, *Hormones: Chemical Communicators*. Garden City, N.Y.: Doubleday/Anchor Press, 1973.

LIFTON, ROBERT JAY, "The Sense of Immortality: On Death and the Continuity of Life," in *Explorations in Psychohistory*. New York: Simon & Schuster, 1974.

LIPETZ, PHILIP D., personal communications.

LIPPMANN, RICHARD D., "Can Maximum Lifespan in Mice Be Extended with Antioxidants That Are More Permeable to the Respiratory Chain of Mitochondria?," presented at American Aging Association, Oct. 1983.

LIU, R. K., and WALFORD, R. L. "The Effect of Lowered Body Temperature on Lifespan and Immune and Non-Immune Processes," *Gerontologia*, Vol. 18, 1972.

———, "Observations on the Lifespans of Several Species of Annual Fishes and the World's Smallest Fishes," *Experimental Gerontology*, Sept. 1970.

LOEB, J., and NORTHROP, J. H. "Is There a Temperature Coefficient for the Duration of Life?," *Proceedings of the National Academy of Sciences*, Vol. 2, 1916.

———, "On the Influence of Food and Temperature upon the Duration of Life," *Journal of Biological Chemistry*, Vol. 32, No. 1, 1917.

LOVENBERG, WALTER, personal communication.

———, et al., "Regulation of Biogenic Amine Synthesis by the Hydroxylase Cofactor and Its Relation to Aging and Parkinsonism," in Regelson and Sinex, *op. cit.*, 1983.

LUCE, GAY GAER, *Your Second Life*. New York: Delacorte Press/Seymour Lawrence, 1979.

LUDWIG, FREDERIC, personal communication.

LUNZER, STEVEN, personal communication.

———, "Aging: Causes and Treatment," unpublished manuscript.

MACIEIRA-COELHO, A., and LORIA, E., "Stimulation of Ribosome Synthesis During Retarded Ageing of Human Fibroblasts by Hydrocortisone," *Nature*, Sept. 6, 1974.

MAKINODAN, TAKASHI, "Mechanism, Prevention, and Restoration of Immunologic Aging," in Bergsma and Harrison, *op. cit.*, 1978.

———, and ADLER, W. H., "The Effects of Aging on the Differentiation and Proliferation Potentials of Cells of the Immune System," prepublication manuscript for *Federation Proceedings*, 1974.

MARANTO, GINA, "Aging: Can We Slow the Inevitable?," *Discover*, Dec. 1984.

MARTIN, GEORGE M., "Genetic Syndromes in Man with Potential Relevance to the Pathobiology of Aging," in Bergsma and Harrison, *op. cit.*, 1978.

———; Sprague, Curtis A.; and Epstein, Charles J., "Replicative Life-Span of Cultivated Human Cells: Effect of Donor's Age, Tissue, and Genotype," *Laboratory Investigation*, Vol. 23, No. 1, 1970.

———; Sprague, Curtis A.; et al., "Clonal Selection, Attenuation, and Differentiation in an In Vitro Model of Hyperplasia," *American Journal of Pathology*, Jan. 1974.

MARX, JEAN L., "A Closer Look at the Genes of the MHC," *Science*, May 27, 1983.

———, "Aging Research. I: Cellular Theories of Senescence," *Science*, Dec. 20, 1974.

———, "Aging Research. II: Pacemakers for Aging?," *Science*, Dec. 27, 1974.

MASTERS, ROBERT, and HOUSTON, JEAN, *Listening to the Body*. New York: Delacorte Press, 1978.

MASTERS, WILLIAM H., "Sex Steroid Influences on the Aging Process," *American Journal of Obstetrics and Gynecology*, Oct. 1957.

MATHEWS, J. D.; WHITTINGHAM, S.; and MACKAY, I. R., "Autoimmune Mechanisms in Human Vascular Disease," *Lancet*, Dec. 14, 1974.

MCCAY, CLIVE M.; MAYNARD, L. A.; et al., "Retarded Growth, Life Span, Ultimate Body Size and Age Changes in the Albino Rat After Feeding Diets Restricted in Calories," *Journal of Nutrition*, Vol. 18, 1939.

MCGRADY, PATRICK M., JR., *The Youth Doctors*. New York: Coward-McCann, 1968.

MCKEAN, KEVIN, "New Parts for Damaged Brains," *Discover*, Feb. 1984.

MEADOW, NORMAN D., and BARROWS, CHARLES H., JR., "Studies on Aging in a Bdelloid Rotifer. II: The Effects of the Various Environmental Conditions and Maternal Age on Longevity and Fecundity," *Journal of Gerontology*, Vol. 26, No. 3, 1971.

———, "Studies on Aging in a Bdelloid Rotifer," *Journal of Experimental Zoology*, March 1971.

MEDAWAR, PETER B. *The Future of Man*. New York: Mentor Books, 1959.

———, *Aging: An Unsolved Problem of Biology*. London: H. K. Lewis, 1952.

———, "Life in the Deep Freeze," *New York Times*, Sept. 6, 1973.

———, "The Growth-Energy and Ageing of the Chicken's Heart," *Proceedings of the Royal Society*, Vol. B129, 1940.

Medical Tribune, "Aging Linked to Decrease in Thymosin Blood Levels," June 13, 1973.

Medical World News, "Mild Overweight Is Risky for Men of 50," Feb. 5, 1979.

———, "Synthesizing Against Senility," June 28, 1974.

———, "Bringing Research on Aging Up to Date," April 19, 1974.

———, "Amyloid—Aging Link Gets Support," Nov. 9, 1973.

———, "Aging: Investigators Probe Biochemical, Genetic Aspects of Universal 'Disease,' " Oct. 22, 1971.

MEDVEDEV, ZHORES A., personal communications.

———, *Protein Biosynthesis and Problems of Heredity, Development, and Ageing*. Edinburgh: Oliver & Boyd, 1966.

———, "Ageing and Lifespan," Royal Institution lecture, London, 1973.

———, "Possible Role of Repeated Nucleotide Sequences in DNA in the Evolution of Life Spans of Differentiated Cells," *Nature*, June 23, 1973.

MEISTER, ALTON, "Selective Modification of Glutathione Metabolism," *Science*, April 29, 1983.

MERRIL, CARL R., personal communications.

MILLER, J. F. A. P., "Endocrine Function of the Thymus," *New England Journal of Medicine*, May 30, 1974.

MILLER, JUDITH K.; BOLLA, ROBERT; and DENCKLA, W. DONNER, "Age-Associated Changes in Initiation of Ribonucleic Acid Synthesis in Isolated Rat Liver Nuclei," *Journal of Biochemistry*, Vol. 188, 1980.

MIQUEL, JAIME, "Morphological Changes in the Aging Drosophila Melanogaster," presented at American Association for the Advancement of Science, San Francisco, 1974.

——, and Fleming, James E., "An Integrated Theory of Cell and Organismic Aging as the Result of Mitochondrial Differentiation and Intrinsic MT DNA Mutagenesis," presented at American Aging Association, Oct. 1983.

——, and Lindseth, Kristin, "Determination of Biological Age in Antioxidant-Treated Drosophila and Mice," in Regelson and Sinex, *op. cit.*, 1983.

——; Bensch, Klaus G., et al., "Natural Aging and Radiation-Induced Life Shortening in Drosophila Melanogaster," *Mechanisms of Ageing and Development*, Vol. 1, 1972.

MOMENT, GAIRDNER, "The Ponce de Leon Trail Today," *BioScience*, Oct. 1975.

MONTAGU, ASHLEY, *Growing Young*. New York: McGraw-Hill, 1981.

MUGGLETON, AUDREY, and DANIELLI, J. F., "Inheritance of the 'Life-Spanning' Phenomenon in *Amoeba proteus*," *Experimental Cell Research*, Vol. 49, 1968.

MUNRO, A. J., and TAUSSIG, M. J. "Two Genes in the Major Histocompatibility Complex Control Immune Response," *Nature*, July 10, 1975.

NAJAFI, HASSAN, "Dr. Alexis Carrel and Tissue Culture," *Journal of the American Medical Association*, Aug. 26, 1983.

NANDY, KALIDAS, personal communications.

——, "Effects of Antioxidant Drugs on Lipopigments," presented at American Aging Association, Oct. 1983.

——, "Further Studies on the Effects of Centrophenoxine on the Lipofuscin Pigment in the Neurons of Senile Guinea Pigs," *Journal of Gerontology*, Jan. 1968.

NETBOY, ANTHONY, "Exit the Salmon," *Esquire*, May 1975.

NEUGARTEN, BERNICE L., "Social Implications of a Prolonged Life-Span," *Gerontologist*, Winter 1972.

——, "Age: Grow Old Along with Me! The Best Is Yet to Be," *Psychology Today*, Dec. 1971.

——, and HAVIGHURST, ROBERT J. (Eds.), *Extending the Human Life Span: Social Policy and Social Ethics*, Washington, D.C., Superintendent of Documents, U.S. Printing Office, 1977.

New Scientist, "What's the Value of Thinking about Ageing?," Sept. 13, 1973.

——, "Ageing: Is It Nature's Intent Rather Than Error?," May 10, 1972.

Newsweek, "Can Aging Be Cured?," April 16, 1973.

NIKITIN, V. N. "The Genetic Apparatus and Aging Processes," in *The Main Problems of Soviet Gerontology*. Kiev, 1972.

NORTHROP, J., "The Effect of Prolongation of the Period of Growth on the Total Duration of Life," *Journal of Biological Chemistry*, Vol. 32, 1917.

OATES, KAREN K., and GOLDSTEIN, ALLAN L., "Thymosins: Hormones of the Thymus Gland," *Trends in Pharmacological Sciences*, Aug. 1984.

OHNO, SUSUMU, and NAGAI, YUKIFUMI, "Genes in Multiple Copies as the Primary Cause of Aging," in Bergsma and Harrison, *op. cit.*, 1978.

ORDY, J. M., "Drugs for Memory in Aging," presented at American Aging Association, Oct. 1983.

ORGEL, LESLIE E., personal communications.

———, "Ageing of Clones of Mammalian Cells," *Nature*, June 22, 1973.

OTT, JOHN N., *Health and Light*. New York: Pocket Books, 1973.

OTTO, A. STUART, personal communications.

———, editorials in *Immortality Newsletter*.

PACKER, LESTER, personal communication.

———, and Smith, James R. "Extension of the Lifespan of Cultured Normal Human Diploid Cells by Vitamin E," prepublication manuscript.

PAPOCONSTANTINOU, JOHN, personal communications.

PARKENING, T. A., personal communications.

———; Collins, T. J.; and Smith, E. R., "Luteinizing Hormone Levels in Aged Female Laboratory Rodents as Measured by a Radioimmunoassay and a Radioreceptor Assay," *Journal of Endocrinology*, Vol. 95, 1982.

———; Collins, T. J.; and Smith, E. R., "Plasma and Pituitary Concentrations of Luteinizing Hormone, Follicle-Stimulating Hormone and Prolactin in Aged, Ovariectomized CD-1 and C57BL/6 Mice," *Experimental Gerontology*, Vol. 17, 1982.

PARKER, ROBERT J., et al., "Vascular Relaxation, Aging and Thyroid Hormones," *Mechanisms of Ageing and Development*, Vol. 8, 1978.

PASSWATER, RICHARD A., personal communications.

———, and Welker, Paul A., "Human Aging Research" (two-part article), *American Laboratory*, April and May, 1971.

PATON, JOHN A., and NOTTEBOHM, FERNANDO N., "Neurons Generated in the Adult Brain Are Recruited into Functional Circuits," *Science*, Sept. 7, 1984.

PATRUSKY, BEN, "Of Mice and Men—and the Aging Factor," *Signature*, Jan. 1971.

PEARSON, DURK, and SHAW, SANDY, *The Life Extension Companion*. New York: Warner Books, 1984.

——, *Life Extension*. New York: Warner Books, 1982.

PECILE, A.; MULLER, E.; and FALCONI, G., "Endocrine Function of Pituitary Transplants Taken from Rats of Different Ages," *Arch. Int. Pharmocodyn.*, Vol. 2, 1966.

PELC, S. R., "Metabolic DNA and the Problem of Ageing," *Experimental Gerontology*, Sept. 1970.

PELLETIER, KENNETH R., personal communications.

——, *Longevity: Fulfilling Our Biological Potential*. New York: Delacorte Press/Seymour Lawrence, 1981.

——, *Holistic Medicine: From Stress to Optimum Health*. New York: Delacorte Press/Seymour Lawrence, 1979.

PENG, MING-TSUNG, and HUANG, HWE-HO, "Aging of Hypothalamic-Pituitary-Ovarian Function in the Rat," *Fertility and Sterility*, Aug. 1972.

PEREZ-POLO, REGINO, personal communications.

PESMEN, CURTIS, and the Editors of *Esquire, How a Man Ages*. New York: Ballantine Books, 1984.

PETES, T. D.; FARBER, R. A.; et al., "Altered Rate of DNA Replication in Ageing Human Fibroblast Cultures," *Nature*, Oct. 4, 1974.

PLATT, DIETER, personal communication.

——; Hering, H.; and Hering, F. J., "Age Dependent Determination of Lysosomal Enzyme Activities in the Liver and Brain as Well as the Measurements of Cytoplasmic Enzyme Activities in the Blood of Piracetam Pre-Treated Rats," *Experimental Gerontology*, Vol. 8, 1973.

——, "Age Dependent Determination of Lysosomal Enzymes in the Liver of Spironolactone and Aldosterone Pretreated Rats," *Experimental Gerontology*, Vol. 7, 1972.

PLUMB, MARK; STEIN, GARY; and STEIN, JANET, "Influence of DNA Synthesis Inhibition on the Coordinate Expression of Core Human Histone Genes During S Phase," *Nucleic Acids Research*, Vol. 11, No. 22, 1983.

——, "Coordinate regulation of multiple histone mRNAs during the cell cycle in HeLa cells," *Nucleic Acids Research*, Vol. 11, No. 8, 1983.

PREHODA, ROBERT W., *Extended Youth*. New York: Putnam's, 1968.

——, "Retardation of Aging," *Medical Opinion & Review*, Oct. 1970.

PRICE, GERALD B.; MODAK, S. P.; and MAKINODAN, P., "Age-Associated Changes in the DNA of Mouse Tissue," *Science*, March 5, 1971.

PRYOR, WILLIAM A., personal communications.

——, "Chemistry of Free Radicals and Implications for Aging," presented at American Aging Association, Oct. 1983.

——, "Free Radicals and Autoxidation," in *Presentation Summaries*. Vitamin Nutrition Information Service, 1983.

——, "Free Radical Biology: Xenobiotics, Cancer and Aging," *Annals of the New York Academy of Sciences*, Vol. 393, 1982.

——, "Free Radicals in Biological Systems," *Scientific American*, Aug. 1970.

——, "Organic Free Radicals," *Chemical & Engineering News*, Jan. 15, 1968.

——, et al., "Reactive Oxy-Radicals from Cigarette Smoke and Their Physiological Effects," in *Oxy-Radicals and Their Scavenger Systems* (Greenwald, Robert A., and Cohen, Gerald, Eds.). New York: Elsevier, 1983.

Public Law 93-296, 93rd Congress, S. 775, "An Act to Amend the Public Health Service Act to Provide for the Establishment of a National Institute on Aging," May 31, 1974.

PYTHILA, M. J., and SINEX, F. MAROTT, "The Effect of Diet on the Composition of Chromatin from Young and Old Rats," *Experimental Gerontology*, March 1970.

QUADRI, S. K.; KLEDZIK, G. S.; and MEITES, J., "Reinitiation of Estrous Cycles in Old Constant-Estrous Rats by Central-Acting Drugs," *Neuroendocrinology*, Vol. 11, 1973.

REGELSON, WILLIAM, personal communications.

——, "Biomarkers in Aging," in Regelson and Sinex, *op. cit.,* 1983.

——, "The Evidence for Pituitary and Thyroid Control of Aging: Is Age Reversal a Myth or Reality? The Search for a 'Death Hormone,' " in Regelson and Sinex, *op. cit.*, 1983.

——, and Sinex, F. Marott (Eds.), *Intervention in the Aging Process*, 2 vols. New York: Alan R. Liss, 1983.

REICHEL, WILLIAM, personal communications.

——, "Premature Aging," presented at 9th International Congress of Gerontology, Kiev, 1972.

——, "Lipofuscin Pigment Accumulation in Five Rat Organs as a Function of Age," *Journal of Gerontology*, April 1968.

——, "The Biology of Aging," *Journal of the American Geriatrics Society*, Vol. 14, 1966.

——; Bailey, Joseph A.; et al., "Radiological Findings in Progeria," *Journal of the American Geriatrics Society*, Aug. 1971.

——; Garcia-Bunuel, Rafael; and DiLallo, Joseph, "Progeria and Werner's Syndrome as Models for the Study of Normal Human Aging," *Journal of the American Geriatrics Society*, May 1971.

REISBERG, BARRY, personal communications.

——, *Brain Failure: An Introduction to Current Concepts of Senility*. New York: The Free Press, 1981.

——; Ferris, Steven H.; and Gershon, Samuel, "An Overview of Pharmacologic Treatment of Cognitive Decline in the Aged," *American Journal of Psychiatry*, May 1981.

———, et al., "Novel Pharmacologic Approaches to the Treatment of Senile Dementia of the Alzheimer's Type (SDAT)," *Psychopharmacology Bulletin*, Vol. 19, No. 2, 1983.

RILEY, JOHN W., JR., personal communications.

———, "Old Age in American Society: Notes on Health, Retirement and the Anticipation of Death," *Journal of the American Society of Chartered Life Underwriters*, Vol. 22, 1968.

RILEY, MATILDA W., personal communications.

———, *Aging and Society*. New York: Russell Sage, 1968.

ROBERT, L.; ROBERT, B.; and ROBERT, A. M., "Molecular Biology of Elastin as Related to Aging and Atherosclerosis," *Experimental Gerontology*, Oct. 1970.

ROBERTS-THOMSON, IAN C.; WHITTINGHAM, S.; et al., "Ageing, Immune Response, and Mortality," *Lancet*, Aug. 17, 1974.

ROBINSON, ARTHUR B.; MCKERROW, JAMES H.; and CARY, PAUL, "Controlled Deamination of Peptides and Proteins: An Experimental Hazard and a Possible Biological Timer," *Proceedings of the National Academy of Sciences*, July 1970.

ROCKSTEIN, MORRIS, "The Genetic Basis for Longevity," in Rockstein, Sussman, and Chesky, *op. cit.*, 1974.

———, and Hawkins, W. Brown, "Thiamine in the Ageing House Fly, *Musca domestica*," *Experimental Gerontology*, July 1970.

———; Sussman, Marvin L.; and Chesky, Jeffrey, *Theoretical Aspects of Aging*. New York: Academic Press, 1974.

RODEHEFFER, RICHARD J., et al., "Exercise Cardiac Output Is Maintained with Advancing Age in Healthy Human Subjects: Cardiac Dilation and Increased Stroke Volume Compensate for a Diminished Heart Rate," *Circulation*, Feb. 1984.

ROSENBERG, BARNETT, personal communications.

———; Kemeny, Gabor; et al., "The Kinetics and Thermodynamics of Death in Multicellular Organisms," *Mechanisms of Ageing and Development*, Vol. 2, 1973.

———, "Quantitative Evidence for Protein Denaturation as the Cause of Thermal Death," *Nature*, Aug. 13, 1971.

ROSENFELD, ALBERT, *The Second Genesis: The Coming Control of Life*. Englewood Cliffs, N.J.: Prentice-Hall, 1969.

———, "Stretching the Span," *Wilson Quarterly*, New Year's issue, 1985.

———, "Aging Well Is the Best Revenge," *GQ* (*Gentleman's Quarterly*), March 1984.

———, "Superpowder," *Omni*, Aug. 1982.

———, "In Search of Youth," *Geo*, June 1982.

———, "Interview—W. Donner Denckla," *Omni*, Nov. 1981.

———, "The Reexamination of a Curious Hormone," *Science/81*, Nov. 1981.

———, "Is Margarine Worse Than Butter?," *Science/81*, Sept. 1981.

———, "The Brain as a Privileged Site," *Science/80*, Nov., 1980.

———, "The Good News & the Bad News About Eating," *Prime Time*, Aug. 1980.

———, "Do You Want to Live to Be 120?," *Prime Time*, Feb. 1980.

———, "Are We Afraid of Living Longer?," *Saturday Review*, May 27, 1978.

———, "Can Humans Be 'Taught' to Hibernate?," *Saturday Review*, June 11, 1977.

———, "The Willy Loman Complex," *Saturday Review*, Aug. 7, 1976.

———, "The Death of Old Age?," in *Nature/Science Annual*. New York: Time-Life Books, 1975.

———, "Thymosin: Breaking the Immune Barrier," *Saturday Review*, June 15, 1974.

———, "The Longevity Seekers," *Saturday Review of the Sciences*, March 1973.

———, (Ed.), "Mind and Supermind: Expanding the Limits of Consciousness," special section in *Saturday Review*, Feb. 22, 1975.

———, and Hills, Alicia, "DNA's Code: Key to All Life," *Life*, Oct. 4, 1963.

Ross, Morris H., "Nutritional Regulation of Longevity," in Behnke, Finch, and Moment, *op. cit.*, 1978.

Rostand, Jean, *Humanly Possible*. New York: Saturday Review Press, 1973.

———, *Can Man Be Modified?* New York: Basic Books, 1959.

Rostovsky, Igor L., "Aging: Oceanography and Geriatrics," *Oceans*, Feb. 1969.

Roth, George S., "Altered Biochemical Responsiveness and Hormone Receptor Changes During Aging," in Behnke, Finch, and Moment, *op. cit.*, 1978.

———, "Hormonal Receptor and Responsiveness Changes During Aging: Genetic Modulation," in Bergsma and Harrison, *op. cit.*, 1978.

Rous, Peyton, "Presentation of the Kober Medal for 1961 to O. H. Robertson," *Transactions of the American Association of Physicians*, 1961.

Russell, Elizabeth S., personal communications.

———, "Analysis of Genetic Differences as a Tool for Understanding Aging Processes," in Bergsma and Harrison, *op. cit.*, 1978.

———, "Genes and Aging," in Behnke, Finch, and Moment, *op. cit.*, 1978.

Sacher, George A., "The Evolutionary-Genetic Approach to Mammalian Longevity and Aging," presented at American Association for the Advancement of Science, San Francisco, 1974.

——, and Hart, Ronald W., "Longevity, Aging and Comparative Cellular and Molecular Biology of the House Mouse, *Mus musculus*, and the White-Footed Mouse, *Peromyscus leucopus*," in Bergsma and Harrison, *op. cit.*, 1978.

SALK, JONAS, personal communications.

——, *Anatomy of Reality*. New York: Columbia University Press, 1983.

——, *The Survival of the Wisest*. New York: Harper & Row, 1973.

Salk Institute Newsletter, "Study on Aging Reported by Dr. Orgel," No. 5, Fall 1973.

SANADI, D. RAO, personal communications.

——; Chen, J. C.; and Warshaw, J. B., "Decline of Mitochondrial Respiration in Senescence," presented at International Study Group for Research in Cardiac Metabolism, Winnipeg, 1972.

SANDERS, HOWARD J., "Human Aging: The Enigma Persists," *Chemical & Engineering News*, July 24, 1972.

SCHLOSS, BENJAMIN, personal communications.

——, *Prolonging Youthfulness*. Brooklyn: Foundation for Aging Research, 1970 (brochure).

——, "Breaking Man's Lifespan Barrier," Foundation for Aging Research, Los Angeles, 1974 (mimeograph).

——, "The Control of Human Aging," Foundation for Aging Research, Los Angeles, 1974 (mimeograph).

SCHMECK, HAROLD M., *Immunology: The Many-Edged Sword*. New York: George Braziller, 1974.

——, "Science: Extending the Life Span," *New York Times*, May 30, 1965.

SCHMID, RUDOLF, and SCHMID, MARVIN J., "Living Links with the Past," *Natural History*, March 1975.

SCHNECK, MICHAEL K.; REISBERG, BARRY; and FERRIS, STEVEN H., "An Overview of Current Concepts of Alzheimer's Disease," *American Journal of Psychiatry*, Feb. 1982.

SCHNEIDER, EDWARD L., "In Vivo Versus In Vitro Cellular Aging," in Bergsma and Harrison, *op. cit.*, 1978.

SCHWARTZ, ARTHUR, personal communications.

——, "The Effects of Dehydroepiandrosterone on the Rate of Development of Cancer and Autoimmune Processes in Laboratory Rodents," in *Brookhaven Symposium in Biology No. 33*, in press, 1984.

——; Pashko, Laura L.; and Tannen, Robert H., "Dehydroepiandrosterone: An Anti-Cancer and Possible Anti-Aging Substance," in Regelson and Sinex, *op. cit.*, 1983.

Sciences, "Slowing the Biological Clock," July 1970.

SCOTT, MITCHELL; BOLLA, ROBERT; and DENCKLA, W. DONNER, "Age-Related Changes in Immune Function of Rats and the Effect of

Long-Term Hypophysectomy," *Mechanisms of Ageing and Development*, Vol. 11, 1979.

SEELIG, MILDRED, personal communications.

——, *Magnesium Deficiency in the Pathogenesis of Disease*. New York: Plenum Medical Book Co., 1980.

——, "Possible Role of Magnesium in Disorders of the Aged," in Regelson and Sinex, *op. cit.*, 1983.

SEGALL, PAUL E., personal communications.

——, and Timiras, Paola S., "Age-related Changes in Thermoregulatory Capacity of Tryptophan-deficient Rats," *Federation Proceedings*, Jan. 1975.

——, "Reproductive and Behavioral Effects of Aging Retardation," prepublication manuscript.

——, and Waitz, Harold D., "Long Term Tryptophan Deficiency and Aging Retardation in the Rat," prepublication report.

SEGERBERG, OSBORN, JR., *Living to Be 100*. New York: Scribner's, 1982.

——, *The Immortality Factor*. New York: E. P. Dutton, 1974.

SHAW, GEORGE BERNARD, *Back to Methuselah*, in *Complete Plays with Prefaces*, Vol. II. New York: Dodd, Mead, 1963.

SHEFER, V. F., "Absolute Number of Neurons and Thickness of the Cerebral Cortex During Aging, Senile and Vascular Dementia, and Pick's and Alzheimer's Diseases," *Zhurnal Nevropatologii i Psikhiatrii imeni S. S. Korsokava*, Vol. 72, No. 7, 1972.

SHELDRAKE, A. R., "The Ageing, Growth and Death of Cells," *Nature*, Aug. 2, 1974.

SHOCK, NATHAN W., "Biological and Physiological Characteristics of Aging in Men and Women," presented at conference on Adaptability and Aging, Quebec, Aug. 1980.

——, "Physiological Theories of Aging," in Rockstein, Sussman, and Chesky, *op. cit.*, 1974.

——, "Will You Live to Be 100?," *Britannica Yearbook*, 1972.

——, "Physiologic Aspects of Aging," *Journal of the American Dietetic Association*, June 1970.

——, "The Physiology of Aging," *Scientific American*, Jan. 1962.

SIAKOTOS, A. N., and ARMSTRONG, DONALD, "Age Pigment: A Biochemical Indicator of Intracellular Aging," in *Neurobiology of Aging* (Ordy, J. M., and Brizzee, K. R., Eds.) New York: Plenum Publishing Co., 1975.

SIERRA, F., et al., "Organization of Human Histone Genes," *Proceedings of the National Academy of Sciences*, March 1982.

SINEX, F. MAROTT, personal communications.

——, "The Molecular Genetics of Aging," prepublication manuscript.

——, "An Overview: Theoretical Considerations as to Intervention in

the Aging Process: Alzheimer's Disease and Aging," in Regelson and Sinex, *op. cit.*, 1983.
————, "The Mutation Theory of Aging," in Rockstein, Sussman, and Chesky, *op. cit.*, 1974.
————, testimony before congressional subcommittee on aging-research needs, 1971.
————, "Genetic Mechanisms of Aging," *Journal of Gerontology*, July 1966.
SMITH, JAMES R., personal communication.
SMITH, JOHN MAYNARD, personal communication.
————, "Molecular Evolution and the Age of Man," *Nature*, Feb. 13, 1975.
————, "Review Lectures on Senescence. I: The Causes of Ageing," *Proceedings of the Royal Society*, Vol. 157, Dec. 18, 1962.
————, "A Theory of Ageing," *Nature*, Vol. 184, 1959.
————; Boscuk, A. N.; and Tebbutt, Susan, "Protein Turnover in Adult Drosophila," *Journal of Insect Physiology*, Vol. 16, 1970.
SMITH-SONNEBORN, JOAN, personal communications.
————; Lipetz, Philip D.; and Stephens, Ralph E., "Paramecium Bioassay of Longevity Modulating Agents," in Regelson and Sinex, *op. cit.*, 1983.
SONNEBORN, TRACY M., "The Origin, Evolution, Nature, and Causes of Aging," in Behnke, Finch, and Moment, *op. cit.*, 1978.
SRIVASTAVA, SATISH, personal communications.
STANLEY, JEAN F.; PYE, DAVID; and MACGREGOR, ANDREW, "Comparison of Doubling Numbers Attained by Cultured Animal Cells with Life Span of Species," *Nature*, May 8, 1975.
STEIN, GARY S., and STEIN, JANET S., personal communications.
————, et al., "Organization and Expression of Human Histone Genes," in *Histone Genes* (Stein, G. S.; Stein, J. S.; and Manziuff, W., Eds.). New York: John Wiley, in press, 1984.
————; Stein, Janet Swinehart; and Kleinsmith, Lewis J., "Chromosomal Proteins and Gene Regulation," *Scientific American*, Feb. 1975.
STEIN, KATHLEEN, "Some of Us May Never Die," *Omni*, Oct. 1978.
————, "Supergene," *Omni*, Dec. 1980.
STEPHENS, RALPH E., and LIPETZ, PHILIP D., "Higher Order DNA Repair in Human Peripheral Leukocytes: A Factor in Aging and Cancer?," in Regelson and Sinex, *op. cit.*, 1983.
STEWART, FRED MUSTARD, *The Methuselah Enzyme*. New York: Arbor House, 1970.
STREHLER, BERNARD L., personal communications.
————, *Time, Cells, and Aging*. New York: Academic Press, 1977 (2nd ed.).
————, "How to Stay Young," prepublication manuscript.

——, "Ageing: Concepts and Theories," in Viidik, *op. cit.*, 1982.

——, "Roles and Mechanisms of rDNA Changes During Aging," in Bergsma and Harrison, *op. cit.*, 1978.

——, "Aging: Transcriptional and Translational Control Mechanisms and Their Alteration," presented at American Association for the Advancement of Science, San Francisco, 1974.

——, "Implications of Aging Research for Society," presented at Federation of American Societies for Experimental Biology, Atlantic City, N.J., 1974.

——, "Lengthening Our Lives," *Science Yearbook*, 1973.

——, "A New Age for Aging," *Natural History*, Feb. 1973.

——, "Men, Molecules and Mortality: Effects of Life Extension," presented at Council for the Advancement of Science Writing, Boulder, Colo., 1972.

——, "Synopsis of an Engram Storage, Retrieval and Manipulation System: A Parsimonious Model for Higher Brain Function," prepublication manuscript, 1972.

——, testimony before congressional subcommittees on aging-research needs, 1967, 1971, and 1972.

——, "Aging at the Cellular Level," in *Clinical Geriatrics* (Rossman, Isadore, Ed.). Philadelphia: J. B. Lippincott, 1971.

——, "Ten Myths About Aging," *Center Magazine*, July 1970.

——, "Information Handling in the Nervous System: An Analogy to Molecular-Genetic Coder-Decoder Mechanisms," *Perspectives in Biology and Medicine*, Summer 1969.

——, "The Prometheus Experiment," *Perspectives in Biology and Medicine*, Winter 1968.

——, "Environmental Factors in Aging and Mortality," *Environmental Research*, Vol. 1, 1967.

——, "Origin and Comparison of the Effects of Time and High-Energy Radiations on Living Systems," *Quarterly Review of Biology*, Vol. 34, No. 2, 1959.

——, "Immortality," in *Science and the Future*. Washington, D.C.: Science Clubs of America, 1943.

——; Hirsch, G.; et al., "Codon-Restriction Theory of Aging and Development," *Journal of Theoretical Biology*, Vol. 33, 1971.

——, and Mildvan, A. S., "General Theory of Mortality and Aging," *Science*, Vol. 132, 1960.

——, "Studies on the Chemical Properties of Lipofuscin Age Pigments," prepublication paper for proceedings of the 5th International Gerontological Congress.

STUART, FRIEND, *How to Conquer Physical Death*. San Marcos, Calif.: Dominion Press, 1968.

STUMPF, WALTER E., personal communication.

———, and Grant, Lester D., "The Brain: An Endocrine Organ and Hormone Target," *Science*, Dec. 20, 1974.

———, and Sar, Madhabananda, "Localization of Thyroid Hormone in the Mature Rat Brain and Pituitary," *Anatomical Neuroendocrinology*, prepublication manuscript.

SULLIVAN, JEROME L., and DEBUSK, A. GIB, "Inositol-less Death in *Neurospora* and Cellular Aging," *Nature New Biology*, May 16, 1973.

SULLIVAN, WALTER, "Scientists Seek Key to Longevity," *New York Times*, Feb. 11, 1973.

———, "Aging: The Eternal Quest for Eternal Youth," *New York Times*, Oct. 24, 1971.

———, "Scientist Foresees a Longer Life Span, Mainly for the Affluent," *New York Times*, Feb. 23, 1971.

———, "Medicine: The Mystery of Aging," *New York Times*, Oct. 30, 1966.

SUMMERFIELD, FRANK W., and TAPPEL, A. L., "Peroxidative Damage to DNA by Polyunsaturated Fats and Protection by Vitamin E," presented at American Aging Association, Oct. 1983.

SWAN, HENRY, personal communications.

———, *Thermoregulation and Bioenergetics*. New York: American Elsevier, 1974.

———, "Metabolic Torpor in Protopterus Aethiopicus: An Anti-Metabolic Agent from the Brain," *American Naturalist*, May–June, 1969.

SZILARD, LEO, personal communications.

———, "On the Nature of the Aging Process," *Proceedings of the National Academy of Sciences*, Vol. 45, 1959.

———, "A Theory of Ageing," *Nature*, Vol. 184, 1959.

TALBERT, GEORGE B., and KROHN, P. L., "Effect of Maternal Age on Viability of Ova and Uterine Support of Pregnancy in Mice," *J. Reprod. Fert.*, Vol. 11, 1966.

TAPPEL, A. L., "Will Antioxidant Nutrients Slow Aging Processes?," *Geriatrics*, Oct. 1968.

———, "Where Old Age Begins," *Nutrition Today*, Dec. 1967.

TATA, J. R., "How Specific Are Nuclear 'Receptors' for Thyroid Hormones?," *Nature*, Sept. 4, 1975.

THOMAS, LEWIS, personal communications.

———, *The Lives of a Cell*. New York: Viking Press, 1974.

———, "Medicine's New Role: Helping the Elderly to Stay Fit in Body, Mind and Spirit," *Discover*, Dec. 1984.

———, "The Future Impact of Science and Technology on Medicine," American College of Surgeons *Bulletin*, June 1974.

TIERNEY, JOHN, "The Aging Body," *Esquire*, May 1982.

Time, "Americans Can—and Should—Live Longer," July 10, 1972.

———, "The Old in the Country of the Young," Aug. 3, 1970.

————, "The Problem of Old Age: Adding Life to Years," July 23, 1956.

TIMIRAS, PAOLA, personal communication.

————, "Neurophysiological Factors in Aging: Recent Advances," presented at International Congress of Gerontology, Jerusalem, 1975.

————, "Aging of Homeostatic Control Systems: Introductory Remarks," *Federation Proceedings*, Jan. 1975.

TOFFLER, ALVIN, *Future Shock*. New York: Random House, 1970.

TOLMASOFF, JULIE M.; ONO, TETSUYA; and CUTLER, RICHARD G., "Superoxide Dismutase: Correlation with Life-Span and Specific Metabolic Rate in Primate Species," *Proceedings of the National Academy of Sciences*, May 1980.

TOMASCH, JOSEPH, "Comments on 'Neuromythology,' " *Nature*, Sept. 3, 1971.

TRAMS, EBERHARD G., personal communication.

————, "Hepatic Insufficiency in Spawning Pacific Salmon," *Marine Biology*, Sept. 1969.

————, "Neurochemical Observations on Spawning Pacific Salmon," *Nature*, May 3, 1969.

TRAVIS, DOROTHY, personal communication.

TREFFERS, HENRY P.; SPINELLI, VIOLA; and BELSER, NAO O., "A Factor (or Mutator Gene) Influencing Mutation Rates in *Escherichia coli*," *Proceedings of the National Academy of Sciences*, Vol. 40, 1954.

TUCCILLE, JEROME, *Here Comes Immortality*. New York: Stein & Day, 1974.

TUMBLESON, MIKE, personal communications.

TURNBULL, COLIN, M., *The Human Cycle*. New York: Simon & Schuster, 1983.

TURNER, MICHAEL D., "Carcinoembryonic Antigen," *Journal of the American Medical Association*, Feb. 17, 1975.

UBELL, EARL, *How to Save Your Life*. New York: Harcourt Brace Jovanovich, 1973.

UNAMUNO, MIGUEL DE, *The Tragic Sense of Life*. New York: Dover Publications, 1954.

VAISRUB, SAMUEL, "Nature's Experiment in Unnatural Aging," *Journal of the American Medical Association*, Dec. 24–31, 1973.

VAN DEN BOSCH, F. J. G., personal communications.

VAN KEUREN, MARGARET L.; MERRIL, CARL R.; and GOLDMAN, DAVID, "Protein Variations Associated with In Vitro Aging of Human Fibroblasts and Quantitative Limits on the Error Catastrophe Hypothesis," preprint from *Journal of Gerontology*, in press, 1984.

VEATCH, ROBERT M. (Ed.), *Life Span: Values and Life-Extending Technologies*, Hastings-on-Hudson, N.Y.: The Hastings Center, 1979.

VIIDIK, ANDRUS, *Lectures on Gerontology*, Vol. IA: *On Biology of Aging*. New York: Academic Press, 1982.

VILLEE, DOROTHY B.; NICHOLS, GEORGE, JR.; and TALBOT, NATHAN B., "Metabolic Studies in Two Boys with Classical Progeria," *Pediatrics*, Feb. 1969.

VON HAHN, HOLGER P., "The Regulation of Protein Synthesis in the Ageing Cell," *Experimental Gerontology*, Oct. 1970.

WALFORD, ROY L., personal communications.

——, *Maximum Life Span*. New York: W. W. Norton, 1983.

——, *The Immunologic Theory of Aging*. Baltimore: Williams & Wilkins, 1969.

——, "Supergenes: Histocompatibility; Immunologic and Other Parameters of Aging," in Regelson and Sinex, *op. cit.*, 1983.

——, et al., "Accelerated Aging in Down's Syndrome: The Concept of Hierarchical Homeostasis in Relation to Local and Global Failure," in *Immunoregulation* (Fabris, N., et al., Eds.). New York: Plenum Press, 1983.

——, "The Immunologic Theory of Aging: Current Status," *Federation Proceedings*, 1973.

——, "Introduction" (section on immune dysfunction and aging), *Gerontologia*, Vol. 18, Nos. 5–6, 1972.

——, testimony before U.S. congressional subcommittee on aging-research needs, 1972.

WALKER, MORTON, *The Miracle Healing Power of Chelation Therapy*. Canfield, Ohio: Fischer Publishing, 1984.

WARA, DIANE W.; GOLDSTEIN, ALLAN L.; et al., "Thymosin Activity in Patients with Cellular Immunodeficiency," *New England Journal of Medicine*, Jan 9, 1975.

WATSON, JAMES D., *The Molecular Biology of the Gene*. New York: W. A. Benjamin, 1970.

——, and Crick, Francis H. C., "A Structure for Deoxyribose Nucleic Acid," *Nature*, April 25, 1953.

WEBB, J. N., "Muscular Dystrophy and Muscle Cell Death in Normal Foetal Development," *Nature*, Nov. 15, 1974.

WEGLICKI, WILLIAM B.; REICHEL, WILLIAM; and NAIR, PADMANABHAN P., "Accumulation of Lipofuscin-like Pigment in the Rat Adrenal Gland as a Function of Vitamin E Deficiency," *Journal of Gerontology*, Oct. 1968.

WEINBACH, E. C., "Oxidative Phosphorylation in Mitochondria from Aged Rats," *Journal of Biological Chemistry*, Vol. 234, 1959.

WEINDRUCH, RICHARD, "Dietary Restriction and the Aging Process," presented at American Aging Association, Oct. 1983.

——; McFeeters, Glenda; and Walford, Roy L., "Food Intake Reduction and Immunologic Alterations in Mice Fed Dehydroepiandrosterone," *Experimental Gerontology*, Vol. 19, 1984.

WEISSMANN, GERALD, personal communications.

WEST, C. E., and REDGRAVE, T. G., "Reservations on the Use of Poly-unsaturated Fats in Human Nutrition," *Search*, March 1974.

WHEELER, K. T., and LETT, J. T., "On the Possibility That DNA Repair Is Related to Age in Non-Dividing Cells," *Proceedings of the National Academy of Science*, May 1974.

WHITE, ABRAHAM, personal communications.

———, "The Endocrine Role of the Thymus and Its Hormone, Thymosin, in Host Immunological Competence," presented at National Foundation–March of Dimes conference, Harbor Springs, Mich., 1975.

———, "Nature and Biological Activities of Thymus Hormones—Prospects for the Future," presented at New York Academy of Sciences, 1974.

———, and Goldstein, Allan L., "Is the Thymus an Endocrine Gland? Old Problem, New Data," *Perspectives in Biology and Medicine*, Spring 1968.

WHITTEN, JOAN M., "Cell Death During Early Morphogenesis: Parallels Between Insect Limb and Vertebrate Limb Development," *Science*, March 28, 1969.

WILKES, MAHLON, personal communication.

WILLIAMS, BERNARD, "The Makropoulos Case: Reflections on the Tedium of Immortality," in *Problems of the Self*. Cambridge: Cambridge University Press, 1973.

WILLIAMS, JERRY R., personal communications.

———, "Alterations in DNA/Chromatin Structure During Aging," in Regelson and Sinex, *op. cit.*, 1983.

WILLIAMSON, A. R., and ASKONAS, B. A., "Senescence of an Antibody-forming Cell Clone," *Nature*, Aug. 11, 1972.

WILLOUGHBY, DAVID P., "Animal Ages," *Natural History*, Dec. 1969.

WILSON, DAVID L., "The Programmed Theory of Aging," in Rockstein, Sussman, and Chesky, *op. cit.*, 1974.

Wilson Quarterly (special issue—James, Timothy, Ed.), "The Elderly in America," New Year's issue, 1985.

WINICK, MYRON, personal communications.

———, "Nutrition for the Elderly," *Nutrition and Health*, Vol. 1, 1979.

WINTER, RUTH, *Ageless Aging*. New York: Crown Publishers, 1973.

WOLF, STEWART, personal communications.

WOOLLCOTT, JOAN, "The Mortal Cell," *Medical Affairs*, Sept. 1967.

WRIGHT, WOODRING E., and HAYFLICK, LEONARD, "Contributions of Cytoplasmic Factors to In Vitro Cellular Senescence," *Federation Proceedings*, Jan. 1975.

———, "Nuclear Control of Cellular Aging Demonstrated by Hybridization of Anucleate and Whole Cultured Normal Human Fibroblasts," prepublication manuscript.

———, "Enucleation of Cultured Human Cells," *Proceedings of the Society for Experimental Biology and Medicine*, Nov. 1973.

———, "Formation of Anucleate and Multinucleate Cells in Normal and SV40 Transformed WI-38 by Cytochalasin B," *Experimental Cell Research*, Vol. 74, 1972.

WYATT, RICHARD J., personal communications.

———, and Freed, William J., "Progress in Neurografting as a Treatment for Degenerative Brain Disease: The Parkinson's Model," in Regelson and Sinex, *op. cit.*, 1983.

WYNDER, ERNST L. (Ed.), *The Book of Health*. New York: Franklin Watts, 1981.

YARBOROUGH, DONALD, personal conversations.

YEN, SAMUEL S. C., "Hypothalamic-Pituitary Discharge," *Reproductive Endocrinology*, 1973.

YOUNG, PETER, "161 Years Old and Going Strong," *Life*, Sept. 16, 1966.

YOUNG, VERNON R.; STEFFEE, WILLIAM P.; et al., "Total Human Body Protein Synthesis in Relation to Protein Requirements at Various Ages," *Nature*, Jan. 17, 1975.

YUNCKER, BARBARA, "Is Aging Necessary?" (a series), *New York Post*, Nov. 18-22, 1963.

INDEX

A NOTE ABOUT THE AUTHOR

Albert Rosenfeld, a distinguished science writer, was science editor of *Life* and *Saturday Review* and is the author of several books, among them *The Second Genesis*. While he continues his journalistic career, he also holds an adjunct professorship in the department of human biological chemistry and genetics at the University of Texas Medical Branch in Galveston, and serves as consultant on future programs for the March of Dimes Birth Defects Foundation.

A NOTE ON THE TYPE

The text of this book was set in a type face called Times Roman, designed by Stanley Morison (1889–1967) for *The Times* (London) and first introduced by that newspaper in 1932.

Among typographers and designers of the twentieth century, Stanley Morison was a strong forming influence—as a typographical adviser to The Monotype Corporation, as a director of two distinguished English publishing houses, and as a writer of sensibility, erudition, and keen practical sense.

Composed by Maryland Linotype
Composition Company,
Baltimore, Maryland.

Printed and bound by
The Haddon Craftsmen, Inc.,
Scranton, Pennsylvania.

Designed by Marysarah Quinn.